June 21–23, 2017
Bangalore, India

**Association for
Computing Machinery**

Advancing Computing as a Science & Profession

SIGMIS-CPR'17

Proceedings of the 2017 ACM SIGMIS Conference on
Computers and People Research

Sponsored by:
ACM SIGMIS

Supported by:
Indian Institute of Management Bangalore

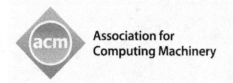

**Association for
Computing Machinery**

Advancing Computing as a Science & Profession

The Association for Computing Machinery
2 Penn Plaza, Suite 701
New York, New York 10121-0701

ISBN: 978-1-4503-5037-2 (Digital)

ISBN: 978-1-4503-5597-1 (Print)

Additional copies may be ordered prepaid from:

ACM Order Department
PO Box 30777
New York, NY 10087-0777, USA

Phone: 1-800-342-6626 (USA and Canada)
+1-212-626-0500 (Global)
Fax: +1-212-944-1318
E-mail: acmhelp@acm.org
Hours of Operation: 8:30 am – 4:30 pm ET

Printed in the USA

ACM SIGMIS CPR 2017 Chairs' Welcome

It is our great pleasure to welcome you to the annual Computers and People Research Conference – ACM SIGMIS CPR 2017. For more than 50 years, ACM SIGMIS CPR has engaged the academic and practitioner communities in understanding the issues related to the interaction of people with computers, what we now broadly refer to as information technology (IT). The current rapidly changing technological landscape is providing organizations and individuals with new tools for working, communication, and collaboration. Increasingly, smartphones and mobile commerce are changing our buying and consumer behaviors; wearable fitness trackers are making us more health conscious; social media and social networks are shifting the ways in which humans interact and collaborate together; start-ups are revamping business models by utilizing digital connections to fuel a sharing economy; and digital transformations are being used to address concerns of health, education, and civic engagement. A variety of social media and mobile technologies are also empowering individuals, communities, and societies to engage and interact with each other to enrich their own lives and to bring about a positive change in the world in which we live. In other words, digital technologies are enabling the transformation not only of business and organizations, but also of how people experience work and life. As a result, we selected the conference theme of Digital Transformation: The Changing Nature of Organizations, Work and Societies for this year's conference.

The papers, posters, keynotes, and the industry-academia panel at the conference address topics and ideas related specifically to the conference theme in addition to the more traditional topics of the interaction between computers and people that the ACM SIGMIS CPR community typically addresses. Several papers and posters this year focus on the thematic topics of digital business and innovation, architecture of digital organizations, social media and social networks, digital empowerment, and digital health in addition to the topics of IT workforce management, software projects and outsourcing, IT security, and institutions and organizations. Of special note this year are two keynote addresses, one by Kris Gopalakrishnan, the co-founder of the iconic Indian IT services company Infosys, chairman of Axilor, and an IT industry pioneer, on the topic Changes in Globalisation & Indian IT Industry Transformation, and the other by Sunil Mithas, a prolific author, a highly-cited scholar, and a professor at the University of Maryland, on the topic Digital Intelligence and Transformations. Also of special note this year is an industry-academia panel that will address issues related to the conference theme and that is comprised of three senior IT executives who are directly shaping through their work the digital world we live in and will live in, and two professors who are engaged in understanding the digital transformation occurring around us and its implications on our work and our lives. To cap it all, an industry visit to Infosys is also planned so participants can see first-hand the Bangalore campus of this iconic Indian IT firm that many of us refer to in our courses, and engage directly with senior executives of this firm to understand their vision and their work in moving to the next stage of digital work. Last but not the least, the doctoral consortium at the conference provides an opportunity to doctoral students, who are the budding scholars of our discipline, to refine their scholarly ideas through their interactions with faculty mentors, many of whom are and were journal editors, and with fellow students, in addition to growing their professional networks.

The various volunteer committees at any scholarly conference play a critical role in making it happen, and this conference is no exception. However, it is the authors, the reviewers, and many other volunteers and supporters who are really critical to the success of any conference. This conference in Bangalore, India would really not have been possible without the many authors and doctoral students who submitted their high-quality work, without the many reviewers who provided their timely and constructive reviews to submitted papers and doctoral proposals, and the faculty mentors who willingly agreed to give their time to interact with invited doctoral students in the doctoral consortium, and we would like to thank them all for their consideration and dedicated efforts.

We are sincerely thankful to the keynote speakers – Mr. Kris Gopalakrishnan and Dr. Sunil Mithas – for readily accepting our request for giving a keynote address on the theme of the conference despite their very busy schedules. We are also very thankful to the panelists on the industry-academia panel – Mr. Pankaj Bagri (Target Corportion, USA), Dr. Prasad Balkundi (SUNY at Buffalo, USA), Mr. Saurabh Chandra (Flipkart, India), Mr. Vishal Shah (Wipro, India), and Dr. Tom Stafford (Louisiana Tech University, USA) – for willingly agreeing to give their time to participate in the panel to discuss issues of direct relevance to the theme of the conference. We are also very thankful to Tejaswini Herath (Brock University, Canada), Pankaj Setia (University of Arkansas, USA), and Tom Stafford (Louisiana Tech University, USA), who are generously giving their time to mentor students in the doctoral consortium. Our sincere thanks also go to the Infosys leadership for opening their campus and making their senior executives available to conference participants as part of an industry visit to their firm. We are also very thankful to Stacie Petter (Baylor University, USA) and Tom Stafford for lending their full support to the conference by way of a special issue of The Data Base for Advances in Information Systems dedicated to the theme of this conference. We are also sincerely thankful to the Indian Institute of Management (IIM) Bangalore for their generous support in allowing us to host this conference at their beautiful campus without any charges for the various conference venues and the audiovisual and other conference infrastructure. Our sincere thanks also go to the Centre for Software and Information Technology Management at IIM Bangalore for providing a generous financial grant to support part of the conference expenses. No conference can be successfully organized without the support of student volunteers, and we wish to recognize Ashay Saxena and Sai Dattatrani of IIM Bangalore for providing their excellent support prior to and during the conference. We would be remiss if we did not acknowledge the ACM SIGMIS leadership including Janice Sipior (Villanova University, USA), Christina Nicole Outlay (University of Wisconsin Whitewater, USA), Jeria Quesenbery (Carnegie Mellon University, USA), Monica Adya (Marquette University, USA), and Indira R. Guzman (Trident University International, USA), who motivated us to organize this conference in Bangalore, India, and who provided their full support throughout the planning and organizing of this conference. Last but not the least, our sincere thanks also go to our supporters at ACM and Sheridan Communications, particularly to Diana Brantuas, Irene Frawley, Adrienne Griscti, Nanette Hernández, Maritza Nichols, Cindy Edwards, and Lisa Tolles, for their support with budgeting, doctoral student travel, conference proceedings, membership, registration, and the many other things that are necessary to make a conference successful. Thank you everyone!

We hope that you will find the conference program interesting and thought-provoking, and that the keynotes, industry-academia panel, and industry visit will provide you with valuable opportunities to learn first-hand from those who are directly engaged in shaping our digital world.

Rajendra K. Bandi
CPR'17 Conference Chair
Indian Institute of Management Bangalore, India

Rajiv Kishore
CPR'17 Conference Chair
State University of New York at Buffalo, USA

Daniel Beimborn
CPR'17 Program Chair
Frankfurt School of Finance
& Management, Germany

Rajeev Sharma
CPR'17 Program Chair
University of Waikato,
New Zealand

Shirish C. Srivastava
CPR'17 Program Chair
HEC Paris, France

Benoit Aubert
CPR'17 Doctoral Consortium
Chair
Victoria University of Wellington,
New Zealand

Geneviève Bassellier
CPR'17 Doctoral Consortium
Chair
McGill University, Canada

Deepa Mani
CPR'17 Doctoral Consortium
Chair
Indian School of Business
Hyderabad, India

Table of Contents

Paper Session 3.1: IT Security
Session Chair: Damien Joseph *(Nanyang Tech. University)*

Paper Session 3.2: Digital Health
Session Chair: Friedrich Holotiuk *(Frankfurt School of Finance & Management)*

Paper Session 4.1: Social Media & Social Networks
Session Chair: Lakshmi Iyer *(University of North Carolina at Greensboro)*

Paper Session 4.2: Software Projects and Outsourcing
Session Chair: Daniel Beimborn *(Frankfurt School of Finance & Management)*

Industry Case Session 5.1
Session Chair: Shirish C. Srivastava *(HEC Paris)*

Paper Session 5.2: Institutions & Organizations
Session Chair: Princely Ifinedo *(Cape Breton University)*

Poster Session
Session Chair: Rajiv Kishore *(State University of New York at Buffalo)*

Doctoral Consortium

ACM SIGMIS CPR 2017 Conference Organization

Conference Chairs: Rajendra K Bandi *(Indian Institute of Management Bangalore, India)*
Rajiv Kishore *(State University of New York at Buffalo, USA)*

Program Chairs: Daniel Beimborn *(Frankfurt School of Finance & Management, Germany)*
Rajeev Sharma *(University of Waikato, New Zealand)*
Shirish C. Srivastava *(HEC Paris, France)*

Doctoral Consortium Chairs: Benoit Aubert *(Victoria University of Wellington, New Zealand)*
Genevieve Bassellier *(McGill University, Canada)*
Deepa Mani *(Indian School of Business, Hyderabad, India)*

Registration Coordinators: Monica Adya *(Marquette University, USA)*
Sangeeta S. Bharadwaj *(Management Development Institute, India)*

Reviewers:

Babak Abedin	Lesley Land
Shahriar Akter	Sven Laumer
Hiyam Al-Kilidar	Diane Lending
Chintan Amrit	Mengxiang Li
Abhijith Anand	Ruochen Liao
Meldie Apag	Sajiv Madhavan
Prasad Balkundi	Charru Malhotra
Shalini Chandra	Poonacha Medappa
Tingru Cui	Luvai Motiwalla
Gay David	Dayasindhu N
Indika Dissanayake	Pankaj Nagpal
Linying Dong	Rohit Nishant
Andreas Eckhardt	Subasinghage Maduka Nuwangi
Shadi Erfani	Kavya P
Jeremy Ezell	Neena Pandey
Mike Gallivan	Vidushi Pandey
Jahyun Goo	Srikanth Parameswaran
Laxmi Gunupudi	Leigh Ellen Potter
Sumeet Gupta	Norah Power
Teju Herath	Sojen Pradhan
Princely Ifinedo	Srinivasan Rao
Vigneswara Ilavarasan	M.N. Ravishankar
Akie Iriyama	Pradeep Kanta Ray
Lakshmi Iyer	Dinesh Reddy
Christian Jentsch	Andreas Reitz
Damien Joseph	Peter Rossbach
Amalendu Jyotishi	Michael Schermann
Kyeong Kang	Peter Seddon
Janina Kettenbohrer	Priya Seetharaman
Anupriya Khan	Anuragini Shirish
Joon Koh	Rahul Singh

Sponsor:

Center for Software and IT Management

Supporter:

Keynote:
Changes in Globalisation & Indian IT Industry Transformation

Senapathy "Kris" Gopalakrishnan
Chairman, Axilor Ventures
Co-Founder, Infosys
kris.gopalakrishnan@outlook.com

ABSTRACT

Indian IT industry was built on a strategy to create the workforce required to scale the industry rapidly. The financial model included the costs of training and retraining the workforce as technology evolves. Today India is the preferred location for knowledge work for the world. How can India continue to evolve the model as the business of IT evolves? How can India evolve with changes in globalisation?

1. BIOGRAPHY

Mr Senapathy "Kris" Gopalakrishnan is the Chairman of Axilor Ventures, an accelerator that helps start-ups during the early stage of their business journey. Kris served as the vice chairman of Infosys from 2011 to 2014 and the chief executive officer and managing director of Infosys from 2007 to 2011. Kris is one of the co-founders of Infosys. Recognized as a global business and technology thought leader, he was voted the top CEO (IT Services category) in Institutional Investor's inaugural ranking of Asia's Top Executives and selected as one of the winners of the second Asian Corporate Director Recognition Awards by Corporate Governance Asia in 2011. He also was selected to Thinkers 50, an elite list of global business thinkers, in 2009. He was elected president of India's apex industry chamber Confederation of Indian Industry (CII) for 2013-14, and served as one of the co-chairs of the World Economic Forum in Davos in January 2014.

In January 2011, the Government of India awarded Mr. Gopalakrishnan the Padma Bhushan, the country's third-highest civilian honor.

Mr Gopalakrishnan serves on the Board of Governors of Indian Institute of Technology, Madras, Indian Institute of

Management, Bangalore, is the Chairman, Board of Governors of IIIT, Bangalore, Board of Governors of National Institute of Technology, Hamirpur, and is on the Board of Trustees of Chennai Mathematical Institute. He is the Chairman of the Vision Group on Information Technology of Karnataka Government and the Chairman of CII Start-up Council.

Mr. Gopalakrishnan holds Master's degrees in physics and computer science from the Indian Institute of Technology, Madras. Kris is a Fellow of Indian National Academy of Engineers (INAE) and an Honorary Fellow of Institution of Electronics and Telecommunication Engineers (IETE) of India.

SIGMIS-CPR '17, June 21-23, 2017, Bangalore, India
© 2017 Copyright is held by the owner/author(s).
ACM ISBN 978-1-4503-5037-2/17/06.
http://dx.doi.org/10.1145/3084381.3084382

Keynote: Digital Intelligence and Transformations

Sunil Mithas

Robert H. Smith School of Business

University of Maryland

smithas@rhsmith.umd.edu

ABSTRACT

Because of changes in competitive and regulatory environment and customer expectations, organizations have to continuously transform their products, services or business models to meet customer needs. Information technology (IT) increasingly plays an important role in many transformations because of significant digitization of business processes and massive investments in IT since 1960s [1, 2]. However, genuine transformations, even if necessary, often face difficulties because of an incomplete understanding of how to drive and manage transformations.

In my talk I will describe some findings and lessons based on my research on transformations [3], and various facets of what I call digital intelligence [4]. I will argue that although information technology is often an important enabler of transformations, sustainable and desirable transformations need much more. They also require attention to leadership; strategic planning; customer, employee and process focus; governance and long-term orientation that balances interests of various stakeholders; and what I call disciplined autonomy. Achieving success often requires an understanding of how to configure these elements optimally in a particular context. I will discuss some of my research on IT human capital, digital skills and its impact at the individual and household levels to suggest implications for policy, managers and IT professionals.

Keywords

Transformations; Digital Transformations; Information Technology; Digital Intelligence

1. BIOGRAPHY

Sunil Mithas is a Professor in the Robert H. Smith School of Business at the University of Maryland, where he is Co-Director of the Center for Digital Innovation, Technology and Strategy and the Center for Excellence in Service. He is the author of the books *Digital Intelligence: What Every Smart Manager Must Have for Success in an Information Age* and *Dancing Elephants and Leaping Jaguars: How to Excel, Innovate, and Transform Your Organization the Tata Way*. He earned his PhD from the Ross School of Business at the University of Michigan and an engineering degree from IIT, Roorkee.

Identified as an MSI Young Scholar by the Marketing Science Institute, Mithas is a frequent speaker at industry events for senior leaders. He has worked on research or consulting assignments with organizations such as Johnson & Johnson, Lear, A.T. Kearney, and the Tata group. His papers have won best-paper awards, and have been featured in practice-oriented publications such as *MIT Sloan Management Review, Bloomberg,* and *CIO.com.*

2. REFERENCES

1. McFarlan, F.W., *Foreword: IT and Management 1960-2020*, in *Digital Intelligence: What Every Smart Manager Must Have for Success in an Information Age, available at* http://a.co/hxsPEJv, S. Mithas, Editor. 2016, Finerplanet: North Potomac. p. xi-xxxiii.

2. Mithas, S. and F.W. McFarlan, *What is Digital Intelligence?,* in *Working paper, Robert H. Smith School of Business.* 2017: College Park.

3. Mithas, S., *Dancing Elephants and Leaping Jaguars: How to Excel, Innovate, and Transform Your Organization the Tata Way* (http://amzn.com/1503011879). 2014, North Potomac: Finerplanet.

4. Mithas, S., *Digital Intelligence: What Every Smart Manager Must Have for Success in an Information Age, available at* http://a.co/hxsPEJv. 2016, North Potomac: Finerplanet.

SIGMIS-CPR '17, June 21-23, 2017, Bangalore, India

© 2017 Copyright is held by the owner/author(s).

ACM ISBN 978-1-4503-5037-2/17/06.

http://dx.doi.org/10.1145/3084381.3087666

Industry Panel
Digital Transformation: The Changing Nature of Organizations, Work and Societies

Rajeev Sharma
University of Waikato, New Zealand
rsharma@waikato.ac.nz
(Moderator)

ABSTRACT

The purpose of the Industry Panel session is to provide attendees with an opportunity to hear the views of a distinguished group of panelists on the theme of the conference, particularly as they relate to the future opportunities and challenges that arise from the changing nature of organizations, work and societies as result of digital transformation.

KEYWORDS

Digital transformation, changing nature of organizations, work and societies.

1 PANEL OVERVIEW

The current rapidly changing technological landscape is providing organizations and individuals with new tools for working, communication and collaboration. Increasingly, smartphones and mobile commerce are changing our buying and consumer behaviors; wearable fitness trackers are making us more health conscious; social media and social networks are shifting the ways humans interact and collaborate together; start-ups are revamping business models by utilizing digital connections to fuel a sharing economy; and digital transformations are being used to address concerns of health, education and civic engagement. IT can empower organizations, communities, and societies to improve the world through positive connection, interaction, and presence. In addition, the way that we engage, understand and communicate around major events in communities, on the national landscape, and in the media has solidified a legitimate role for technology for years to come. Hence, digital technologies are enabling the transformation not only of business and organizations, but also

of how people experience work and life. It is an important issue for both research and practice.

This industry panel will include a distinguished group of industry executives from global IT services firms and firms in industry verticals as well as distinguished academics. The panel discussion will focus on the challenges of transformation that individuals, organizations and societies face. The intent is to provide insights from real world examples of these challenges and the practices that have generated positive outcomes from those challenges. The panelists have a wide variety of experiences, approaches, and practices. This session is designed to provide a rich, multi-faceted view on the benefits, challenges, and lessons learned from real-world examples of digital transformation.

2 PROFILE OF PANELISTS

Dr. Pankaj Bagri: Pankaj is currently Senior Director, Business Intelligence & Analytics at Target Corporation (a $70 bn US retailer). His team located in Bangalore and Minneapolis, is responsible for providing business insights for improvements in the operations of over 1800 stores in the chain. Prior to joining Target in 2011, Pankaj worked with GE/Genpact for 8 years in various roles across Analytics, Six Sigma and Learning &Development domains with a proven track record of setting and delivering on business goals in a variety of leadership roles. Pankaj is an alumnus of IIM Bangalore, from where he has done his masters level and doctoral degrees in Management.

Dr. Prasad Balkundi: Prasad is an associate professor of management in the University at Buffalo, State University of New York. He received his Ph.D. in business administration from Pennsylvania State University. His research interests include social networks and leadership in teams and his work has appeared in the *Academy of Management Journal, Academy of Management Review, Journal of Applied Psychology and Leadership Quarterly*. He is on the editorial board of *Organization Science and Leadership Quarterly*.

Saurabh Chandra: Saurabh is currently the CIO for FlipKart Group Companies. He has relocated from Bay Area and has also

SIGMIS-CPR '17, June 21-23, 2017, Bangalore, India
© 2017 Copyright is held by the owner/author(s).
ACM ISBN 978-1-4503-5037-2/17/06.
DOI: http://dx.doi.org/10.1145/3084381.3098611

worked extensively in UK & Philippines. He has worked with and helped companies establish their R&D centers - DRDO, Oracle, CA Technologies. He was also heading one of the BU's for the world's largest bank - J P Morgan Chase. His experience cuts across varied functions & domains - i.e. R&D, IT & Engineering, Data Science, Strategy, Sales, Product Management & Investment Banking. Currently, he is on the board of 3 startups, on the advisory for few incubators across India & UK and is a "Tech Mentor" for Google Incubators & NASSCOM. Visiting Professor to India's top most & Tier 1 Engineering and B-Schools. Saurabh is the founder of a SaaS firm, author of 2 books on automation, and has 3 patents. He is an alumnus of BITS Pilani and IIM Lucknow.

Dr. Vishal Shah: Vishal is currently Vice President-Leadership & People Sciences at Wipro. He is responsible for leadership development and organization effectiveness initiatives. Vishal has a mix of academic and corporate backgrounds. A passion for people and people development is the common thread that runs through his career. Prior to Wipro, he has worked in multiple industries like IT, BPO and Retail. He has also had the opportunity to work in different roles in Sales, HR and Consulting. Vishal is an alumnus of IIMB's masters and doctoral programs in management. He has published papers in international journals and presented in international conferences.

Dr. Rajeev Sharma: Rajeev currently serves as Professor and Associate Dean of Strategic Projects at Waikato Management School, University of Waikato. Rajeev has previously served as Professor and Head of School in the School of Information Systems and Technology at the University of Wollongong. His research interests include business analytics, the implementation of IS innovations, the management of IS projects, the strategic management of IS and method bias. His published research includes articles in *MIS Quarterly, Journal of Association of Information Systems, Journal of Information Technology, European Journal of Information Systems, Information Systems Journal, and Information and Organization.* Rajeev is currently serving as an Associate Editor of *MIS Quarterly.* He has served as a Guest Editor of a Special Issue of the *Journal of Information Technology* on IT Alignment and as a Guest Editor of a Special Issue of the *European Journal of Information Systems* on 'Transforming Decision-Making Processes: The Next IS Frontier'. Rajeev also serves on the Editorial Boards of *Journal of Information Technology and Journal of Strategic Information Systems.* Rajeev has previously held faculty positions at University of Technology Sydney, University of Melbourne, University of Oklahoma, University of North Carolina at Greensboro, and University of New South Wales. Rajeev is a graduate of the Australian Graduate School of Management at The University of New South Wales, the Indian Institute of Management Bangalore, and the University of Delhi.

Dr. Tom Stafford: Tom is J.E. Barnes Professor at the College of Business of Louisiana Tech, and is Editor of the prestigious journal *Data Base for Advances in Information Systems.* He has earned doctorates in Marketing and in Management Information Systems, and his research involves perceptions of information systems security practices, user motivations of technology use, outsourcing, and technology use in global contexts.

Do IT Professionals Attend to Internal and External Distributive Justice?

Full Paper

Damien Joseph
Nanyang Technological University
adjoseph@ntu.edu.sg

Tenace K. Setor
Nanyang Technological University
tenacekw001@ntu.edu.sg

Shirish C. Srivastava
HEC Paris
srivastava@hec.fr

ABSTRACT

The purpose of this study is to ascertain whether IT professionals attend to the different referents in distributive justice evaluations. This study achieves its purpose by drawing on distributive justice theory to differentiate two important referents for IT professionals' distributive justice evaluations: organizational or internal referents, and professional or external referents. Data for this study was collected through a survey research design in a large multinational organization headquartered in India. Analysis of the data indicates that IT professionals distinguish internal distributive justice from external distributive justice. Internal distributive justice evaluations were higher than external distributive justice evaluations in this sample. Both internal and external distributive justices are positively related to pay level satisfaction, thereby validating the former construct's multidimensional nature. We conclude the paper by discussing the implications of the findings for research and offer recommendations for the management of IT professionals.

CCS CONCEPTS

• **Social and professional topics** → **Computing profession** → Employment issues; Computing occupations

KEYWORDS

Management, Human factors, Theory.

1 INTRODUCTION

The amount of pay a worker receives is typically considered a hygiene factor that motivates outcomes [17]. But, a worker's comparison of pay with similar others appears to be a stronger motivator [9]. The comparison of pay with similar others is

SIGMIS-CPR '17, June 21-23, 2017, Bangalore, India
© 2017 Association for Computing Machinery.
ACM ISBN 978-1-4503-5037-2/17/06...$15.00
http://dx.doi.org/10.1145/3084381.3084389

termed, distributive justice [7]. The "similar others" that workers compare their pay to are known as referents [24]. Prior research on distributive justice has typically examined respondents' reactions to distributive justice evaluations based on either internal referents [e.g. 4] or external referents [e.g. 14]. However, prior studies have hinted that workers attend to multiple referents in distributive justice evaluations [10, 23]. Yet, there have been few studies, which we know of, that have simultaneously examined internal and external references of distributive justice evaluations and its associated outcomes [e.g. 23]. IS research has yet to corroborate or to support the generalizability of findings of this small set of studies.

Hence, this study's purpose is two-fold: (1) to ascertain whether IT professionals simultaneously attend to different referents on distributive justice evaluations; and (2) to validate our proposition that IT professionals consider both internal and external referents in distributive justice evaluations by associating these constructs with pay level satisfaction. Pay level satisfaction is a proximal reaction to distributive justice evaluations [21, 23]. This study, therefore, aims to contribute to distributive justice research by differentiating distributive justice evaluations by referents—internal and external. Prior research on distributive justice has typically examined respondents' reactions to distributive justice evaluations based on either internal referents [e.g. 4] or external referents [e.g. 14]. However, prior studies have hinted that workers attend to multiple referents in distributive justice evaluations [10, 23]. Yet, there have been few studies, which we know of, that have simultaneously examined internal and external references of distributive justice evaluations and its associated outcomes [e.g. 23]. IS research has yet to corroborate or to support the generalizability of findings of this small set of studies.

2 THEORETICAL FOUNDATION

2.1 Dimensionality of Distributive Justice

Distributive justice is defined as the balance in the ratio of a person's contributions and outcomes, compared to referents [11]. Distributive justice differs from pay equity or pay fairness evaluations because distributive justice involves an additional component – the comparison of pay with referents [3].

Referents used in distributive justice evaluations are either internal, i.e. comparable others in similar job roles within the same firm [23]; or external, i.e. comparable others in similar job roles in the external labor market [24]. The fact that referents are utilized in distributive justice evaluations implies that workers are sensitive to and will react to pay levels that affect their relative standing with different groups [10].

Prior research has theorized and found evidence that external comparisons within the same occupation are most pertinent to workplace outcomes, more so than internal and similar comparisons [20]. As noted by Greenberg et al. [12, p. 24] on the importance of external over internal equity comparisons: "Indeed, these external referents have been found to be more predictive of perceptions of inequity than local, person-to-person comparisons." As noted in Trevor and Wazeter [24, p. 1261], "...external pay comparisons have a considerable history in the relative deprivation, distributive justice, pay discrepancy, and pay referent literatures, where they have been related to numerous employee attitudes and behaviors."

There is a wealth of evidence supporting the assertion that individuals access external sources of pay information such as salary surveys. Goodman [10, pp. 172-173] notes that "participation in a professional society (e.g. accounting) provides information about input/pay ratios of others who are in different organizations. ... The media, corporation reports, and publicity given to union contracts highlight other comparison points for pay evaluation." Goodman goes on to find that the greater the level of professionalism of an occupation, the greater the access and selection of referents such as published pay information.

As such, we expect that external referents are as important as internal referents to IT professionals because the IT profession has an established external labor market [15]. An external IT labor market provides the context within which trade journals may collect pay data and publish annual salary surveys for most IT job roles. These salary surveys provide detailed job descriptions, and pay related information by education levels, work experience, and regions. There are also numerous websites (e.g. Payscale.com and Salary.com) that provide information to benchmark current pay with pay received by comparable others. Consequently, IT professionals may readily obtain pay related information for their specific IT job roles from these multiple sources to accurately arrive at distributive justice evaluations and to react to their evaluations [14]. Thus, we hypothesize that:

Hypothesis 1. IT professionals distinguish internal distributive justice from external distributive justice.

2.2 Distributive Justice and Pay Level Satisfaction

Distributive justice is upheld when the pay a worker receives is perceived to be consistent with norms for the allocation of such rewards. Inequity arises when pay received is inconsistent with these norms. Distributive justice theory proposes that perceived pay inequity creates a sense of dissatisfaction with pay received. It follows that pay level satisfaction is dependent on pay comparisons with referents. The positive relationship between

distributive justice evaluations and pay level satisfaction has been established by empirical research [23].

In this study, we relate distributive justice to pay level satisfaction as the criterion variable. Pay level satisfaction represents the "amount of overall positive or negative affect (or feelings) that individuals have toward their pay" [16, p. 246]. The arguments for both internally referenced and externally referenced distributive justice are similar in nature. When there is internal distributive justice, IT professionals will hold a positive affect towards pay received for work done. Similarly, when there is external distributive justice, IT professionals will also hold a positive affect towards pay received for work done.

Studies that simultaneously examine internal and external pay comparisons [22, 23] cast pay level satisfaction as the dependent variable. These studies are in consensus that internal and external distributive justice is positively related to pay level satisfaction. Thus, we hypothesize that:

Hypothesis 2.1. Internal distributive justice is positively related to pay level satisfaction.

Hypothesis 2.2. External distributive justice is positively related to pay level satisfaction.

3 METHOD

The key objective of this paper is to ascertain whether IT professionals distinguish between internal and external distributive justice; and to relate distributive justice to a well-established criterion measure. Accordingly, we conducted a large-scale field study of IT professionals.

3.1 Data Collection

In this section, we present information about the data collection procedure, sample, and instruments used in this study. The statistical analysis technique utilized, to test the theoretical model is also presented.

3.2 Sample

We collected survey data in two waves from a sample of IT professionals working in technical roles in a large multinational IT organization headquartered in India. In both waves, email invitations were sent to the list of 1,964 IT professionals within the organization; three reminders were subsequently sent to increase participation. Participants were assured anonymity in both the initial invitation as well as in all the reminders.

The dataset used for this study included 663 responses; representing a final response rate of 33.76%. The sample is predominantly male (76%), and attaining at least a bachelor's degree. All IT professionals surveyed were in IT technical roles. This sample of IT professionals possess, on average, four years (Mean: 4.27 years, SD: 4.56 years) of organization tenure.

3.3 Measures

The questionnaire contained multiple measurement items relating to each of the constructs in the research model. Where possible, validated scales from prior studies were used. All items were measured using a seven-point Likert-type scale (1=strongly disagree; 7=strongly agree).

Table 1. Descriptives, Reliabilities, and Inter-correlations

Constructs	Mean	SD	α	CR	AVE	1	2	3	4	5	6
1 Distributive Justice - Internal	3.72	1.63	0.89	0.97	0.89	0.95					
2 Distributive Justice - External	3.58	1.69	0.93	0.98	0.93	0.84 **	0.96				
3 Pay Satisfaction	3.22	1.62	0.92	0.98	0.92	0.72 **	0.71 **	0.96			
4 Pay	2.04	2.13				0.00	-0.02	0.01			
5 Work Week (Hours)	39.59	15.58				-0.10 *	-0.12 *	-0.05	0.20 **		
6 Education Level	1.12	0.50				-0.02	0.00	0.00	0.02	0.05	
7 Organization Tenure	4.27	4.56				-0.05	-0.09 *	-0.04	0.42 **	0.28 **	0.01

3.3.1 Distributive Justice. We operationalized internal and external distributive justice with four items each adapted from Colquitt [4]. Internal Distributive Justice elicited evaluations comparing to other IT professionals at their current organization, at the same level of the respondent, and undertaking similar IT work. External Distributive Justice elicited evaluations comparing to other IT professionals at other organizations, at the same level of the respondent, and undertaking similar IT work.

3.3.2 Pay Level Satisfaction. This was measured with four items adapted from Heneman and Schwab [13]

3.3.3 Controls. We controlled for pay level, work week, education level, and organization tenure (years). Data for all control variables were extracted from the organization's human resource database. Pay information was retrieved from organizational pay records. Due to the confidential nature of the information, the organization reported respondents' pay as a quartile value, i.e. whether pay was in the first, second, third or fourth quartile in their job role and job level. Work Week represents the total number of hours logged at work. Education Level was measured with a three level ordinal variable representing associate degree (1), bachelor's degree (2), and postgraduate degree (3). Organization Tenure was computed using the organization's reported employment start dates for each respondent.

3.4 Analysis

A structural equation modeling (SEM) technique, using Rosseel's [19] lavaan package (version 0.5-20) in R, was used to analyze the theoretical model. SEM enables the assessment of the measurement model through a confirmatory factor analysis (CFA) technique. The structural modeling capability of SEM enables the specification and testing of the hypothesized model.

4 RESULTS

This section presents the results that answer our research question of: Do IT professionals perceive internal distributive justice as different from external distributive justice. This section also presents results to validate the thesis that internal distributive justice is perceived as different from external distributive justice.

4.1 Distributive Justice

4.1.1 Confirmatory Factor Analysis. We conducted a confirmatory factor analysis to ascertain the dimensionality or factor structure of distributive justice. Given our proposal that IT professionals differentiate internal distributive justice from external distributive justice, we develop and compare rival models. Specifically, we compare a single factor structure to a two factor structure. In models with correlated errors, we correlated the errors for mirror items and so on, as these items would have similar sources of errors. We find that a two factor oblique structure with correlated errors fits the data best (χ^2 = 70,05, df = 15; RMSEA = 0.07, *90% Confidence Interval:* 0.06 to 0.09; SRMR = 0.01; CFI = 0.99; GFI = 0.97), according to existing rules of thumbs. All factor loadings of the items for internal and external distributive justice are above conventional cut-off values [i.e. 0.60, 20].

The internal consistencies (*Cronbach α*), composite reliabilities (*CR*), average variance extracted (*AVE*) and its square root are presented in Table 1. Convergent validity is indicated by *Cronbach α* values and *CR*s of constructs greater than 0.70 [2]; and *AVE*s of constructs greater than 0.50 [8]. Discriminant validity is indicated when the square root of the average variance extracted for a focal construct is greater than the correlations between the focal construct and other constructs in the model. Following these guidelines, we find all contracts possessing convergent and discriminant validities. The mean of internal distributive justice is significantly larger than the mean of external distributive justice (t = 3.0174, df = 5302, $p < 0.01$). Descriptives and correlations are reported in Table 1.

4.2 Pay Level Satisfaction

We relate internal and external distributive justice to ascertain criterion validity. Criterion validity refers to the extent to which a measure is related to an outcome [5]. The relationship between internal and external distributive justice was tested using a structural model as well as multiple regression analysis.

4.2.1 Structural Model. The structural model demonstrated a good fit with the data (χ^2 = 212.61, df = 87; RMSEA = 0.05, *90% Confidence Interval:* 0.04 to 0.06; SRMR = 0.04; CFI = 0.99; GFI = 0.96). The results of the structural model are presented in Table 2. The standardized betas (β) in Table 2 represent the magnitudes of the path coefficients in the model. Both internal (β = 0.47, se = 0.08, t = 5.94, $p < 0.01$) and external (β = 0.35, se = 0.08, t = 4.54, $p < 0.01$) are in the expected direction, i.e. positively and significantly related to pay level satisfaction.

Table 2. Results of Structural Model

	β	se	t	p
Pay	0.00	0.03	0.12	
Work Week (Hours)	0.03	0.04	0.68	
Education Level	0.01	0.03	0.33	
Organization tenure	0.01	0.03	0.32	
Distributive Justice - Internal	0.47	0.08	5.94	**
Distributive Justice - External	0.35	0.08	4.54	**

N=663, $* p < 0.5$; $** p < 0.01$

5 DISCUSSION

The purpose of this study was to ascertain whether IT professionals attend to internal and external referents when making distributive justice evaluations. Building on current conceptualizations of distributive justice and its theory, this study differentiated internal distributive justice from external distributive justice. In addition, this study validated the revised conceptualization with pay level satisfaction with the data collected from a sample of IT professionals working in IT roles in a large multinational IT organization. The data was analyzed using structural equation modeling.

The analyses of the factor structures indicate that IT professionals, in this sample, differentiate between referents when evaluating distributive justice. The referents - internal and external - correspond to similar others in the organization and in the external labor market. Overall, both referents of distributive justice are positively related to pay level satisfaction. We expect that favorable evaluations of distributive justice tend to reduce the desire of IT professionals to withdraw from their employer through increased pay level satisfaction. Higher pay level satisfaction should, in turn, reduce turnover intentions leading to a lowered likelihood of voluntary turnover.

However, this sample reports greater internal distributive justice compared to external distributive justice. Lower levels of external distributive justice reported by this sample may trigger thoughts that the "grass is greener on the other side" [6]. A significant disparity between internal and external distributive justice may yet lower pay level satisfaction; and subsequently lead to an increased likelihood of voluntary turnover. The current state of distributive justice theory provides little guidance about the interplay of internal and external distributive justice evaluations on work outcomes.

Subsequent research should examine the interplay of internal and external distributive justice on the turnover process. Such a study would provide a richer understanding of why and how distributive justice leads to voluntary turnover in professions with an external labor market. For the practice of human resource management, it may not be enough to focus on either referent in managing pay equity. It may be critical, especially for jobs with a robust external labor market, to benchmark pay internally as well as externally.

5.1 Implications for Research

Research on distributive justice in professions with an external labor market should include internal and external referents as these referents may have different effects on criterion variables. Moreover, theorizing the role of the external labor market answers repeated calls for incorporating context into theory building [1]. The effects of distributive justice may be far more complex and dynamic requiring different theoretical perspectives for a deeper understanding of distributive justice influences work outcomes. Although we find positive associations of distributive justice evaluations with pay level satisfaction, it may be that the significant difference in distributive justice evaluations may lower pay level satisfaction triggering voluntary turnover. This next research would contribute to research and raise important implications for practice.

5.2 Implications for Practice

One clear implication for practice is that the compensation of IT professionals should benchmark IT salaries in the internal and external labor markets. Even if firms focus on pay equity policies within the firm, there may be attrition of valuable IT talent when the influence of the external labor market is stronger and/or disregarded. Valuable IT talent would easily move to other firms willing to pay a premium for IT experience with prior employers [18]. It is possible that this implication is generalizable to occupations with an established external labor market.

Managing external pay equity is understandably a challenging task. Managers may find themselves constrained in attempting to influence external pay equity because compensation budgets are limited. One strategy towards retaining IT professionals could be to embed them deeper into the organization by facilitating the development of richer links to colleagues, strengthening fit with the organization and increasing the perceived cost of turnover. These strategies, however, need to be tested and are recommended directions for future research.

6 CONCLUSION

This study adds to the literature by differentiating distributive justice evaluations by referents—internal and external. Research has long hinted that workers attend to referents within their firms (internal) and beyond the firm (external) in distributive justice evaluations. IT professionals attend to the organizational and professional interfaces in comparing pay.

In closing, IT research may extend "borrowed" theories in directions that explain phenomenon idiosyncratic to IT, e.g. the organization-profession tensions inherent in the IT profession. Distributive justice theory, for one, does not explicitly address this organization-profession tension. But, as demonstrated in this study, established theories may be expanded and successfully applied to the IT context. The use and extension of organizational behavior and human resource theories would facilitate their generalizability across context and identify boundary conditions previously unrecognized.

ACKNOWLEDGMENTS

The authors would like to thank Dhiren Joseph for his contributions to early versions of this study. This work was partially supported by a Ministry of Education, Singapore, Tier 1 Grant (RG62/14).

7 REFERENCES

[1]　Ang, S. and Slaughter, S. *The Missing Context of Information Technology Personnel: A Review and Future Directions for Research.* Pinnaflex Educational Resources, City, 2000.

[2]　Carmines, E. G. and Zeller, R. A. *Reliability and Validity Assessment.* Sage Publications, [1979], Beverly Hills, 1979.

[3]　Colquitt, J. A. *Two Decades of Organizational Justice: Findings, Controversies, and Future Directions.* Sage, City, 2008.

[4]　Colquitt, J. A. and Rodell, J. B. Justice, Trust, and Trustworthiness: A Longitudinal Analysis Integrating Three Theoretical Perspectives. *Academy of Management Journal*, 54, 6 (2011), 1183-1206.

[5]　Cronbach, L. J. and Meehl, P. E. Construct Validity in Psychological Tests. *Psychological Bulletin*, 52, 4 (July) (1955), 281-302.

[6]　Dinger, M., Thatcher, J. B., Stepina, L. P. and Craig, K. The Grass Is Always Greener on the Other Side: A Test of Present and Alternative Job Utility on IT Professionals' Turnover. *Ieee Transactions on Engineering Management*, 59, 3 (Aug 2012), 364-378.

[7]　Folger, R. and Konovsky, M. A. Effects of Procedural and Distributive Justice on Reactions to Pay Raise Decisions. *Academy of Management Journal*, 32, 1 (1989), 115-130.

[8]　Fornell, C. and Larcker, D. F. Evaluating Structural Equation Models with Observable Variables and Measurement Error. *Journal of Marketing Research*, 18, 1 (February 1981), 39-50.

[9]　Gerhart, B. and Rynes, S. *Compensation: Theory, Evidence, and Strategic Implications.* SAGE Publications, Inc., New Jersey, NY., 2003.

[10]　Goodman, P. S. An Examination of Referents Used in the Evaluation of Pay. *Organizational Behavior and Human Performance*, 12, 2 (1974), 170-195.

[11]　Greenberg, J. A Taxonomy of Organizational Justice Theories. *Academy of Management Review*, 12, 1 (Jan 1987), 9-22.

[12]　Greenberg, J., Ashton-James, C. E. and Ashkanasy, N. M. Social Comparison Processes in Organizations. *Organizational Behavior and Human Decision Processes*, 102, 1 (Jan 2007), 22-41.

[13]　Heneman, H. G. and Schwab, D. P. Pay Satisfaction: Its Multidimensional Nature and Measurement. *International Journal of Psychology*, 20, 2 (1985), 129-141.

[14]　Joseph, D., Ang, S. and Slaughter, S. A. Turnover or Turnaway? Competing Risks Analysis of Male and Female IT Professionals' Job Mobility and Relative Pay Gap. *Information Systems Research*, 26, 1 (2015), 145-164.

[15]　Joseph, D., Boh, W. F., Ang, S. and Slaughter, S. A. The Career Paths Less (or More) Traveled: A Sequence Analysis of IT Career Histories, Mobility Patterns, and Career Success. *MIS Quarterly*, 36, 2 (Jun 2012), 427-452.

[16]　Miceli, M. P. and Lane, M. C. *Antecedents of Pay Satisfaction: A Review and Extension.* JAI Press, 1991.

[17]　Milkovich, G. T., Newman, J. M. and Milkovich, C. *Compensation.* Irwin/McGraw-Hill, New Jersey, NY, 2007.

[18]　Mithas, S. and Krishnan, M. S. Human Capital and Institutional Effects in the Compensation of Information Technology Professionals in the United States. *Management Science*, 54, 3 (March 2008), 415-428.

[19]　Rosseel, Y. Lavaan: An R Package for Structural Equation Modeling. *Journal of Statistical Software*, 48, 2 (2012), 1-36.

[20]　Sweeney, P. D. and McFarlin, D. B. Workers' Evaluations of the "Ends" and the "Means": An Examination of Four Models of Distributive and Procedural Justice. *Organizational Behavior and Human Decision Processes*, 55, 1 (1993), 23-40.

[21]　Tekleab, A. G., Bartol, K. M. and Liu, W. Is It Pay Levels or Pay Raises That Matter to Fairness and Turnover? *Journal of Organizational Behavior*, 26, 8 (Dec 2005), 899-921.

[22]　Terpstra, D. E. and Honoree, A. L. The Relative Importance of External, Internal, Individual, and Procedural Equity to Pay Satisfaction. *Compensation and Benefits Review*, 35, 6 (2003), 69-74.

[23]　Till, R. E. and Karren, R. Organizational Justice Perceptions and Pay Level Satisfaction. *Journal of Managerial Psychology*, 26, 1-2 (2011), 42-57.

[24]　Trevor, C. O. and Wazeter, D. L. Contingent View of Reactions to Objective Pay Conditions: Interdependence among Pay Structure Characteristics and Pay Relative to Internal and External Referents. *Journal of Applied Psychology*, 91, 6 (Nov 2006), 1260-1275.

Analyzing Gender Pay Gap in Freelancing Marketplace

Full Paper

Alpana Dubey
Accenture Labs
Bangalore, INDIA
alpana.a.dubey@accenture.com

Kumar Abhinav
Accenture Labs
Bangalore, INDIA
k.a.abhinav @accenture.com

Mary Hamilton
Accenture Labs
San Jose, USA
mary.hamilton @accenture.com

Alex Kass
Accenture Labs
San Jose, USA
alex.kass @accenture.com

ABSTRACT

Diversity and inclusion are becoming major focus areas for most of the organizations these days. It has shown to bring several positive impacts to organizations such as highly engaged and motivated employees, improved team dynamics, sustainable team structure, and better work outcome. Pay and career opportunity are some of the indicators to assess diversity and inclusion practice. In this paper, we study gender pay gap in freelancing marketplace. Freelancing marketplaces are open to everyone and gender neutral; hence, it is expected that gender pay gap should not be much over these platforms as freelancers can quote or negotiate the price for the jobs as per their wish. However, our study, performed on 37,599 freelancers, reveals a gap in pay between male and female freelancers. Moreover, the study shows that female freelancers undervalue themselves compared to male freelancers having similar profile. Our study suggests that there is a need to address this large scale pay gap issue by guidance and counselling of female freelancers.

CCS CONCEPTS

• **Social and professional topics**→ **Computing and business**

KEYWORDS

Freelancing; Gender diversity; Gender pay gap

SIGMIS-CPR '17, June 21-23, 2017, Bangalore, India
© 2017 Copyright is held by the owner/author(s). Publication rights licensed to ACM.
ACM ISBN 978-1-4503-5037-2/17/06...$15.00
http://dx.doi.org/10.1145/3084381.3084402

1 INTRODUCTION

Diversity and inclusion are one of the focus areas for high performance organizations these days [1, 3, 12]. According to a report from McKinsey [2], diverse organizations show better financial returns when compared to organizations that are less diverse. Moreover, it is found to be one of the top talent management practices in organizations [4]. A diverse workforce involves people from different ethnicity, age group, gender, etc. It has been shown that a diversity focused organization can attract top talents, have better customer orientation, employee satisfaction, and decision making [2]. One of the main indicators of diversity is that people from different gender, ethnicity, age group, etc. are treated equally. This equal treatment can be in terms of hiring opportunities, career progression, pay scale, etc. Therefore, these are considered some of the important indicators of a diversity focused organization. As lack of diversity and inclusion is mainly due to unconscious biases inherent in humans, most of the organizations deploy various diversity and inclusion programs for their employees to remove these biases. Despite these efforts, we still do not witness encouraging diversity indicators. For instance, a study done on paycheck.in data shows gaps in pay scale between male and female population [5]. Although, the study shows that gap has been declining over the years mainly because of diversity and inclusion programs run by the organizations.

Online labor marketplaces, such as Freelancer.com, Upwork, Taskrabbit, etc. [13, 14, 15] bring another kind of workforce which is not controlled by an organizational setup. Online labor marketplace is commonly known as freelancing marketplace and it has grown rapidly in the recent years. Intuit has forecasted that by 2020, 43% of workforce in US will be freelancers [26]. Online marketplaces provide a medium for buyers and providers of labor market. Freelancers join and leave a marketplace as per their convenience and ask for pay based on the complexity of job. Given these flexibilities, it is worth studying if the online marketplaces naturally demonstrate positive diversity indicators. In this paper, we study the pay gap and career progression gap between male and female freelancers on online labor marketplace. This study helps in understanding whether the gender pay gap exists due to social factors, such as women generally undervalue themselves and men negotiate more aggressively than women. We answer the following two research questions in this paper:

RQ1: Does a pay gap exist among freelancers of different genders?
RQ2: Does pay increase at different rates for the freelancers of different genders?

We answer the above questions for different job categories and countries. The analysis is done on the freelancers having similar profiles. With this study, we asses if the problem of gender pay gap needs to be addressed for freelancing workforce which is growing rapidly every year.

The report by Jessica et al. [16] shows that gender pay gap persists even after accounting for similar occupation, experience level, etc. The report stresses on the role of society and females bearing other responsibilities behind this gap. Our hypothesis is that gender pay gap is a social issue. Therefore, we expect to see gender pay gaps on freelancing market place even though they are open and gender neutral. To validate the above hypothesis, first, we study the pay gaps between male and female freelancers having comparable experience and profile. Second, we study to what extent the pay gaps exist and investigate whether or not it differs for the jobs of different types. Third, we study how freelancers' career progress in terms of pay increase for different genders. Through this study, we intend to empirically evaluate our hypothesis about the pay gap. The study is performed on top five countries in terms of freelancers' population. In addition, the pay comparison is performed on freelancers having similar profile, experience, and capabilities. Our results show that females earn less than males across job categories and countries. For every dollar a man earns, a woman, with similar profile and capability, earns 62-89 cents for the similar job. Except few exceptions, this gap is consistently observed across all job categories. Therefore we conclude that pay gap is indeed an important problem in the context of online labor market and need to be addressed through proper career guidance and counselling of female freelancers.

Rest of the paper is organized as follows. Section 2 discusses related work. Section 3 describes diversity and inclusion and its indicators. Section 4 covers the study setup, and section 5 discusses the results. The paper is concluded with a final remark in section 6.

2 RELATED WORK

There have been several studies on gender biasness in organized sectors. For instance, Varkkey et al. [5] assess gender pay gap in formal sector in India. The study has been done from the data coming from Paycheck India [5]. They observed that pay gap exists in almost all the sectors. Further, they have found that the gap has been declining over the years. Similar statistics are observed from the data available for employees in USA [17]. Blau et al. [23] observed a reduction in the gender pay gap over the period 1980-2010. They identified women's education, experience and occupational representation as important factors for this. Heckert et al. [19] revealed that the female workers expect lower pay in comparison to their male counterparts. They also found out that entry-level pay expectations of women was approximately 80% of those reported by men and the peak-career pay

expectations were only 60% of men's pay expectation. O'shea et al. [22] observed that job applicants with low pay expectations often receive low pay offers relative to equally qualified applicants with higher pay expectations. They further identified that starting salaries can have a career-long impact on actual pay. Hogue et al. observed that females expect less pay as compared to male counterparts both at the beginning and at the peak of their careers [20]. Schweitzer et al. [21] observed that females expect low pay for themselves and a longer time for their promotion despite their better educational and experience qualifications. Leibbrandt et al. [25] noticed that women are less likely to negotiate over salary than men and this negotiation gap plays an important role in the gender pay gap. They also observed that when they did not make an explicit statement that wages are negotiable, men were more likely to negotiate than women. However, when they explicitly mentioned the possibility that wages are negotiable, this difference disappeared. Chamberlain et al. [24] observed that there is statistically significant difference between male and female pay when they compared workers with similar job titles, similar employers, with comparable education, experience and locations. They also observed that male earn 24.1 percent higher base pay than female on average. In other words, women earn about 76 cents per dollar men earn.

In the online marketplace context, there are studies on evaluating hiring biasness based on geography and gender. Chan et al. [7] observed a positive hiring bias towards female workers in online labor platforms. They further noticed that hiring bias diminishes as employers gain more hiring experience on the platform. They also reported that female hiring bias appears only from the applicants from developing countries, and not those from developed countries [9]. Agrawal et al. [8] observed that applicants from less developed countries (LDCs) are more likely to be hired by task posters from developed countries (DCs) when compared to applicants from DCs. Ghani et al. [10] outlined that Indian workers are more likely to be hired by members of the Indian diaspora than other employers on Upwork.

Even though gender pay gap has been extensively studied in the organized sector, there is a lack of study in context of unorganized sectors such as online labor market. Our study is the first attempt to evaluate gender pay gap in online labor marketplace. As we see a rapid growth in freelance economy [26], this study is highly relevant in today's context. In this paper, we study freelancer pay gap and pay progression gap to understand gender equality.

3 DIVERSITY AND INLCUSION

3.1 Definition

Diversity and inclusion implies acknowledging that each individual is different [6]. The above difference can be on various dimensions such as race, ethnicity, gender, sexual orientation, age, physical abilities, socio-economic status, political belief, or other ideologies. Besides acknowledging the differences, it also includes accepting and respecting those differences. Organizations often focus on bringing more diversity in terms of composition of the teams, i.e. having a balanced participation from different groups and they lack inclusion practices which is very crucial to bring the benefits of diversity [12]. A report from Deloitte shows that organizations that adopt Diversity and

Inclusion practices are likely to produce 80% improvement in their performance [12]. An organization is assessed high on diversity practice if it compositionally maintains a workforce with people from different groups whereas it is assessed high on inclusion if its employees feel part of the organization, feel valued, and feel treated equally with regard to the career progression and pay scale

3.2 Indicators of Diversity and Inclusion

A diversity and inclusion problem exists, in an organization, if business policies, or practices have different impact on individual groups in terms of remuneration, payment, opportunity, etc. The reasons behind the same may not always be the organization's policies but the practices employees may follow due to unconscious biases that may come from societal structure or employees' background. To remove such biases, several organizations run gender sensitization programs and introduce policies which specifically addresses the needs of various groups [1].

Lack of Diversity and Inclusion is often reflected when different groups statistically show different values for various metrics. For instance, a significant difference in turnover, number of terminations, number of promotions, number of disciplinary cases, and number of role models, etc., among different groups may indicate lack of diversity [6]. Typically Diversity and Inclusion practices are assessed based on the organization's practices, various metrics, and surveys performed on the employees.

3.3 Diversity and Inclusion in Organizational Workplace and Freelancing Marketplace

Organizations employ business policies, recruitments, training programs, gender sensitization programs to improve diversity and inclusion. This goal is driven from top to bottom. Freelancing marketplace differs from Organizational workplace along several dimensions: firstly, there is no single leadership which drives diversity and inclusion agenda for all the freelancers subscribed to freelancing platform. Secondly, these marketplaces are open to everyone. Thirdly, freelancers can quote the price for the work based on their own assessment. Lastly, freelancers' relationship with employer (or client) is contractual and short term. As employer hires freelancers for short term and not responsible for freelancers' long term career, whether or not freelancers feel included within the team of the employer does not matter much compare to a full time employee feeling included in an organization. Moreover, as freelancers can quote and negotiate the price for their work, it is often freelancers' responsibility to ask the right price for a job.

In freelancing marketplace, freelancers choose how they want to grow their career in terms of acquisition of new skills. Whereas, in an organization career growth is business driven and the organization makes sure that career aspiration of employee is fulfilled and is in line with the organization's business goals. Ensuring a good career progression of employees is very important in the organizational context as the organizations focus on having a long term relationship with employees.

Now a days, organizations are also considering to engage freelancing workforce as their extended resource pool. Given these differences and increased growth of freelancing workforce, there is a need to study the freelancing marketplace from diversity and inclusion perspective so that right actions could be taken to ensure diversity and inclusion for such extended workforce.

4 STUDY SETUP

4.1 Data

We used freelancers' data from a popular freelancing platform to perform this study. We chose the platform based on the accessibility of the data and wide variety of job types supported over the platform. We fetched the jobs of five different categories from the jobs posted from Jan 2012 – Dec 2015 along with the freelancers' information. The job categories were as follows:

1. Administrative: This job category includes jobs such as data entry, personal/virtual assistant, project management, etc. We refer such jobs as "Admin" jobs.
2. Design: This job category includes jobs that requires multimedia content creation and design activities such as graphic and logo design, animation, etc.
3. Business service: This job category includes customer services, technical support, etc.
4. Networking and Infrastructure management: This job category includes jobs such as network configuration, IT infrastructure creation, customization, database administration, system administration, ERP/CRM Software management, etc.
5. Sales and marketing: as the name suggests, this category includes all the jobs related to sales and marketing such as market and customer research, public relations, etc.
6. Writing and translation: includes writing and translation jobs. For instance, blog writing, technical writing, general and technical translation, etc.
7. Software development: This category includes jobs such as web development, mobile development, game development, testing etc.

As gender information was not available on the freelancers' profile, we used gender resolution APIs to resolve gender based on freelancers' first name [18]. Out of 68,000 freelancers, gender of only 37,599 freelancers' could be resolved. The gender resolution was done only for two types of genders, male and female, as the other gender categories cannot be revealed by names. Table 1 shows the statistics on % freelancers whose gender were resolved. A significant number of names (45%) could not be resolved to either of the genders. We did not consider them in our study. These were mostly the misspelt names. Also, we considered only those names where API's confidence score was more than 95%. Table 2 shows the country wise distribution of freelancers.

Table 1: Gender Resolution Stats

Number of freelancers	% Male	%Female
37599	81%	19%

Table 2: Country wise distribution of freelancers

Number of freelancers	India	USA	Pakistan	Bangladesh	Ukraine	Others
37599	45%	8%	6%	6%	5%	30%

4.2 Analysis Methodology

To study the pay gap, we followed the process as described in Algorithm 1. First, freelancers are grouped based on countries and job categories. The above grouping is done because countries may have different price range for the same job due to difference in the purchasing power of countries. Also, price range differs based on the job category. Next, we create a set of male, female freelancer pairs for each of the above groups. A two level filtering is performed on each set of freelancers' pairs. In the first level filtering, we remove all the pairs where the number of matching skills between male and female freelancer is less than five. Freelancers' skills are identified from the profile of freelancers. In the second level filtering, a similarity score is calculated between the male and female freelancers, for each pair, using Algorithm 2. Pairs that have similarity score below a threshold are removed. The similarity calculation is done based on similarity between freelancers' profiles which is a textual description and similarity between other numerical attributes such as freelancers' rating, billing rate, total hours worked, and number of billed assignments. For textual description, we use TF-IDF approach [11] and for numerical attributes we use Euclidean distance to measure similarity. The above similarity computation is done after normalizing the data. Finally, we calculate the Earning Ratio and Billing Ratio for each set which now contains freelancer pairs with similar profiles.

Algorithm 1: Pay Gap Calculation

Input: List of Freelancers
Output: Pay gap between male and female freelancers
Begin
    Group freelancers based on countries and job category
    For each group of freelancers
        Create a set of pairs of freelancers, G, where for each pair $(m, f) \in G$, m is a male freelancer f is a female freelancer
        Remove those pairs, (m, f), from G, where matching skills between m and f is less than 5
        Remove those pairs, (m, f), from G where $FreelancerSimilarity(m, f) < Threshold$
        Calculate   EarningRatio(G)

Algorithm 2: Freelancer Similarity

Input: Freelancer1, Freelancer2
Output: Similarity between Freelancer1 and Freelancer 2
Begin
    $Profile1 \leftarrow$ Fetch public profile of Freelancer 1
    $Profile2 \leftarrow$ Fetch public profile of Freelancer 2
    $ProfileSimilarity \leftarrow$ Compute textual similarity between $Profile1$ and $Profile2$ using TF/IDF based approach
    $OtherAttributes1 \leftarrow <Rating_1, BillingRate_1, TotalHoursWorked_1, Billed Assignment_1>$
    $OtherAttributes2 \leftarrow <Rating_2, BillingRate_2, TotalHoursWorked_2, Billed Assignment_2>$
    $OtherAttributesSimilarity \leftarrow$ Euclidean Distance($OtherAttributes1$, $OtherAttributes2$)
    Return $ProfileSimilarity + OtherAttributesSimilarity$
End

There are two price indicators in a freelancer's profile:

Hourly earning rate: captures how much a freelancer earns on an hourly basis. It is calculated using the following formula:

$$HourlyEarningRate(w) = \frac{\sum_{j \in Job_w} Pay(j)}{|Job_w|} \dots \dots \dots (1)$$

Here w is a freelancer, Job_w is a set of all the jobs perform by w and $Pay(j)$ is payment done after the completion of job j.

Billing rate: captures how much price per hour a freelancer quotes for him/herself. It, in some way, captures the self-assessment of a freelancer.

Earning gap for a set is calculated as ratio of medians of male earning rate and female earning rate in the set. Similarly, billing gap is calculated as ratio of medians of male billing rate and female billing rate in the set. We use ratio of medians of hourly earning of males and females to measure the earning gap as shown in Eq. 2. Similarly, we use ratio of medians of hourly billing rate of males and females to measure gap in billing rate (Eq. 3). Instead of mean, we used medians because we observed huge variation in the earning and billing rates. Earning and billing rates are captured in US dollars. An earning ratio less than one would indicate that females earns less than males. For instance, a value of 0.6 would imply that a female earns 60 cents for every dollar a male, with similar experience and expertise, earns.

$$EarningRatio(G) = \frac{Median(\bigcup_{f \in Female(G)}\{HourlyEarning(f)\})}{Median(\bigcup_{m \in Male(G)}\{HourlyEarning(m)\})} \cdot (2)$$

$$BillingRatio(G) = \frac{Median(\bigcup_{f \in Female(G)}\{BillingRate(f)\})}{Median(\bigcup_{m \in Male(G)}\{BillingRate(m)\})} \dots \dots \dots (3)$$

5 ANSWERS TO RESEARCH QUESTIONS

In this section, we discuss the research questions stated earlier.

5.1 Does a pay gap exist among freelancers of different gender?

Here, we discuss the pay gap analysis done on the freelancers from five countries, namely India, United States, Pakistan, Bangladesh, and Ukraine. These are the top five countries in terms of freelancers' population over the platform. Gender wise distribution of freelancers for each country is captured in Table 3.

Table 3: Gender wise distribution of freelancers across countries

	India	USA	Pakistan	Bangladesh	Ukraine
Male	77%	78%	89%	80%	88%
Female	23%	22%	11%	20%	12%

Table 4: Overall pay gap

	India	USA	Pakistan	Bangladesh	Ukraine
Earning ratio	0.84	0.89	0.78	0.62	0.79
Billing ratio	0.94	0.85	0.84	0.80	0.85

The average earning ratio and billing ratio for each country are shown in Table 4. The figures demonstrate that there is a pay gap between male and female freelancers. Table 4 also shows an interesting insight in which except USA, the billing ratio is lower than the earning ratio for all the countries. This implies that females from rest of the countries are not good at wage negotiation; i.e. even though they start with a self-assessment which is not much lower than male, but at the end they get paid less. Pay gap for individual job categories for each country is captured in Table 5. Table 5 shows data only for those job categories where the sample size (i.e. number of male, female freelancers' pairs) was at least 1000. Therefore, we see that several job categories from Ukraine has no values. Earning ratio for individual job categories show that, except few exceptions (highlighted bold), male earns more than female across all the job categories. Even for those exceptions, the gap is not too high and can be considered comparable. Results for billing ratio is also captured in Table 5 and show the similar observations. The earning ratio ranges from 0.3 to 1.19 and billing ratio ranges from 0.54 to 1.17.

5.2 Does pay increase at different rates for the freelancers of different genders?

Here we study the rate of increase in hourly earning for male and female freelancers over a period and assess if there is any difference between male and female earning progression. We evaluate if the rate of change in pay scale is comparable for both. In this analysis, we calculate average hourly pay for male and female freelancers in a given job category over different years. For this study, we selected those freelancers who have good experience on the platform (i.e. they have completed atleast ~100 jobs) and have worked consistently on the platform. We performed this study on two groups – freelancers in Software development job category and freelancers in design jobs category, both from India. For rest of the groups, we could not get a representative number of freelancers having good experience over the platform.

The results for the two job categories are shown in Figure 1 and Figure 2. We observed that male freelancers' career progression is much faster than female freelancers for both the job categories. Hence, there is not just the pay gap, but also a career progression gap in male and female freelancers.

We also captured the difference in earning between male and female freelancers over a period. As the rate of increase in earning for female freelancers is significantly less than the rate of increase in earning for male, the earning difference between male and female freelancers is getting wider over the years as shown in Figures 1 and Figure 2. The chart in Figure 3 shows the earning ratio, which is decreasing over the years.

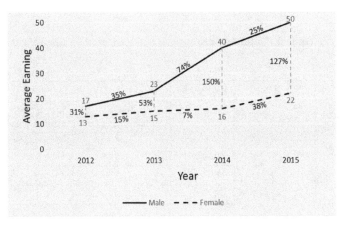

Figure 1: Pay progression of Indian freelancers for Software Development jobs

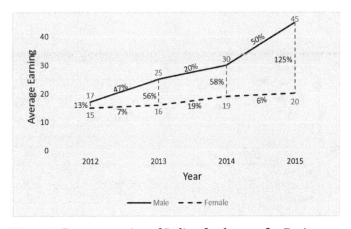

Figure 2: Pay progression of Indian freelancers for Design jobs

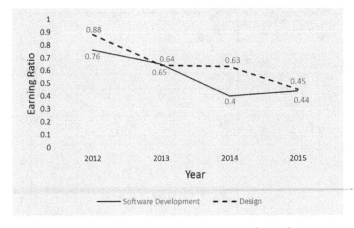

Figure 3: Earning Ratio of Indian freelancers for Software Development and Design jobs.

Table 5: Detailed Earning gap and Expectation Gap for different job categories

Job Category	Country	Earning per hour (in USD)					Billing Rate (in USD)				
		Male		Female		Earning Ratio	Male		Female		Billing Ratio
		Median	Std. Dev.	Median	Std. Dev.		Median	Std. Dev.	Median	Std. Dev.	
Administrative	India	31	60.6	36	80.7	**1.16**	11.03	6	10.99	5.36	0.99
	Pakistan	28	68.9	31	33.4	**1.10**	11.6	8.3	13	38.7	**1.12**
	Bangladesh	14	39.1	10	30	0.71	8.62	6.02	7.04	5.28	0.81
	Ukraine	-	-	-	-	-	-	-	-	-	-
	United States	39	86.3	30	88	0.77	27	19.3	23.31	17.9	0.86
Design	India	37	83.2	34	53.8	0.91	12.34	6.82	11.73	4.59	0.95
	Pakistan	35	167.8	30	147.5	0.86	14.53	14.3	14.29	10.89	0.98
	Bangladesh	20	38.1	7	61.1	0.35	11.32	7.28	8.85	4.74	0.78
	Ukraine	-	-	-	-	-	-	-	-	-	-
	United States	46	246.3	55	139	**1.19**	37.48	28.35	31.83	17.76	0.85
Business Services	India	34	101.2	30	117.5	0.88	14.5	15.02	12.48	5.25	0.86
	Pakistan	52	113.3	36	63.8	0.69	14.3	11.41	8.89	7.07	0.62
	Bangladesh	23	38	19	62.3	0.82	9.34	7.4	6.28	4.13	0.67
	Ukraine	60	136.3	45	149.3	0.75	27	14.72	21	11.64	0.78
	United States	75	240.4	53	82.3	0.70	36	31.5	32.53	21.58	0.90
Networking & Infrastructure management	India	41	72	35	52.6	0.85	16.51	8.04	14.68	7.52	0.89
	Pakistan	51	160.7	20	13.7	0.39	17.29	9.7	9.47	5.6	0.54
	Bangladesh	24	54.4	13	30	0.54	13.54	8.28	10.24	8.85	0.76
	Ukraine	-	-	-	-	-	-	-	-	-	-
	United States	55	144.3	64	68	**1.16**	43.93	31.30	42	20.23	0.95
Sales & Marketing	India	25	87.9	17	91.8	0.68	10.66	6.27	9.26	4.34	0.86
	Pakistan	28	81.3	18	52.8	0.64	10.4	7.5	9.64	9.60	0.92
	Bangladesh	10	33.5	3	86.1	0.3	7.33	5.3	6.43	5.74	0.88
	Ukraine	-	-	-	-	-	-	-	-	-	-
	United States	62	191.4	43	127.8	0.69	43.19	43.4	26.82	20.61	0.62
Writing & Translation	India	33	75.5	22	77	0.66	11.48	9.3	13.49	17.8	**1.17**
	Pakistan	37	131.1	33	135.8	0.89	11.76	8.48	9.29	8.18	0.79
	Bangladesh	13	44.8	12	39.2	0.92	8.28	6.6	6.9	5.9	0.83
	Ukraine	-	-	-	-	-	-	-	-	-	-
	United States	48	113.9	38	122.8	0.79	32.24	29.62	25.75	20.25	0.79
Software Development	India	32	194.1	24	164.1	0.75	12.83	8	11.53	4.7	0.90
	Pakistan	49	184.4	44	111.5	0.89	13.85	8.81	12.61	8.96	0.91
	Bangladesh	23	97	17	59	0.73	11.4	7.2	10.1	6.9	0.88
	Ukraine	31	236	26	274	0.83	25	36.4	23	12.26	0.92
	United States	57	212.4	56	188.3	0.98	39.2	30.39	38.71	24.8	0.98

6   CONCLUSIONS AND FUTURE WORK

In this paper, we studied gender pay gap and career progression gap in freelancing marketplace. We observed that there is a pay gap between male and female freelancers having similar profiles. We also found out that male freelancers earn comparatively more than female freelancers across all the job categories. The study also reveals that female freelancers undervalue themselves in comparison to male freelancers. Further, we observed that career progression of male freelancers increase at a faster rate than that of female freelancers for some job categories. The observation on career progression is contradictory to the observations made for the same in organized sectors. The data from organized sectors show that pay gap has been decreasing over the years. This may be due to various initiatives taken by the organizations over the years. Hence, a set of initiatives are needed to address gender pay gap in unorganized sectors that consists of mainly freelancers whose population is growing at rapid pace. With the emergence of online labor markets, reaching to a large population of freelancers is now much easier. Hence, there is an urgent need for studying various aspects of an unorganized sector, starting diversity initiatives, and equipping freelancers with tools and guidance to promote gender equality at a large scale.

REFERENCES

[1]   http://www.forbes.com/sites/joshbersin/2015/12/06/why-diversity-and-inclusion-will-be-a-top-priority-for-2016/2/#399a416064bb. Last accessed 17-Jan-2017.

[2]   http://www.mckinsey.com/business-functions/organization/our-insights/why-diversity-matters. Last accessed 17-Jan-2017.

[3]   http://www.catalyst.org/media/companies-more-women-board-directors-experience-higher-financial-performance-according-latest. Last accessed 17-Jan-2017.

[4]   Diversity and Inclusion Top the List of Talent Practices Linked to Stronger Financial Outcomes. http://www.bersin.com/News/PressArticles.aspx?id=19377. Last accessed 17-Jan-2017.

[5]   B. Varkkey, and R. Korde. Gender Pay Gap in the Formal Sector: 2006 - 2013, Wage Indicator Data Report Preliminary Evidences from Paycheck India Data. Available at http://www.paycheck.in/files/gender-pay-gap-in-india-2006-2013. Last accessed 20-Jan-2017.

[6]   Diversity definition. http://www.qcc.cuny.edu/diversity/definition.html. Last accessed 17-Jan-2017.

[7]   C. Jason, and J. Wang. Hiring biases in online labor markets: The case of gender stereotyping. 2014. In Proc. 35th International Conference on Information Systems "Building a Better World Through Information Systems", ICIS.

[8]   A. K. Agrawal, N. Lacetera, and E. Lyons. 2013. Does Information Help Or Hinder Job Applicants from Less Developed Countries in Online Markets?. http://dx.doi.org/10.3386/w18720.

[9]   C. Jason and J. Wang. 2015. Hiring Preferences in Online Labor Markets: Evidence of a Female Hiring Bias.

[10]   Ejaz Ghani, R. Kerr William, and Christopher Stanton. 2014. Diasporas and outsourcing: evidence from oDesk and India. Management Science 60.7 (2014): 1677-1697.

[11]   B. Y. Ricardo, and B. Ribeiro-Neto. 1999. Modern information retrieval. vol. 463. New York: ACM press.

[12]   Waiter, is that inclusion in my soup? A new recipe to improve business performance. http://www2.deloitte.com/content/dam/Deloitte/au/Documents/human-capital/deloitte-au-hc-diversity-inclusion-soup-0513.pdf. Last accessed 17-Jan-2017

[13]   https://www.freelancer.com/. Last accessed 17-Jan-2017.

[14]   https://www.upwork.com/. Last accessed 17-Jan-2017.

[15]   https://www.taskrabbit.com/. Last accessed 17-Jan-2017.

[16]   J. Schieder, and E. Gould. "Women's work" and the gender pay gap. http://www.epi.org/publication/womens-work-and-the-gender-pay-gap-how-discrimination-societal-norms-and-other-forces-affect-womens-occupational-choices-and-their-pay/. Last accessed 17-Jan-2017.

[17]   http://www.aauw.org/research/the-simple-truth-about-the-gender-pay-gap/. Last accessed 17-Jan-2017.

[18]   https://genderize.io/. Last accessed 17-Jan-2017.

[19]   Teresa M. Heckert, et al. 2002. Gender differences in anticipated salary: Role of salary estimates for others, job characteristics, career paths, and job inputs. Sex roles. 47. 3 139-151.

[20]   H. Mary, C. L Dubois, and L. Fox-Cardamone. 2010. Gender difference in pay expectations: The roles of job intention and self – View. Psychology of Women Quarterly 34.2 (2010): 215-227.

[21]   Schweitzer, Linda, et al. 2014. The gender gap in pre-career salary expectations: a test of five explanations. Career Development International. 19.4 (2014): 404-425.

[22]   O'. P. Gavan, and D. F. Bush. 2002. Negotiation for starting salary: Antecedents and outcomes among recent college graduates. Journal of Business and Psychology 16.3 (2002): 365-382.

[23]   B. D. Francine, and L. M. Kahn. 2016. The gender wage gap: Extent, trends, and explanations. No. w21913. National Bureau of Economic Research, 2016.

[24]   Chamberlain, Andrew. 2016. Demystifying the Gender Pay Gap. Mill Valley, CA: Glassdoor (2016).

[25]   L. Andreas, and J. A. List. 2014. Do women avoid salary negotiations? Evidence from a large-scale natural field experiment. Management Science 61.9 (2014): 2016-2024.

[26]   Intuit Forecast: 7.6 Million People in On-Demand Economy by 2020. http://investors.intuit.com/press-releases/press-release-details/2015/Intuit-Forecast-76-Million-People-in-On-Demand-Economy-by-2020/default.aspx. Last accessed 20-Jan-2017.

The Failure of Success Factors: Lessons from Success and Failure Cases of Enterprise Architecture Implementation

Full Paper

Tom Hope
True Technology Partners Pty Ltd
Sydney
New South Wales 2000 Australia
+61 411 250 901
tom.hope@truetechnologypartners.com.au

Eng Chew
University of Technology, Sydney
15 Broadway
Ultimo, Sydney
New South Wales 2007
Australia +61 2 9514 4504
Eng.Chew@uts.edu.au

Rajeev Sharma
University of Waikato, Hamilton
Gate 1 Knighton Road
Hamilton 3240
New Zealand +64 838 4628
rsharma@waikato.ac.nz

ABSTRACT

Many Enterprise Architecture programmes fail to meet expectations. While much has been written about the factors influencing the success of EA programmes, there are few empirical investigations of the role of critical success factors (CSFs) in the success of EA programmes. This study condensed the very broad literature on CSFs for EA identifying six key CSFs that share a broad consensus in the literature. A qualitative case study was conducted to test the hypothesis that the six key CSFs would distinguish between the successful and the unsuccessful programmes. Analysis of the case study data reveals that three key CSFs associated with the use of EA tools did not distinguish between successful and unsuccessful cases while three key CSFs related to the process of EA programme implementation did so. The study concludes that success in EA programmes comes more from how architecture is practiced than what is practiced. The findings have important implications for EA suggesting that the methodological skills of architects need to be supplemented with an understanding of practice.

Keywords

Enterprise Architecture; Critical Success Factor; CSF; Practice; Routines; Ostensive; Performative; Reflexivity

ACM Reference format:

Tom Hope, Eng Chew and Rajeev Sharma. 2017. The Failure of Success Factors: Lessons from Success and Failure Cases of Enterprise Architecture Implementation. In *Proceedings of Computers and People Research Conference, Bangalore, India, June 21-23, 2017 (SIGMIS-CPR '17), 7 pages.*
DOI: 3084381.3084392

Acknowledgement

This research was partly supported by Australian Research Council's Discovery Project funding scheme (project number DP140100248) to Rajeev Sharma.

INTRODUCTION

Doing Enterprise Architecture (EA) well is an important capability for organizations as it ensures an alignment between IT and business strategy by creating an internal coherence between the various IT artifacts and business applications. It achieves this by reflecting the *"organizing logic for business processes and IT infrastructure"* [4]. However, despite more than twenty five years of practice, deriving value from EA remains an important managerial challenge [1].

Anecdotal evidence suggests that many programmes fail to *"get beyond the end of the runway"* [2] and that 40% of programmes are predicted to shut down within three years [3]. What makes EA an important capability for organizations is that *"only a small percentage of companies do it well"* [4].

An extensive amount of academic and practitioner literature has examined the question of what leads to success in EA programmes. A notable stream addressing that question is the critical success factors (CSF) literature, which identifies a very large number of factors associated with the success of EA programmes ([5], [6], [7], [8]). A key proposition of the CSF literature is that the presence of certain CSFs, such as a Strategy for the Development of Architecture, the Use of a Formal Methodology and Architectural Tools is important for ensuring the success of EA programmes. However, the conclusions and recommendations from that literature can only be considered speculative as its propositions are rarely grounded in theory and have hardly been the subject of rigorous empirical enquiry.

The objective of this paper is to address the above limitation by empirically examining the core proposition of the CSF literature, viz. "that success of EA programmes is associated with the presence of certain CSFs while failure is associated with the absence of those CSFs". To do that, this paper begins with a thematic analysis of a large eclectic body of the EA literature to identify a few key CSFs from the large number mentioned in the literature. The analysis identifies six key CSFs that are mentioned independently by a large number of sources. The empirical validation of the CSF literature is based on the analysis of eight case studies of EA implementation, four of which were successful and the other four were unsuccessful. The case data is then analyzed to identify the roles that the six key CSFs identified in our thematic analysis play in those cases. The expectation is that each of the six key CSFs would distinguish between the successful and the unsuccessful cases. Our analysis finds that three of the six key CSFs do so, while the other three fail to do so. The Discussion speculates on the reasons for the failure of CSFs to distinguish between the cases. It also speculates on alternative theories that could explain EA success. In particular, we discuss the possibility that differences between the *ostensive* and the *performative* [9] aspects of the routines underpinning the practice of EA in organizational contexts could explain EA success better than the absence or presence of key CSFs.

LITERATURE REVIEW

While the term EA has been defined and described in multiple ways, for the purpose of this research we consider it as an umbrella term that encompasses the multitude of activities that are required to realize a business concept as a socio-technical system. The multitude of definitions and descriptions arise from multiple perspectives employed by various scholars in defining and describing the term. Some of those are presented in Table 1. For instance, Nakakawa, van Bommel and Proper [10] define EA as "*the normative restriction of design freedom*" and "*a consistent and coherent set of design principles,*" which they draw from Dietz [11]. Bernus, Nemes and Schmidt's Handbook of Enterprise Architecture [12] employs multiple perspectives, each of which, Corporations, Consultants and Engineers, Managers and Project Leaders, Researchers and Graduates, Business Managers and IT Vendors is assigned a chapter in the book. Similarly, TOGAF describes EA from the perspectives of Business Process, Applications, Data and Technology [13]. The Nolan Norton Framework, in contrast, defines EA from five technical perspectives, Content and Goals, Architecture development process, Architecture process operation, Architectural competencies and Costs/Benefits [14]. Tambouris, Zotou, Kaalpokis and Tarabanis [15] employ a different perspective and define architecture as activity considered from an observer's perspective. Despite the multiple perspectives, there is reasonable consensus that doing EA well contributes to improved organizational performance through aligning "*business objectives with information technology infrastructure in an organization*" [15].

Table 1: Perspective-Based Definitions of Architecture

Perspective	Definition
Business Owner	A structure for value creation
Business Planner	A strategic management tool used to create the architectural blueprint for value creation and an attendant sustainable competitive advantage.
Business System Designer	The architectural blueprint that fuses organization, process and information technology into an integrated business whole.
Business System Builder	Provides the methodology to develop business solutions to achieve the integrated business whole.
Architect	The activity (practice) necessary to design and implement the architectural blueprint.
Enterprise	"*creates the ability to understand and determine the continual needs of integration, alignment, change and responsiveness of the business to technology and the market place*". [16]

Thematic Analysis of EA CSFs

The literature identifies a number of critical factors for the successful implementation of EA. To enable a critical review of the utility of the CSF approach, we begin with a thematic review of the EA literature to identify the key themes from this body of work. A number of electronic databases, including Academic Search Premier (EBSCO), the ACM Digital Library, Computer Source and ProQuest 5000 were searched to identify relevant publications. In addition, a number of commercially published architecture books were also searched.

The search identified over 500 observations relating to CSFs from over 100 distinct publications, authored by over 330 scholars. An initial analysis revealed an absence of a cumulative tradition: a number of different terms are employed for the same concept and the same labels are used to represent different concepts. Such a pattern is not uncommon in emerging research fields [17].

In order to reduce the plethora of CSFs identified in the literature to a manageable number, we employed a classification tool to sort similar concepts into overarching categories of CSFs. Specifically, we employed van den Berg and van Steenbergen's [18] assessment model, which identifies "*18 areas that must be represented in performing the architectural functions*" [18]. van den Berg and van Steenbergen divide the 18 areas (Table A, included after the Discussion section) into two sets of 9 areas. They label one set of 9 areas as representing "Thinking", i.e. the level architectural thinking in the organization. The other set of

9 areas is labeled by them as representing "Integration", i.e. the degree of organizational integration achieved by architecture [18]. Without being stringently prescriptive, the Key Areas provide sufficient guidance to ensure a high degree of classification consistency, while accommodating a range of interpretations.

The publications identified in the search were manually scanned for text that mentioned factors important for the success of EA implementation. The identified portions of text were classified into one of the 18 areas of van den Berg and van Steenbergen's model.

Results of Thematic Review

The CSFs were identified and ordered according to the frequency of their occurrence in the thematic review. The analysis (Table 2) revealed six Key CSFs that account for 72% of all observations that were cited by more than 25 independent sources. Three of the six Key CSFs are from the Thinking Area: Strategy for the Development of Architecture (T1), Use of Formal Architectural Methodology (T7), and Architecture Tools (T9). The other three are from the Integration Area: Monitoring and Compliance (I6), Commitment and Motivation (I7), and Consultation and Communication (I9).

Table 2: Top Six Key CSFs Identified through Thematic Review

Label	Critical Success Factor	% Sources citing CSF*
T1	Strategy for the Development of Architecture	33
T7	Use of Formal Methodology	63
T9	Use of Architecture Tools	25
I6	Monitoring and Compliance	30
I7	Commitment to the Use of Architecture	42
I9	Consultation and Communication	51

*Sources typically cite more than one CSF.

EMPIRICAL VALIDATION OF THE UTILITY OF THE CSFS

The above review has identified the consensus in the literature around the six Key CSFs that are considered important for the success of EA programmes. However, our review also identified that the validity of the CSFs has rarely been subjected to a rigorous empirical investigation. To address that limitation, this research employs a case study approach to investigate the validity of the CSFs.

Methodology

We employed a comparative case technique to evaluate the validity of the CSFs as predictors of success or failure. Specifically, we investigated multiple cases, some of which were seen by the informants and their organizations as successes while the others were seen as failures. Interviews were conducted with architects currently employed by those programmes. Overall, we conducted interviews with 10 architects across 8 organizations covering 8 independent EA programmes. The interviews typically lasted between 45 minutes and an hour, and were digitally recorded and transcribed, with one exception where the participant declined to be recorded. The interviews included questions on the history of the cases and the success factors present or absent.

Analysis

The eight EA programmes investigated were selected based on purposive sampling in order to maximize the chances of finding insights. Specifically, four successful and four unsuccessful programmes were chosen for investigation. The organizations come from banking, insurance and government sectors and range in size from approximately 45,000 employees to as few as 1,600 with the average being around 25,000.

All interviewees held long term senior permanent positions. All had more than a decade's architecture experience, with most having twenty or more years' experience.

The success or failure classifications were confirmed with the interviewees. Key words representing success and failure were searched for in the text of the interviews and the cumulative evidence was then employed to corroborate judgments regarding success and failure (Table 3).

The case evidence was then interrogated for the extent to which the six Key CSFs were presented within each of the eight cases. Key words related to each of the six Key CSFs (Table 2) were searched for across the transcripts. Each case was ranked for the extent of presence of each Key CSF. The ranking was done on a 0-5 scale (Table 4), where 5 represents 'Present to a very high degree' and 0 represents 'Not present at all'. Given the space limitations, the details of that analysis are not presented here.

Table 3: Classification of Cases as Successful/Unsuccessful

Case ID.	Supporting Comments (Programme outcome)
S1	**Organization**: Merging Government Super Department **Interviewee**: Chief Enterprise Architect "So now we find after four years we've returned about 100 million dollars after four years of cost avoidance." "and every year above and beyond that we've gone about 50 million extra so we started with 100 after 4 and I think it's now 200 or 250 which is where we are (unclear) and we do that every year." (Merge widely considered as one of the most successful ever done. Chief Architect rewarded with a directorship.) **Outcome: Successful**
S2	**Organization**: Financial services company **Interviewee**: Chief Enterprise Architect "I was recently appointed group architect by the managing director" (Transformation considered successful. Chief Architect Promoted.) **Outcome: Successful**
S3	**Organization**: A Major Bank **Interviewee**: Senior Domain Architect "... we are very mature architecture thinking organization." "... As in we all value architecture from the senior executives down to the ops developers etc." (Bank completed a multi years business transformation including the integration of a competitor) **Outcome: Successful**
S4	**Organization**: Another Major Bank **Interviewee**: Manager Enterprise Architecture team "It's almost like it's got its own brand recognition now. I want an architect telling me if I should even be looking at this business strategy. Tell me better ways of doing it." (Bank completed a seven year core system replacement programme.) **Outcome: Successful**
U1	**Organization**: Global Insurance Company **Interviewee**: Solutions Architecture Manager "those PMs then set up their teams and set up the project accordingly. If, for example, if they believe in architecture then they'll put an architect on the project. If they don't believe in it, there's no mandate to make them do it." (Architecture programme abolished most architects made redundant.) **Outcome: Unsuccessful**
U2	**Organization**: Federal Government Agency **Interviewee**: Last Surviving Full Time Architect "there is now two managers in charge of the architecture area one of whom has been here six months if not more, twelve months. The other one's been here three months and neither of them has yet seen or tried to look at our TO BE architecture and roadmap. They didn't even know they existed, yet they are managing the architecture and they've been here for a year, didn't know we had a target architecture or a roadmap for it, had not asked whether we had one, so that's the depth of the churn, the depth of the discontinuity." (Architect resigned, architecture function ceased.) **Outcome: Unsuccessful**
U3	**Organization**: Large Insurance Company **Interviewee**: Senior Enterprise Architect "It's a question of empowerment and the balance of power in that relationship. If the PM has more power than the architect then you get individual solutions that are not optimized." "Because they don't know and they don't care on time on budget delivery even if that means sacrificing some of the features some time in the future." (Architecture programme abolished ALL architects made redundant.) **Outcome: Unsuccessful**
U4	**Organization**: Very Large Insurance Company **Interviewee**: Manager Enterprise Architecture "You can have supply side architecture and demand side architecture. Supply side architecture where the CIO gets some architects and says "go and fix the business" fails. Supply side architecture doesn't work" "Demand side where the business says "we need to change works". Why does architecture need sponsorship? Infrastructure doesn't, applications don't." (Architecture programme abolished, function passed to consulting organization.) **Outcome: Unsuccessful**

Results

The core hypothesis of this study is that the six Key CSFs identified in the thematic review will distinguish between successful versus unsuccessful cases, i.e. the CSFs will be present to a greater extent in the successful cases than in the unsuccessful cases. To test this hypothesis, the interviews were analyzed for the extent to which each of the six Key CSFs was present in each of the eight cases (Table 4). Columns 2 and 3 of Table 4 report the scores on the extent of presence of each Key CSF for each of the successful and unsuccessful cases. Columns 4 and 5 report the mean scores for the extent of presence of each Key CSF for each of the successful and the unsuccessful cases. The last column reports the differences between the mean scores of the successful cases and the unsuccessful cases (Delta Mean Score). For the validity of the CSFs to be empirically established based on the analysis of the case evidence, the mean scores for the successful cases should be systematically and substantially higher than those for the unsuccessful cases, i.e. the Difference score should be high and positive across all the six Key CSFs.

Table 4: Differences in Extent to which Key CSFs were Present between Successful and Unsuccessful Cases

CSF	Case Scores		Mean Score		Delta
	Success-ful cases	Unsuccess-ful cases	Success-ful cases	Unsucce ss-ful cases	Mean Score
T1	2, 3, 4, 4	2, 4, 5, 5	3.25	3.75	-0.50
T7	2, 2, 3, 4	1, 2, 3, 4	2.75	2.50	+0.25
T9	0, 0, 1, 1	0, 0, 0, 3	0.50	0.75	-0.25
I6	4, 4, 5, 5	0, 1, 1, 1	4.50	0.75	+3.75
I7	4, 5, 5, 5	0, 1, 1, 2	4.75	1.00	+3.75
I9	4, 5, 5, 5	0, 0, 1, 1	4.75	0.25	+4.50

* 0 = 'Not present at all'; 1 = 'Present to a minimal degree'; 2 = 'Present inconsistently'; 3 = 'Present consistently but weak'; 4 = 'Present to a high degree'; 5 = 'Present to a very high degree'

Analysis of the pattern of Delta scores suggests two overarching conclusions. First, the Delta scores for all three Thinking Key CSFs are close to zero, suggesting that they were present to equal degrees in the successful and the unsuccessful cases, i.e. they do not distinguish between the successful and unsuccessful cases. Two, the Delta scores for all three Integration Key CSFs are systematically and substantially higher than zero, suggesting that the presence/absence of Integration Key CSFs is associated with the success/failure of EA programs.

DISCUSSION

Our analysis finds that only three of the six CSFs distinguish between successful and unsuccessful cases, i.e. they were present to a greater degree in the successful cases than in the unsuccessful cases. Further, there is plausible evidence to suggest those CSFs contributed to the outcomes (for space considerations that analysis is not presented here).

The three CSFs whose role was validated across the cases are Monitoring and Compliance, Commitment to the Use of Architecture and Consultation and Communication. The three CSFs whose role was not validated are Strategy for the Development of Architecture, Use of Formal Methodology and Use of Architectural Tools.

The pattern of validated and unvalidated CSFs reveals an interesting conclusion. All three unvalidated CSFs represent the technical sophistication of EA tools i.e. "Thinking" CSFs employed in the methodological execution of the projects. In contrast, all three validated CSFs represent the sociological processes of EA implementation, i.e. "Integration" CSFs. We speculate below on the implications of this pattern of findings.

Zachman's framework, perhaps the most influential commentary on the practice of EA, privileges the engineering imperative focusing on tools and techniques for the creation of EA artifacts. However, it ignores how EA is practiced and the role of sociological factors in the practice of EA within organizational contexts. This is particularly important as the analysis of the cases shows success perhaps comes less from "what" is done, as Zachman's framework would have us believe than from "how" it is done, i.e. the sociological process involved in the implementation of EA [27]. In both those respects, Zachman's perspectives mirror the shortcomings of an Information Engineering framework [28], which is about creating technical artifacts to produce organizational outcomes.

We speculate that the theory of routines [29] may offer an interpretation of the pattern of findings revealed in this study. Feldman and Pentland [29] define routines as the "*repetitive, recognizable patterns of interdependent actions, carried out by multiple actors.*" Pentland and Feldman [9] identify two aspects of routines, the ostensive and the performative. The ostensive aspect of routines is the understandings of the participants, the "*embodied and cognitive understandings that guide actions taken in the enactment of routines*" [9]. In contrast, the performative pertains to their actual execution.

The separation of *ostensive* and *performative* is crucial to understanding the findings of this study. Feldman and Pentland [29] explain that the *performative* modifies the *ostensive* aspect as "*participants construct routines from a repertoire of possibilities*". The self-monitoring (reflexivity) of participants [30] makes the *performative* aspect "*inherently improvisational*" [28]. From the perspective of EA methodologies, the architects' *performative* execution of the *ostensive* aspect of the methodologies is assumed to be unproblematic. Success is assumed to rest on the competent and faithful execution of the methodology. However, the need for *performative improvisation* that arises when fluid methodologies meet fluid organizational contexts [31] suggests that the process of execution becomes critical for success, rather than the methodological repertoire of the architects. It seems that having a methodology is less important than how it is executed.

In summary, this research empirically reinforces a key proposition of the practice perspective [32], [33], [34] that success rests on *performative improvisation*. The practice perspective may be another useful theoretical lens through which to understand the findings of this study.

The findings of this study have important implications for the practice of EA. It suggests that the methodological skills of architects need to be supplemented with process (or social) skills so that architects might be able to attend to key aspects of the organizational context to assure the success of EA programmes as well as their own success, rather than be the victims of circumstances.

REFERENCES

[1] Ernst, Alexander M. 2008. Enterprise Architecture Management Patterns. 15th Conference on Pattern Languages of Programs (PLoP), *Plop '08*, October 18-20, 2008, Nashville, TN, USA.

[2] Schekkerman, Jaap 2005. *The Economic Benefits of Enterprise Architecture.* Trafford Publishing, Victoria, British Columbia.

[3] Sessions, Rodger 2008. *Simple Architectures for Complex Enterprises.* Best Practices, Microsoft Press. Redmond.

[4] Ross, Jeanne W., Weill, Peter and Robertson, David C. 2006. *Enterprise Architecture as Strategy.* Harvard Business School Press, Boston.

[5] Perkins, Alan 2003. *Critical Success Factors for Enterprise Architecture Engineering.* Visible Systems Corporation, Lexington. Available at: www.visible.com/Company/whitepapers/EACSF.PDF, *accessed 23/2/2013.*

[6] Ylimaki, Tanja and Halttunen Veikko 2005. Method engineering in practice: A case of applying the Zachman framework in the context of small enterprise architecture oriented projects. *Information Knowledge Systems Management 5,* IOS Press, 189-209.

[7] Doucet, Gary, Gotze, John, Saha, Pallab and Bernard Scott 2008. Coherency Management: Using Enterprise Architecture for Alignment, Agility and Assurance. *Journal of Enterprise Architecture,* vol. 4, no. 2, 9-20.

[8] Lapalme, James, 2011. Three Schools of Enterprise Architecture. IT Professional, IEEE Computer Society Digital Library. IEEE Computer Society, Accessed 21/06/2013.

[9] Pentland, Brian T. and Feldman, Martha S. 2008. Designing routines: On the folly of designing artifacts, while hoping for patterns of action. *Information and Organization,* vol. 18, 235-250.

[10] Nakakawa, A. , van Bommel P. and Proper, H. A. 2011. Definition and Validation of Requirements For Collaborative Decision – Making In Enterprise Architecture Creation. *International Journal of Cooperative Information Systems,* vol. 20, no. 1, 83-136.

[11] Dietz, J. 2008. *Building Strategy into Design.* Netherlands Architecture Forum Academic Service SDU, The Hague, The Netherlands, ISBN-139789012580861, http://www.naf.nl

[12] Bernus, P., Nemes, L. and Schmidt, G. (Eds) 2003. *Handbook on Enterprise Architecture.* International Handbooks on Information Systems, Springer-Verlag, Berlin.

[13] Schekkerman, Jaap 2004. *How to survive in the jungle of Enterprise Architecture Frameworks,* 3rd Edition. Trafford Publishing, Victoria, British Columbia.

[14] Lankhorst, Marc, et al. 2005. *Enterprise Architecture at Work: Modelling, Communication, and Analysis.* Telematica Instituut, Springer-Verlag, Berlin.

[15] Tambouris, Efthimios, Zotou, Maria, Kalampokis, Evangelos and Tarabanis Konstantinos 2012. Fostering enterprise architecture education and training with the enterprise architecture competence framework. *International Journal of Training and Development,* vol. 16, issue 2, 128-136.

[16] O'Rourke, C., Fishman, N. and Selkow, W. 2003. *Enterprise Architecture, Using the Zachman Framework,* Thomson Course Technology, Boston.

[17] Hirsch, P. M., & Levin, D. Z. 1999. Umbrella advocates versus validity police: A life-cycle model. *Organization Science, 10, 2,* 199-212.

[18] Van den Berg, Martin and van Steenbergen, Marlies 2006. *Building an Enterprise Architecture Practice,* Sogeti, Springer, Dordrecht, Netherlands

[19] Rico, David F. 2006. A Framework for Measuring ROI of Enterprise Architecture, *Journal of Organizational and End User Computing,* Apr-Jun 2006, 18, 2.

[20] Strang, C. J. 2005. Next generation systems architecture - the Matrix, *BT Technology Journal,* vol. 23, no. 1, January 2005.

[21] Gruman, Galen 2006. The Four Stages of Enterprise Architecture; An exclusive MIT survey maps the evolution of IT architecture and explains why you can't skip any steps. *CIO,* vol. 20, issue 5, 1.

[22] Hungerford, Peter 2007. The Syngenta Architecture Story, in *Handbook of Enterprise Systems Architecture in Practice.* Saha, Pallab (Ed), Idea Group Inc, Hershey, 331-350.

[23] Van den Hoven, John 2003. DATA ARCHITECTURE: BLUEPRINTS FOR DATA, *Information Systems Management,* WINTER 2003, 90-92.

[24] Raths, David 2007. The People Side of IT Architecture, *Computerworld,* October 29, 2007, 44-48.

[25] Schekkerman, Jaap 2008. *Enterprise Architecture Good Practices Guide.* Trafford Publishing, Victoria, British Columbia.

[26] Strnadle Christoph F. 2006. ALIGNING BUSINESS AND IT: THE PROCESS DRIVEN ARCHITECTURE MODEL, *Information Systems Management,* FALL 2006, 67-77.

[27] Whittington, Richard 2007.Completing the Practice Turn in Strategy Research, *Organization Studies,* 27, 5, 613-634. SAGE publications.

[28] Beath, Cynthia Mathis, and Wanda J. Orlikowski 1994. The contradictory structure of systems development methodologies: Deconstructing the IS-user relationship in information engineering. *Information Systems Research* 5.4 (1994), 350-377.

[29] Feldman, Martha S. and Pentland, Brian T 2003. Reconceptualizing Organizational Routines as a Source of Flexibility and Change, *Administrative Science Quarterly,* 48, 94-118.

[30] Giddens, Anthony 1984. *The Constitution of Society.* Polity Press, Cambridge.

[31] Leonardi, Paul M. 2011. When Flexible Routines Meet Flexible Technologies: Affordance, Constraint, and the Imbrication of Human and Material Agencies, *MIS Quarterly,* 35, 1,147-167.

[32] Whittington, Richard 1996. Strategy as Practice, *Long Range Planning,* 29, 5, 731-735. Pergamon, Elsevier Science Ltd.

[33] Bourdieu, Pierre 1990. *The Logic of Practice.* Polity Press, Cambridge, United Kingdom.

[34] Felin, Teppo, Foss, Nicolai J., Heimeriks, Koen H., and Madsen, Tammy L. 2012. Microfoundations of Routines and Capabilities: Individuals, Processes, and Structure. *Journal of Management Studies,* 49, 8, December 2012, 1351-1374.

Table A: van den Berg and van Steenbergen's (2006) Key Areas

Label	CSF: Definition	Examples (Reference)
T1	Strategy for the Development of Architecture: "Any process, technique, methodology, activity, organization or artefact that directs or influences the way that architects operate might be considered strategic."	"have a clear understanding of what one is trying to achieve" [19]
T2	Alignment with Business: Architecture is the control instrument to make sure that the content of such developments is coordinated. Of course, architecture must then be employed for this purpose.	"The beginning of architecture is business strategy, and its end is business change. The Matrix is driven by analytical insight into BT's business strategy." [20]
T3	Coordination of Developments: Architecture is the control instrument to make sure that the content of such developments is coordinated. Of course, architecture must then be employed for this purpose.	"We do rip and replace," he says. That way he says, platform heterogeneity can't get a toehold in the organization." [21]
T4	Quality Management: Artefacts and outputs must be fit for purpose and appropriate for their audience and delivered in a timely fashion. Ultimately QM is about the usability of the outputs of the EA practice.	"monitored primarily through the adoption of the standard quality gate framework" [20]
T5 & T6	Maintenance of the Architectural Process and Artefacts: Maintenance of the architecture means that a cycle of evaluation, development, improvement and implementation is periodically rerun and that artefacts are assessed for currency.	"There are some diagrams that are always referred to within the organization and give structure to many discussions. It is important that once the organization has taken to these (in fact assumed ownership) that they are not lightly changed" [22]
T7	Use of Architectural Method: Architecture is developed in a methodical procedure made up of activities, techniques, tools and artefacts	"The Enterprise architecture is the overall framework or blueprint for how the enterprise uses information technology to achieve its business objectives" [23]
T8	Use of Architectural Tools: Using tools in an integrated manner, preferably with the support of a repository, maximizes their efficiency and effectiveness.	"make effective use of tools and automation, and may in turn be influenced by the available features of the tools" [20]
T9	Budgeting and Planning: Budgeting and planning can range from drafting occasional plans to collecting past experiences with architecture.	"Create a system for measuring and reporting measures for the return on investment …" [19]
I1	The Purpose of Architecture: Architecture has a goal: it must accomplish something; it needs to be detail the means of execution.	"it's also important to get involved in strategic planning with business units,…" [24'
I2	Alignment with Development Process: Architecture needs to channel changes in such a way that the business goals are achieved in the most effective manner.	"follow a standard life-cycle model and delivery process, create the major deliverables listed within each lifecycle stage, and to justify any exceptions" [20]
I3	Alignment with Operations: Architecture is not only important for development – the alignment with operations and maintenance is also important.	"Eliminate duplicating technology, reducing costs" [25]
I4	Relationship to the AS-IS State: Most organizations have to deal with an existing situation based on historical growth (frequently without architecture). In assessing the suitability of the architecture, it is important to realize that a set of circumstances already exists, which has its own range of possibilities and impossibilities.	"identification, specification, and elaboration of cause–effect relations necessary to demonstrate the return on investment (ROI) for any change initiative" [26]
I5	Roles and Responsibilities: If the roles and responsibilities concerning architectural thinking and taking actions are clearly defined and unambiguously outlined to everyone, discussions and differences of opinion about architecture are prevented from falling into limbo.	"There is a standard set of roles defined to support projects in establishing delivery teams to fulfill the main activities expected" Strang [20]
I6	Monitoring and Compliance: Without a control mechanism, the temptation will be too great to choose the path of least resistance and to ignore the architecture at certain points.	"Exceptions are evaluated in case they justify improvements to governance or IT domains." [20]
I7	Commitment and Motivation: Business and IT managers are primarily responsible for creating a favourable atmosphere. This ensures that the architectural process is given sufficient time, money and resources.	"Senior business managers share responsibility with IT managers for delivering business value from IT" [20]
I8	Architectural Roles and Training: Acquiring this skill set takes training. Hence defining the architect's role and providing the necessary training is an important concern.	"Have a training program, which includes presentation, influencing, and negotiation skills" [22]
I9	Consultation and Communication: A great deal of consultation with various stakeholders is required in developing architecture.	"Managers are educated to understand and play their role in the governance process and decisions are widely communicated" [20]

27

The Impact of Process and IT Modularity for Mutual Understanding among Business and IT

Short Paper

Christian Jentsch
University of Bamberg
c.jensch@uni-bamberg.de

Andreas Reitz
Frankfurt School of Finance &
Management
a.reitz@fs.de

Daniel Beimborn
Frankfurt School of Finance &
Management
d.beimborn@fs.de

ACM Reference format:
Christian Jentsch, Andreas Reitz, and Daniel Beimborn. 2017. The Impact of Process and IT Modularity for Mutual Understanding among Business and IT. In *Proceedings of SIGMIS-CPR '17, Bangalore, India, June 21-23, 2017*, 3 pages.
https://doi.org/http://dx.doi.org/10.1145/3084381.3084412

1 INTRODUCTION

In most organizations, many people are contributing to one specific business object or process. To maximize the performance of the process, it is important that the manager and the IT personnel have a mutual understanding of the tasks, problems and characteristics of the process. Mutual understanding between business and IT personnel has been frequently raised as one of the critical aspects to achieve high performance in IT projects [13] and strategically align the IT with the business system [8]. In addition, most of these studies highlight the significance of business/IT mutual understanding especially in 'complex' systems [5]. We argue that mutual understanding is more difficult to achieve in highly complex systems and combine this idea with the assumption that modularity reduces complexity. Thus, our research question is:

RQ: Does modularity facilitate mutual understanding?

2 THEORETICAL BACKGROUND

Modularity: Modularity is a well-known concept from general systems theory [10]. It describes the decomposition of a complex system into separated loosely coupled constructs. In this context, we use IT architecture and business process modularity as measurements for modularity.

IT architecture modularity can be described as "degree of decomposition of an organization's IT portfolio into loosely coupled subsystems that communicate through standardized interfaces" [12]. So, changes to one subsystem affect others only to a certain level [2, 6]. IT modularity is driven by standardization, which specify communication and interaction rules between different applications [14]. A business process can either be modular itself, if its single process

steps are loosely coupled and only interact through its interfaces or modular in relation to other business processes (the processes are loosely coupled [9]). Single processes are isolated from each other and self-contained [11]. The processes encapsulate all their required information and hide them to others [7].

Business/IT Mutual Understanding (BITMU): We define mutual understanding (MU) as intersection of individual cognitive models, which are formed and adjusted by experiences and sense-making processes. In literature, there is no doubt regarding the importance of a MU between business and IT professionals in high performing companies [4]. However, it appears that previous conceptualizations are tightly linked to their respective research stream [4]. For example, BITMU in alignment research mainly focuses on the MU of business and IT strategies [8] and so on.

To overcome this context-based conceptualization, we apply a more theoretical approach by describing the dimensions of MU through the lens of the work system theory proposed by Alter [1]. Basically, the framework of this theory differs between two perspectives in an organization - artefacts which are inside the work system and the artefacts which are outside the work system. The work system itself consists of processes and activities between participants to perform a task using information and technologies. These artefacts are inside the work system, because they are all necessary conditions to complete the underlying task. Artefacts which are outside the work system are environment, infrastructure and strategies. Depending on the context of the respective work system, the artefacts product/services and customer can be inside or outside the work system.

Thus, we conceptualize BITMU by differing between elements which are inside the work system - like MU of the business processes and activities - and elements that are outside the work system - like business strategies.

3 MODEL DEVELOPMENTS

We differ between modularity of business processes and IT architecture; on the other hand, we differ between MU of the business process (MU inside the work system) and MU of the business strategy (MU outside the work system). For an employee, it is much easier to apply a cognitive pattern to interpret the environment (cf. template theory by Gobet [3]) on a structured (e.g. modularized) system than on an unstructured system; especially, if this involves common standards for modules and interfaces. Now, if two employees perceive the same modular system in the environment it is very likely that their cognitive patterns of how they interpret their environment converge. Therefore, our first hypothesis is:

Hypothesis 1: Modular business processes lead to a higher level of mutual understanding regarding the business processes.

In our research setting, the involved employees are members of the business or and IT unit. While the main work domain of business professionals is the business process itself, the IT personnel interprets the business process through the lens of the IT architecture. We argue that IT personnel possess a larger set of cognitive patterns in their domain than in the business domain. A modular IT architecture which matches the structure of the process especially facilitates business understanding of IT personnel which in turn leads to a MU between business and IT professionals regarding the business processes.

Hypothesis 2: A modular IT architecture leads to a higher level of mutual understanding regarding the business processes.

The theory of templates [3] argues that employees possess several different cognitive templates to interpret the environment. Depending on the perceived elements in the environment, the individual will apply different templates for interpretation. That allows a hierarchical scrolling through different abstraction levels. Thus, an individual will use different hierarchical templates to recognize environmental patterns from an abstract business system to a concrete step in a business process. We argue that employees who are able to recognize the abstract business system are rather able to interpret the strategy of the business system.

Hypothesis 3: Modular business processes lead to a higher level of mutual understanding regarding the business strategies.

Similar to our argumentation for H2, we argue that the IT personnel interprets the business processes through the lens of the IT systems. Thus, if the modular IT systems map the whole network of business processes (see H3), the IT personnel will develop an understanding of the strategic intent of the business much faster than in an environment with non-modular IT systems.

Hypothesis 4: Modular IT systems lead to a higher level of mutual understanding regarding the business strategies.

4   RESEARCH METHODOLOGY

We conducted a survey with participants from the banking industry. We received 202 filled questionnaires (response rate of 10.8%). Due to missing values our tests are based on 119 responses.

The items for our measurement instrument has been derived from literature whenever possible. As controls, we used process type (type of credit), country, size (categories of firm size based on balance sheet total), bank sector (commercial banks, cooperatives, public savings banks), and age of the respondent.

5   DISCUSSION AND CONCLUSION

Higher levels of MU of the business processes and strategy can be achieved, if business processes and IT architecture are modular. Business process modularity can explain the development of MU of business strategy but not of the respective business processes. Employees apply different cognitive templates to interpret the environment. Related to business process modularity, single modules can either be interpreted within the respective business process or

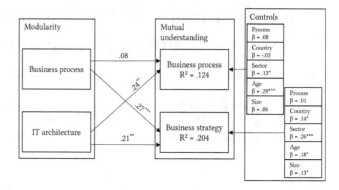

Figure 1: Estimation Results
Notes: N=119. *** $p < 0.001$; ** $p < 0.01$: * $p < 0.05$.

across different business processes. Individuals only seem to apply similar templates in a modularized business process environment when it comes to the overall business strategy (i.e. H3 supported) but not regarding the modularity within a business process (i.e. H1 rejected). Work systems theory explains, that different business units work systems while IT has a work system that covers all the work systems. Business process modularity does not imply that the MU of every single brick in the system will increase. This is because not every single brick is part of the joint work system of business and IT professionals. This interpretation can be applied for the findings of the IT architecture modularity as well. Since the IT architecture modularity, which matches the modularity of the business process, is part of the IT unit's work system, the business process itself becomes a critical component in IT's work system. This implies that the IT personnel's understanding for the business strategy on a global level will increase likewise. In the process of aligning IT architecture to the modular business processes, the IT unit's understanding of the business process will increase likewise (H2 confirmed). The IT unit aligns the IT architecture not only to one business module but to the whole system of business modules, for which reason the understanding of business strategy also increases (H4 confirmed).

The linkage between modularity and MU can be explained by the template theory that indicates why modularity in general can potentially impact MU. But, only combined with the work system theory it can explain why business process modularity does not enable MU of the business process (H1) but MU of the business strategy (H3). This research shows, that not only a modular business system is an important antecedent of MU, but as well the inclusion of all stakeholders (business and IT) on one work system. In our study, we could cover the two different work systems by focusing on business processes on one hand and IT architectures on the other hand. We can conclude, that profound MU is facilitated by process modularity only in combination with an IT architecture which matches the modular. These results can be used for further research regarding a more differentiated view on the modularity as a driver of BITMU.

REFERENCES

[1] Steven Alter. 2013. Work System Theory: Overview of Core Concepts, Extensions, and Challenges for the Future. *Journal of the Association for Information Systems*

14, 2 (2013), 72–121.

[2] Martin Fowler. 2001. Reducing coupling. *IEEE Software* 18, 4 (2001), 102.

[3] Fernand Gobet. 1998. Expert memory: a comparison of four theories. *Cognition* 66, 2 (1998), 115–152.

[4] Christian Jentsch and Daniel Beimborn. 2014. Shared Understanding Among Business and IT - A Literature Review and Research Agenda. In *22th European Conference on Information Systems*.

[5] Christian Jentsch and Daniel Beimborn. 2016. IT is all about the Game - An Exploratory Study on the Impact of Task Characteristics on the Dimensions of Business/IT Shared Understanding. In *Proceedings of the 24nd European Conference on Information Systems*.

[6] Satish Nambisan. 2002. Complementary product integration by high-technology new ventures: The role of initial technology strategy. *Management Science* 48, 3 (2002), 382–398.

[7] D. L. Parnas. 1972. On the Criteria to Be Used in Decomposing Systems into Modules. *Communications on ACM* 15, 12 (1972), 1053–1058.

[8] Blaize Horner Reich and Izak Benbasat. 2000. Factors that influence the Social Dimension of Alignment between Business and Information Technology Objectives. *MIS Quarterly* 24, 1 (2000), 81–113.

[9] Ron Sanchez and Joseph T. Mahoney. 1996. Modularity, flexibility, and knowledge management in product and organization design. *Strategic management journal* 17, S2 (1996), 63–76.

[10] Melissa A. Schilling. 2000. Toward a general modular systems theory and its application to interfirm product modularity. *Academy of management review* 25, 2 (2000), 312–334.

[11] Hüseyin Tanriverdi, Prabhudev Konana, and Ling Ge. 2007. The Choice of Sourcing Mechanisms for Business Processes. *Information Systems Research* 18, 3 (2007), 280–299. https://doi.org/10.1287/isre.1070.0129

[12] Amrit Tiwana and Benn Konsynski. 2010. Complementarities Between Organizational IT Architecture and Governance Structure. *Information Systems Research* 21, 2 (2010), 288–304. https://doi.org/10.1287/isre.1080.0206

[13] Paul W. L. Vlaar, Paul C. van Fenema, and Vinay Tiwari. 2008. Cocreating Understanding and Value in distributed Work: How Members of Onsite and Offshore Vendor Teams give, make, demand, and break sense. *MIS Quarterly* 32, 2 (2008), 227–255.

[14] Peter Weill and Jeanne Ross. 2005. Designing IT governance. *MIT Sloan Management Review* 46, 2 (2005), 26–34.

The Effects of Modularity on Effective Communication and Collaboration

Full Paper

Chintan Amrit
IEBIS Department
University of Twente
The Netherlands
c.amrit@utwente.nl

Elody Hutten
APG Asset Management
Amsterdam
The Netherlands
elody.hutten@gmail.com

ABSTRACT

In this article we explore the consequences associated with a lack of coordination between the requirements engineering process and the development process. We conduct a detailed case study of an ICT department of a large European bank that develops software using the agile software development method. Our current study reveals that the application of a modular organizational design in a dynamic agile environment has a negative effect on the communication and coordination between members of different modules. More specifically, the modular design creates both a semantic and a pragmatic boundary among members of different modules, which is primarily caused by the fact that modules have differentiated tasks and often misaligned interests.

CCS CONCEPTS

•Software and its engineering~Agile software development   • Software and its engineering~Programming teams • Software and its engineering~Agile software development

KEYWORDS

Agile Software Development, Modular organization, knowledge sharing boundaries

1 INTRODUCTION

Conway's law states that "organizations which design systems are constrained to produce designs which are copies of the communication structures of these organizations" [1]. This organization pattern [2, 3] implies that the interface structure of an information system will mirror the social structure of the organization that designed it [4-6]. The importance of

coordination between the requirement engineering process and the development process has also been demonstrated [7]. Frank and Hartel (2009) [8] conducted a study with respect to the application of a modular organizational design within an agile software development context and found that a reintegration of different modules resulted in an increase in both team morale and team performance. These findings could indicate that splitting a tightly coupled system (e.g. a development team) into autonomous modules within an agile software development environment reduces the performance of such a system. An explanation for these observations could be the fact that modules have their own goals which might cause two different modules to become highly differentiated. This is clearly evident in the study by Frank and Hartel (2009) [8, 9], one of the modules was responsible for writing user stories while the other module was responsible for actually developing the software. A consequence of these differentiated roles could be that the development of shared mental models, which is the overlapping of the cognitive representation of the external reality between team members [9], is inhibited, due to a semantic boundary between the modules, interpretive differences despite a common lexicon [10]. Another consequence of the differentiated roles modules could have, is that it creates a pragmatic boundary, which could inhibit effective communication. Finally, the separation of a tightly coupled system into different modules could result in a decrease of relational capital between members of different modules. These hypotheses suggest that applying a modular design in an agile software development context might lead to a decrease in coordination between the different modules which, as reasoned above, is crucial in software development and especially in agile software development. It is therefore questionable whether a modular organization design can be applied effectively within an agile software development context. This leads to the following research question: *Can a modular organizational design be applied in an agile software development context?*The current study will investigate the role of a modular organizational design with respect to its effect on communication and coordination between modules composed from a tightly coupled system within an agile software development context.

2 Literature Background

The framework of Carlile (2004) [10] provides an understanding of communication and boundaries affecting effective communication. Carlile (2004) constructed a framework regarding knowledge sharing within organizations. He proposed three boundaries of knowledge sharing with increasing complexity due to increasing novelty, specialized (domain-specific) knowledge and dependency: syntactic, semantic and pragmatic with the corresponding capabilities: transfer, translation and transformation see figure 1. The first boundary, the syntactic knowledge boundary, is concerned with the lack of a common lexicon, which prevents knowledge from being processed across a (functional) boundary. A shared, stable syntax could serve as a boundary object and enable the transfer of knowledge (boundary spanning). The second boundary is the semantic boundary which is concerned with interpretive differences despite a common lexicon that decreases effective collaboration and coordination. It is necessary to consider tacit, context-specific knowledge in order to be able to span the semantic boundary and really understand the meaning of knowledge that is being transferred (called translation). Purpose of semantic boundary spanning is, thus, the development of a shared meaning. The final boundary is the pragmatic boundary which refers to conflicts that arise due to consequential interaction in the presence of conflicting interests. The purpose of pragmatic boundary spanning is to achieve a common interest.

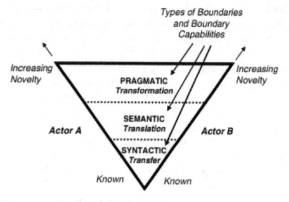

Figure 1, Integrated framework regarding knowledge sharing [10]. There are three levels of boundaries and corresponding required capabilities.

A study by Hsu, Chu, Lin, And Lo (2014) [11] investigated the integrated framework regarding knowledge sharing by Carlile (2004) [10] in an agile software development context. More specifically, they tested an extension of the model which included three aspects of intellectual capital and their influence on effective boundary spanning and the influence of effective boundary spanning on information system performance

Ernst (2006) [12] conducted a study with respect to the limits of modularity. He hypothesizes that modularity has been taken too far and that the limits to modularity are not taken into account appropriately. The conclusion that he draws from his research in the chip industry is that inter-firm collaboration requires more coordination through corporate management when codification does not reduce the complexity.

The application of a modular design in software development in an agile environment has been observed in a case study by [7]. Besides studying the consequences of lacking customer involvement, they also report on how organizations dealt with this issue. One of the strategies they found was the use of a definition of READY. This means that the requirements provided by the customer (or representatives or surrogates for that matter) need to conform to a certain standard (the definition of READY) before the developers are prepared to work on it [7].

Frank and Hartel (2009) [8] conducted a study in a company that used a modular organizational design by creating a requirement engineering model (READY) and a development module (DONE). Originally, separate teams were responsible for constructing user stories (READY) and development teams (DONE) who were responsible for building the actual software. Frank and Hartel (2009) concluded that the increased collaboration between the READY and DONE part increased team morale and more predictable results while maintaining a constant velocity. This study, thus, questions the application of a very modular design in an agile software development context [8].

Currently, a new conceptual framework with respect to software development is emerging: DevOps. DevOps extends agile methodologies and principles outside of the field of development in order to integrate two departments: development and operations[13]. DevOps clearly views the different aspects of an information system as interdependent which is an indication that these are not loosely coupled systems. The fact that the emerging conceptual framework in IS research, DevOps, advocates more integration and collaboration could be seen as another indication that a modular organizational design might be less appropriate in an agile software development environment.

As mentioned above, a modular organization design can be inappropriate in an Agile development environment, as parts of an organization are not loosely coupled systems with weak interdependency. Moreover, customer involvement is highly important in requirements engineering, which implies that the READY and DONE part are highly dependent, and thus tightly coupled [7]. So, creating modules out of a tightly coupled system can lead to a decrease in the effectiveness of the modularity. So, from an organizational design perspective, the results obtained by Frank and Hartel (2009) can be explained by the fact that modules are created from a tightly coupled system (scrum team) which results in a decrease in coordination and, consequently, a decrease in performance [8].

Our research question will be answered using a case study approach within a program concerned with agile software development. Data were primarily collected using qualitative interviews.

3. Case Study

Our case study setting is at a bank in Europe, referred to as 'European bank' in this paper. The ICT group of European bank have adopted agile software development practices based on the scaled agile framework (SAFe) [14]. Just as in many agile projects, this case followed a modular organizational design [8]. Two modules were created from the scrum teams, a READY part which is responsible for getting user stories "READY" and a DONE part which is responsible for getting the user stories "DONE". One of the core reasons for implementing the agile model was to remove project management from the development part. This was achieved by dividing the original scrum teams in both a READY and a DONE team whereby the project manager was included in the READY team. It was thought that, by decoupling the DONE teams from a certain project and thus single project manager, teams would become more stable since they do not have to be abrogated after a project has finished, but the DONE teams can now be assigned to another project, or used for different projects at the same time. Another benefit was that the DONE teams would now be coordinated by one person who would become responsible for the continuity of these teams and, thus, the HR. It was therefore hypothesized that the program would be able to add more value by being able to give priority to features and stories at program level instead of giving priority to user stories within projects. Another consequence of this arrangement was supposed to be improved scalability, the teams could become more able to respond to changes. When a higher demand for developers occurs, new teams could be created and when demand drops, teams could be send home.

The design of the Agile model occurred using working groups, consisting of all the people that were interested. In total, there were six themes and six working groups. These themes were: communication, process decisions, governance, team/aligned functions, environments and scrum of scrums. Each working group thus worked on how the new model should address the issues related to their theme. After approximately one year, the design of the Agile model was finished and the new agile process model was made definite and implemented. The actual implementation consisted of a presentation to inform the people of the program about the new model.

The scrum teams (also called "DONE teams") were responsible for building the software and consists of a scrum master, product owner and developers and tester. There were approximately 18 DONE teams. All members of the DONE teams were externals and both European and Indian nationalities were present in (some) of the teams, although no DONE team were entirely made up of people from India. Most of the DONE teams were collocated, with the exception of teams including Indian developers or tester since these team members were often located in India. Contact with these globally distributed team members was established via telephone, email, chat and videoconferencing. In principle, the Indian team members participated in all scrum rituals.

The READY teams were responsible for transforming business requirements (from different projects) into user stories that could be built by DONE teams. These teams consisted of a product manager, project manager, application engineer, test manager, interaction designer and a business analyst. These READY teams were organized among six themes: financial insight, cross-channel functionalities (one theme is concerned with banking related functionalities and the other theme with the remaining functionalities), content interaction and design, cross-channel marketing, integration of the client's world and cross-channel contact. The exact composition of the READY teams was not rigid and varied per theme.

The current study uses semi-structured interviews using the framework provided by Myers and Newman (2007) to conduct semi-structured or unstructured interviews in an information systems context. We use the interview method to gain a better and more in depth understanding of the effect of a modular organizational design on the knowledge sharing in an Agile development enviroment. We engaged both a "maximum variation" and a "snowball" sampling strategy in line with the typologies provided by Miles and Huberman (1994). The aim of a maximum variation strategy is to compose a sample that is heterogeneous. The logic behind this is that the results of the extremes will aggregate to a result that is representative for the entire population. After each interview, the researcher asked the interviewee who would also be interesting to interview, hence the snowballing. These strategies and the quota of at least one informant per function resulted in a total sample of 21 different informants. More detailed information with respect to the composition of the sample can be found in Appendix A (table 1).

All interviews were face-to-face and took place in a familiar location for the interviewee. With permission of the interviewee, the entire interview was recorded with a laptop and no notes were made in order to contribute to the feeling of a natural conversation. Afterwards, transcripts were made of the interviews. The script used during the interview can be found in Appendix B.

The data analysis process occurred according to Miles and Huberman (1994)[15]. All codes were assigned using the software "Atlas TI". The coding process resulted in 58 unique codes (see Appendix C). Coding occurred by assigning anything from words to short sentences to meaningful pieces of transcript. Despite the fact that the sample size was predominantly determined by quota sampling, it was checked whether saturation of the codes had occurred after all interviews were conducted. The saturation process is illustrated by Figure 2.

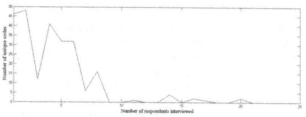

Figure 2. The saturation process.

Figure 2 illustrates that saturation of the codes occurred relatively early in the process. The dip that can be observed from the second respondent until the fifth can be explained by the fact that these interviews were conducted with line management. Their interviews contained relatively large amounts of context information because they are further removed from the actual process in comparison to members of both modules and the data they provided was more concerned with how they expected the agile process to work, compared to how it actually worked in practice.

After all transcripts had been coded, all codes thematically related were clustered and, if necessary, refined (Figure 3). From these clusters of codes, categories with respect to the research question were constructed.

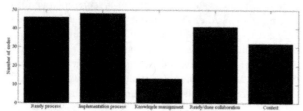

Figure 3 Number of codes per category. Categories from left to right: ready process, implementation process, knowledge management, ready/done collaboration and context.

Figure 3 illustrates that the READY process, implementation process and READY/DONE collaboration were mentioned approximately equally often across all the interviews. Knowledge management was discussed less often which could indicate that knowledge management is less important and/or less of an issue within the process.

4. Results

This section contains the results obtained by the current study. As part of the results section, quotations were added. Since the interviews were conducted in a western European language, the quotes were translated. The results section will explain what the interviews revealed the consequences of the modular design.

4.1 The semantic boundary

During the interview, people were asked about the implementation of the modular design and the consequences thereof. One of the things that popped up during the interviews is that people perceived the implementation process of the new

modular design that was chosen to be insufficient. The implementation consisted of a presentation that was given to all members of the program. During the presentation, the philosophy of the new modular agile model was discussed, as well as the benefits it was supposed to bring in terms of flexibility at the program level. However, the presentation did not explain the impact of the model beyond the operational level, in terms of changes in the different roles (like the business analyst), the requirement engineering process and the development process. One interviewee indicated that they had expected a more active implementation containing change management. The perception that the presentation was not sufficient to cover the entire implementation process is illustrated by quote 1.

Q1: *"We were given a presentation containing the general idea of what they were aiming for and I've got the feeling that it has not sunk in, at least not sufficiently. You have to really implement it."* (P07 – Test Manager)

An example of a concept that does not have the same meaning across the entire department but is used by all the teams of both modules is a "feature". Customer demand is captured in a business case which describes broadly what new functionality should be able on the company's website for example. This business case is split up in features and from these features, user stories are created. The three concepts are distinguishable by the amount of time needed to realize them whereby the business case requires the most time and the user stories the least. This broad distinction is known across the department but exact definitions of the different concepts are not the same. This is illustrated by quote 2 by a Business Analyst:

Q2: *"How can you, if you cannot even uniformly determine the weight of a feature, compare features across teams? (..) It becomes very difficult to exchange a feature from team one to team two when team one and team two think differently."* (PO8 – Business Analyst)

This quote illustrates the semantic boundary between members of different teams, apparently the concepts are known across the entire department but their meaning is different for teams and thus also varies between both modules. These results are also in line with the model as proposed by [11], who concluded that a common understanding positively affected effective communication.

An Application Engineer mentioned (quote 3) that the semantic boundary has to be spanned using very elaborate specifications in the modular organizational design. These specifications are needed in order to create a common understanding and to enable DONE teams to build software.

Q3: *"The way we have it [modular organizational design] is that a DONE team has to be able to build software without the context that we [READY] have. Practice shows that when you conduct the process like this [modular organizational design] is that specifications need to be very elaborate or a DONE team will not be able to estimate the work and execute it."* (PO 20 – Application Engineer)

Apparently, the implementation of a modular design in the case that was investigated has resulted in a lack of shared mental models between the teams. The meaning attached to different concepts as well as representations of the development process are not necessarily similar across all the teams. In conclusion, it appears that the modular design had created a semantic boundary thereby causing a lack of shared mental models across the teams. The effect of this lack of shared mental models caused by the semantic boundary between teams, had caused a decrease in the effective communication and coordination between teams. The interdependencies between the teams of the READY and DONE module created the necessity to coordinate and communicate between them. However, effective communication and coordination was inhibited by the lack of shared mental models since a shared understanding has to be reached before any coordination can occur.

4.2 The pragmatic boundary

Another topic discussed during the interview was the split of responsibility between the READY and DONE teams. Although both modules worked on the same product, this common goal/responsibility was not experienced in practice. When, for example, a new function for the mobile application had to be developed the READY module solely felt responsible for writing the user stories and after they had finished, their responsibility for the application ended. The same could be applied to the DONE module: they are merely responsible for actually developing the application and they did not feel responsible for the user stories.

Q4: *"Now, they [READY] do not have the responsibility to deliver something. That responsibility now lies solely with us [done] and they merely prepare at the moment (...). Maybe that should be more aligned so that the people that create the specifications also feel responsible for the delivery."* (PO12 – Developer)

This modular design and the relatively strict division of the responsibilities of both modules was also perceived to be very "waterfall like" by some of the participants in line with the observations of Frank and Hartel (2009)[8]. With this, participants were most often referring to the tendency of both parties to "throw it over the wall", meaning that READY "throws" their user stories over the wall and that DONE has to figure out what they are supposed to build but the other way around also occurs, DONE throws "not READY" user stories back over the wall and READY has to fix it. This effect is illustrated by a scrum master in quote 5.

Q5: *"READY and DONE is a waterfall. You have got the preparatory work [writing user stories] and it is just thrown over the wall and it has to be done."* (PO 9 – Scrum master)

This finding indicates a pragmatic boundary that is negatively affecting collaboration. Like mentioned before, Carlile (2004) defines the pragmatic boundary as conflicts that arise due to consequential interaction in the presence of conflicting interests meaning that conflicts arise when their goals regarding knowledge delivery contradict [10]. Another factor that was used to explain the pragmatic boundary was the fact that READY and DONE were not working in parallel but sequential. READY first wrote user stories and after they are finished, DONE would build them. During the development process, however, READY was already working on something else which could decrease their interest in the user story that DONE was working on.

It appears that both the semantic boundary and the pragmatic boundary indeed cause a decrease in effective communication and that the semantic boundaries occurs both within and between modules and that the pragmatic boundary solely occurs between modules. No evidence was found with respect to the occurrence of a syntactic boundary based on the results of the current study.

4.3 Intellectual capital: the state of relational capital

Besides the "throw it over the wall" effect, the modular design also had an impact on the relationship across members between different modules. The results reveal that an "us and them" feeling could be observed between the modules meaning that members from the READY module felt little affiliation with members from the DONE module and vice versa. This lack of affiliation has negatively influenced the relationship between members of both modules. Quote 6 by a business analyst illustrates what the effect of the modular design is on the relationship between the ready and done modules.

Q6: *"I do not have a relationship with them [DONE]. I'm so far removed from them; I just have to deliver user stories".* (PO8 – Business Analyst)

This view is similar to another quote by a member of a DONE team that also stresses the consequences of the decreased relationship between both parts (quote 7).

Q7: *"I do not consider them [READY] to be part of us [DONE]. The way you look at them and approach them does differs."* (PO12 – Developer)

The fact that the quality of their relationship has decreased due to the fact that they have become members of different modules has affected the way they approach and interact with each other. One of the consequences mentioned during one of the interviews is reluctance from both parties to initiate face-to-face contact. This face-to-face contact is often replaced by emails which delays the response and decreases the richness of information thereby causing inefficiencies. This effect was illustrated by a Developer (quote 8) who indeed felt that not knowing each other and being located at different floors inhibits the initiation of face-to-face contact. As a consequence, this contact was initiated using emails whereby important nuances of the message are lost.

Q8: *"At first, you do not know each other. They say that it does not matter whether you have a development team on the second floor and you have to take the stairs (...). But when you do not know each other, you would rather send an email but then you will miss the nuance."* (PO 14 – Developer)

The fact that a decrease in the quality of the relationship between both modules has led to a decrease in effective communication between the modules which, in turn, has caused ineffective coordination is in line with the results obtained by [11] who found that a decrease in relational capital negatively affect communicational effectiveness which results in a decrease in project efficiency.

These results further confirm the theory that the strictly separate responsibilities of both modules causes a pragmatic boundary and a decrease in effective communication by proving that this decrease in effective communication does not happen when the responsibilities are not strictly separated. The same reasoning applies to the theory that a decrease in relational capital results in a decrease in effective communication since the current study found that effective communication remained when the quality of the relationship between both modules remained intact. This finding is also in line with the literature on DevOps which advocates a culture of open communication and trust in order to enhance collaboration.

5. Conclusion and discussion

The aim of the current study is to investigate the degree to which a modular organizational design can be applied effectively in an agile software development context. More specifically, the current study tried to explain the limits of a modular design in an environment where technologies change fast and unpredictably as found by Ernst (2006) [12]. In order to gain more understanding with respect to this finding, the effects of applying a modular design in an agile software development context on effective communication was researched.

One of the results was that the modular design caused a semantic boundary between members of different modules which indicates a lack of shared understanding. It appeared that this semantic boundary was caused primarily by the different goals assigned to each module. Due to the fact that each module had its own goal(s), each module had its own processes and methodologies which were not known by heart by members outside of the specific module. So, the different concepts and processes applied by different modules causes a semantic boundary between modules. Another effect of the modular design is that, although some concepts and processes are used across all modules, the meaning attached to these concepts and processes differs across modules. This means that the modules

have a common lexicon but do not necessarily have a shared meaning. This lack of shared understanding implies that the semantic boundary caused by the modular design also inhibits the development of shared mental models between modules. The effect of the lack of shared mental models caused by the semantic boundary is that a decrease of effective communication between members of different modules can be observed. This result is in line with the studies by [10, 11, 16]. The differentiated roles of the different modules could explain the lack of shared mental model development between members of different modules.

Another result of the current study is that the modular design resulted in a pragmatic boundary between the modules. More specifically, the different goals of the different modules resulted in misaligned interests thereby decreasing the incentive of members of different modules to communicate with each other. This effect appears to be very similar to the "throw-it-over-the-wall" effect as observed by [17]. After each module had completed their task, they "threw their work over the wall" to the other module who had to figure out how to deal with it. For example, the READY module was responsible for writing user stories which the DONE module had to build. After the READY module had completed their task, they presented their user story to the DONE module which had to deal with it relatively autonomously. Due to the fact that the formal responsibility of the READY module ends after the user story is completed, they lack an incentive to help and guide the DONE module during software development. Therefore, in this case, a modular design causes a pragmatic boundary between modules which inhibits effective communication between members of different modules. These results are in line with the study by [10]. Further, these findings are also in line with the literature on DevOps, which advocates aligned responsibilities among the parties involved in information systems.

Finally, the results of the current study revealed that the modular design decreases the relational capital between members of different modules. In practice this decrease in relational capital resulted in an "us and them" feeling between members of the different modules. The effect of this group thinking is that members of other modules were approached different from members of the same module. Communication between members of different modules with relatively low relationship quality were often approached either through other, better known people or via communication channels with lower quality compared to face-to-face communication like email. The effects of these coping strategies resulted in a decrease in effective communication between the members of different modules with a relatively low quality relationship. This negative effect of a decrease in relational capital on effective communication is in line with the results found by [11]. Again, this finding is in line with the literature on DevOps which stressed the importance of a culture of open communication and trust.

In conclusion, the current study has revealed that the application of a modular organizational design in a dynamic agile environment is limited due to the fact that a modular design has a negative effect on the effective communication and coordination between members of different modules. More specifically, the modular design creates both a semantic and a pragmatic boundary between members of different modules which is primarily caused by the fact that modules have differentiated tasks and often misaligned interests. Another consequence of modularity is a decrease in the quality of the relationships between members of different modules which are thought to be caused by group thinking. The effects of the decrease in effective communication and coordination between members of different modules are more severe for modules that are highly interconnected.

Acknowledgements

The authors would like to acknowledge the contribution of Dr. Michel Ehrenhard for his guidance of this research project.

REFERENCES

[1] Conway, M. E. How do committees invent. *Datamation*, 14, 4 (1968), 28-31.
[2] Amrit, C. and Van Hillegersberg, J. Detecting coordination problems in collaborative software development environments. *Information Systems Management*, 25, 1 (2008), 57-70.
[3] Coplien, J., O. and Harrison, N., B. *Organizational Patterns of Agile Software Development*. Prentice-Hall, Upper Saddle River, NJ, USA, 2004.
[4] Amrit, C. *Improving coordination in software development through social and technical network analysis*. University of Twente, 2008.
[5] Herbsleb, J. D. and Grinter, R. E. *Splitting the organization and integrating the code: Conway's law revisited*. ACM, City, 1999.
[6] Amrit, C., van Hillegersberg, J. and Kumar, K. Identifying coordination problems in software development: finding mismatches between software and project team structures. *arXiv preprint arXiv:1201.4142* (2012).
[7] Hoda, R., Noble, J. and Marshall, S. The impact of inadequate customer collaboration on self-organizing Agile teams. *Information and Software Technology*, 53, 5 (2011), 521-534.
[8] Frank, A. and Hartel, C. *Feature teams collaboratively building products from ready to done*. IEEE, City, 2009.
[9] Klimoski, R. and Mohammed, S. Team mental model: Construct or metaphor? *Journal of management*, 20, 2 (1994), 403-437.
[10] Carlile, P. R. Transferring, translating, and transforming: An integrative framework for managing knowledge across boundaries. *Organization science*, 15, 5 (2004), 555-568.
[11] Hsu, J. S.-C., Chu, T.-H., Lin, T.-C. and Lo, C.-F. Coping knowledge boundaries between information system and business disciplines: An intellectual capital perspective. *Information & Management*, 51, 2 (2014), 283-295.
[12] Ernst, D. Limits to modularity: reflections on recent developments in chip design. *Industry and Innovation*, 12, 3 (2005), 303-335.
[13] Erich, F., Amrit, C. and Daneva, M. *Cooperation between information system development and operations: a literature review*. ACM, City, 2014.
[14] Laanti, M. *Characteristics and principles of scaled agile*. Springer, City, 2014.
[15] Miles, M. B. and Huberman, A. M. Qualitative data analysis: A sourcebook. *Beverly Hills: Sage Publications* (1994).
[16] Espinosa, J. A., Slaughter, S. A., Kraut, R. E. and Herbsleb, J. D. Team knowledge and coordination in geographically distributed software development. *Journal of management information systems*, 24, 1 (2007), 135-169.
[17] Al-Rawas, A. and Easterbrook, S. Communication problems in requirements engineering: a field study (1996).

Appendix A

Table 1 Overview with respect to the composition of the sample used in the current study.

Function/role	Number	Percentage (%)
Line manager	3	14,3
Project manager	1	4,8
Test manager	2	9,5
Application engineer	1	4,8
Product manager	1	4,8
Business analyst	3	14,3
Interaction designer	1	4,8
Scrum master	3	14,3
Product owner	1	4,8
Tester	1	4,8
Developer	3	14,3
Total	21	100

Appendix B

The interview protocol:

1. Opening
a) Introduction of the interviewer and the research
b) Aim of the interview and explanation of the structure
c) Emphasis of confidentiality and permission regarding recording was asked

2. General information interviewee
a) Interviewee was asked to introduce his/herself
b) The following topics had to be discussed:
- Number of years active in Rabobank
- Different functions the interviewee has been operating in
- Current function and responsibilities

3. Rabobank and agile
a) Implementation of the scrum process
Topics that were included are:
- Construction of user stories
- Relevant rituals
b) Issues related to the current implementation of the scrum process

4. Definition of both READY and DONE
a) The READY/DONE process
- Goal of the division
- Implementation of the new model
- Responsibilities of both
- Formal/informal meetings
b) Issues related to the READY/DONE division

c) Solution for these issues
- Solutions within the current process
- Solutions outside of the current process

5. Ending
a) The interviewee is asked whether he or she would like to add something to the interview
b) Check whether the interviewer knows other people that might be interesting to interview
c) Thank the interviewee for his/her time

Appendix C

The codes and their nesting displayed in relational context. The core concept displayed in the center, with high-level concepts.

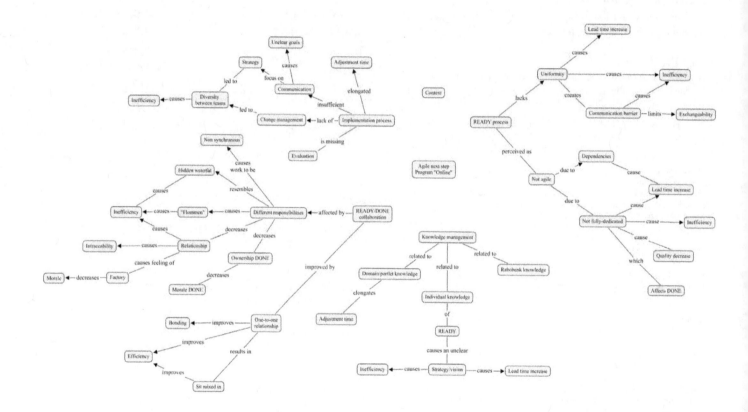

Community Journalism & Empowerment:
Do they go hand in hand?

Full Paper

Neena Pandey
Decision Sciences & Information Systems
Indian Institute of Management, Bangalore
neena.pandey@iimb.ernet.in

ABSTRACT

With the credibility of mainstream journalism[1] decreasing each passing day, Community Journalism (CJ), assisted by Information and Communication Technologies (ICTs), stands out as a workable and interesting alternative. Using Rowland's Empowerment framework, this paper analyzes what impact CJ has on individual empowerment. The study is based on CGNet-Swara, a CJ project launched for tribal and marginalized communities of India. The study uses case study research design following hermeneutics as the method of data analysis. The study indicates that CJ projects do not strive to provide empowerment to the individuals in all its manifestations. Moreover, although these projects do empower individuals to certain extent, they sometimes also create false consciousness of attaining power.

CCS CONCEPTS

• Human-centered computing → Collaborative and social computing; Empirical Studies in HCI

KEYWORDS

Community Journalism, ICT; CGNet-Swara, individual empowerment; hermeneutics; Rowland's empowerment framework

1 INTRODUCTION

Researchers have identified various reasons that lead marginal communities all over the world to live in abject poverty

SIGMIS-CPR '17, June 21-23, 2017, Bangalore, India
© 2017 Copyright is held by the owner/author(s). Publication rights licensed to ACM.
ACM ISBN 978-1-4503-5037-2/17/06...$15.00
http://dx.doi.org/10.1145/3084381.3084404

and deprivation. One of the main problems identified is the extremely low level of communication between them and the authorities responsible for taking any step forward, leading to a cycle of deprivation. Saha [14] argues that even though poverty and human development are governance problems for the most part, the lack of communication can aggravate this cycle of deprivation. For such marginal communities where communication, both to and fro, is a grave concern, informatics assisted CJ is being posed as a tool to achieve individual and community empowerment.

However, what is empowerment? Although in practice it is defined in various ways, the notion of empowerment is complex as it appears differently in a range of literature with varied interpretations. This lack of clarity or coherence is mainly caused by the various different interpretations of power as well as the contrasting views on power centrality [6].

Thus, to analyze the impact of community journalism on individual empowerment, we borrow from Rowland's empowerment framework which she developed during her study on women empowerment in Honduras. On developing her framework, she encouraged its use in other development studies. Since the context of this study is the empowerment of the marginalized population, her definition and conceptualization seems well-suited in the context of this paper.

The paper proceeds as follows. The next section presents a literature review of theories/topics of concern in the current paper which is followed by a section on research design. Finally along with an explanation on data collection, the case is analyzed ending the paper with conclusions and insights from the study.

2 LITERATURE REVIEW

2.1 Individual Empowerment

In practice, empowerment is defined in various terms. As per the World Bank's Sourcebook of 2002, Empowerment is "the expansion of assets and capabilities of poor people to participate in, negotiate with, influence, control and hold accountable institutions that affect their lives". For practical requirements, access to information, inclusion and participation, accountability and local organizational capacity are the four key elements of empowerment [7].

However, defining it theoretically is complex as it varies with different conceptualizations of power and growing and diverse literature on the topic is a testimony to that [6]. The roots of thinking on empowerment lie in feminist theory and popular education work of the radical educationist Paulo Freire, who stressed on the personal and inner dimensions of power.

As per Freire (1970), to build a liberated society where people are free from all forms of oppression, 'conscientisation', and with that transformation of the self has to be brought. This, he suggested, can happen only through an appropriate dialogical form of education [7]. This basic idea of empowerment retains its meaning even in feminist theories, which believe that empowerment can be brought upon only through changed perceptions and through the transformation of the self [7]. However, both these approaches to empowerment focus on the cognitive process of the individual and downplay the influence of situational or social structural factors in favor of a focus on individual perceptions [12].

Focusing on the situational and social structural factors, empowerment is defined as "the expansion in people's ability to make strategic life choices in a context where this ability was previously denied to them". This definition highlights both the actor's ability to make choices and the process of change in the achievement of these abilities [6]. This notion of empowerment is close to Amartya Sen's Capability Approach [16] which encompasses empowerment of individuals and communities to achieve overall human development. In accordance with his Capability Approach, Sen mentions "greater freedom enhances the ability of people to help themselves and to influence the world, and these matters are central to the process of development." [17].

In her Empowerment framework, Rowlands [13] argues that empowerment can be conceptualized in different ways depending upon the conceptualization of 'power' it is based upon. When power is conceptualized as 'power over', "it is exercised by dominant social, political, economic, or cultural groups over those who are marginalized." In this context, power is available in finite supply and is also considered a zero-sum game, i.e. more power for one will inevitably lead to less for someone else. Thus, the powerful group always feels threatened of any change in power equation [13]. Under this conceptualization, empowerment means bringing people who are outside the decision making process into it. This concept of 'power' views empowerment more as an outcome than a process and supposedly leads to socio-political empowerment by radically changing the structural inequalities and focusing on the broader political and socio-economic context [6].

The other conceptualizations of empowerment view it as a process and are derived from various other interpretations of power as 'power to', 'power with' or 'power from within'. **'Power to'** is often considered *"generative or productive power which creates new possibilities and actions without domination"* [13]. This aspect of power leads to the kind of leadership where a group sets its own collective agenda and there is no conflict of interest. By enhancing the capabilities of the poor and improving their participation in decision-making process, the interpretation of empowerment with this conceptualization of power is similar to what Sen [16] discusses in his Capability Approach [6] as discussed earlier.

'Power with' refers to *'a sense of the whole being greater than the sum of the individuals, especially when a group tackles problems together'* [13]. In this case, empowerment is concerned with the processes by which people become aware of their own interests and how those relate to the interests of others, so as to be actually able to influence such decisions along with being able to participate in decision making from a position of greater strength [13]. The collective empowerment in this case is achieved by social mobilization, building alliances and coalitions [6].

Finally, **power from within,** refers to *'the spiritual strength and uniqueness that resides in each one of us and makes us truly human. Its basis is self-acceptance and self-respect which extend, in turn, to respect for and acceptance of others as equals'* [13]. This conceptualization is close to psychological empowerment when individual's awareness and self-esteem is strengthened and involves giving scope to the full range of human abilities and potential.

In this context of individual empowerment in marginalized communities, Laverack & Wallerstein [10] contend, *'communities consists of heterogeneous individuals who may collectively take action towards shared and specific goals of the group'*. However, they warn against conditions when dominant minority may dictate the community unless adequate precautions of involving as many people as possible are taken.

In the studies on critical assessment of empowerment, Riger [12] contends that the usage of empowerment sometimes confounds a sense of efficacy or esteem with actual control over resources. This 'false consciousness' of empowerment, although enhances the self-esteem, does not do much to affect people's power over resources or policies.

2.2 ICTs Enabled Community Journalism

The traditional view on understanding the role of ICTs on individuals and communities empowerment emphasizes on closing the 'knowledge gaps' and transferring the knowledge from 'north' to 'south' by completely ignoring the value of indigenous local knowledge (World Bank, 1999 as cited in Gigler, 2004). However, as early as 1973, Schumacher [15] criticized direct transfer of the technologies of developed work to developing countries. He brought in the concept of 'intermediate technologies' which should be ideally used in developing countries. Recently many other researchers are recognizing the nature of knowledge gaps whereby not only the poor communities lack access to information, policymakers based in capital cities and towns also lack knowledge about the local and cultural context of the poor and marginalized groups. Thus, discussion on the role of information and knowledge for development has to be seen under the broader context of structural inequalities and the social exclusion of marginalized groups within developing countries [6].

The role of ICTs on development and empowerment in the development discourse is a strongly contested issue. There is a stream of researchers who emphasize the importance of cultural, social and economic context on the impact of ICTs on development [2, 18]. Gigler [6], on the other hand, emphasizes on the 'people-centered' approach to development where he stresses on the capability of poor or marginalized people to define their own development priorities and goals, and then should the work of 'outside support' start. In this context, he develops an alternative evaluation framework of ICT interventions by operationalizing Sen's CA.

Traditionally, journalism has been attached to the institution of the media, where the news available for public consumption passes through paid journalists who are often referred to as "gatekeepers". This is because of the authority residing with the journalists in terms of which news, in what shape and how much quantity will be presented to the reader [5].

Altschull [1], a veteran journalist questions the press' arrogance, its faith in objectivity and argues for allowing the bigger role of public in the news decision making process. A few other contemporary critics of the mainstream model of journalism have proposed alternative models such as public journalism (Massey & Haas, 2002 as cited in [5]) that asked for a more reciprocal relationship between reporters and their audience, suggesting news should be conversation, rather than a lecture [20].

However, even with all these shortcomings highlighted in mainstream journalism, the development of new participatory models does not solely depend upon its internal differentiation. Various other external factors such as economy, emergence of technology, and the larger cultural and societal framework influence its emergence [5]. Over the past few decades, with the availability of new ICT tools like Internet, mobile communications and Web 2.0, it has become possible for others (non-journalists) to publish content for a potentially global audience.

These developments have led to the field of community journalism, which is also known as Participatory/Citizen/Alternative Journalism. The working definition of the domain is provided by Bowman & Willis [3] is: *"The act of a citizen, or group of citizens, playing an active role in the process of collecting, reporting, analyzing and disseminating news and information. The intent of this participation is to provide independent, reliable, accurate, wide-ranging and relevant information that a democracy requires"*

The proliferation of community journalism projects all over the world, and more so in the developing regions where the reach of mainstream media is limited, with most of those systems claiming to be 'empowering' people and communities they serve, motivates the need to understand the impact of CJ on individuals and communities.

3 RESEARCH DESIGN AND METHODOLOGY

3.1 Research Method

Since this study of impact of CJ on individual empowerment tries to understand individuals and communities' perception of different dimensions of power they achieve because of CJ, qualitative research can provide rich insights into the research question.

The case study will be examined following hermeneutics as the mode of analysis, following the set of seven principles suggested by Klein & Myers [9] for conducting and reporting of research.

3.2 Research Data

The data for this study is from a running Community Journalism project, CGNet Swara, which is implemented in the state of Chhattisgarh in India. Interviews, reports and news items are the primary and secondary sources of data. The web site of CGNet Swara is also studied extensively which along with providing the details of the project, also highlights various achievements of the project which is also used for our analysis.

3.3 Case History

India has a dismal record of poverty and human development, more so in its remotest regions. This has led to many *adivasi*[2] and *dalits*[3] led rebellion in those areas. Owing to the remoteness of the area, the issues afflicting the *adivasis* or extremely marginalized are very different from those affecting the rest of the country. However, lack of media publications in the language which the locals speak and understand leads to much of the discussion about *adivasis* in the Indian media to happen through the prism of people who were themselves raised in privileged backgrounds and have no idea about the ground realities [11]. Thus, even though some of their problems can be attributed to ineffective governance, lack of communication, both to and fro between those communities and government, aggravates the deprivation [14]. Since most of these languages the *adivasis* use do not even have a written script, the print and the visual mainstream media do not hold much significance for this group.

CGNet Swara, thus, is an Internet and mobile based CJ project, started by Shubhranshu Choudhary in 2004 (as CGNet), based in the state of Chhattisgarh. In his own words, Choudhary mentions, "CGNet is the people's website of Chhattisgarh, where everybody is a journalist. It is a citizen's journalism forum whose mission is the democratization of journalism, where journalism is not restricted only to journalists." [4].

In its earlier version, CGNet was planned to be a web and community radio based project. Due to changes in government regulations and Internet connectivity issues, the system now

---

[2] *adivasi* is a member of any of the aboriginal tribal peoples living in India before the arrival of the Aryans in the second millennium BC
[3] *dalit* (in the traditional Indian caste system) a member of the lowest caste

works on one of the cheapest and highly penetrated form of communication, i.e. mobile phones. This latest version of the application is termed CGNet Swara, meaning 'voice' in Sanskrit. Currently, CGNet Swara is a voice-based portal, which enables ordinary citizens to report and discuss issues of local interest. Reported stories are moderated by journalists and after rigorous checks of authenticity, become available for playback online as well as over phone.

Since its inception (Swara version) in Feb 2010 till December 2011, more than 74,000 calls have been made on Swara for either publishing or listening to new reports from 9000 unique callers. About 1,100 messages were released on the system during this time period. The content of the posts is quite diverse, the single biggest use being to report on the issues of governance. By 2012, news published had gone to about 3 new posts per day, on receiving approximately 240 calls per day, which indicates that most of the callers are only listening to the content (Mudliar et al., 2012).

3.4 Case Data Collection

Data collection for the study involved a detailed look at the project's official website as well as other Internet resources reporting on the project. I also interviewed Mr. Shubhranshu Choudhary, the founder of CGNet-Swara on two occasions. Thus the study is based both on primary and secondary sources of data. The author also studied the work of a few other researchers who have analyzed CGNet Swara, mainly to understand the viewpoints and multiple interpretations coming through other stakeholders of the project.

Once the data was collected, it was coded in two ways. One was done using free coding where the codes were generated considering data content for individual under Rowland's empowerment framework. This led to about 26 codes. Since the different conceptualizations of power were not clearly indicated in those codes, pre-defined codes which were the different conceptualizations of power was also done (Please refer Appendix A for the detailed list of codes).

4 CASE ANALYSIS

The limited reach of mainstream journalism and extreme dearth of communication of local issues in Chhattisgarh motivated a group of community journalism believers to look for a technological solution to address the problem. As the founder mentions "We were trying to move from J of vested interest to J of concern, where the work doesn't stop at publishing the report but extends the support in lobbying the person responsible".

We analyze the main findings in context of empowerment as analyzed from the available data. We first analyze the codes obtained through the free coding performed during data collection and then analyze them further through the Rowland's power framework.

Capability Building and Participation - CGNet Swara offers courses on basics of journalism (learning who, what,

where, when, why and how), and trains the participants on interviewing processes. Some news items supporting this include:

"*Lingaram Kadopi and one of his friend were initially trained at CGNet Swara and were awarded a fellowship by the Washington-based International Center for Journalists to study journalism..... He was probably the first Gondi-speaking journalist in India.*"

"*Choudhary has trained more than 100 citizen journalists to produce audio news reports through CGNet Swara...*"

and "*Samir Xalxo, 32, a tribal farmer, said his interest in citizen journalism was sparked after a local reporter for a mainstream media outlet refused to run a story about an incident that happened in his region.*"

Decision Making - Most of the conceptualizations of power, barring 'power from within', discuss individuals and groups being part of decision making process in one way or the other in the process of achieving empowerment. There is no indication of any movement of individuals or communities in that direction from the available and analyzed data. Thus, though CGNet Swara seems to be a strong mediator of communication between citizens and administrators, achieving the state of being part of decision making is still distant. However, considering CGNet Swara is posed as being more of a news sharing platform encouraging communication, both among community population and between communities and administrators, achieving to be a part of decision making might not be a top priority.

System Usage - Mudliar et al. (2012) profiled the contributors to the system and found indications that a savvy subset of residents took advantage of the system. During a particular study period, about 80% of the posts were found to be in Hindi and about 10% in Kurukh and the remainder in other tribal languages. Hence, it looked like that the Hindi-speaking activists and NGO workers, rather than disadvantaged members from the community are the extensive users of the system. Does it mean that the marginalization of the poorest of the poor is still there, it has only moved from the state level to local level? It appears that the local administrators are prioritizing the tasks they deem more important, which might be more community related than individual specific.

Identity Revelation and fear of retaliation - During initial periods of the project, news providers had the flexibility of whether or not they wanted to provide their personal identity information. In due course, the mandatory requirement of identity revelation came up as an unintended consequence of two steps which CGNet Swara had to take. Firstly, CGNet Swara servers were closed down twice through 'back door', which made them lose all the data and hence made it difficult to recollect the news from the data sources. Secondly, with the success of CGNet Swara, many other such entities were established which are more concerned about higher number of incoming calls than the news/call quality. This led to projects based on CJ being tagged as 'rumor-mongering entities'. Hence CGNet Swara decided to very strictly regulate its authentication process. Both these events led to the requirement of mandatory revelation of the news-provider.

Although this was a step with good intentions, it led to people moving away from reporting more and more news, as specifically mentioned by the project coordinator, Shubhranshu. There have been instances of false implication of CGNet Swara moderator by state police, when a moderator and another of his family member were sent to custody claiming them to be supporting insurgency. The retaliation can come both from and higher level administrators or from the locally influential people. Thus, the unintended consequence of preventing false news items is leading to lesser complaints regarding local influential people or administrators in fear or repercussions.

Institutional Support – The institutional (mainstream journalism) support is beneficial to CGNet Swara for their success in solving local problems and getting them empowered, as they can increase the reach of local news of significance to the global audience. As Mr. Shubhranshu mentioned that *"We can't and don't want to compete with mainstream journalism"*.

The conceptualization of CGNet Swara was based on various discussion sessions held between mainstream and proponents of CJ. The founder himself had been a mainstream journalist for a couple of decades. But data from the case study suggests that even though some of the mainstream journalists praise CJ for the work they do, CJ is not credited by mainstream media if the story is picked up by them. Local journalists feel that this acknowledgement, if offered, could have worked for the sustainability of their project. The following report from Columbia Journal Review mentions similar sentiment:

"Many journalists who use Swara to get their leads to big stories hardly ever acknowledge the original source. In Jharkhand, we approached leading newspapers like Prabhat Khabar and Hindustan to enter into a formal content-sharing agreement but it has not taken off at all. While journalists are willing to utilize the system to get rare stories no mainstream media organization is willing to help such initiatives to sustain itself."

Hence the talk of support by mainstream media appears false as they do not really believe in the model.

Entertainment - One very interesting aspect of CJ is the presence and encouragement of entertainment in their system. White (2004) talks about how citizen's media, without questioning power relationships, and by simply celebrating local culture and local people can be effective for the community. He mentions that building up of confidence about the value of one's culture lays the groundwork for legitimating contestatory action. These programming and themes are contingent upon the response and support community provides and might die out in case of no response (Dervin & Huesca, 1997 as cited in White, 2004).

During initial periods of CGNet Swara launch, when all residents were allowed to put data on the server, an interesting unintended outcome was people expressing their creative instincts via this channel. Various users offered poems to the common pool which are a hit among listeners. Considering White's view as discussed above, the entertainment dimension of CJ projects can be extremely beneficial to the community. Even now, when the Sandesh 4 items go through a rigorous authentication process, the flow of cultural contents still continues at a regular pace.

False Consciousness - One of the reports on CGNet Swara website presents a poem by one of the contributors which goes *"ShivrajSingh bhaiya se kehna hai ho bhaiya hum to gariba hain"*. This literally translates in English to *"Tell brother Shivraj Singh that we are poor"*. Shivraj Singh was the Chief Minister of the state of Chhattisgarh and thus a post like this indicates the illusion of common tribal people who are under the impression that the reports they are generating are reaching the head of the state.

In another incidence, Markam, a person from Chhattisgarh, said that *"CGNet Swara has made him feel powerful, as if he had the support of powerful people"*. This a case of "false consciousness", which Marx (as cited in [12]) mentions is this individual's experience of power or powerlessness may be unrelated to actual ability to influence, and an increase in the sense of empowerment does not always reflect an increase in actual power (Riger, 1993).

Belief in Self or the System - Each impact report available on the website thanks the system so profusely and so many times, it gives a feeling that the users have started believing in a system to solve their problems or in themselves.

Insurgent's Reaction - Since the presence of CGNet Swara has reduced the approach of local population to insurgents to some extent, the insurgents do not like this. They consider power as a zero-sum game where if the locals achieve power, the insurgents will lose their power over them. Hence, there's a constant effort to disrupt the system, which can be another reason for locals to fear retaliation from insurgents.

Global Reach - CGNet Swara has enabled the reach of local news to global audiences along with better reach among locals. The attached internet platform of Swara and a few news feed to mainstream news outlets have enabled the reach of local problems to the outside world and provided them with an opportunity to take a position on those issues. Some of the instances include:
"Villagers and activists who heard the report called administrators to find out why the food deliveries had stopped."

---

4 *Sandesh* means 'message' which CGNet Swara team uses for news items

"The CGNet Swara platform provides a crucial missing link between rural and urban communities, and provides key information for people who often don't have knowledge of what's happening in the outlying areas," said Choudhary.

Sustainability - The technical and political constraints have led to the discussions on the sustainability of CGNet Swara. The placement of server in an outstation location (Bangalore) because of security and political reasons have made the calls to the system (the cost of which is borne by the project and not by contributing members) costly and hence making it difficult to sustain for a long period of time. Although the data doesn't give any indications of the users of the system being apprised of these complications, it might act as a dampener in getting the complaints to the forefront because of the fear of retaliation when the system is no more working for them.

Expansion by Partnership - Recognizing the grass root level reach of CGNet Swara, various other socially oriented groups like Change.org are moving towards partnerships with them to highlight various other issues in rural India.

"It was important for us to adapt to Indian conditions where Internet penetration is still very low. We work with Video Volunteers and CGNet Swara to identify issues in their areas which could be promoted online and hence bridge the gap between rural and urban population."

These outlets use audio and video to highlight various issues in rural India.

5 DISCUSSION

The overall analysis of the data suggests that technology assisted community journalism projects do not aim to provide empowerment as derived by all the conceptualizations of power by Rowlands [13]. The system is launched clearly for not aiming 'power over' the mainstream journalism and the authorities concerned. They also do not consider power as a zero-sum game in which more power by individuals and communities under deprivation will lead to loss of power by the targets of community journalism.

The main contribution of community journalism projects is providing psychological empowerment by enhancing various capabilities of people, i.e. providing 'power from within' and collective empowerment by creating social mobilization, i.e. by providing 'power with'.

The capability to produce and publish local news is created and enhanced by training locals and enabling their participation in communication between locals and administrators. The ability of getting the local news reach global audience either through mainstream media or through mobile/Internet provides informational capabilities which leads to psychological empowerment [6]. Secondly, as White [19] suggests, the ability of being able to share poems and other outlets of cultural expression strengthens the cultural identity of people. It helps in building up of confidence about the value of one's culture lays

the groundwork for legitimating contestatory action and hence is a factor in enhancing psychological empowerment.

Although CJ does have an impact on certain aspects of empowerment, enabling the decision making aspect of empowerment is still far-fetched. In fact, there are possibilities of the shift in marginalization from community level to the individual level. The team of 'moderators' use their discretion in authenticating and releasing the reports. This leads to loss in transparency between the people whom the system is claiming to serve and the final output. Although these steps are adopted for logistic reasons, their unintended consequences can hinder the opening up of various people against someone in the community. Similarly, identity revelation issues also hinder the process, more so in a community where intra-community social issues can be extremely complex and discriminatory.

A related question of significant interest is that, in communities with a long history of marginalization, is it even possible to achieve individual empowerment (participate from a position of greater strength in decision making and actually to influence those decision) unless the community is empowered. Unless the individual feels that the community is empowered enough to back him in case of any retaliation from supposedly higher authorities, or they see things working out for communities, only then will an individual be ready to take a chance with self-related issues.

6 CONCLUSION

As discussed above, the community journalism projects cannot be assessed on all conceptualizations of power to assess their impact on empowerment since the aim itself of the project might be limited in terms of providing empowerment of a certain kind. Moreover, studies on empowerment will be able to achieve better understanding when community level empowerment is studied along with individual empowerment. Moreover, the impact of individual empowerment on community empowerment and vice-versa will be an interesting relationship to indulge upon.

Although financial sustainability of the project does not seem to impact the empowerment of individuals, it does have a significant impact. The uncertainty regarding sustainability can dampen the spirit of the system-users in fear of retaliation which can happen when the system is not in use. Finally, even though the impact of such CJ projects is not as strong as the society or even the individual users might want to believe and does seem to cause 'false consciousness' of empowerment, it seems to have some positive impact.

A APPENDIX

A.1 Codes arrived at during data analysis

Pre-defined codes – which come from Rowland's empowerment framework.

    a. 'Power over'
    b. 'power to'
    c. 'power with'
    d. 'power within'

Free coding

    a. Institutional Response
    b. Sustainability
    c. Training and Capacity Building
    d. Entertainment
    e. Rights Awareness
    f. Belief in system
    g. Individual Self-belief
    h. Collective Strength
    i. Technical Capabilities and Limitations
    j. Impact
    k. Alternative to insurgency
    l. Feeder to mainstream media
    m. Retaliation
    n. Global reach
    o. Alternative/Local view
    p. Oppression
    q. Illusions
    r. Reverting back with results
    s. Transformed Communication/ Media democratization
    t. Empowerment through Power
    u. Participation
    v. Government Accountability/Response
    w. Quick response
    x. Transparency
    y. Loopholes
    z. Expansion

A.2 Questions posed to Mr. Shubhranshu Chaudhary, the founder of CGNet-Swara

The interview with Mr. Shubhranshu Chaudhary was semi-structured where the researcher asked the following basic questions. However, in many cases, one question led to another question and the interaction, for most part of it, was free-wheeling.

Questions:

1. What motivated you to start an organization like CG-Net Swara?
2. Tell me something about the journey that CGNet-Swara has gone through.
3. What has been the response of local population to this project?
4. How do local reporters gain skill in reporting?
5. What kind of interaction you have had with the mainstream media in the context of CG-Net Swara? Has it changed over the years?
6. What has been the response of various government institutions that you interact with?
7. Has the system, in any way, impacted the interaction between the locals and the insurgent groups of the area?
8. How do you manage the finances for the project? What do you think about its sustainability?

REFERENCES

[1] Altschull, J. H. 1996. A crisis of conscience: Is community journalism the answer? *Journal of mass media Ethics*, *11*(3), 166-172

[2] Avgerou, C. 2001. The significance of context in information systems and organizational change. *Information systems journal*, *11*(1), 43-63.

[3] Bowman, S. and C. Willis. 2003. We Media: How Audiences Are Shaping the Future of News and Information. The Media Center at The American Press Institute, URL (consulted June 2005): http://www.hypergene.net/wemedia/download/we_media.pdf - accessed on 30th April, 2014

[4] Choudhary, S. 2009. CGNet and Citizen Journalism in India. *eJournal USA*. http://iipdigital.usembassy.gov/ st/english/publication/2009/06/20090616175845mlenuhret0.1840588.html#ax zz2zzvFYNMf – accessed on 26th April 2014

[5] Domingo, D., Quandt, T., Heinonen, A., Paulussen, S., Singer, J. B,, & Vujnovic, M. 2008. Participatory journalism practices in the media and beyond: An international comparative study of initiatives in online newspapers. *Journalism practice*, *2*(3), 326-342.

[6] Gigler, B. S. 2004. Including the Excluded-Can ICTs empower poor communities? Towards an alternative evaluation framework based on the capability approach. In *4th International conference on the capability approach* (Vol. 5, No. 7).

[7] Harriss, J. 2007. Antinomies of empowerment: observations on civil society, politics and urban governance in India. *Economic and Political Weekly*, 2716-2724.

[8] Key Terms. http://www.trentu.ca/academic/nativestudies/courses/nast305/keyterms.htm - accessed on May 1, 2014

[9] Klein, H. K., & Myers, M. D. 1999. A set of principles for conducting and evaluating interpretive field studies in information systems. *MIS quarterly*, 67-93.

[10] Laverack, G., & Wallerstein, N. 2001. Measuring community empowerment: a fresh look at organizational domains. *Health Promotion International*, *16*(2), 179-185.

[11] Mudliar, P., Donner, J., & Thies, W. 2012. Emergent practices around CGNet Swara, voice forum for citizen journalism in rural India. In *Proceedings of the Fifth International Conference on Information and Communication Technologies and Development* (pp. 159-168). ACM.

[12] Riger, S. 1993. What's wrong with empowerment? *American Journal of Community Psychology*, *21*(3), 279-292.

[13] Rowlands, J. 1997. Questioning empowerment: Working with women in Honduras. Oxfam.

[14] Saha, A. 2012. Cellphones as a Tool for Democracy: The Example of CGNet Swara. *Economic and Political Weekly*, *14*, 23-6.

[15] Schumacher, E. F. 1973. Small is beautiful: A study of economics as if people mattered. Random House.

[16] Sen, A., & Nussbaum, M. 1993. "Capability and Well-being", in *The Quality of Life*. Oxford: Clarendon Press.

[17] Sen, A. 1999. *Development as Freedom*, New York: Knopf Press

[18] Walsham, G. 1995. The emergence of interpretivism in IS research. *Information systems research*, *6*(4), 376-394.

[19] White, R. A. 2004. Is 'empowerment' the answer? Current theory and research on development communication. *Gazette*, *66*(1), 7-24.

[20] Gillmor, D. (2004). We the media: The rise of citizen journalists. *National Civic Review*, *93*(3), 58-63.

"RISE IT for Social Good" – An Experimental Investigation of Context to Improve Programming Skills

Full Paper

L.S. Iyer
The University of North Carolina at
Greensboro
Lsiyer@uncg.edu

I. Dissanayake
The University of North Carolina at
Greensboro
i_dissan@uncg.edu

R.T. Bedeley
The University of North Carolina at
Greensboro
rtbedele@uncg.edu

ABSTRACT

Despite increases in female labor force participation, Information Technology (IT) remains heavily male-dominated field. Given the rapid growth in IT career opportunities, it is important find ways to increase the IT female talent pipeline. As a solution that might help mitigate the problem, we proposed the "RISE IT for Social Good" project to examine possible pedagogical interventions to improve the experience female students have in programming. Specifically, this paper uses experimental method to examine whether context plays a role on enhancing female students' performance in IT related tasks.

KEYWORDS

Programming Skills; Self-efficacy; Retention; Gender; Experiment; Context

1 INTRODUCTION

Literature continues to show the underrepresentation of women in Information Technology[1] (IT) and challenges researchers to examine factors that affect this trend and/or solutions that might help alleviate the problem. The motivation for the study stems from the noted attrition of female students (from a bit over 40% in late 1990s to about 20% in recent years) in IT[2]. Factors such as lack of female role models, misconceptions such as lack of social interactions in IT careers or ability to help people, lack of job opportunities due to outsourcing have been examined as reasons for female students not choosing IT education [18, 35, 36]. Other studies have shown that female students tend to drop out of IT majors around sophomore or junior year when they take the programming class [29, 34]. In addition, others in IS have focused on examining gender stereotyping in IT skills and knowledge among students [36], power relationships in IT work and education, and gender differences among IT students based on importance of job attributes [25]. Given that we live in a technologically driven world and that IT related job prospects are growing significantly (Bureau of Labor Statistics 2016), it is astounding to discover that fewer female students are participating in IT education. Despite the under representation of women in the work force, literature on technology-business-performance show that presence of women on organizational teams leads to higher performance. Specifically, women perform well on social sensitive tasks [4].

Based on a seed funding to examine possible pedagogical interventions to improve the experience that female students have in programming, we first examined literature for factors that impact programming skills of students. According to [9,11,13,15, 25, 27,31] female students lacked exposure to programming, perceived programming to be taught in a very abstract manner making it difficult to relate to, and lack of ability to help people [35]. We proposed the "RISE IT for Social Good" project to address this issue. The basic idea was to recruit, inspire, sustain, and engage students in IT through involvement in projects for social good. The study aimed to address the following research questions:

a. Does involving students in problems with social context increase their project quality, satisfaction, confidence in performance, and change in the level of programming self-efficacy?

b. Does project team homogeneity (teams with same or mixed gender) affect the above?

c. Are there differences among factors between female students who worked on social vs non-social themed projects?

To answer the above questions, we conducted an 2x3 factorial experiment outlined in the methodology section. Students were assigned to teams with same or mixed gender and assigned to projects with social and non-social context. Survey was conducted before and after the project. This paper presents the background, details of the methodology and data collection. The findings of the study will provide insights on how to design programming courses that encourages student to achieve higher levels of performances. Currently, analysis is in progress and we anticipate to present the results of the pilot study. It will help us refine the research approach and conduct a full study in Fall 2017.

---

[1] IT is used here to refer to Information Technology, Information Systems (IS), Computer Information Systems and related areas.

[2] National Center for Women & Information Technology, By the Numbers. Retrieved from www.ncwit.org/bythenumbers

SIGMIS-CPR '17, June 21-23, 2017, Bangalore, India
© 2017 Association for Computing Machinery.
ACM ISBN 978-1-4503-5037-2/17/06...$15.00
http://dx.doi.org/10.1145/3084381.3084415

2 BACKGROUND

2.1 Women and IT

Women continue to remain a minority in IT representing only about 25% as compared to 58% in other professional occupations held by women. Efforts to understand the factors that affect this disparity is important so appropriate intervention mechanisms can be put in place to improve the representation of women in IT.

Education in a relevant discipline is generally a strong indicator of the respective career path a person may choose. The enrollment of women in IT education in U.S. has also been steadily decreasing in the recent decades dropping from about 36.8% in the 1980s to about 18.6% in 2007 [17, 21]. Given the opposite direction of trends there are clearly gender issues that deserve study and understanding [1] Because the enrollment of women in computing education is decreasing, it is no surprise that women are underrepresented in IT careers. Without an education in the computing field, they have a narrower chance of making the type of impact that they are capable of. The number of women who majored in computing related areas declined by 80% in the last decade, which ultimately represents a 93% decrease since its peak in 1982 [39]. Broadening the role of women in computing education requires a close examination of factors that shape a student's (1) education, (2) learning, and (3) career choice.

2.2 Theoretical Background & Research Model

This research is grounded in multiple theories such as social cognitive career theory (SCCT) [5], 1986), the theory of planned behavior (TPB) [2], Social Learning Theory [6], the theory of identity [14] and gender theory [1, 37]. Due to page limitation for submission we provide a brief overview of each relevant theory and list the constructs drawn from these theories (see Table 1).

SCCT, based on social cognitive theory (SCT), seeks to explain how environmental and cognitive factors affect a person's intended and actual behavior. TPB proposes that behavior is influenced by specific personal traits and environmental factors [2]. It considers two sets of personal traits—attitudes and perceived behavioral control (PBC). The attitude toward the behavior refers to an individual's predisposition towards the behavior and PBC is an individual's perception of their ability to perform a given behavior [2]. Social norm, as the environmental factor in TPB, refers to the social pressures an individual perceives to engage or not to engage in a behavior [2]. Social Learning Theory (SLT) [6] is proposes a three-way relationship between cognitive factors, environmental influences, and behavior. Carlone and Johnson [14] use identity lens to propose relation between identify and meaningful knowledge to gain requisite skills to perform scientific practices; and recognize herself or himself, while also being recognized by others in the field. In IS literature, genuine interests and motivation were found as salient factors affecting the decision to major in IS [37] Through a thorough analysis of the role of theory in gender and IS research [14], the study provides recommendations on how to conduct gender and IS research.

The constructs under consideration for the study, it's definition in the study context, the theoretical source it is drawn from, and sources from which the instruments are adapted from

as shown in Table 1. In particular, the study will examine how confidence in programming, intrinsic motivation, social norm, IT identity impacts programming self-efficacy, task satisfaction, confidence in performance, and solution quality. Figure 1 summarizes the research model.

Table 1: Constructs and Definitions as adapted to current study and Key Sources.			
Constructs used in the study	Definition adopted for the study	Theoretical Source	Key Sources adopted from
Confidence in Programming	A student's predisposition towards Programming	Theory of planned behavior (TPB)	[2,20]
Social norm	Their perception of family or friend's views on their choice of IT	Theory of planned behavior (TPB)	[20,25]
Intrinsic Motivation	A student's perception of their ability to handle challenging tasks	Social Learning Theory	[6, 33]
Programming Self-efficacy	A student's perception of his or her capability towards Programming	Social Cognitive Career Theory (SCCT)	[5,16,20, 23]
IT Identity	A student's perception of himself or herself as an IT person.	Identity theory	[14, 22]

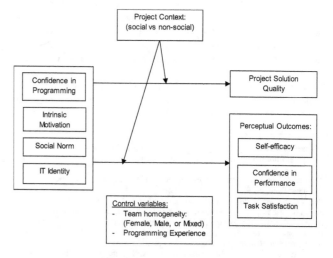

Figure 1: Research Model

3 METHODOLOGY

3.1 Experimental Design

An Experiment, employing 2x3 factorial design (Figure 2), was conducted to examine the effect of software project context (social vs non-social) and project team homogeneity (Female, Male, and Mixed) on project quality, satisfaction, confidence in programming, and change in the level of programming self-efficacy. The experiment task was a semester-long software development project. The participants were undergraduate students enrolled in a Business programming course at a public university in the United States. Subjects earned class credit for participating on the project. In the social context condition, participants were instructed to select a project with a social context (Ex: an application for a non-profit organization). In the non-social context condition, participants were instructed to select a project with a commercial context (Ex: an application for a car rental company). 66 subjects (24 females and 42 males) participated in the experiment. They were assigned into 6 females only, 10 males only and 8 mixed gender groups. Equal number of groups within each gender category were assigned into projects with social and non-social contexts. 31 subjects worked in projects with social contexts and 35 subjects participated in projects with non-social contexts. The average group size was 3.

	Context	
	Social	Non-Social
Female only	3 teams	3 teams
Male only	5 teams	5 teams
Mixed	4 teams	4 teams

Figure 2: Experimental Design

At the beginning (pre-project) and at the end (post-project) of the semester the participants were asked to complete an online survey individually. 50 participants completed the pre-survey (24 social, 26 non-social), 40 participants completed the post-survey (19 social, 21 non-social), and 34 participants completed both pre and post surveys (16 social, 18 non-social). The pre-survey assessed their programming self-efficacy, programming experience, educational and career goals, IT identity, social norm, and intrinsic motivation. The post-survey assessed their confidence in task performance, task satisfaction, and self-efficacy. The confidence in task performance indicates the participant's perception about the quality of his/her solution. This measure was adapted from the previous literature [7, 8, 12, 19]. The task satisfaction represents participant's level of satisfaction with the overall task. The measure for satisfaction also borrowed from the existing literature [7, 10]. The programming self-efficacy represents participant's perception about the level of confidence in programming and information technology (IT) [28]. We measured the programming self-efficacy before and after completion of the project to see whether the project experience has any impact on the participant's level of self-efficacy.

Project quality refers to the assessment of quality of the programming task. Points were awarded based on how well the application satisfy the project requirements. The projects were graded by an independent grader (Teaching Assistant) who was not a part of this experiment.

4 IMPLICATIONS AND LIMITATIONS

We are currently analyzing results of the pilot study and hence unable to present discussions. However, we anticipate the study findings will contribute to both literature and practice. The findings from the experiment will show if this intervention is useful or not. If results do show that context plays a role, then it will provide some useful guidance to how programming courses can be designed with contexts that are meaningful to students. This will also provide some strategies for institutions with low enrollment of female students to use to recruit, retain and grow female students in their programs.

The study limitations will be more clear when we do the analysis. However, as is evident with pilot data collection that getting students to complete both pre- and post-survey will be very critical to having a good ample size for meaningful analysis and results. There may be group dynamics factors that can influence outcomes.

ACKNOWLEDGMENTS
This work is partially supported by the National Center for Women in Information Technology's (ncwit.org) Microsoft Research Grant.

REFERENCES
[1] M. Ahuja. Women in the information technology profession: A literature review, synthesis and research agenda. *European Journal of Information Systems*, 11, 20–34, 2002.

[2] I. Ajzen. The theory of planned behavior. *Organizational Behavior and Human Decision Processes, 50*, 179-211, 1991.

[3] M. Alavi, G.M. Marakas, and Y. Yoo. A Comparative Study of Distributed Learning Environments on Learning Outcomes. Information Systems Research 13 (4):404-415. 2002. http://dx.doi.org/10.1287/isre.13.4.404.72

[4] C. A. Baker, E. Peterson, S. Pulos, and R. A. Kirkland. Eyes and iq: a meta-analysis of the relationship between intelligence and reading the mind in the eyes, *Intelligence* 44, 78–92. 2014.

[5] A. Bandura. *Social foundations of thought and action: A social cognitive theory*, NJ, US: Prentice-Hall 1986.

[6] A. Bandura. Social learning theory. Englewood Cliffs (NJ): Prentice-Hall 1977.

[7] V. Balijepally, R. Mahapatra, S. Nerur, and C.H. Price. Are Two Heads Better than One for Software Development? The Productivity Paradox of Pair Programming, *MIS Quarterly*, Vol. 33, No. 1, pp. 91-118. March 2009.

[8] V. Balijepally. Task Complexity and Effectiveness of Pair Programming: An Experimental Study, *Doctoral Dissertation, The University of Texas at Arlington*, May 2006

[9] S. Beyer. Gender Differences and Intra-Gender Differences amongst Management Information Systems Students, *Journal of Information Systems Education*, 19 (3), 301-310. 2008

[10] A. Bhattacherjee. Understanding information systems continuance: An expectation-confirmation model, *MIS Quarterly*; 25, 3; SciTech Premium Collection pg. 351. Sep 2001

[11] S.J. Bock, L.J. Taylor, Z.E. Phillips, and W. Sun. Women and Minorities in Computer Science Majors: Results on Barriers from Interviews and Survey, *Issues in Information Systems*, 14, 1 143-152 2013

[12] M.B. Brewer, and R.M. Kramer. Choice Behavior in Social Dilemmas: Effects of Social Identity, Group Size, and Decision Framing, Journal of Personality and Social Psychology, 50, 3 543-549. 1986

[13] N. Buzzetto-More, O. Ukoha, and N. Rustagi. Unlocking the Barriers to Women and Minorities in Computer Science and Information Systems Studies: Results from a Multi-Methodological Study Conducted at Two Minority Serving Institutions. *Journal of Information Technology Education*, 2010.

[14] H.B. Carlone, and A. Johnson. "Understanding the science experiences of successful women of color: Science identity as an analytic lens," *Journal of Research in Science Teaching*, (*44:8*), pp.1187-1218. 2007.

[15] J. Carter, and T. Jenkins. Gender and Programming: What's Going On? ACM 1999.

[16] D.R. Compeau and C.A. Higgins. "Computer self-efficacy: Development of a measure and initial test," *MIS Quarterly*, (*19:2*), pp.189-211, 1995.

[17] G.A. Davis, T.L. Lenox, and C.R. Woratschek, Exploring declining CS/IS/IT enrollments. *Information Systems Educational Journal, 6(44)*, 1-11, 2008.

[18] A. Fisher and J. Margolis. Unlocking the Clubhouse: The Carnegie Mellon Experience, SIGCSE Bulletin, 34, 2, 79-83, 2002

[19] F.J. Jourden and C. Heath. The Evaluation Gap in Performance Perceptions: Illusory Perceptions of Groups and Individuals, Journal of Applied Psychology, 81, (4) 369-379. 1996.

[20] N. Heinze and Q. Hu. "Why college undergraduates choose IT: A multi-theoretical perspective," *European Journal of Information Systems*, 18, pp.462-475, 2009.

[21] C. Hill, C. Corbett, and A. Rose. Why So Few: Women in Science, Technology, Engineering, and Mathematics, AAUW Publishing, 2010.

[22] L.S. Iyer, X. Zhao, A. Chow, and S. Tate. Computer Science and Information Technology (CSIT) Identity: An Integrative Theory to Explain Gender Gap in IT, *Proceedings of the International Conference on Information Systems*, (2011).

[23] R.D. Johnson, D. Richard and M. George Marakas. "Research Report: The Role of Behavioral Modeling in Computer Skills Acquisition: Toward Refinement of the Model", Information Systems Research, 11, 402-417, (2000)

[24] K.D. Joshi, L. Kvasny, S. McPherson, E. Trauth, and S. Kulturel-Konak. Choosing IT as a career: Exploring the role of self-efficacy and perceived importance of IT skills. *Proceedings of International Conference on Information Systems, paper 154* 2010.

[25] K.D. Joshi and K. Kuhn. "Gender differences in IS career choice: Examine the role of attitudes and social norms in selecting IS profession," *Proceedings of the 2001 ACM SIGCPR Conference on Computer Personnel*, 2001. *Research.* doi:10.1145/371209.371224

[26] C. Kelleher and R. Pausch. Using Storytelling to Motivate Programming, Communication of the ACM, 50, 759-64, 2007

[27] L. Ma, J. Ferguson, M. Roper, and M. Wood. Investigating the Viability of Mental Models Held by Novice Programmers, ACM, pp. 499-503, 2007.

[28] G.M. Marakas, M.Y. Yi, and R.D. Johnson, he Multilevel and Multifaceted Character of Computer Self-Efficacy: Toward Clarification of the Construct and an Integrative Framework for Research, *Information Systems Research* 9 (2), 126-163, 1998. http://dx.doi.org/10.1287/isre.9.2.126

[29] J. Margolis and A. Fisher. Unlocking the Clubhouse Women in Computing, The MIT Press, Cambridge, Massachusetts, 2002.

[30] J. Nandhakumar, N.S. Panourgias, and H. Scarbrough. From Knowing It to "Getting It": Envisioning Practices in Computer Games Development. *Information Systems Research* 24(4):933-955, 2013. http://dx.doi.org/10.1287/isre.2013.0482

[31] M. Papastergiou, Are computer science and information technology still masculine fields? High school students' perceptions and career choices. *Computers & Education*, 51(2), 594-608, 2008.

[32] R.D. Pea and D.M. Kurland. On the Cognitive Effects of Learning Computer Programming, New Ideas Psychology, 2, (2) 137-168, 1984.

[33] S. Ravi, C. Subramaniam, and M.L. Nelson. Determinants of the Choice of Open Source Software License, *Journal of management Information Systems*, 25, 207-239, 2008.

[34] G. Scragg, and J. Smith. A study of barriers to women in undergraduate computer science. *Proceedings of SIGCSE'98 conference, Atlanta, 1998*

[35] G. C. Townsend, S. Menzel, and K. A. Siek. Leveling the CS1 playing field. Paper presented at the 38th SIGCSE technical symposium on Computer science education, Covington, KY., 2007.

[36] E.M. Trauth, C. Cain, K.D. Joshi, L. Kvasny, and K. Booth. The Influence of Gender-Ethnic Intersectionality on Gender Stereotypes about IT Skills and Knowledge. The Data Base for Advances in Information Systems, 47:3, 9-39 2016.

[37] E.M. Trauth. The Role of Theory in Gender and Information Systems Research. Information and Organization, 23, 277-293, 2013.

[38] K.A. Walstrom, T.P. Schambach, and W.J. Crampton. Why are students not majoring in information systems? *Journal of Information Systems Education 19(1)*, 313-319, 2008.

[39] S. Zweben. Taulbee Survey Report, 2009-2010, Computing Research Association, April 5, 2011

Acceptance of Warehouse Picking Systems – A Literature Review

Full Paper

Jendrik Haase
Frankfurt School of Finance & Management
Germany
Jendrik.Haase@fs-students.de

Daniel Beimborn
Frankfurt School of Finance & Management
Germany
D.Beimborn@fs.de

ABSTRACT

This paper reports the findings from a structured review of the research literature on individual warehouse workers' (pickers') acceptance of order picking support systems (OPSS), such as Pick by Vision, Pick by Voice, or Pick by Light. Summarizing 17 publications, it becomes clear that OPSS deliver significant value with regard to performance increases but that social influences among workers and various facilitating conditions have to be taken into account when implementing such solutions and expecting warehouse workers to use them.

KEYWORDS

Order picking support systems (OPSS); user acceptance; adoption determinants; literature review

1 INTRODUCTION

In an increasingly interconnected world, distribution and warehouse operations have become critical for managing supply chain operations [41]. Warehouses have to execute an increasing number of transactions and handle more products within shorter and shorter time windows. This especially affects order picking, the activity of retrieving items from storage upon customer demand. Order picking, which has traditionally been performed using error-prone paper lists, accounts for up to 55% of total warehouse operating expenses in many warehouses [47]. Accordingly, advanced IT plays a critical role: order picking support systems, like Pick by Vision where pickers wear a head mounted augmented reality device, are increasingly implemented [35] and show promising effects on performance [8; 37; 54].

However, IT implementation projects frequently fail, often because of user resistance. In response to the implementation, users may reject the new system and cause delays in the project duration, budget overruns, and underutilization of the new system [7; 27]. Accordingly, to take potential acceptance inhibitors into ac-

count when designing and implementing new order picking systems, human factors and acceptance determinants of those systems should be explored in detail [13; 19]. However, the literature does yet not provide an overarching analysis of the adoption of different warehouse picking support technologies. Addressing this research gap, our paper analyzes and consolidates existing but fragmented research on the acceptance of IT-based picking systems, answering the following research question: *What are the determinants driving the acceptance of order picking support systems by individual workers?*

In the following, we analyze 17 research articles, containing case studies and experiments, from which we will derive adoption drivers and barriers. In the following, we will first summarize the basics of order picking systems, then describe our literature review approach, and finally present and discuss the findings addressing the research question.

2 BASICS

2.1 Order Picking Support Systems

Order picking is the operation of retrieving goods from specified warehouse storage locations based on customer orders [40]. In manually operated warehouses, it is the most labor-intensive operation, whereas in automatically operated warehouses it is considered a very capital-intensive activity [35; 47]. Despite the possibility of implementing fully automated storage and retrieval systems, 80% of all warehouses are to some extent still manually operated [2; 33]. Humans are better able to respond rapidly to varying requirements and urgent requests in the order picking process; they can retrieve items of different shape, weight and volume from their storage locations, which is still difficult and/or comparably expensive to imitate by IT and robots [18].

The main objective of order picking is to maximize picking accuracy and minimize delivery response times with an efficient amount of resources such as labor, machines, and capital [20; 31]. Order picking is pivotal to reach short lead times and high customer satisfaction and, in order to succeed, an efficient and flexible order picking process needs to be implemented [19].

Traditionally, order pickers, or warehouse operators, perform the picking task by using carts and being guided by lists printed on paper or presented on tablets that contain all relevant information. The advantage is that they can start without further action and with minimal training.

The downside of list-based picking is an error rate of about .35% to 1.5% [21; 22; 46][1]. Picking errors mainly occur due to subjective task overload influenced by an inadequate amount of information [50]. The minimization of picking errors is one of the main challenges in order picking.

Besides customer satisfaction, an efficient picking process contributes significantly to the balance sheet. Order picking activities are responsible for more than half of the warehouse operating expenses in many warehouses [3; 47], while half of the order picking time is spent on non-value adding activities such as navigating to and searching for specific storage locations [9; 14; 39]. Given that order picking is such a costly and crucial operation within warehousing, many organizations continuously examine how their processes can be made more efficient. Today, many technical tools exist to support operators and thus to increase quality and productivity. A growing number of firms implement mobile Order Picking Support Systems (OPSS), such as *Pick by Vision* and *Pick by Voice*, or stationary OPSS, such as *Pick by Light*, to combine human pickers' flexibility with technological precision [48]. In the following, these three main types of OPSS are introduced:

-   *Pick by Vision (PbVision).* PbVision uses augmented reality (AR) to support the picking process. Operators wear a head mounted display (HMD) or technologically modified glasses which contain an augmented reality compatible lens and overlay the real world with virtual objects [34]. During the picking process, the operator wears the device, which visualizes all required picking information, including storage location and quantity, directly into the picker's field of view [34]. The warehouse management system (WMS) constantly provides the device with real-time information. Depending on the system's level of sophistication, the device either guides the operator through the warehouse aisles based on his or her current position or solely visualizes picking information in a text based format [22]. Results from a laboratory experiment confirmed a decrease in picking errors by up to 75% and a decrease in picking time by 30% compared to paper list-based picking systems [6].

-   *Pick by Voice (PbVoice).* PbVoice supports the picking process by using audio and voice commands. The picker wears a headset with an integrated processing unit. The processing unit continuously exchanges data with the WMS and translates the received information, which consists of all information required for the picking operation, into spoken voice [4]. After collecting an item, the picker confirms the pick by repeating the name and quantity of the picked product. The processing unit recognizes the spoken words, converts them into data and transmits them to the WMS. Most voice picking systems require only a short training to ensure that user and system understand each other's commands [13]. The usage

of PbVoice systems can lead to a very low error rate of 0.18% [23; 32][2].

-   Pick by Light (PbLight): PbLight uses stationary light signals to guide the picker. Each storage location is equipped with a small digital display and buttons or sensors. The display lightens up if an item has to be retrieved from that particular location and indicates the required quantity. To confirm a pick, the operator pushes the display and the corresponding lights will fade out. The operator then moves towards the next indicated storage location. Contrary to PbVision and PbVoice systems, PbLight systems indicate all relevant storage locations at the same time. Thus, the operator has some flexibility regarding the chosen picking sequence. Usually, each storage location is equipped with only one display, which implies that only one picker can work in a particular picking area at a time. Therefore, PbLight is best suited for picking strategies where operators are assigned to specific zones. The PbLight system can increase productivity by up to 50% compared to traditional paper list systems [31].

All OPSS create a link between the operator and the WMS as they are continuously exchanging data among them. In order to support the operator as desired, the IT devices have to automatically provide and collect relevant and context-dependent information, such as a product location or a picking confirmation. That data is transmitted to the WMS, which immediately updates the inventory level for that item and in return provides the OPSS with information for the next picking tour. This allows the operator to retrieve items based on real-time information. Thus, late modifications on customer orders, more economic picking sequences, and the latest inventory levels can be considered. Furthermore, OPSS allow operators to perform their picking activities "hands and eyes free", meaning they neither have to carry a list nor need to take their eyes off the aisles or storage locations. This enables them to focus on the actual order picking process [42]. Most OPSS are further able to immediately inform operators about picking errors, either verbally or optically.

Being linked to the WMS, the usage of an OPSS allows warehouse managers to continuously monitor the picking process and to track performance indicators [31]. Several studies confirmed that the introduction of IT to order picking enhances productivity by up to 30% [30] and also improves operational flexibility as the handling of late stage customization and other value added services can be integrated [12][3]. Table 1 summarizes the advantages and disadvantages of OPSS vs. paper-based order picking.

---

[1] According to Gudehus (2010), the most frequent picking errors are (1) picking the wrong item (37 to 42% of all picking errors), (2) picking the wrong quantity (44 to 46%), and (3) skipping an item (10%).

[2] An extension to PbVision and PbVoice systems includes gloves or wristbands equipped with RFID tags that will send alerts if the operator reaches into a wrong storage location.

[3] Interestingly, none of the studies compared the performance of all the different OPSS using the same experimental setup. Thus, research has provided no empirical evidence on the superiority or inferiority of any of the OPSS, so far.

Table 1: Advantages and Disadvantages of Evaluated Picking Systems

	Advantages	Disadvantages
Paper-based picking	- Easy and cheap to implement - Limited training required, due to intuitive usage	- Time consuming due to longer searching times of storage location - Does not allow real time data exchange. WMS will be not be updated before picking tour is completed.
Pick by Light	- Allows for a "hands and eyes free" order picking operation	- High cost for initial installation and modification - Only one picker can work in one zone at a time
Pick by Voice	- Limited training required, due to its intuitive usage	- Difficult to use in noisy industrial environments - Decreased interaction with co-workers
Pick by Vision		- Decreased interaction with co-workers

2.2 Technology Acceptance Determinants

The decision of individuals to accept and use a certain technology introduced to their personal or workplace environment has been extensively researched [26; 45]. In this paper, we consolidate the determinants of OPSS acceptance by individual workers from earlier studies. Therefore, it is useful to use the theoretical determinants from adoption research as a categorization framework. Basically, there exist two academic strands that try to explain the factors leading to the adoption or rejection of a new IT system. The user resistance literature mainly sees expected threats, such as loss of power, higher efforts or reduced outcome as the main barriers to the adoption of IT.

The technology acceptance literature on the other hand looks at factors influencing the adoption and usage of a new technology. One of the most comprehensive and best-established technology acceptance frameworks is the UTAUT [49]. It has a strong theoretical basis as it builds on eight previous technology acceptance theories. In our work, we will use the main acceptance determinants of the UTAUT – performance expectancy, effort expectancy, social influence, and facilitating conditions – to categorize influencing factors and possible barriers to OPSS acceptance.

Within the user resistance literature, Joshi [25] developed the equity-implementation model that deals with perceived mismatches between inputs and outcomes of the new system.Users evaluate expected changes in outcomes and input; a decrease in outcome and/or an increase in input will be felt as a loss and cause distress, which will lead to user resistance [25]. This basic idea is partially covered by two of the determinants of the UTAUT: Performance Expectancy and Effort Expectancy. Performance Expectancy describes the changes in outcome and deals with the question to what extent the individual believes that the system will help her attain gains in job performance [10]. Effort expectancy deals with the expected ease of use and as such also with the degree to which an individual believes using the system will be free of effort [11; 25].

In the following, empirical research on workers' acceptance of OPSS will be consolidated and analyzed in a literature review structured along the determinants of the UTAUT framework.

3 METHODOLOGY

Aim of this paper is to provide a consolidation of the findings of existing studies on the adoption of OPSS. Our literature review considered the guidelines recommended by Webster & Watson, Kitchenham, and Levy & Ellis [28; 29; 52].

Prior to the analysis, neither viable keywords nor robust details on a rational timeframe for a successful query were evident. Therefore, an initial Google Scholar search was performed in order to find commonly used key words related to OPSS.

This initial search revealed a set of distinct keywords, which were then used to find relevant research articles in the following databases: ABI/Inform Collection, EBSCO Business Source Premier, Emerald Insight, JSTOR, and Science Direct. In addition, ResearchGate, Google Scholar and Springer Link were used.

Basically, the following generic query was used: «(Title OR Abstract OR Text) CONTAINS ("pick by vision" OR "pick to vision" OR "pick by voice" OR "pick to voice" OR "pick by light" OR "pick to light") AND (Title OR Abstract OR Text) CONTAINS (warehouse AND NOT "data warehouse") AND (Article Type)=(Peer Reviewed)». This search came up with 36 hits, which were then used as basis for a backward search.

Finally, the retrieval process resulted in 51 articles. The articles were analyzed in detail to select those works that were relevant for our research question. Thereby, only works that provided original empirical research were considered, eventually leading to 17 publications (two of them referring to the same study).

4 RESULTS

The literature search revealed that no data dealing with the application of OPSS has been published before 2007, probably because there had been no sufficiently developed OPSS solutions available before. Since then, a number of studies were published; however, notably, none of the studies was published in a top-ranked journal. 15 of the 17 publications considered are findings from laboratory experiments (involving both unexperienced subjects and experienced warehouse workers), whereas two of them are studies performed in a real warehouse environment. PbVision was the most frequently examined system. 11 of the articles compared at least one OPSS with the traditional paper-based picking approach. Interestingly, none of the articles linked its research findings to any theoretical underpinning.

Table 2 gives a detailed overview about the publications considered for the identification of determinants of the adoption of OPSS. In the following section, the results of these studies will be summarized along the UTAUT determinants.

Table 2: Overview of Articles Included in the Analysis Ordered by Publication Date

Article (ordered by year of publication)	Publication type	Research Method	# of Subjects	Studied Picking System
Berger & Ludwig 2007 [8]	Journal article	Case study	132	PbVoice, Paper
Schwerdtfeger et al. 2007 [42]	Book	Lab experiment	18	PbVision
Reif & Walch 2008 [38]	Journal article	Lab experiment	17	PbVision, PbVoice, Paper
Günthner et al. 2009 [22] Reif et al. 2009 [36][a]	University report Conference paper	Lab experiment	16	PbVision, Paper
Schwerdtfeger et al. 2009 [44]	Conference paper	Lab experiment	19	PbVision, Paper
Weaver et al. 2010 [51]	Conference paper	Lab experiment	8	PbVision, PbVoice, Paper
Schwerdtfeger et al. 2011 [43]	Journal article	Lab experiment	34	PbVision
Baumann & Lawo 2012 [6]	Book section	Lab experiment	n/a	PbVision, PbLight, Paper
Ehmann 2012 [15]	Book section	Lab experiment	n/a	PbVision
Günthner & Rammelmeier 2012 [23]	University report	Lab experiment	17	PbVision, Paper
Baumann 2013 [5]	University report	Case study	20	PbVision, PbLight, Paper
Guo et al. 2014 [24]	Conference paper	Lab experiment	8	PbVision, PbLight, Paper
Wu et al. 2015 [53]	Conference paper	Lab experiment	8	PbVision, PbLight
Funk et al. 2015 [17]	Conference paper	Lab experiment	16	PbVision, PbVoice, PbLight, Paper
De Vries et al. 2016 [13]	Journal article	Lab experiment	101	PbVoice, PbLight
Baechler et al. 2016 [1]	Conference paper	Lab experiment	24	PbLight, Paper

[a] Günthner et al. 2009 and Reif et al. 2009 refer two different publications reporting results from the same study.

4.1 Performance Expectancy

Performance Expectancy is defined as the degree to which an individual believes that using a specific system will help him or her to improve job performance [49]. The two most important performance criteria in order picking are picking speed and picking accuracy. Therefore, several articles examined how subjects perceive the influence of OPSS to their work performance along these dimensions. Picking Speed: Various experiments confirm that the usage of PbVision, PbVoice and PbLight significantly increased the perceived picking speed compared with traditional lists [24; 51; 53]. Picking Accuracy: Participants in lab experiments ranked PbVision and PbLight significantly more accurate than picking based on paper lists and emphasized the potential to significantly reduce the share of picking errors [23; 24; 51; 53]. Continuously available picking information and "hands and eyes free" usage were perceived as especially supportive among subjects [22; 53]. Order pickers who used PbVoice for fourteen weeks stated that it became significantly easier to identify the correct storage location of an item [8]. Professional order pickers in a laboratory environment reported that the application of PbVision would especially be useful in large warehouses and for extensive orders [22]. Confirming the pickers' perceptions, research analyzing performance data predominately found improvements in picking speed and picking accuracy.

4.2 Effort Expectancy

Effort Expectancy can be described as the degree to which an individual perceives a particular technology to be easy to use and of low complexity [11]. Three aspects were identified during the literature review: required subjective task load, its learnability and the individuals' motivation to use the systems.

Subjective Task Load: The subjective task load of a particular action is influenced by the individuals' mental, physical, and temporal demand while performing the action as well as the perceived effort and level of frustration. In the studies, we found some contradictions in the perceived subjective task load related with the different OPSS. In some experiments, paper-based picking was perceived as less demanding, whereas in others it was perceived as more demanding. These contradictions make it impossible to rank the picking methods based on their subjective task load.

However, we found some interesting insights. A four-week study on PbVision showed that the subjective task load was high in the beginning but decreased over time [5]. In particular, operators reported that it was, at least in the beginning, significantly harder to navigate through the aisles wearing a HMD and that they suffered from eyestrain and headache [5]. By contrast, pickers also reported that paper-based lists required much higher concentration than PbLight and PbVision [5]. With growing familiarity, order pickers started to appreciate the new technology and began to use it predominately [5]. Continuous use led to an easier handling and reduced the uncomfortable feeling caused by the

HMD [5; 44]. Further, some experienced operators rated the paper list to be less demanding than PbVision. The fact that these operators are experts in performing their tasks assisted by a paper list possibly explains why they do not perceive the traditional method as exhausting [23]. Therefore, it is hardly surprising that the traditional paper list received high scores on usability, as it is intuitive and self-explanatory. By contrast, participants also reported that the available information in PbVision reduced task complexity [36]. Physical examination of participants' subjective state of well-being indicated that there is no significant difference in the perceived subjective task load for PbVision compared with using a traditional paper list [44]. Notably, participants across all types of research used their both hands for picking when using any of the paperless systems. This indicates that the hands-free usage is well accepted, confirming previous expectations [17; 36; 51].

Learnability: The degree to which a new system is perceived as easy to learn contributes significantly to the overall Effort Expectancy. The easier the system is to learn, the less likely will learnability represent a barrier to the adoption of IT. Professional order pickers reported that PbVision is easy to learn. However, a viable and comparable comparison was not possible, as the order pickers were already familiar with that system [23]. Various experiments confirmed these results. Among participants without relevant technology and picking experience, all OPSS systems were perceived as equally easy to learn [24; 51]. But, those participants perceived the learnability of paper-based picking as more demanding [24; 51].

Interestingly, research did not provide consistent results on whether previous experiences with augmented reality increase the perceived learnability of PbVision [24; 42].

Age, a moderator to Effort Expectancy, proved to have a negative influence on PbVoice picking performance, implying that it is more difficult to learn for older people [13].

The results on learnability and subjective task load suggest that the use of list-based approaches is indeed difficult for beginners. As it requires a high degree of concentration and knowledge on the warehouse layout, the perceived time for learning is longer. Researchers expect an average lead-time of three months until PbVision reaches the expected productivity levels [15].

Motivation: An individual's motivation to perform a particular behavior is a good indicator for how that individual perceives its ease of use. Humans tend to have a higher motivation to engage in a particular behavior if they perceive it as challenging but achievable. Too easy as well as too complex tasks cause frustration, loss of interest, and lead to rejection [16].

Professional order pickers who started to use PbVoice instead of paper-based picking reported after fourteen weeks of usage that their motivation to come to work each day had decreased significantly and that they received considerably less constructive feedback on their work performance. They further criticized that the PbVoice system left them with notably less opportunity to pick items in the sequence they prefer and that interaction with peers was no longer possible [8]. This outcome emphasizes that these operators suffer from the loss of their autonomous working style, which to some extent means that they felt disempowered. Operators emphasized that the monotonous verbal input of PbVoice caused them to be less motivated to perform the picking tasks. Additionally, operators prefer to have an overview of the whole operation, a feature that PbVoice cannot offer. By contrast, operators who used PbVision in a three-week trial reported that their motivation to use the system increased over time [5], probably due to growing familiarity with the system.

In general, participants in laboratory experiments were significantly more motivated to perform the picking tasks using IT [22]. This might be because humans tend to be curios to try new technology. However, it seems that order pickers perceive the IT systems differently (i.e., more positively) when they know that they use it for experimental purposes only.

4.3 Social Influence

Social Influence is the degree to which an individual feels social pressure to use the new system [49]. Social pressure can be created by co-workers and supervisors and is reported to directly affect an individual's behavior towards a particular technology.

Field research revealed that co-workers indeed have a significant influence on pickers' adoption and usage behavior. Researchers noticed that pickers are far more reluctant to wear an HMD in their working environment than when they are in a research laboratory. Even though researchers expected some skepticism, the intensity of a negative attitude towards the IT support was surprising. Further, during a voluntary trial, some workers tried to convince their co-workers to not try PbVision as they saw it as a potential threat to their job security [5]. Group dynamics evolved and the wearable computer device was denigrated [5]. As a result, many workers tried to avoid using the HMD and some refused to wear them at all. Possibly, due to this atmosphere, most operators stopped using PbVision before becoming familiar with it.

Notably, during the PbVoice case study, no similar problems had been reported [8]. However, it cannot be concluded whether this disparity is caused by the difference in technologies or the fact that the usage in the PbVoice case study was mandatory. Finally, during one lab experiment, several operators expressed that they would not feel comfortable wearing a HMD in front of peers as they expect their co-workers to make fun of them [17].

4.4 Facilitating Conditions

Facilitating Conditions are defined as the degree to which an individual believes that his or her organization and environment is supporting the change [49]. A supportive organization is likely to face less adoption barriers. The studies suggest that two aspects are particularly relevant for facilitating conditions: training and guidance provided by the organization as well as the technological maturity of the implemented system.

Training: Operators who received sufficient trainings utilized PbVoice better than others did. This effect is even larger for employees who were previously considered as low-performers [8]. However, providing extensive training did not always increase acceptance of OPSS [17]. Research also revealed, that operators who had experiences with any kind of 3D virtual reality applications (e.g., computer games), compared to their unexperienced peers, are faster and more accurate using PbVision [22; 44]. This implies that the organization has to provide more training to employees who are unfamiliar with certain technologies – which sounds trivial but is often not considered by firms.

Technological Maturity: Apart from training, technological maturity plays an essential role for adoption. Most systems used in the studies were not yet fully market-ready. Therefore, the findings could only serve as guiding propositions, which might cause a bias in the participants' evaluation of the subjective experience.

Participants across various laboratory experiments reported to have problems with the PbVision devices. Immature augmented reality software led to difficulties with changing brightness and an insufficient focus. Bulky and non-ergonomically designed hardware was considered disturbing and caused headaches. Some participants had to suspend their tasks as they did not feel comfortable using the device [22; 44]. The level of IT affinity did not have an influence on the likelihood of these perceptions. Participants who considered themselves as IT affine also experienced head-

aches and eye strain [44]. Furthermore, one experiment emphasized that physical constraints of the individual picker have to be considered when visualizing the way towards the storage location (e.g., the mathematically shortest way to turn is not always the best way to guide the user) [43].

Similar problems were reported for PbVoice systems. Participants experienced problems with the speech recognition and audio output of the PbVoice device. In particular, they criticized that instructions were given too slowly and that the devices did not always understand verbal input correctly [38]. Hence, researchers who experienced that the devices used in their experiments contained bugs or improvable ergonomics recommended further development to improve the technology. It is important to ensure that the device suits the users' demands. Its weight, size and ergonomic shape should allow for a comfortable interaction.

Table 3: Overview of Barriers to OPSS Adoption (asterisk (*) indicates statistically significant result)

		Pick by Vision	Pick by Voice	Pick by Light
Performance Expectancy	**Perceived Picking Speed**	Faster than paper-based picking [24]*, [51]* Faster than PbVoice [51]* Faster than PbLight [24]*	Faster than paper-based picking [51]	Faster than paper-based picking but slower than PbVision [24]
	Perceived Picking Accuracy	More accurate than paper-based picking [24]*, [23], [51*] More accurate than PbLight [24], [53] Equal to PbVoice [51]	Equal to PbVision [51]	More accurate than paper-based picking [24] Less accurate than PbVision [53]
Effort Expectancy	**Subjective Task Load**	Less than paper-based picking [24]*, [22], [38], [44], [51]* Higher than paper-based picking [23] Less than PbLight [24], [53]* Less than PbVoice [38], [6]*	Higher than PbVision [38], [6] Lower than PbVision [17] Higher than paper-based picking [38], [17]	Less than paper-based picking [1], [5], [17]*, [24] Less than PbVoice [17]* Less than PbVision [17]* Higher than PbVision [53]*
	Learnability	Harder than paper-based picking [23] Easier than paper-based picking [24]*, [51] Equal to PbLight [24] Equal to PbVoice [51] Easier than PbLight [51]	Equal to PbVision [51] Easier than paper-based picking [51] Age has a negative influence on PbVoice performance [13]*	Harder than PbVision [51] Easier than paper-based picking [24] Equal to PbVision [24]
	Motivation	Higher than paper-based picking [22]*, [38] Higher than PbVoice [38] Perceived as exciting [15]	Less than paper-based picking [8] Higher than paper based picking [38]	
Social Influence		Colleagues tried to convince their peers not to wear a HMD [5] Participants said they would dislike to wear HMD in real working environment [17]		
Facilitating Conditions	**Training**	3D VR experienced subjects achieved faster picking times than their unexperienced peers [22; 23;42;44] 3D VR experienced subjects achieved more accurate picking results than their unexperienced peers [44]		
	Technological Maturity	HMD moved during picking task [17], [22] Device not ergonomically designed [38] Information hard to read when brightness changed [15] Mathematically shortest way to turn is not always the best way to guide the user [43]		

As individuals differ in age, cognitive capabilities and perception of comfort, the device should ideally be adjustable to one's personal preferences. Recent studies with more advanced devices confirmed the progress in development and importance of comfort and ease of use. Participants in those studies reported that wearing the HMD for eight hours felt unusual but not painful [5].

4.5 Summary of Findings

Table 3 on the previous page summarizes the results from the analyzed studies. The richest results exist regarding PbVision, which also represents the technologically most advanced concept.

5 DISCUSSION AND CONCLUSION

Our literature review provides a consolidation of the scarce literature on warehouse workers' acceptance of order picking support systems. Although order picking is such an essential and costly part of the overall supply chain process, only a few studies on adoption and usage determinants of OPSS have been conducted, so far. In our consolidated review, we found seven barriers to OPSS adoption: (1) an overwhelmingly high subjective task load, (2) loss of autonomy, (3) loss of social interaction, (4) negative influences from co-workers, (5) high complexity in handling the technology, (6) a lack of training and (7) a lack of maturity of the technology. In summary, this paper contributes to the adoption literature by presenting the first synthesis of existing studies about the implementation of order picking technology in warehouses.

Two significant managerial implications can be derived from these findings:

The implemented OPSS technology should be mature and intuitive: The adoption of a new technology requires changing old habits and routines. The performance and effort expectations play an important role for the adoption of picking technology. When the new picking technology does not work properly, no performance increase or easement of the task will occur. Instead, a lack of technological maturity will very likely be a strong adoption barrier. It should also be ensured that the new OPSS runs smoothly and free of errors in conjunction with the WMS.

The implementation of a new OPSS is a multifaceted and complex process: The analyzed studies show that various barriers throughout the implementation phase can occur. The concerns and emotions of the pickers can lead to rejection of the technology. Communication is very important to lessen the fear of job loss or influences from co-workers. Having a pilot phase where a group of employees can test the new technology and give feedback can be very advantageous – but, negative experiences will inevitably lead to negative word of mouth and increase the social influence barrier (calling again for mature technology). Further, the loss of autonomy and social interaction are important points and should be compensated for (e.g., longer breaks for allowing sufficient social interaction among the workers).

Directions for Future Research: Despite the potential limitation that we oversaw studies on OPSS adoption, we can conclude that there is only little, immature, and inconclusive research available, so far. First, hardly any field studies evaluated OPSS in real environments. Most works are lab experiments, which furthermore have only partly included professional pickers – comparing the studies has clearly shown that picking experience has an impact on the results and that workers behave differently in lab vs. their own environments. Therefore, the most straightforward implication for future research is that more robust insights on OPSS acceptance require more and broader field experiments with experienced pickers in real warehouse settings. These field experiments should also involve more mature OPSS technology since some of the lab experiments suffered from problems with the software and hardware of the used picking support systems. Future studies should also include multiple different OPSS to allow comparisons among them.

Further, almost all of the analyzed studies remained atheoretical. Many of them were industry reports; they did not take our rich theoretical understanding of technology adoption and usage into account nor did they ground their hypotheses in the well-established theories on individual action and attitudes. In the future, scholars should take these and other theories (e.g., work characteristics theory and others from work psychology) into account to get a more reliable and deeper understanding about the attitudes and behaviors of the pickers.

Finally, the research field on OPSS adoption seems to be quite isolated so far. In the future, it should link to and integrate with findings from related research fields; for instance, research on wearable devices, ambient computing, or augmented reality will likely inform future theorization and more facetted empirical studies on OPSS adoption by the individual workers.

Overall, we hope that our analysis will help stimulate further research on the digitalization of the order picking process. Such research is highly needed and will help firms to make effective decisions on selecting and implementing the right OPSS.

REFERENCES

[1] BAECHLER, A., BAECHLER, L., AUTENRIETH, S., KURTZ, P., HOERZ, T., HEIDENREICH, T., and KRUELL, G., 2016. A Comparative Study of an Assistance System for Manual Order Picking - Called Pick-by-Projection - with the Guiding Systems Pick-by-Paper, Pick-by-Light and Pick-by-Display. In *49th Hawaii International Conference on System Sciences (HICSS)*, Koloa, Hawaii, 523-531.

[2] BAKER, P. and PEROTTI, S., 2008. *UK Warehouse Benchmarking Report*. Cranfield School of Management.

[3] BARTHOLDI III, J.J. and HACKMAN, S.T., 2016. *Warehouse & Distribution Science*. Georgia Institute of Technology.

[4] BATTINI, D., CALZAVARA, M., PERSONA, A., and SGARBOSSA, F., 2015. A comparative analysis of different paperless picking systems. *Industrial Management & Data Systems 115*, 3, 483-503.

[5] BAUMANN, H., 2013. *Order picking supported by mobile computing*. University of Bremen.

[6] BAUMANN, H. and LAWO, M., 2012. Evaluation grafischer Benutzerschnittstellen für die Kommissionierung unter Verwendung von Head Mounted Displays. In *Datenbrillen – Aktueller Stand von Forschung und Umsetzung sowie zukünftiger Entwicklungsrichtungen* Bundesanstalt für Arbeitsschutz und Arbeitsmedizin, Dortmund, 19-22.

[7] BEAUDRY, A. and PINSONNEAULT, A., 2005. Understanding user responses to information technology: A coping model of user adaptation. *MIS Quarterly 29*, 3, 493-524.

[8] BERGER, S.M. and LUDWIG, T.D., 2007. Reducing warehouse employee errors using voice-assisted technology that provided immediate feedback. Journal of Org. Behavior Management 27, 1, 1-31.

[9] ÇELIK, M. and SÜRAL, H., 2014. Order picking under random and turnover-based storage policies in fishbone aisle warehouses. IIE Transactions 46, 3, 283-300.

[10] COMPEAU, D.R. and HIGGINS, C.A., 1995. Computer self-efficacy: Development of a measure and initial test. *MIS Quarterly 19*, 2, 189-211.

[11] DAVIS, F.D., 1989. Perceived usefulness, perceived ease of use, and user acceptance of IT. *MIS Quarterly 13*, 3, 319-339.

[12] DE KOSTER, R., LE-DUC, T., and ROODBERGEN, K.J., 2007. Design and control of warehouse order picking: A literature review. *European Journal of Operational Research 182*, 2, 481-501.

[13] DE VRIES, J., DE KOSTER, R., and STAM, D., 2016. Exploring the role of picker personality in predicting picking performance with pick by voice, pick to light and RF-terminal picking. International Journal of Production Research 54, 8, 2260-2274.

[14] DEKKER, R., DE KOSTER, R., ROODBERGEN, K.J., and VAN KALLEVEEN, H., 2004. Improving order-picking response time at Ankor's warehouse. Interfaces 34, 4, 303-313.

[15] EHMANN, M., 2012. Visual Guided Picking – Ergonomische und wirtschaftliche Unterstützung in der Intralogistik. In Datenbrillen – Aktueller Stand von Forschung und Umsetzung sowie zukünftiger Entwicklungsrichtungen Bundesanstalt für Arbeitsschutz und Arbeitsmedizin, Dortmund, Germany, 23-28.

[16] FISHERL, C.D., 1993. Boredom at work: A neglected concept. Human relations 46, 3, 395-417.

[17] FUNK, M., SHIRAZI, A.S., MAYER, S., LISCHKE, L., and SCHMIDT, A., 2015. Pick from here! An interactive mobile cart using in-situ projection for order picking. In ACM International Joint Conference on Pervasive and Ubiquitous Computing, Osaka, 601-609.

[18] GROSSE, E.H. and GLOCK, C.H., 2015. The effect of worker learning on manual order picking processes. International Journal of Production Economics 170, 882-890.

[19] GROSSE, E.H., H., G.C., and NEUMANN, W.P., 2015. Human Factors in Order Picking System Design: A Content Analysis. IFAC-Papers OnLine 48, 3, 320-325.

[20] GU, J., GOETSCHALCKX, M., and MCGINNIS, L.F., 2010. Research on warehouse design and performance evaluation: A comprehensive review. European Journal of Operational Research 203, 3, 539-549.

[21] GUDEHUS, T., 2010. *Logistik Grundlagen - Strategien - Anwendungen*. Springer-Verlag, Berlin et al.

[22] GÜNTHNER, W.A., BLOMEYER, N., REIF, R., and SCHEDLBAUER, M., 2009. *Pick-by-Vision: Augmented Reality unterstützte Kommissionierung*. Technical University of Munich.

[23] GÜNTHNER, W.A. and RAMMELMEIER, T., 2012. Vermeidung von Kommissionierfehlern mit Pick-by-Vision. Tech University of Munich.

[24] GUO, A., RAGHU, S., XIE, X., ISMAIL, S., LUO, X., SIMONEAU, J., GILLI-LAND, S., BAUMANN, H., SOUTHERN, C., and STARNER, T., 2014. A comparison of order picking assisted by head-up display (HUD), cart-mounted display (CMD), light, and paper pick list. In ACM Internat. Symposium on Wearable Computers, Seattle, 71-78.

[25] JOSHI, K., 1991. A model of users' perspective on change: the case of IS technology implementation. MIS Quarterly 15, 2, 229-242.

[26] JOSHI, K., 2005. Understanding user resistance and acceptance during the implementation of an order management system: A case study using the equity implementation model. Journal of Information Technology Cases and Application Research 7, 1, 6-20.

[27] KIM, H.W. and PAN, S.L., 2006. Towards a process model of information systems implementation: the case of customer relationship management (CRM). ACM SIGMIS Database 37, 1, 59-76.

[28] KITCHENHAM, B., 2004. Procedures for performing systematic reviews. Keele University Press, Keele.

[29] LEVY, Y. and ELLIS, T.J., 2006. A systems approach to conduct an effective literature review in support of information systems research. International Journal of an Emerging Transdiscipline 9, 1, 181-212.

[30] LOLLING, A., 2003. Analyse der menschlichen Zuverlässigkeit bei Kommissioniertätigkeiten. Shaker, Einbeck.

[31] MARCHET, G., MELACINI, M., and PEROTTI, S., 2015. Investigating order picking system adoption: a case-study-based approach. International Journal of Logistics Research and Applications 18, 1, 82-98.

[32] MILLER, A., 2004. Order picking for the 21st Century. Tompkins.

[33] NAPOLITANO, M., 2012. 2012 Warehouse/DC Operations Survey. Logistics management 51, 11, 54-63.

[34] ONG, S.K., YUAN, M.L., and NEE, A.Y.C., 2008. Augmented reality applications in manufacturing: a survey. International Journal of Production Research 46, 10, 2707-2742.

[35] POON, T.C., CHOY, K.L., CHOW, H.K., LAU, H.C., CHAN, F.T., and HO, K.C., 2009. A RFID case-based logistics resource management system for managing order-picking operations in warehouses. Expert Systems with Applications 36, 4, 8277-8301.

[36] REIF, R., GÜNTHNER, W.A., SCHWERDTFEGER, B., and KLINKER, G., 2009. Pick-by-Vision comes on age: evaluation of an augmented reality supported picking system in a real storage environment. In 6th International Conference on Computer Graphics, Virtual Reality, Visualisation and Interaction in Africa, Pretoria, 23-31.

[37] REIF, R., GÜNTHNER, W.A., SCHWERDTFEGER, B., and KLINKER, G., 2010. Evaluation of an augmented reality supported picking system under practical conditions. Computer Graphics Forum 29, 1, 2-12.

[38] REIF, R. and WALCH, D., 2008. Augmented & Virtual Reality applications in the field of logistics. The Visual Computer 24, 11, 987-994.

[39] RICHARDS, G., 2014. Warehouse Management: A complete guide to improving efficiency and minimizing costs in the modern warehouse. Kogan Page Publishers, London.

[40] ROODBERGEN, K.J. and DE KOSTER, R., 2001. Routing order pickers in a warehouse with a middle aisle. *European Journal of Operational Research 133*, 1, 32-43.

[41] ROY, D., KRISHNAMURTHY, A., HERAGU, S.S., and MALMBORG, C.J., 2012. Performance analysis and design trade-offs in warehouses with autonomous vehicle technology. *IIE Transactions 44*, 12, 1045-1060.

[42] SCHWERDTFEGER, B., REIF, R., FRIMOR, T., and KLINKER, G., 2007. Neue Techniken zur Informationsbereitstellung in der Kommissionierung. Neue Wege in der Automobillogistik. Springer, Berlin et al.

[43] SCHWERDTFEGER, B., REIF, R., GÜNTHNER, W.A., and KLINKER, G., 2011. Pick-by-vision: there is something to pick at the end of the augmented tunnel. Virtual Reality 15, 2-3, 213-223.

[44] SCHWERDTFEGER, B., REIF, R., GÜNTHNER, W.A., KLINKER, G., HAMACHER, D., SCHEGA, L., BRÖKELMANN, I., DOIL, F., and TÜMLER, J., 2009. Pick-by-Vision: A first stress test. 8th IEEE Internat. Symposium on Mixed and Augmented Reality, Washington, 115-124.

[45] STRAUB, E.T., 2009. Understanding technology adoption: Theory and future directions for informal learning. *Review of Educational Research 79*, 2, 625-649.

[46] TEN HOMPEL, M. and SCHMIDT, T., 2004. Warehouse Management – Organisation und Betrieb von Kommissionier-und Lagersystemen. Springer, Berlin et al.

[47] TOMPKINS, J.A., WHITE, J.A., BOZER, Y.A., and TANCHOCO, J.M.A., 2010. *Facilities planning*. John Wiley & Sons, Hoboken.

[48] TSAROUCHI, P.M.S. and CHRYSSOLOURIS, G., 2016. Human–robot interaction review and challenges on task planning and programming. *Internat. Journal of Computer Integrated Manufacturing 29*, 8, 916-931.

[49] VENKATESH, V., MORRIS, M.G., DAVIS, G.B., and DAVIS, F.D., 2003. User Acceptance of Information Technology: Toward a Unified View. *MIS Quarterly 27*, 3, 425-478.

[50] VOGT, G., 1997. *Das neue Kommissionierhandbuch*. Moderne Industrie GmbH, Landsberg, Germany.

[51] WEAVER, K.A., BAUMANN, H., STARNER, T., IBEN, H., and LAWO, M., 2010. An empirical task analysis of warehouse order picking using head-mounted displays. In *SIGCHI Conference on Human Factors in Computing Systems*, Atlanta, 1695-1704.

[52] WEBSTER, J. and WATSON, R.T., 2002. Analyzing the Past to Prepare for the Future: Writing a Literature Review. *MIS Quarterly 26*, 2, xiii-xxiii.

[53] WU, X., HAYNES, M., ZHANG, Y., JIANG, Z., SHEN, Z., GUO, A., STARNER, T., and GILLILAND, S., 2015. Comparing order picking assisted by head-up display versus pick-by-light with explicit pick confirmation. In ACM International Symposium on Wearable Computers, Osaka, 133-136.

[54] YEOW, P.H. and GOOMAS, D.T., 2014. Ergonomics improvement in order selection in a refrigerated environment. *Human Factors and Ergonomics in Manufacturing & Service Industries 24*, 3, 262-274.

Trust and Risk in E-Commerce: A Re-examination and Theoretical Integration

Short Paper

Ruochen Liao
State University of New York at Buffalo
rliao2@buffalo.edu

Rajiv Kishore
State University of New York at Buffalo
rkishore@buffalo.edu

1 INTRODUCTION

In the context of e-commerce, buyers often possess little directly accessible information about e-vendors prior to purchase. E-vendors respond to this problem by investing in a combination of marketing campaigns, advertisements, and offering guarantees and return policies, both to foster trust in themselves and to assure buyers of reduced risk in conducting transactions on their websites [1, 2]. However, dishonest or fraudulent e-vendors are economically incented to advertise about themselves falsely as high quality firms. The buyers' ability to verify the credibility of information provided by e-vendors in online buying environment is thus essential in their buying decision-making process.

Feedback systems that allow buyers to provide feedback about their buying experiences play an important role as decision support systems in e-commerce and enable buyers to cross validate the information provided by e-vendors. A substantial body of research has examined the effect of feedback systems in building buyers' confidence and willingness in making purchase decisions, boosting sales, and generating price premiums [3-6]. However, as a mechanism that is provided and operated by the e-vendor/website owner, a feedback system is also not immune to fake reviews and comment frauds [7-9]. Jindal and Liu [10] pointed out that nearly one third of the comments on Amazon can be fake, and the ratio for Yelp is around 16% [11]. Moreover, previous literature has shown that e-vendors may be economically incented to commit review fraud and deliberate manipulate feedback information by choosing which reviews to display on their websites with the goal of creating false impressions in the minds of potential buyers that their products are high quality and that their sales and post-sales service is superior [11]. Thus, this raises the research question: How does a potential first-time buyer know if the reviews provided by a feedback system on an e-vendor website are true?

2 THEORETICAL FOUNDATIONS

In this paper, we adopt signaling theory to open the black box of the cognitive process buyers may go through when they face a mixture of true and fake signals from an e-vendor in terms of advertisements, guarantees, assurance seals, etc., and examine how buyers assess the credibility of such signals from the e-vendor. In signaling theory, credibility of a signal is established through *signaling cost*. The cost of the signal can be the upfront cost and difficulty in sending high-quality signals (e.g., high costs incurred in building a store in prime location, high advertising costs incurred in advertising during prime time on national TV channels, etc.), and the possible future negative consequences in sending fake signals (e.g., high replacement/return costs incurred as part of warranties provided if the product/service does not live up to the promised quality, or sanctions imposed by governmental agencies for not providing warranty services as advertised, etc.). Thus, signaling costs serve as a hostage or bond for signal credibility [12-14].

However, the effectiveness of signaling cost as a bond for signal credibility has been greatly reduced in e-commerce due to the ease with which an e-commerce website or a virtual store front can be set up and taken down. Other fake signals can also be coined at little or no cost, and breaches in promises of quality and service suffer minimal future consequences. Further, the lack of indirect social cues, such as those conveyed by brick-and-mortar retail stores, impedes buyers' ability to authenticate and cross-validate signals sent by an e-vendor in the e-commerce environment [3, 15-17].

To address the signal credibility problem, e-vendors generally provide a feedback system on their websites where previous buyers can provide feedback to future buyers about the quality of the products and/or sales/post-sales service provided by those e-merchants. We propose that such systems make up for the reduced bonding power of e-vendor signals in the e-commerce context. This is because a feedback system provides an alternative source of signals for future buyers in terms of the positive/negative experience of other buyers that can be used to evaluate the trustworthiness of an e-vendor and the risk in conducting e-commerce transactions on that e-vendor's website [18]. Essentially, by incorporating a feedback system on its website, an e-vendor is ceding part of the control over what to display on its website, thereby voluntarily increasing the difficulty in sending out fake signals and increasing the bonding power of its signals.

However, as discussed above, an e-vendor can manipulate the feedback system itself. We propose that the credibility of the feedback system is increased when it affords previous buyers the opportunity to increase their *social presence* on the system. Gunawardena [19] defined social presence as "the degree to which a person is perceived as a 'real person' in IT-mediated communication." Similar to the traditional face-to-face, word of mouth systems, where people seek out advice from friends, family members, and acquaintances [20, 21], strong social cues embedded within the feedback system in terms of identity association, peer recognition, etc. can significantly increase the difficulty in creating fake reviews and comments, serving as the bond for the credibility of the feedback system itself. When perceived credibility of feedback system is high, the cost of sending out fake signals about the quality of the product will also be high, as reviewers in the feedback system will expose the cheating behavior of the seller. Based on these notions, we develop an integrated model of trust and risk in e-commerce incorporating the concepts of feedback system and social presence that is shown in figure 1 below.

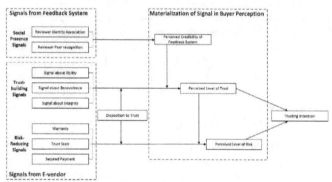

Figure 1: Conceptual Model of Signal Materialization.

3 IMPLICATIONS

This paper extends the previous literature on trust and risk in e-commerce by integrating the literature on marketing signals that are used to promote trust in an e-vendor and mitigate risk for future buyers with the literature on e-commerce fraud and feedback systems. By examining each type of signal and the type of bond needed for its credibility, we propose that instead of being parallel constructs, social presence, feedback system, trust-building signals, and risk-reducing signals are in an iterative, reinforcing structure where the former serves as the bond for the credibility of the latter. This paper also offers insights to practitioners of e-commerce because buyer habituation, i.e., constant and repeated exposure to a mixture of true and fake e-vendor signals of quality claims, is leading to a decrease in

response to the stimulus, and creating a concern that businesses are "overinvesting" in sending out these signals with only marginal increase in their effectiveness [22]. By understanding the underlying cognitive process of buyers, e-commerce websites can focus their investment on building effective feedback systems to enhance their credibility.

REFERENCES

[1] Gefen, D. E-commerce: the role of familiarity and trust. *Omega*, 28, 6 (2000), 725-737.

[2] McKnight, D. H., Choudhury, V. and Kacmar, C. Developing and validating trust measures for e-commerce: An integrative typology. *Information systems research*, 13, 3 (2002), 334-359.

[3] Ba, S. and Pavlou, P. A. Evidence of the effect of trust building technology in electronic markets: Price premiums and buyer behavior. *MIS quarterly* (2002), 243-268.

[4] Chevalier, J. A. and Mayzlin, D. The effect of word of mouth on sales: Online book reviews. *Journal of marketing research*, 43, 3 (2006), 345-354.

[5] Mudambi, S. M. and Schuff, D. What makes a helpful review? A study of customer reviews on Amazon. com. *MIS quarterly*, 34, 1 (2010), 185-200.

[6] Panniello, U., Gorgoglione, M. and Tuzhilin, A. Research Note—In CARSs We Trust: How Context-Aware Recommendations Affect Customers' Trust and Other Business Performance Measures of Recommender Systems. *Information Systems Research*, 27, 1 (2016), 182-196.

[7] Mishra, D. P., Heide, J. B. and Cort, S. G. Information asymmetry and levels of agency relationships. *Journal of marketing Research* (1998), 277-295.

[8] Jensen, M. L., Averbeck, J. M., Zhang, Z. and Wright, K. B. Credibility of anonymous online product reviews: A language expectancy perspective. *Journal of Management Information Systems*, 30, 1 (2013), 293-324.

[9] Dong, B., Liu, Q., Fu, Y. and Zhang, L. *A research of Taobao cheater detection*. Springer, City, 2014.

[10] Jindal, N. and Liu, B. *Review spam detection*. ACM, City, 2007.

[11] Luca, M. and Zervas, G. Fake it till you make it: Reputation, competition, and Yelp review fraud. *Management Science* (2016).

[12] Connelly, B. L., Certo, S. T., Ireland, R. D. and Reutzel, C. R. Signaling theory: A review and assessment. *Journal of Management*, 37, 1 (2011), 39-67.

[13] Kirmani, A. and Rao, A. R. No pain, no gain: A critical review of the literature on signaling unobservable product quality. *Journal of marketing*, 64, 2 (2000), 66-79.

[14] Ippolito, P. M. Bonding and nonbonding signals of product quality. *Journal of Business* (1990), 41-60.

[15] Gupta, A., Su, B.-C. and Walter, Z. An empirical study of consumer switching from traditional to electronic channels: A purchase-decision process perspective. *International Journal of Electronic Commerce*, 8, 3 (2004), 131-161.

[16] Jiang, Z. and Benbasat, I. Virtual product experience: Effects of visual and functional control of products on perceived diagnosticity and flow in electronic shopping. *Journal of Management Information Systems*, 21, 3 (2004), 111-147.

[17] Bigley, G. A. and Pearce, J. L. Straining for shared meaning in organization science: Problems of trust and distrust. *Academy of management review*, 23, 3 (1998), 405-421.

[18] Fan, M., Tan, Y. and Whinston, A. B. Evaluation and design of online cooperative feedback mechanisms for reputation management. *IEEE Transactions on Knowledge and Data Engineering*, 17, 2 (2005), 244-254.

[19] Gunawardena, C. N. Social presence theory and implications for interaction and collaborative learning in computer conferences. *International journal of educational telecommunications*, 1, 2/3 (1995), 147-166.

[20] Dellarocas, C. The digitization of word of mouth: Promise and challenges of online feedback mechanisms. *Management science*, 49, 10 (2003), 1407-1424.

[21] Cheung, C. M. and Thadani, D. R. The effectiveness of electronic word-of-mouth communication: A literature analysis. *Proceedings of the 23rd Bled eConference eTrust: implications for the individual, enterprises and society* (2010), 329-345.

[22] Gefen, D. and Pavlou, P. A. The boundaries of trust and risk: The quadratic moderating role of institutional structures. *Information Systems Research*, 23, 3-part-2 (2012), 940-959.

Understanding Mobile Banking Usage:
An Integrative Perspective

Full Paper

Mousa Albashrawi
U Mass Lowell
USA
Mousa_Albashrawi@uml.edu

Luvai Motiwalla
U Mass Lowell
USA
Luvai_Motiwalla@uml.edu

ABSTRACT

Increasingly, smartphones and mobile commerce are changing consumer transaction behaviors and shifting the ways in which users interact with business. Similarly, the banking and financial industry is now empowered by FinTech applications to improve their consumer experience and banking services to solidify the role for mobile banking (MB) for years to come. In this study, we are taking an integrated approach by combining two IT adoption models: UTAUT and IS Success, and using both subjective and objective measures for mobile banking usage. Our regression results for a sample of 472 bank users in a mid-size US bank find a strong support for satisfaction, objective actual use, and loyalty but not for subjective actual use. These results provide interesting implications for both IS adoption theory and banking institutions for improving satisfaction and use of MB.

KEYWORDS

System usage; IT adoption; UTAUT; IS Success model

1 INTRODUCTION

Mobile systems are rapidly changing financial technology (FinTech) landscape which is providing banking industry and bank customer new banking tools for transactions and communication [1]. This is providing opportunities for new business models that utilizes technology to fuel the digital economy. "*People will use their phones, increasingly stacked with artificial intelligence and behavior monitoring services, in place of the various financial services products we've come to expect from banks. In the next 10 years, technology is going to have more impact on the banking industry than we've seen for the last 100 years*"[21]. Today, Mobile banking (MB) is enabling the digital transformation of banks and how people use and experience banking services. Understanding the changing nature of MB usage is therefore an important issue for both research and practice.

MB is already considered an important difference-maker and a strategic technology in banking industry [20]. It provides anywhere and anytime access to various banking services like instant access to account balances, fund transfers, bill payment, account alerts, ATM locations, P2P transfers, and mobile deposits through a users' mobile device. This emerging technology has been adopted and used on a large scale by customers; more customers are using mobile banking services now than going to bank branch or ATM [29]. Yet, banks have very little insights on their customer use and satisfaction of MB services [36]. Retaining existing customers and attracting new users will require banks a deeper understanding of user perception and use of MB. We are therefore applying the IS adoption and use theoretical models to examine the factors influencing user satisfaction and use of MB system. System use will be measured objectively and subjectively.

Prior research on IS adoption has been criticized for focusing mainly on subjective measures of system use over relying on self-reported survey data [2, 6]. A big concern associated with self-reported studies, besides validity threat, is the potential bias generated from overestimating or underestimating the perceived system usage [9], thereby leading to wrong conclusions [10]. One way to reduce self-reported bias is by combining the subjective measurement (survey data) with objective measurement (system log data) approaches. Objective measurement captures the rich measures of the system usage, which includes use intensity and appropriateness in addition to usage frequency and duration [11, 27].

Few research studies have attempted a deeper analysis of MB usage and understand reasons behind this high acceptance rates by bank users: 1) *are bank users satisfied and use MB due to the system functionality and usability features of the MB system?* Or, 2) *are users satisfied and use MB for their own convenience, social influence, better performance, or customer support from the banks?* The first question helps us understand whether end-users are influenced by system-oriented factors such as the quality of MB system, service, and information, key constructs of the IS success model have been used to predict user satisfaction and use [11]. This could be considered as the *system influences* on MB use. The second question helps us understand whether end-users are influenced by non-system factors such as their expected performance or productivity with MB system, community influences, and facilitating resources provided by banks to support and encourage MB use, which are the key constructs of the unified theory of acceptance and use (UTAUT) model [33]. These are considered as cognitive influences on MB use. User satisfaction has been considered a reliable dependent variable in post-adoption use environment [3] and replaced the behavioral intention in the UTAUT model by [5] for examining e-government usage. Although the previous two studies have a non-voluntary use setting, Venkatesh and Davis [32] highlight that the effect on usage behavior does not change across voluntary and non-voluntary use settings, and therefore not often a determinant factor. We have thus employed satisfaction here as a centric hub for MB system use with both IS Success and UTAUT.

One goal of our paper is to combine these two established IS adoption models to provide a deeper understanding of MB user satisfaction and use. We believe these two models are complementary because they are different focuses and predictor variables. Once combined, the integrated models provide a comprehensive framework for the understanding MB use, and perhaps for system usage. Yet, research remains sparse on integrating the two models. We believe they collective can provide a higher explanatory power of satisfaction and the actual system use. Similarly, attention to objective measurement of system usage has faded in the IS domain, especially since 2011 and hardly ever used in the context of mobile innovation usage [35]. This motivates us, towards our second goal, to use both the subjective and objective measures for MB usage. It also allows us to compare the two approaches to determine which provides a better measure for MB usage. Finally, we have added loyalty in our research model to determine how MB satisfaction and use affects user loyalty towards the banks. Loyalty can help the banks retain their customers in this competitive industry [8]; [17].

This study, in brief, contributes to IS adoption theory and practice by providing a holistic framework that incorporates system and human-cognition factors affecting satisfaction and actual system use. Second is to communicate the significant results to practitioners so that they work on improving the embedded services and promoting a higher MB usage. The rest of the paper reviews the previous works in UTAUT and IS success models, compares objective versus subjective measures of system usage, develops our research model and hypotheses, discuss our findings and finally, conclude with our study's limitations and future work.

2   AN INTEGRATIVE FRAMEWORK: IS SUCCESS AND UTAUT

The IS adoption theory, such as the unified theory of acceptance and use of technology (UTAUT) model focuses on performance expectancy, social influence, and facilitating conditions and similarly the IS success model focuses on system quality, service quality, and information quality, as predictors to customer satisfaction and use [11]; [33]; [5]; [2]. These two models have been widely used and validated across different

contexts including measuring the usage of mobile technologies [6]; [16]; [7]; [42]; [2].

Within the MB context, we have not found any post-adoption studies that have combined both models. There are two studies in IS context that have combined these two models. The first study suggests IS success's factors to be antecedents of UTAUT2's factors to examine the adoption of government e-services [24]. The second study suggests to partially combine technology acceptance model (TAM), IS success, and UTAUT to examine IS behavioral intention [19]. Besides the different context and different endogenous variable, both studies lack an empirical analysis to validate the integrated models limiting their theoretical contributions.

Venkatesh et al. [33]; [34] emphasizes the importance of integrating their UTAUT with other models, particularly in consumer voluntary use context to expand its theoretical boundaries and gain a greater cognitive understanding of system use behavior. Driven by this perceptive, we integrate to widely used IS adoption models: the UTAUT with the IS Success model and empirically validate its authenticity in mobile use research. The IS success model addresses technical, semantic and service quality success in predicting the system use [11]. These three system factors are more attached to what the system reflects, for example, providing attractive interfaces, personalized services, and relevant information. In contrast, the UTAUT model addresses the instrumental beliefs of the users on the extent MB use can decrease their time for banking transactions, MB use is influenced by their community and social contacts, and MB use is facilitated by the supporting resources, like help desk, collectively known as UTAUT pillars for predicting behavioral intention and use [42]. "Effort expectancy is excluded because it significantly overlaps with system quality capturing the easiness part of the system". Behavioral intention was replaced with user satisfaction because this factor is also used by IS success model and prior studies have found it to be a better predictor of use in e-government and e-business studies [3]; [5]. Complementing the IS success model, which focuses more on system success factors, with the UTAUT, which focuses more on human acceptance factors allows us to evaluate whether this integration framework can provide a solid theoretical foundation for examining MB use considering that UTAUT accounts for 70% of the variance in the outcome variable [33], while IS success model accounts for about 36% of the variance [42]. The different underlying assumptions and emphasis, of both these models makes their integration plausible for higher variance and explanation.

In sum, prior research has assessed the state of knowledge in this area by employing the IS success, UTAUT, and UTAUT2 individually, but they have not provided a holistic explanation for MB use behavior [6]; [39]; [2]. We are therefore shifting our theoretical model into more comprehensive framework by combining contributions of two IS adoption models. Aligned with Venkatesh et al.'s [33] goal of developing UTAUT for greater variance, our integrative model would allow moving towards a deeper understating of this phenomenon.

3   OBJECTIVE SYSTEM USAGE

System usage, which represents the success of information systems, is defined as to what extent system capabilities are utilized by customers [25]. Prior research on actual system use has been abundantly investigated by estimating the system usage via self-reported data. Few studies have explored objective system usage across different IT innovations through measuring usage via computer-recorded data in the past 19 years.

For example, Straub et al. [27] measured the usage of a voice mail system objectively through computer-recorded data and subjectively through self-reported data using TAM with the purpose of addressing conceptual and methodological issues associated with system usage measurement. Szajna [28], similar to Straub et al. [27], highlighted the issues between self-reported and computer-recorded data through measuring the usage of an electronic mail system. Klein [15] adapted theory of reasoned action (TRA) to measure the objective usage of web-based patient–physician communication application via capturing the number of e-mails sent. Ma and Yuen [18] applied UTAUT to predict the usage of e-learning system in a university setting with the help of system log. Joo et al. [13] used the access frequency to objectively measure the usage of a mobile learning system among students from South-Korean online university. Although objective measure is considered more accurate than subjective measure of system usage, there are few studies employing objective measures in IS literature [35]. Our study addresses this gap and develops a comparison case with prior research using subjective measures.

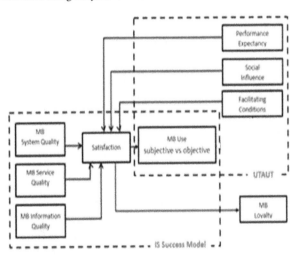

Figure 1: Research model.

4   RESEARCH MODEL AND HYPOTHESES DEVELOPMENT

The two adoption models: IS success and UTAUT have been adapted to help in understanding MB usage subjectively, through a survey, and objectively, by analyzing a computer-recorded data log file which records MB use. The IS success model is capable to determine satisfaction and system usage of IT innovations [11]

based on its three quality factors. Similarly, UTAUT can also predict system usage but has a higher explanatory power [33]. Both models have been applied to measure adoption of various information systems, hence, they exhibit a higher generalizability [5]; [42]. As per our goals above of providing a comprehensive theoretical perspective, we have integrated the IS success and UTAUT as complementary models to understand MB use from two contradictory angles. Figure 1 visualizes our integrative framework followed by the development of our hypothesis.

4.1   MB System Quality (TQ)

System quality refers to what extent MB systems are visually appealing and easy to use and navigate [42]. System quality is manifested in the easy access of different and trustworthy services. Reliability and flexibility aspects can be crucial to promote MB services and leverage customers' gratification level while poor interface and difficulty to navigate lower such level. Past research empirically validates this relationship across different IT applications, in mobile payment [42], electronic service [37], and e-government system [30]. MB shares a number of similarities with the above mentioned information systems, therefore we suggest that:

H1: MB system quality will influence positively customer satisfaction

4.2   MB Service Quality (SQ)

Service quality refers to what extent MB system provides reliable, timely, responsive, and personalized services [42]. Over the past 20 years, the dimensions of assurance, reliability, empathy, and responsiveness, infrastructure and/or appearance emerge to form service quality [38]. Hence, IT innovations that are associated with such dimensions may increase customer satisfaction. Prior IS research confirms that high service quality can predict customer satisfaction on the empirical plane [4]; [38]. This relationship is also supported in the context of mobile technology [42]. Therefore, we suggest that:

H2: MB service quality will influence positively customer satisfaction.

4.3   MB Information Quality (IQ)

Information quality refers to what extent MB system provides sufficient, relevant, and accurate information [42]. Timeliness is another valuable quality that provides customers the capability to easily access their information when they need to. As customers may struggle to find their banking information because of the small screen size, how information is organized and presented in MB can influence their level of satisfaction. An empirical support has been found to relate information quality and customer satisfaction in a context of electronic service [38]. As MB is an electronic banking service in its core, we suggest that:

H3: MB information quality will influence positively customer satisfaction.

4.4 Performance Expectancy (PE)

Performance expectancy is defined by Venkatesh et al. [33: p. 447] as *"the degree to which an individual believes that using the system will help him or her to attain gains in job performance"*. Performance expectancy, developed from TAM's usefulness, indicates ones' personal feelings about efficiency and productivity. For example, when customers are easily accessing their MB system and efficiently conducting their banking transactions, they most likely will be satisfied towards using the system. System usefulness revealed by performance expectancy has been significantly considered and found to be related to positive attitude and satisfaction in several IS studies including mobile services [31] and banking information system [3] contexts. Therefore, we suggest that:

H4: Performance expectancy will positively influence customer satisfaction for using MB.

4.5 Social Influence (SI)

Social influence refers to what extent a person feels that a MB technology should be used by his/her social network [22]. Normative beliefs for individuals are highly impacted by their social circle and hence the individuals' attitude towards system use could also be affected by their family and friends. For instance, when the individual is surrounded by family members, friends, or work mates who show a positive attitude towards MB use, their attitude will turn positive towards MB use. Satisfaction is basically a positive attitude formed over a course of time with the habitual use of system or services [14], we can suggest that social influence will impact individual's satisfaction. Chan et al. [5] provide a supportive case where social influence is significantly impacts user satisfaction in the adoption of e-government system. We therefore extend this relationship to our MB system context and hypothesize that:

H5: Social influence will positively influence customer satisfaction for using MB.

4.6 Facilitating Conditions (FC)

Facilitating conditions show to what extent a person perceives that the use of MB system is supported with organizational and technical infrastructure [22]. Facilitating conditions for technological innovations, which include (but are not limited to) help-desk support, peer support, institutional encouragement to use the system all provide a strong foundation to both positive feeling and system usage. A causal link between facilitating conditions and satisfaction has been empirically validated in prior research in the contexts of e-government services [5] and mobile banking [2]; thus we suggest that:

H6: Facilitating conditions will positively influence customer satisfaction for using MB.

4.7 Satisfaction (SAT) and Loyalty (LY)

Satisfaction reflects the affective reaction that individuals have when interacting with MB services [4]. When banks sustain the satisfaction level among MB users, this can impact the level of MB usage positively. Rationally speaking, users who feel they are being well-served will show a greater level of satisfaction towards MB, which in turn leads to build up their loyalty and use. The positive relationship between satisfaction, loyalty and system usage has an empirical support in mobile learning system [23]. which overlaps with MB in many features. Additionally, loyalty implies long relationships between banks and their customers, which is very beneficial to banks interested in retaining their customers in a highly competitive environment. Loyalty is also a significant indicator of customer retention and satisfaction has been validated as a determinant of loyalty in mobile phone usability [17] and mobile platforms [26]. Hence we propose that:

H7: Customer satisfaction will influence positively MB loyalty
H8: Customer satisfaction will influence positively MB use.

5 METHOD

Our method used a field survey to test the hypothesized relationships and analyzed computer-recorded data for MB users extracted from bank log files. The survey was conducted by the bank through an online survey with all their online users, our target population. The questionnaire was developed by use to measure all our factors and items of interest.

5.1 Measurement

All constructs items were adapted from previous research to ensure face validity. The items were measured via a seven-point Likert-scale with 7 "Strongly agree" and 1 "Strongly disagree". Quality factors (system, information, and service) and satisfaction were adapted from Zhou [42]. While loyalty was adapted from Zhou and Lu [41]. UTAUT factors of performance expectancy, social influence, and facilitating conditions were adapted from Chan et al. [5]. Subjective and objective MB usage were adapted from Straub et al. [27]. Subjective MB usage will reflect customers' perceived usage derived from the survey while objective MB usage will reflect customers' actual usage derived from system log data. The questionnaire was pilot tested with about 10 MB users and preliminary evidence had been found for scales' validity and reliability.

5.2 Data Collection and User Demographics

Participants were recruited from a US mid-sized bank, headquartered in the northeastern region. The reason for selecting this bank was convenience and bank's willingness to collect and provide us the data. Besides, this bank is representative a typical US bank as demonstrated from the user demographics (Table 1). The targeted sample was the customers who are currently using online banking and were aware of MB. A questionnaire was administrated by the bank with an

Paper Session 2.2: Digital Business and Innovation

SIGMIS-CPR'17, June 21-23, 2017, Bangalore, India

invitation email to their customers to participate in the study. The bank, also, offered an incentive for its customers for completing the survey, which helped to obtain a response rate of 16%. The system usage data was collected via an online survey and from the banks' log data files. The log data was for a period of 9 months and shared with us without any personal identifiers to protect customers' privacy. The bank matched the customers from system log use with the survey responses and provided us the combined data with system generated user IDs. We signed a non-disclosure agreement with the bank and this was approved by our university IRB office.

Our sample consisted of 1,165 users, of which 760 are MB users while the remaining 355 are non-users. From the 760 survey responses, we ended up with 472 valid respondents due to missing values and matching the surveyed users with users from the log files. This final sample was demographically similar to the overall demographics of the bank customers (Table 1). Gender is well-balanced, age of the participants was generally skewed towards the elderly population. Similarly, in education and work, the majority of the respondents were literate and employed with a full-time job. In all the demographic characteristics it maps well to the bank's typical customer profile.

Table 1: User Demographics

Variable	Frequency	Percentage
Gender		
Male	224	47.46
Female	248	52.54
Age		
15-25	48	10.17
26-35	60	12.71
36-45	81	17.16
46-55	115	24.36
56-60	57	12.08
>60	111	23.52
Education		
High school	55	11.65
Some college	131	27.75
College degree	148	31.36
Graduate degree	134	28.39
Other	4	0.85
Work Status		
Full-time	309	64.47
Part-time	59	12.50
Unemployed	16	3.39
Retired	77	16.31
Student	11	2.33

6 DATA ANALYSIS

Before testing the structural model, the variables were statistically described in terms of mean and standard deviation as well as checked for confirmatory factor analysis (CFA) to evaluate reliability of the instruments through factor loadings (Table 2).

Table 2: Descriptive Statistics and Factor Loadings

Factors	Items	Mean	S.D	Factor loadings
System Quality	TQ1	5.797	1.042	0.732
	TQ2	5.981	1.054	0.909
	TQ3	5.949	1.001	0.893
	TQ4	5.436	1.287	0.767
Service Quality	SQ1	5.879	1.126	0.798
	SQ2	5.809	1.109	0.857
	SQ3	5.761	1.052	0.773
	SQ4	5.443	1.176	0.817
Information Quality	IQ1	5.850	1.030	0.873
	IQ2	5.782	1.082	0.870
	IQ3	6.242	0.782	0.815
	IQ4	6.163	0.869	0.773
Performance Expectancy	PE1	6.017	0.996	0.923
	PE2	5.928	1.127	0.953
	PE3	5.773	1.152	0.937
Social Influence	SI1	4.290	1.539	0.964
	SI2	4.358	1.535	0.966
	SI3	4.284	1.497	0.949
Facilitating Conditions	FC1	6.144	0.824	0.955
	FC2	6.239	0.701	0.806
Satisfaction	SAT1	5.869	1.168	0.956
	SAT2	5.799	1.214	0.971
	SAT3	5.809	1.181	0.965
Loyalty	LY1	6.324	0.840	0.875
	LY2	5.953	1.191	0.916
	LY3	5.801	1.360	0.887
Actual Use (Survey)	AU1	1.892	1.260	1.000
Actual Use (Log Data)	AU2	1.288	0.671	1.000

As per Table 3, Cronbach's alpha, and composite reliability were evaluated for further proof of instruments' reliability. Convergent validity was tested with average variance extracted (AVE) and collinearity between variables was assessed via variance inflation factor (VIF). As per Table 4, discriminant validity was checked by comparing the square root of AVEs with other variables coefficients. Common method variance was tested through conducting a Harman's single-factor test.

Table 3: Instrument Reliability and Validity

Factors	Cronbach's	*Composite*	*AVE*	*VIF*

	Alpha	*Reliability*		
TQ	0.846	0.897	0.687	2.467
SQ	0.828	0.886	0.660	2.579
IQ	0.855	0.901	0.695	2.520
PE	0.932	0.956	0.880	2.050
SI	0.957	0.972	0.921	1.169
FC	0.745	0.876	0.781	1.434
SAT	0.962	0.975	0.929	1.000
LY	0.873	0.922	0.798	1.000

The above tables show that all factors and their respective items have values above the acceptable thresholds in literature, for example, 0.7 for Cronbach's alpha, 0.5 for AVE, and 0.7 for factor loading. This indicates that instruments' reliability and validity have been established. For common method variance, the Herman's single factor test showed that the large factor explains 43.979% of the total variance. Hence, there is no dominant single factor since this percentage was less than 50%, confirming our data is not affected by common method variance.

Table 4: Fornell-Larcker Criterion

	1	2	3	4	5	6	7	8	9
1. AU	1.000								
2. FC	0.028	0.884							
3. IQ	-0.017	0.451	0.834						
4. LY	0.096	0.362	0.663	0.893					
5. PE	0.162	0.500	0.555	0.636	0.938				
6. SAT	0.053	0.335	0.731	0.812	0.678	0.964			
7. SQ	0.068	0.429	0.708	0.655	0.609	0.688	0.812		
8. SI	0.156	0.149	0.214	0.337	0.343	0.334	0.305	0.960	
9. IQ	0.093	0.354	0.692	0.743	0.604	0.770	0.688	0.307	0.829

7   RESULTS

7.1   Structural Model and Hypotheses Testing

Structural equation modeling – partial least square (SEM-PLS) was employed because of multiple mediation terms. With the help of SmartPLS software, this technique reveals the significant relationships with path coefficients in the tested model. We tested the hypothesized relationships in two separate models; the first structural model has subjective system usage (Table 5) while the second structural model has objective system usage (Table 6) so that we can effectively compare the findings of this outcome variable.

Under subjective system usage, SEM-PLS results indicate that system quality ($\beta = 0.347$, $p < 0.01$) and information quality ($\beta = 0.310$, $p < 0.01$) are highly significant but service quality is not that significant ($\beta = 0.093$, $p < 0.10$). Also, as hypothesized, both of performance expectancy ($\beta = 0.279$, $p < 0.01$) and social influence ($\beta = 0.052$, $p < 0.05$) have a significant and positive impact on user satisfaction while facilitating conditions ($\beta = -0.113$, $p < 0.01$) has a significant but negative impact instead. On

the other side, satisfaction ($\beta = 0.813$, $p < 0.01$) is an important predictor for users' loyalty but not for the perceived MB system usage ($\beta = 0.054$, $p > 0.10$).

Under objective system usage, it appears that SEM-PLS results of the significant factors in model 2 are similar for those in model 1 except for MB system usage, which turned to be significant ($\beta = 0.090$, $p < 0.05$). Hence, it is important to note that MB system usage retrieved from computer-recorded data is significant but MB system usage retrieved from the survey is not. However, subjective system usage weakly correlates with objective system usage; 0.495. Those two constructs are basically the same; one is perceived and the other is actual, and accordingly they should be highly correlated. Thus, it is very unexpected to reach at such conclusion.

Table 5: Model 1 (Subjective System Usage)

Path	Estimate	Std. Error	t-statistics	p-Value
H1: TQ → SAT	0.347	0.055	6.265***	0.000
H2: SQ → SAT	0.093	0.052	1.802*	0.072
H3: IQ → SAT	0.310	0.045	6.938***	0.000
H4: PE → SAT	0.279	0.045	6.175***	0.000
H5: SI → SAT	0.052	0.022	2.410**	0.016
H6: FC → SAT	-0.113	0.039	2.924***	0.004
H7: SAT → LY	0.813	0.022	36.262***	0.000
H8: SAT → AU1	0.054	0.043	1.246	0.213

Note: n= 472, ***$p < 0.01$, **$p < 0.05$, * $p < 0.10$
Explained variance in satisfaction = 73.2%
Explained variance in loyalty = 66.1%

Table 6: Model 2 (Objective System Usage)

Path	Estimate	Std. Error	t-statistics	p-Value
H1: TQ → SAT	0.348	0.054	6.360***	0.000
H2: SQ → SAT	0.093	0.052	1.796*	0.073
H3: IQ → SAT	0.308	0.045	6.965***	0.000
H4: PE → SAT	0.279	0.042	6.600***	0.000
H5: SI → SAT	0.054	0.023	2.376**	0.018
H6: FC → SAT	-0.114	0.035	3.275***	0.001
H7: SAT → LY	0.810	0.024	33.839***	0.000
H8: SAT → AU2	0.090	0.036	2.437**	0.015

Note: n= 472, ***$p < 0.01$, **$p < 0.05$, * $p < 0.10$
Explained variance in satisfaction = 73.3%
Explained variance in loyalty = 65.7%
Explained variance in actual use = 0.9%

Our integrated framework of IS success and UTAUT accounted for 73.3% of the variance in user satisfaction, outperforming the standalone models (IS success = 68% and UTAUT = 47%) and confirming the authenticity and validity of this integration. While satisfaction accounts for about 66% of the variance in loyalty but unexpectedly 0.9% of the total variance in actual system use. Contrasting this with behavioral intention, user satisfaction is an important antecedent to loyalty and thus reflects the increase customer retention. This result confirms our appropriate utilization of satisfaction instead of behavioral intention in UTAUT.

8 DISCUSSION

8.1 Major Findings

Majority of our hypothesized relationships were significant and consistent with prior IS research. IS success factors (system quality, service quality, and information quality) are positively significant and in line with results reached by Xu et al. [38] and Zhou [42]. The UTAUT model factors of performance expectancy and social influence were significant predictors of user satisfaction similar to prior IS studies of Brown et al. [3] and Chan et al. [5]. Facilitating conditions was also significant, consistent with Chan et al. [5] and Baptista and Oliveira [2], but it was unexpectedly associated with a negative sign. This negative direction may be attributed to the easy-to-use characteristics of the MB, which means that the majority of users do not access the help resources when using the MB system.

8.2 Theoretical and Practical Implications of MB Use

Based on our SEM-PLS analysis, subjective measures were not strongly related to objective measures of MB use even though we measured them with the same users. Additionally, objective usage was significantly predicted, while subjective usage was not significantly predicted by satisfaction. This leads us to doubt the authenticity of subjective measures used as a dependent variable in prior IS research [12]; [23]; [40]. Due to the errors in human judgment, this perceived construct may not reflect the actual usage by the users and affected by self-reported bias [9]; [10], leading to false conclusions. Moreover, the low correlation between subjective and objective system usage has augmented our concern. As a result, it is plausible to infer that some of past IS studies employing subjective system usage had been implicated by using inadequate measure for this construct. Therefore, future studies should shift towards objective measurement of system use by obtaining computer-recorded data for the system usage. This would enhance the reliability of the reported results.

On the other hand, integrating IS success's system factors with UTAUT's human acceptance factors increases the theoretical boundaries of these two models, hopefully leading to a greater understanding of user's behavior. With 73% of the explained variance, this integrative model has outperformed the two standalone models and provided a higher explanatory power, leading us to answer our research questions with higher validity: bank users were satisfied and using MB for its system and information quality features (68%) and were similarly influenced by their performance, social influence and facilitating conditions with MB (47%). Hence, our integrated framework is a robust theoretical model for examining the MB system usage but this model must be mediated by satisfaction and focus on objective use measures.

In sum, this study provides practical insights by highlighting the key factors to increase the level of satisfaction and loyalty of MB users. The latter is more significant because it helps banking industry improve their customer retention rate. For example, because social influence is significant, the bank's marketing channels should encourage their customers in recommending the MB app informally to their social circles. Similarly, their focus should be on increasing the level of satisfaction which increases loyalty and customer retention.

9 LIMITATIONS AND CONCLUSION

The major limitations of our study are: *sample diversity* and *cross-sectional sample*. While our sample size was good, all users were from one bank at a single point of time, which affects external validity. However, these results can be generalized to many US mid-sized banks with similar customer demographics. We still recommend further research in this area by including banks of different sizes from various geographic regions of US to enhance the external validity, and expand to banks in other countries to address cultural influences. In addition, this study used cross-sectional sample that analyzed data by association rather than cause-and-effect; this causal relationship weakness should be addressed in future research through a longitudinal or experience-based study.

In conclusion, this study contributes to the theory of IS acceptance and use by 1) incorporating system-oriented factors (IS success) with human acceptance factors (UTAUT) to evaluate the robustness of these models combined in the MB context, and 2) compares objective and subjective usage measures to determine system success; such measurement approach has not been employed in the MB system use context. Accordingly, this paper provides insightful feedback for IT adoption researchers and financial institutions on how their users are coping with the digital transformation of banking services through their use and experience of mobile devices.

REFERENCES
[1] Anonymous, "The Fintech revolution: A wave of startups is changing finance—for the better," The Economist, Leaders section, May 9th, 2015.

[2] Baptista, G., and Oliveira, T. 2015. "Understanding Mobile Banking: The Unified Theory of Acceptance and Use of Technology Combined with Cultural Moderators," *Computers in Human Behavior* (50), pp. 418-430.

[3] Brown, S. A., Venkatesh, V., Kuruzovich, J., and Massey, A. P. 2008. "Expectation Confirmation: An Examination of Three Competing Models," *Organizational Behavior and Human Decision Processes* (105:1), pp. 52-66.

[4] Cenfetelli, R. T., Benbasat, I., and Al-Natour, S. 2008. "Addressing the What and How of Online Services: Positioning Supporting-Services Functionality and Service Quality for Business-to-Consumer Success," *Information Systems Research* (19:2), pp. 161-181.

[5] Chan, F. K., Thong, J. Y., Venkatesh, V., Brown, S. A., Hu, P. J., and Tam, K. Y. 2010. "Modeling Citizen Satisfaction with Mandatory Adoption of an E-Government Technology," *Journal of the Association for Information Systems* (11:10), pp. 519-549.

[6] Chatterjee, S., Chakraborty, S., Sarker, S. Sarker, S., and Lau, F. Y. 2009. "Examining the Success Factors for Mobile Work in Healthcare: A Deductive Study," *Decision Support Systems* (46:3), pp. 620-633.

[7] Chung, N., and Jae Kwon, S. 2009b. "Effect of Trust Level on Mobile Banking Satisfaction: A Multi-Group Analysis of Information System Success Instruments," *Behaviour & Information Technology* (28:6), pp. 549-562.

[8] Cody-Allen, E. and Kishore, R., 2006. "An extension of the UTAUT Model with E-Quality, Trust, and Satisfaction Constructs". *In Proceedings of the*

2006 ACM SIGMIS CPR conference on computer personnel research: Forty-four years of computer personnel research: achievements, challenges & the future, pp. 82-89.

[9] Collopy, F. 1996. "Biases in Retrospective Self-Reports of Time Use: An Empirical Study of Computer Users," *Management Science* (42), pp. 758–767.

[10] de Reuver, M., and Bouwman, H. 2015. "Dealing with Self-Report Bias in Mobile Internet Acceptance and Usage Studies," *Information & Management* (5:3), pp. 287–294.

[11] Delone, W. H., and McLean, E. R. 2003. "The DeLone and McLean Model of Information Systems Success: A Ten-Year Update," *Journal of Management Information Systems* (19:4), pp. 9-30.

[12] Hou, C. K. 2012. "Examining the Effect of User Satisfaction on System Usage and Individual Performance with Business Intelligence Systems: An Empirical Study of Taiwan's Electronics Industry," *International Journal of Information Management* (32:6), pp. 560-573.

[13] Joo, Y. J., Lim, K. Y., and Lim, E. 2014. "Investigating the Structural Relationship among Perceived Innovation Attributes, Intention to Use and Actual Use of Mobile Learning in an Online University in South Korea," *Australasian Journal of Educational Technology* (30:4), pp. 427-439.

[14] Kim, C., Oh, E., Shin, N., and Chae, M. 2009. "An Empirical Investigation of Factors Affecting Ubiquitous Computing Use and U-business Value," *International Journal of Information Management* (29:6), pp. 436-448.

[15] Klein, R. 2007. "Internet-Based Patient-Physician Electronic Communication Applications: Patient Acceptance and Trust," *E-Service Journal* (5:2), pp. 27-51.

[16] Lee, K. C., and Chung, N. 2009. "Understanding Factors Affecting Trust in and Satisfaction with Mobile Banking in Korea: A Modified DeLone and McLean's Model Perspective," *Interacting with Computers* (21:5–6), pp. 385–392.

[17] Lee, D., Moon, J., Kim, Y. J., and Yi, M. Y. 2015. "Antecedents and Consequences of Mobile Phone Usability: Linking Simplicity and Interactivity to Satisfaction, Trust, and Brand Loyalty," *Information and Management* (52), pp. 295-304.

[18] Ma, W., and Yuen, A. 2011. "E-Learning System Acceptance and Usage Pattern," *Technology Acceptance in Education*, pp. 201-216.

[19] Mardiana, S., Tjakraatmadja, J. H., and Aprianingsih, A. 2015. "DeLone-McLean information system success model revisited: The separation of intention to use-use and the integration of technology acceptance models," *International Journal of Economics and Financial Issues* (5), pp. 172-182.

[20] Marous, J. 2013. "Building A Winning Mobile Banking Strategy," *The Financial Brand*. URL: http://thefinancialbrand.com/37199/building-winning-mobile-banking-strategy/

[21] Michael J. Casey, "Bold Bet That Banking Industry Is Poised for Serious Disruption," WSJ, Jun 5, 2015

[22] Miltgen, C. L., Popovič, A., and Oliveira, T. 2013. "Determinants of End-User Acceptance of Biometrics: Integrating the "Big 3" of Technology Acceptance with Privacy Context," *Decision Support Systems* (56), pp. 103-114.

[23] Mohammadi, H. 2015. "Investigating Users' Perspectives on E-Learning: An Integration of TAM and IS Success Model," Computers in Human Behavior (45), pp. 359-374.

[24] Molnar, A., Weerakkody, V., El-Haddadeh, R., Lee, H., and Irani, Z. 2013. "A framework of reference for evaluating user experience when using high definition video to video to facilitate public services," *In International Working Conference on Transfer and Diffusion of IT*. pp. 436-450.

[25] Petter, S., DeLone, W., and McLean, E. A. 2013. "Information Systems Success: the Quest for the Independent Variables," *Journal of Management Information Systems* (29:4), pp. 7–62.

[26] Ryua, M. H., Kim, J., and Kim, S. 2014. "Factors Affecting Application Developers' Loyalty to Mobile Platforms," *Computers in Human Behavior* (40), pp. 78-85.

[27] Straub, M., Limayem, M., and Karahanna-Evaristo, E. 1995. "Measuring System Usage: Implications for IS Theory Testing," *Management Science* (41:8), pp. 1328-1342.

[28] Szajna, B. 1996. "Empirical Evaluation of the Revised Technology Acceptance Model," *Management science* (42:1), pp. 85-92.

[29] Telis Demos, "For the First Time, More Are Mobile-Banking Than Going to a Branch," WSJ, Jan 12, 2016.

[30] Teo, T. S., Srivastava, S. C., and Jiang, L. 2008. "Trust and Electronic Government Success: An Empirical Study," *Journal of Management Information Systems* (25:3), pp. 99-132.

[31] Thong, J. Y., Hong, S., and Tam, K. Y. 2006. "The Effects of Post-Adoption Beliefs on the Expectation-Confirmation Model for Information Technology Continuance," *International Journal of Human-Computer Studies* (64:9), pp. 799-810.

[32] Venkatesh, V., and Davis, F. D. 2000. "A Theoretical Extension of the Technology Acceptance Model: Four Longitudinal Field Studies," *Management Science* (46:2), pp. 186-204.

[33] Venkatesh, V., Morris, M. G., Davis, G. B., and Davis, F. D. 2003. "User Acceptance of Information Technology: Toward a Unified View," *MIS Quarterly* (27:3), pp. 425-478.

[34] Venkatesh, V., Thong, J. Y., and Xu, X. 2012. "Consumer Acceptance and Use of Information Technology: Extending the Unified Theory of Acceptance and Use of Technology," *MIS Quarterly* (36:1), pp. 157-178.

[35] Walldén, S., Mäkinen, E., and Raisamo, R. 2015. "A Review on Objective Measurement of Usage in Technology Acceptance Studies," *Universal Access in the Information Society*, pp. 1-14.

[36] Wannemacher, P., Ensor, B., Ask, J. A., Clarke, A., Roizen, R., and Blumstein, A. 2015."The Mobile Banking Imperative," *Forrester*, URL: https://www.forrester.com/The+Mobile+Banking+Imperative/fulltext/-/E-RES75581

[37] Wu, J., and Du, H. 2012. "Toward a Better Understanding of Behavioural Intention and System Usage Constructs," *European Journal of Information Systems* (21), pp.680–698.

[38] Xu, J. D., Benbasat, I., and Cenfetelli, R. T. 2013. "Integrating Service Quality with System and Information Quality: An Empirical Test in the E-Service Context," *MIS Quarterly* (37:3), pp. 777-794.

[39] Yu, C. 2012. "Factors Affecting Individuals to Adopt Mobile Banking: Empirical Evidence from the UTAUT Model," *Journal of Electronic Commerce Research* (13:2), pp. 104-121.

[40] Zhou, T., Lu, Y., and Wang, B. 2010. "Integrating TTF and UTAUT to Explain Mobile Banking User Adoption," *Computers in human behavior* (26:4), pp. 760-767.

[41] Zhou, T., and Lu, Y. 2011. "Examining Mobile Instant Messaging User Loyalty from the Perspectives of Network Externalities and Flow Experience," *Computers in Human Behavior* (27:2), pp. 883-889.

[42] Zhou, T. 2013. "An Empirical Examination of Continuance Intention of Mobile Payment Services," *Decision Support Systems* (54:2), pp. 1085-1091.

Note:

Survey items/constructs available upon request.

IT Enabled Frugal Effectuation

Full Paper

Prem B. Khanal
Victoria University of Wellington
Wellington, New Zealand
prem.khanal@vuw.ac.nz

Jean-Gregoire Bernard
Victoria University of Wellington
Wellington, New Zealand
jean-gregoire.bernard@vuw.ac.nz

Benoit A. Aubert
Victoria University of Wellington
Wellington, New Zealand
benoit.aubert@vuw.ac.nz

ABSTRACT

To succeed, entrepreneurs operating in frugal contexts tend to adopt an effectual logic of action. Such entrepreneurs also increasingly rely on digital technologies to pursue opportunities. Yet, despite a flurry of scholarly attention to effectuation tactics and their outcomes, surprisingly little is known about how digital technologies support effectuation, and with what outcomes. This paper sketches a theoretical model of how IT affordances support effectuation in frugal contexts. The model extends entrepreneurship and information systems theories of frugal entrepreneurship by linking specific IT affordances to dimensions of effectuation. The paper also discusses how the model could be refined by empirical studies and extended across levels of analysis.

CCS CONCEPTS

• **Social and professional topics** → **Socio-technical systems**;

KEYWORDS

Effectuation, Entrepreneurship, Frugality, Frugal Innovation, IT Affordances, Experimentation

ACM Reference format:
Prem B. Khanal, Jean-Gregoire Bernard, and Benoit A. Aubert. 2017. IT Enabled Frugal Effectuation. In *Proceedings of SIGMIS-CPR '17, June 21-23, 2017, Bangalore, India,* , 8 pages.
DOI: http://dx.doi.org/10.1145/3084381.3084396

1 INTRODUCTION

Rajesh, an engineering graduate, wanted to help the millions of Nepalese citizens who have no access to conventional banking services. His knowledge of payment systems was limited to what he could learn through Wikipedia, YouTube videos, and other online resources. He used his savings of 14000 Rupees (about $140 USD) to put together a network from commoditized hardware parts sourced from a cousin that runs a local computer store. He relied on open source technologies to setup a development environment and offered a partnership to his friend Asgar Ali in exchange of a spare room at Asgar's home to serve as an office. He often found

himself tied up in red tape when dealing with central bank and other government agencies for licenses and other formal approvals, but managed to glean enough information from government websites to get his venture off the ground. After many trials and errors attempting to offer a payment gateway he ended up developing a mobile payment solution when a local telecom vendor began offering a new low-cost mobile data service in the country. Following a successful crowdfunding campaign on Kiva (www.kiva.org), the solution spread quickly across all 75 districts by exploiting existing mobile networks.

This stylized case provides a glimpse of the role of information technology (IT) in an entrepreneurial venture. Rajesh could expand his knowledge corridors through digital repositories. Constrained by limited resources he could rein expenses to minimum by using free open source technology and his immediate contacts. He found partners who could share the risks and aid in experimentation. Finally, IT provided a reach to millions of customers and investors in no time.

The relationship between IT and entrepreneurship is enabling, inspiring, and long standing [22]. Effectuation theory can provide insights to understand this relationship. Effectuation draws attention to the logic of action underlying entrepreneurial behavior when creating new ventures: "When using effectuation processes, entrepreneurs start with a generalized aspiration and then attempt to satisfy that aspiration using the resources they have at their immediate disposal ... The overall objective is not clearly envisioned at the beginning, and those using effectuation processes remain flexible, take advantage of environmental contingencies as they arise, and learn as they go" [40, p. 837]. Nowadays, entrepreneurs like Rajesh who pursue innovation opportunities in frugal contexts characterized by extreme resource constraints and institutional voids (lack of regulatory/institutional/legal norms or safeguards) can leverage the potential of IT for ideation and launch of products and services in much faster, affordable, scalable ways than ever before.

Entrepreneurs often come up with creative and affordable solutions when impinged by resource scarcity and institutional voids. A separate branch of innovation studies which acknowledges scarcity as both constraint and opportunity has emerged under the label of frugal innovation [21]. Effectuation is at the core of frugal innovation, which consists in the creation of "good-enough, affordable products that meet the needs of resource-constrained consumers" [63, p. 1]. Affordable improvisation to solve grass-root level problems in resource scarce environment distinguishes frugal from traditional innovation, which relies on resource abundance [4]. Typically, western companies used to ignore resource constrained consumers and targeted minority affluent class in emerging markets [63]. It was only after Prahalad and Hart [42] came up with the concept of fortune at the bottom of the pyramid (BoP) that this bottom segment got more serious attention. Recent data reflects that people earning less than $10 a day (Purchasing Power Parity) represent 71% of world population [11] [1]. Most of these people live in Africa, Asia and South Pacific. This particular market segment has its own peculiar challenges and opportunities. These markets are characterized by harsh development/deployment environments, a semi/un-educated customer base, the need for radical improvement on value/price ratio, and institutional constraints [7, 41]. Providers of products and services in these emerging market segments face unique types of opportunities: provide acceptable (not high) performance at a much lower price point, introduce a solution without worrying about compatibility since there is usually no infrastructure in place, offer sustainability, operate in minimally regulated markets, and adjust to distinct preferences of emerging markets [23]. Frugal innovators find creative workarounds to aforementioned constraints and exploit these opportunities to "reinvent, recycle and reuse ideas, resources, technologies and even people" [28, p. 252]. To succeed in such difficult situations, an effectual orientation toward entrepreneurial action becomes unavoidable [20, 45].

The academic research on frugal innovation is still at a nascent stage [58]. A number of terminologies have emerged such as jugaad innovation [46], Gandhian innovation [43], inclusive innovation [19], BoP innovation [14], reverse innovation [23], and grass-root innovation [54]. These terms are sometimes used interchangeably and sometimes used to refer to slightly different concepts and contexts. In this particular research frugal context is characterized by four fundamental pillars of frugality namely resource scarcity, uncertainty, affordability, and sustainability.

Ever since Sarasvathy's initial conceptualization of effectuation back in 2001, academic interest in its role in entrepreneurial action has swelled [2]. Attempts have been made to compare and contrast effectuation with other entrepreneurial concepts like causation, bricolage, and frugal engineering [12, 18, 49, 50, 62]. Efforts have been made to understand the role of effectuation in R&D processes and outcomes, as well as its relationship with entrepreneurial orientation and firm performance [9, 35]. In a meta-analytic review Read, Song and Smit [48] not only suggest a measure of effectuation but also conclude that three dimensions of effectuation are positively related to new venture performance, namely means driven action, partnership orientation, and leverage contingency. No significant effect was observed between a fourth dimension, affordable loss, and performance. In another review Perry et al. [40] conclude that the research on effectuation is moving towards an intermediate state of theoretical maturity. Surprisingly, despite this growing volume of research about effectuation, no formal attempt has been made to investigate how and when information technology facilitates effectuation.

In this conceptual paper we examine how entrepreneurs who follow the principles of effectuation can leverage IT to seek opportunities in the context of frugal innovation. Our primary contribution

is to extend effectuation theory to acknowledge the role of information technology in frugal contexts. The unit of analysis for our proposed model is the frugal entrepreneur who employs digital technologies to enact the effectuation method as a way to transcend constraints in the design of creative and sustainable solutions.

Moving forward, the core concepts of effectuation and IT affordances are discussed in the next sections, then a set of propositions is developed to explain how IT affordances influence each dimension of effectuation. This is followed by a discussion of the key ideas and conclusion.

2 CONCEPTUAL FRAMEWORK AND PROPOSITIONS

In this section existing literature on effectuation is explored to understand how IT influences the behavior of an effectuator while pursuing an innovation opportunity.

2.1 What is Effectuation?

Two distinct approaches to entrepreneurial action have been proposed in the literature: causation and effectuation. Causation considers a specific effect as given and focuses on selecting the appropriate means to create the effect. Effectuation takes the opposite view: the set of means is given and the innovator is selecting between possible effects that could be created with the means [50]. Causation underlies planned, outcome-driven activities like market analysis and business plan development. Effectuation, on the contrary, involves emergent and adaptive strategies of opportunity creation [12]. Sarasvathy [50] uses the example of a chef to illustrate the difference between causation and effectuation. With causation, the chef thinks about a recipe, purchases the required ingredients, and follows the set of steps to prepare the meal. On the other hand, if effectuation is followed, the chef just opens the refrigerator, looks at the ingredients available, and prepares a dish using the ingredients on hand. The entrepreneurship literature considers effectuation as an intuitive entrepreneurial function and causation as a goal-oriented managerial function [15, 47, 50].The enactment of causation and effectuation is situational: both logics may interlace in entrepreneurial actions and decisions to varying degrees [50].

According to Sarasvathy [50, p. 250] effectual action consists of:

(1) A given set of means (that usually consists of relatively unalterable characteristics/circumstances of the decision maker);
(2) A set of effects or possible operationalization of generalized aspirations (mostly generated through the decision process);
(3) Constraints on (and opportunities for) possible effects (usually imposed by the limited means as well as by the environment and its contingencies);
(4) Criteria for selecting between the effects (usually a predetermined level of affordable loss or acceptable risk related to the given means); and
(5) The creation of new markets together with customers, suppliers, and even prospective competitors [51, p. 390].

---

[1]Prahalad & Hart [42] categorize the people earning less than $4 a day (PPP) as bottom of the economic pyramid (BOP).
[2]reflected by 2859 citations that appear in Google Scholar as of 26-12-2016 to [50].

Table 1: Effectuation Dimensions and Descriptions used in the literature

Effectuation Dimensions	Unit of Analysis	Description	Authors
Affordable loss, Experimentation, Flexibility, Pre-commitments	High-technology Firms	Effectuation have been linked with entrepreneurial outcomes and firm performance under dynamic and hostile environments	Mthanti & Urban [35]
Resource focus, Affordable loss, Strategic Alliance, Exploit Contingencies, Control Logic	Entrepreneur or Emerging Firm	Effectuation should be measured as a reflective construct when research centers around effectuation and as a formative construct when effectuation is part of a complex research model.	Perry et al. [40]
Means-driven, Affordable loss, Partnership, Acknowledge unexpected	R&D Project	Effectuation and causation dimensions have been linked with R&D process efficiency and output.	Brettel et al. [9]
Experimentation, Affordable Loss, Flexibility, Pre-Commitments	Startup Phase of Venture	Initial empirical validation of effectuation as a formative construct.	Chandler et al. [12]
Means: What I know, Who I am and Whom I know, Partnership, Affordable loss, Leverage contingency	New Venture	Meta-analysis relationships with entrepreneurial outcomes. All sub-dimensions except affordable loss influence new venture performance positively.	Read et al. [48]

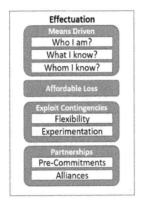

Figure 1: Effectuation (Sub) Dimensions

Significant efforts have been made by researchers to articulate the construct of effectuation as a multidimensional latent variable based on aforementioned theoretical principles [9, 12, 35, 40, 48]. Table 1 lists some of those research works along with unit of analysis and a short description. The following paragraphs discuss the key points in the effectuation construct as shown in Figure 1.

Means Driven: Entrepreneurs start with aspirations and limited means: who they are (traits, identity, preferences, resource endowments), what they know (abilities, knowledge corridors), and whom they know (social networks) [50]. Entrepreneurs rely on these means, are aware of their own strengths and limitations, and utilize their social network to kickoff innovation.

Affordable Loss: Entrepreneurs assess an innovation opportunity based on the loss they could absorb in case of failure rather than the potential returns [15]. In other words effectuators look for frugal ways of doing things to minimize downside risk first and foremost [18].

Exploit Contingencies: Effectuators seek to turn unexpected events into profitable outcomes [18] by exploiting environmental contingencies through flexibility and experimentation [40].

Flexibility: Effectuators tend to remain flexible to choose and adapt contingent opportunities.

Experimentation: "A series of trial and error changes pursued along various dimensions of strategy, over a relatively short period of time, in an effort to identify and establish a viable basis for competing [37, p. 496]."

Partnerships: The last dimension is concerned with establishing pre-commitments and alliances with customers, suppliers, and other strategic partners which help reduce the uncertainty associated with the venture. Diversifying risk among multiple stakeholders minimize potential loss for each one [35, 50].

2.2 Information Technology: Artifact, Relationship or Property

Our goal is to identify how IT influences the behavior of frugal effectuator. These influences will be complex and hence a multifaceted construct to represent the various ways information technology is likely to influence effectuation is needed.

IS researchers have adapted different terminologies to understand human technology interactions. These terminologies include (but are not limited to) artifact, artifact properties, artifact capabilities, artifact functionalities, perceived functionalities, emergent functionalities, and properties of relationship between artifact and end user etc. Ever since Gibson's inception of affordance to understand animal environment interactions, IS researchers have adapted the analogy to study human technology interactions. Slightly varied definitions of IT affordances could be found in IS literature. For example: according to Markus & Silver [34, p. 622] functional affordance is offered by technical objects; "the possibilities for goal-oriented action offered to specified user groups by technical objects". Similarly Volkoff & Strong [59, p. 823] define affordance as a function of relationship as "The potential for behaviors associated with achieving an immediate concrete outcome and arising from the relation between an object (e.g., an IT artifact) and a goal-oriented actor or actress." The concept of IT affordances have been adapted in various contexts; for example Schultze [53] explains that IT affordances provide a sense of presence in virtual world and Leonardi [29] explores the implication of IT affordances in collective action of a group (individualized, collective and shared affordances).

In order to illustrate the notion of affordances a few examples are provided. Social media offers to shape the identity of someone who is trying to create/change an impression to others. Also, social media offers entertainment to someone who is looking for some pastime. Interestingly, we can see that, the same technology can exhibit different affordances depending on the goal of end user(s). Therefore affordances not only change with the technology or artifact but also with the goal of the end user. Hence influence of technology on actions and on decisions of frugal effectuators could be studied using the concept of affordances.

In this particular research both aforementioned definitions have been considered where appropriate.

2.3   Information Technology and Effectuation

We now turn our attention to how IT affordances can influence each of the sub-dimensions of effectuation.

Modern day entrepreneurs have access to ubiquitous and cheap technology. By drawing on past literature that has examined how IT affordances are enacted, it is possible to assess which dimensions of effectuation are possibly affected by IT affordances. The list of affordances considered is not comprehensive nor is it applicable in all cases. Affordances were chosen according to their relevance with each dimension. Our objective is to open up an initial line of inquiry about how IT affordances can enable various aspects of effectual action. Table 2 maps effectuation dimensions with IT affordances in frugal context.

2.3.1   How IT Affordances Enable Means Driven Action.

Digital-Self. Effectuation starts with the limited means/resources of the entrepreneur where s/he knows her own traits, preferences, and resource endowments [50]. In other words: effectuators draw on their identity as a resource to recognize and exploit opportunities. Frugal effectuators are driven by the aspiration to do more with less resources for more people [7]. Also, entrepreneurial identity plays a major role in securing resources and acquiring trust and investment [36]. We propose that effectuators' identity involves an IT component too: a cyber-extension of oneself. IT identity is a novel identity created when one associates IT as an integral part of his/her sense of self [10]. IT in this context means a unit of technology (hardware, software, platform) accessible to a conscious end user over time and space to produce, store and communicate information [10]. Stein, Galliers and Markus [56] identify five different ways of how IT shapes professional identity: creation, translation, management, illustration, and utilization of IT artifacts. These so called cyber extensions of the self can help sharpen the skills or abilities, convey the thought process in graphical ways, and create an image of the person (entrepreneur). For example effectuators might project their entrepreneurial identity through their personal or professional websites, blogs, and presence in social media. In short digital projection of the identity of the effectuator creates an extended self which in turn extends entrepreneurial resources. This leads to our first proposition:

PROPOSITION 1. *In frugal contexts, IT affordances can extend self-identities of effectuators by creating digital persona.*

Digital-Knowledge. Effectuators are aware of the knowledge corridor they are in [50]. Said differently they masterfully utilize what they know to create something new (contingent effects). Frugal innovators also exploit the deep knowledge of contextual problems and the local workarounds to those problems [32]. The knowledge corridors the entrepreneurs are in could be extended, influenced and/or established through digital repositories of information. Combination of computing resources and existing knowledge if properly utilized increases the chances of entrepreneurial endeavors [22]. Multimedia repositories like Youtube and Wikipedia are useful to extend explicit knowledge. Online communities and blogs help extending/spreading tacit knowledge. Self-paced, customized online courses like MOOC (Massive Open Online Course) can be source of both tacit and explicit knowledge. In short publicly/proprietary available digital repositories deepen the breadth of effectuator's knowledge. Which leads us to our second proposition:

PROPOSITION 2. *In frugal contexts, IT affordances can extend (positively) the limited entrepreneurial knowledge by enabling contextual knowledge seeking.*

Digital-Connections. Effectuators lean on their immediate contacts to create/exploit opportunities. In other words they rely on people they know, personally or professionally, to kick off their venture. Being embedded in local networks has been identified as one of the major driving forces for frugal innovations [16]. Digital connections can expand the effectuator's network not only by linking people with people but also by linking people with objects and objects with objects. Ever expanding digital network known as "Internet of things (IoT)" encompasses the interconnectivity of things, data and people [6]. Pilot IoT projects like 'physical-web'at the slums of Dharavi (Mumbai, India) are being developed to help entrepreneurs and customers in BoP markets [24]. Platforms like social media help entrepreneurs to coordinate and collaborate not only with people to whom that are in their immediate network vicinity, but also with the people that are remotely located - socially, physically, and culturally. For example effectuators develop personal contacts over social media like Facebook and professional contacts over LinkedIn. In short digital networks and platforms extend effectuator's social capital. Which leads to our third proposition.

PROPOSITION 3. *In frugal contexts, IT affordances can extend the reach and breadth of effectuators' social network by enabling local embeddedness.*

2.3.2   How IT Affordances Limit Affordable Losses.   Seasoned entrepreneurs start by estimating the loss they could afford rather than thinking about possible returns from an opportunity [50]. In the same vein, affordability is the defining feature of almost any innovations in frugal contexts [5, 52, 55, 57] where success can only be achieved by failing cheap [46]. With modern day technologies like cloud computing, entrepreneurs can get an affordable and scalable world class IT infrastructure "on demand". It is not long ago that investing in a fully operational datacenter and sophisticated software was a mandatory requirement for entrepreneurs seeking to exploit IT. Economic, scalable and customizable solutions are

Table 2: Mapping Effectuation Dimensions, IT Affordances, and Frugal Innovation Context

Effectuation Dimensions	Dimension Description	IT (Affordances and *Artifacts*)	Description of IT (Artifact and Affordances)	Explanation	Frugal Innovation Context
Means-who am I	Their own traits, tastes, and resource endowments	Shaping Identity - *Digital Persona Systems*	"IT identity is the extent to which an individual views use of an IT as integral to his or her sense of self - as a new form of identity" [10, p. 931].	Presence in social media, blogs, websites as an extension to who they are or how do they project themselves in the digital world	Aspiration to create product/service/process/system that is profitable, sustainable and affordable for more people
Means-what do I know	Abilities and knowledge corridors	Seeking Knowledge - *Digital Repositories, Online Communities*	Organizational knowledge repositories, academic knowledge repositories, big data repositories, online communities	The knowledge corridors are expanded by digital repositories	Aspects of domestic marketplace [5]
Means-whom do I know	Social network they are part of	Seeking Connections - *Social Media/Platforms*	"Web-based services that allow individuals to (1) construct a ...profile within a bounded system, (2) articulate a list of other users with whom they share a connection, and (3) view and traverse their list of connections and those made by others within the system. The nature and nomenclature of these connections may vary from site to site" [8, p. 211].	Social networking platforms generate social capital by expanding the reach and breadth of an entrepreneur's network	Non-traditional partnering, localizing value creation, positive social action, local business unit [17]
Affordable Loss	Loss that could be absorbed in case of failure	Seeking Solutions on Demand - *Cloud Technology /Open Source Technology*	"'On demand' refers to the fact that users of IT resources access them when they need them, for how long they need them, and only pay for this actual usage" [31, p. 163].	Economic IT solution for budding entrepreneurs which might help to keep expenses low	Fail cheap, fail fast, fail often [46]
Exploit Contingencies - Flexibility	Flexible to choose and adapt contingent opportunities	Seeking Flexibility - *Real Time Communication/ Simulation/Modeling*	"Modeling is the process of producing a model; ... One purpose of a model is to enable the analyst to predict the effect of changes to the system" [33, p. 7].	Simulation and modeling of the system provides flexibility to choose among contingent opportunities	Flex your assets, MacGyver Spirit [45]
Exploit Contingencies - Experimentation	Trial and error	Evaluating Alternatives - *Simulation/Modeling/3D Printing*	"A simulation ...can be reconfigured and experimented with; usually, this is impossible, too expensive or impractical to do in the system it represents. The operation of the model can be studied, and hence, properties concerning the behavior of the actual system or its subsystem can be inferred" [33, p. 7].	Simulation/modeling and/or 3D printing could be an economic way of experimentation of complex systems.	Engage and Iterate [45]
Partnership - Pre commitments	Risk sharing	Finding Supporters - *Social Media/Platforms/Crowd Funding*	"Crowd-funding is an initiative undertaken to raise money for a new project proposed by someone, by collecting small to medium-size investments from several other people (i.e. a crowd)" [38, p. 444].	Funding could be obtained in the form of pre commitments from crowd (Partnership redefined)	Make innovative friends [45]
Partnership - Alliances	Reduce uncertainty	Seeking Alliances - *Social Media/Platforms/Crowd Sourcing*	"The fundamental idea of crowdsourcing is that a crowdsourcer ...proposes to an undefined group of contributors ...the voluntary undertaking of a task presented in an open call. The ensuing interaction process unfolds over IT-based crowdsourcing platforms. The power of crowdsourcing lies in aggregating knowledge from a multitude of diverse and independent contributors. Crowdsourcing enables crowdsourcers to obtain solutions that are beyond the boundaries of their established mindset" [39, p. 200].	Transient alliances could be created using crowd sourcing or a long lasting one could be created using platforms or social connections on world wide web.	Co-create value with prosumers [45], collaborative efforts with local market partners [3]

nowadays available through internet connections. Entrepreneurs do not need to put at risk excessive amount of resources upfront while facing an uncertain future payoff: if the innovation succeeds then costs rise as the innovation is scaled, and if the innovation fails then the loss is limited to the cost of the on-demand services consumed. Also, social media platforms provide a cheap (and sometimes free) reach to the millions of potential customers and/or partners. A plethora of open source technologies is available for free, which further limit the magnitude of investments required. Hence frugal information systems using minimal of resources [61] help reducing losses in case of venture failure, an observation which leads to our fourth proposition:

PROPOSITION 4. *In frugal contexts, IT affordances can lower the potential losses associated with entrepreneurial action by providing on-demand solutions.*

2.3.3 How IT Affordances Enable Experimentation and Flexibility. Effectuators perform trial and error with multiple business model variations [18]. Moreover they are flexible enough to choose one or more among those variations based on their aspirations. Frugal innovators engage customers in experimentation with products or services; they are flexible enough to choose one among many contingencies as they come along [45]. Nowadays, the entrepreneurs' ability to simulate reality using sophisticated software systems facilitates both experimentation and flexibility to choose among contingencies. For example, India was able to launch a satellite to Mars "Mangalyan" within 15 months and $74 million USD whereas the budget for the NASA's satellite to the Mars "Maven" was $670 million USD [13] [3]. One of the secrets to achieving this for a 10 times lower cost and 3 times less time was the experimentation using sophisticated simulation and modeling software instead of physical prototypes [44]. Ideas could be evaluated in no time on world wide web using control experiments like A/B testing [where users are randomly exposed to a single factor with two values control(A) and treatment(B)] or MultiVariable testing (where users are exposed to multiple factors at the same time) [27]. In short, digital effectuators perform virtual experiments to generate contingencies (often referred as effects) and to evaluate those, which increases flexibility. This potential leads to our fifth proposition:

PROPOSITION 5. *In frugal contexts, IT affordances can facilitate flexibility and experimentation by allowing virtual experiments.*

2.3.4 How IT Affordances Help Building Partnerships. Rather than focusing on competitors and/or competitive analysis, effectuators focus on a) building strategic alliances to reduce uncertainty and b) obtaining pre-commitments to share risks. Frugal innovators rely on non-traditional partnerships, local business units [17], local networks [16], strong local presence [63], and collaboration with prosumers [45]. Platforms like AirBnb and Uber help forming a partnership among millions of users and reach out to billions of customers. In addition to traditional forms of partnership using social media, websites, emails, and mobile technologies, significant growth has been observed in alternative finance markets like crowdfunding or peer-to-peer lending [60, 64]. In short digital partnerships and alliances, often done through social media and platforms, extend

[3] Authors acknowledge that Mavan was highly advanced science mission and Mangalyaan was a technology demonstration mission.

the reach to partners and potential users. This leads us to our sixth proposition:

PROPOSITION 6. *In frugal contexts, IT affordances can facilitate partnerships by connecting with local allies.*

In sum, we sketched a preliminary theoretical model of how effectuators can leverage IT affordances while pursuing an innovation opportunity in frugal contexts. We have selected only a few of the trending IT artifacts and affordances nowadays, and we acknowledge that there may be unforeseen affordances that could affect entrepreneurial behavior as new IT artifacts become available over time. There may also be IT affordances that influence entrepreneurial effectuation negatively (or do not affect it at all) such as traditional reporting and analyzing tools which effectuators do not seem to bother about because those tools are aligned with a goal-based causation logic.

3 DISCUSSION

Technology has infiltrated every aspect of human life, be it self-identity, be it aspirations, be it relations, be it the way we see and evaluate opportunities or be it the way we conduct businesses. Traditional usage of information technology to automate and operate treats it as a logical intellectual tool. So does the traditional view of entrepreneurship where a predefined goal is pursued in a logical way keeping return on investments in mind. Effectuation challenges the traditional view point of entrepreneurship by arguing that entrepreneurs are driven by intuition. They can switch and adopt new goals. In this paper we have investigated the potential use of IT to support emergent strategies of effectuation in frugal contexts. The growth of global income inequality [11]; the reduction of purchasing power in the developed world [23]; and the increasingly pervasive role of IT to reduce the cost of experimentation, improvisation and innovation [2] make the study of digital effectuation in frugal contexts particularly relevant and timely.

As explained earlier effectuation and causation are intermingled in entrepreneurial decisions and actions. Hence it is difficult to observe the effect of IT on effectuation in isolation. This examination of digital frugal effectuation as an archetype contributes to effectuation theory by acknowledging the role of IT affordances in frugal innovation approaches of entrepreneurial actions.

To the best of our knowledge this is the only conceptual work that explores the influence of digital affordances on effectuation principles. It is opening up new possibilities to study digital effectuation.

From our explanations and propositions we identify four key characteristics of digital effectuators as shown in Figure 2. Digital effectuators are equipped with digital means (Digital Identity, Digital Knowledge, and Digital Connections). They utilize digital (on-demand/open source) solutions to curb losses. Digital experiments facilitate trial and error to create new effects and provide flexibility to choose among the contingent effects. Partnerships on digital platforms facilitate risk sharing and strategic alliances.

Sarasvathy [50] has explained that effectuation principles are applicable at individual, organization, and macroeconomic levels. In this conceptual research we have explored the technologies and traits at the individual level but it is possible to imagine that IT-enabled effectuation follows the same pattern and thus could

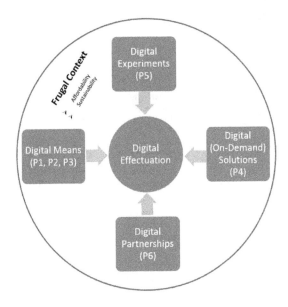

Figure 2: Key Characteristics of Digital Effectuators

also be applied at different level of analysis. Macroeconomic level effectuation principles have not yet been a research focus at all, but it would be interesting to study how national and international economies are influenced by digital effectuation principles.

Entrepreneurial and frugal practices within established organizations are gaining popularity among both academicians and practitioners (e.g., intrapreneurship, amoeba management techniques [1], increasing number of R&D centers in emerging markets [25, 26]). Study of digital effectuation principles/dimensions in the context of frugal intrapreneurship is another potential research area for exploration.

One aspect that was not considered in this paper is the negative influence of IT affordances on effectuation. Our primary interest was in identifying the nature of the affordances that can support specific dimensions of effectuation as a first step, rather than examine the directionality of the influences. The examination of IT affordances that negatively influence effectuation principles have been left for future research. Conceptually, it is conceivable that such negative influences exist. It is unclear if the effectuators would be able to avoid such influences.

Further understanding of the effect of IT affordances on effectuation will be derived from empirical work. Case studies to establish conceptual foundation of digital effectuation could further unpack how frugal entrepreneurs rely on IT affordances for effectuation. Studies examining the moderating or mediating effects of IT affordances on new venture performance is another potential research area. Our model complements comparative case studies of 'born-digital' versus 'grown-digital' ventures [30], and help further the IS field's collective understanding of digital effectuation.

It becomes increasingly important to understand the influence of digital technologies on effectuation principles given the centrality of IT in today's emerging business models that aim to provide sustainable solutions to some of the world's most complex problems. More broadly, the spread of agile and lean approaches to innovation

suggests that ignoring IT-enabled effectuation in theories of frugal innovation could become a crucial error of exclusion.

4 CONCLUSION

Nature has sustained the exponential growth of human population from 5 million (8000 BC) to 7 billion (2016 AD). This growth has brought an unprecedented use of scarce and finite resources. Yet about 71% of world population is bound to live in despair conditions [11]. Hence entrepreneurs who could do more with less resources for more people in sustainable way are desperately needed. That is the reason why we have developed a conceptual framework to study the influence of IT affordances on effectuators in frugal context. Frugal context stimulates the industrious effort for sustainable and affordable solutions for more people in entrepreneurial endeavors.

In this theoretical paper we set out to explore if intuition based effectuation principles could be supported by emerging information technologies. By mapping relevant IT affordances to the corresponding dimensions of effectuation we conclude that specific IT affordances have positive influence on each effectuation sub-dimension. Effectuation is basically trying to control the future based on today's contingent choices. It follows the principle of you don't need to predict the future if you can control it from your choices [50]. IT affordances facilitate creating and evaluating contingent effects from digitally extended means to fulfill entrepreneurial aspirations.

Frugal digital effectuation viewpoint helps understanding the actions and decisions of new generation tech-savvy entrepreneurs and prosumers who not only care about value for money but also care about value for many.

REFERENCES

[1] Ralph W. Adler and Toshiro Hiromoto. 2012. Amoeba Management: Lessons From Japan's Kyocera. *MIT Sloan Management Review* 54, 1 (2012), 83–89.
[2] Suchit Ahuja and Yolande E. Chan. 2014. The Enabling Role of IT in Frugal Innovation. In *Thirty Fifth International Conference on Information Systems*. 1–20.
[3] Peter Altmann and Robert Engberg. 2016. Frugal Innovation and Knowledge Transferability: Innovation for Emerging Markets Using Home-Based R&D. *Research-Technology Management* January-Februrary (2016), 48–55.
[4] Preeta M. Banerjee. 2013. The "Frugal" in Frugal Innovation. In *Evolution of Innovation Management*, Alexander Brem and Eric Viardot (Eds.). Palgrave Macmillan UK, 290–310.
[5] Radha R. Basu, Preeta M. Banerjee, and Elizabeth G. Sweeny. 2013. Frugal Innovation: Core Competencies to Address Global Sustainability. *Journal of Management for Global Sustainability* 2 (2013), 63–82.
[6] Anandhi Bharadwaj, Omar A. El Sawy, Paul A. Pavlou, and N. Venkatraman. 2013. Digital Business Strategy: Toward a Next Generation of Insights. *MIS Quarterly* 37, 2 (2013), 471–482.
[7] Yasser Ahmad Bhatti and Marc Ventresca. 2013. How Can "Frugal Innovation" Be Conceptualized? *SSRN* (2013), 1–26. DOI:http://dx.doi.org/10.2139/ssrn.2203552
[8] Danah m. Boyd and Nicole B. Ellison. 2007. Social Network Sites: Definition, History, and Scholarship. *Journal of Computer-Mediated Communication* 13, 1 (oct 2007), 210–230.
[9] Malte Brettel, René Mauer, Andreas Engelen, and Daniel Küpper. 2012. Corporate Effectuation: Entrepreneurial Action and Its Impact on R&D Project Performance. *Journal of Business Venturing* 27, 2 (2012), 167–184.
[10] Michelle Carter and Varun Grover. 2015. Me, Myself, and I(T): Conceptualizing Information Technology Identity and Its Implications. *MIS Quarterly* 39, 4 (2015), 931–957.
[11] Pew Research Center. 2015. World Population by Income: How Many Live on How Much, and Where. (2015). http://www.pewglobal.org/interactives/global-population-by-income/
[12] Gaylen N. Chandler, Dawn R. DeTienne, Alexander McKelvie, and Troy V. Mumford. 2011. Causation and effectuation processes: A validation study. *Journal of Business Venturing* 26, 3 (2011), 375–390.
[13] National Geographic Channel. 2015. India's Mission To Mars Video By National Geography. (2015). https://www.youtube.com/watch?v=FPQkasiqVkw

[14] Carl Dahlman and Yevgeny Kuznetsov. 2014. Chapter 4- Innovation for the " Base of the Pyramid": Developing a Framework for Policy Experimentation. In *Making Innovation Policy Work: Learning From Experimentation*. OECD/World Bank, Chapter 4, 71–123.

[15] Nicholas Dew, Stuart Read, Saras D. Sarasvathy, and Robert Wiltbank. 2009. Effectual Versus Predictive Logics in Entrepreneurial Decision-Making: Differences Between Experts and Novices. *Journal of Business Venturing* 24, 4 (2009), 287–309.

[16] Holger Ernst, Hanna Nari Kahle, Anna Dubiel, Jaideep Prabhu, and Mohan Subramaniam. 2015. The Antecedents and Consequences of Affordable Value Innovations for Emerging Markets. *Journal of Product Innovation Management* 32, 1 (2015), 65–79.

[17] Siim Esko, Mindaugas Zeromskis, and Juliana Hsuan. 2013. Value chain and innovation at the base of the pyramid. *South Asian Journal of Global Business Research* 2, 2 (2013), 230–250.

[18] Greg Fisher. 2012. Effectuation, Causation, and Bricolage: A Behavioral Comparison of Emerging Theories in Entrepreneurship Research. *Entrepreneurship: Theory and Practice* 36, 5 (2012), 1019–1051.

[19] Christopher Foster and Richard Heeks. 2013. Conceptualising Inclusive Innovation: Modifying Systems of Innovation Frameworks to Understand Diffusion of New Technology to Low-Income Consumers. *European Journal of Development Research* 25, 3 (2013), 333–355.

[20] Michael Gibbert, Martin Hoegl, and Liisa Välikangas. 2007. In Praise of Resource Constraints. *MIT Sloan Management Review* Spring, 48308 (2007), 1–5.

[21] Michael Gibbert, Martin Hoegl, and Liisa Valikangas. 2014. Introduction to the Special Issue: Financial Resource Constraints and Innovation. *Journal of Product Innovation Management* 31, 2 (mar 2014), 197–201.

[22] Manlio Del Giudice and Detmar Straub. 2011. IT and Entrepreneurism: An On-Again, Off-Again Love Affair or a Marriage? *MIS Quarterly* 35, 4 (2011), III–VII.

[23] Vijay Govindarajan and Chris Trimble. 2012. Reverse Innovation: a Global Growth Strategy That Could Pre-empt Disruption at Home. *Strategy & Leadership* 40, 5 (2012), 5–11.

[24] HindustanTimes. 2017. Internet of Things: Dharavi Market Taps into Virtual World for Gains. (2017). http://www.hindustantimes.com/mumbai-news/internet-of-things-dharavi-market-taps-into-virtual-world-for-gains/story-S2KDFsgRJ8MFk0QBp9gJ3O.html

[25] Jeffrey R Immelt, Vijay Govindarajan, and Chris Trimble. 2009. How GE Is Disrupting Itself. *Harvard Business Review* October (2009), 56–65.

[26] Barry Jaruzelski, Kevin Schwartz, and Volker Staack. 2015. The Innovation's New World Order. *Strategy + Business* 27, 81 (2015).

[27] Ron Kohavi, Roger Longbotham, Dan Sommerfield, and Randal M Henne. 2009. Controlled Experiments on the Web : Survey and Practical Guide. *Data Minining and Knowledge Discovery* 18 (2009), 140–181.

[28] Charles Leadbeater. 2014. *The Frugal Innovator: Creating Change on a Shoestring Budget* (1st ed.). Plgrave Macmillan UK.

[29] Paul M Leonardi. 2013. When Does Technology Use Enable Network Change in Organizations? A Comparative Study of Feature Use and Shared Affordances. *MIS Quarterly* 37, 3 (2013), 749–775.

[30] Carmen Leong, Shan L Pan, and Jie Liu. 2016. Digital Entrepreneurship of Born Digital and Grown Digital Firms: Comparing the Effectuation Process of Yihaodian and Suning. In *Thirty Seventh International Conference on Information Systems*. Dublin, 1–11.

[31] Frank Leymann. 2011. Cloud Computing. *it - Information Technology* 53 (2011), 163–164. arXiv:1003.4074

[32] Ted London and Stuart L Hart. 2004. Reinventing Strategies for Emerging Markets: Beyond the Transnational Model. *Journal of International Business Studies* 35, 5 (2004), 350–370.

[33] Anu Maria. 1997. Introduction to Modeling and Simulation. *Proceedings of the 29th conference on Winter simulation - WSC '97* (1997), 7–13.

[34] M Lynne Markus and Mark S. Silver. 2008. A Foundation for the Study of IT Effects: A New Look at DeSanctis and Poole's Concepts of Structural Features and Spirit. *Journal of the Association for Information Systems* 9, 10 (2008), 609–632.

[35] Thanti Sibonelo Mthanti and Boris Urban. 2014. Effectuation and Entrepreneurial Orientation in High-Technology Firms. *Technology Analysis & Strategic Management* 26, 2 (2014), 121–133.

[36] Chad Navis and Mary Glynn. 2011. Legitimate Distinctiveness and the Entrepreneurial Identity: Influence on Investor Judgments of New Venture Plausibility. *Academy of Management Review* 36, 3 (2011), 479–499.

[37] Charlene L Nicholls-Nixona, Arnold C Cooper, and Carolyn Y Woo. 2000. Strategic Experimentation: Understanding Change and Performance in New Ventures. *Journal of Business Venturing* 15, 6-6 (2000), 493–521.

[38] A. Ordanini, A., Miceli, L., Pizzetti, M., & Parasuraman. 2011. Crowd-Funding: Transforming Customers into Investors Through Innovative Service Platforms. *Journal of Service Management* 22, 4 (2011), 443–470.

[39] Joe Peppard, Chris Edwards, and Rob Lambert. 2011. Crowdsourcing: How to Benefit From (Too) Many Great Ideas. *MIS Quarterly* 10, 2 (2011), 115–117.

[40] John T. Perry, Gaylen N. Chandler, and Gergana Markova. 2012. Entrepreneurial Effectuation: A Review and Suggestions for Future Research. *Entrepreneurship: Theory and Practice* 36, 4 (2012), 837–861.

[41] C. K. Prahalad. 2006. *The Fortune at The Bottom of the Pyramid: Eradicating Poverty Through Profits*. Wharton School Pub.

[42] C. K. Prahalad and Stuart L Hart. 2002. The Fortune at the Bottom of the Pyramid. *Strategy+Business Magazine* 26 (2002), 1–16.

[43] C. K. Prahalad and R. A. Mashelkar. 2010. Innovation's Holy Grail. *Harvard Business Review* 88, 7-8 (2010), 1–10.

[44] Navi Radjou. 2015. Navi Radjou: "Frugal Innovation: How To Do More With Less" | Authors at Google. (2015). https://www.youtube.com/watch?v=fI-KPJKrfRY

[45] Navi Radjou and Jaideep Prabhu. 2015. *Frugal Innovation: How to do more with less*. The Economist.

[46] Navi Radjou, Jaideep Prabhu, and Simone Ahuja. 2012. *Jugaad Innovation*. Jossey-Bass.

[47] Stuart Read and Saras D. Sarasvathy. 2015. Knowing What to Do and Doing What You Know: Effectuation as a Form of Entrepreneurial Expertise. *Journal of Private Equity* Winter (2015), 45–62.

[48] Stuart Read, Michael Song, and Willem Smit. 2009. A Meta-Analytic Review of Effectuation and Venture Performance. *Journal of Business Venturing* 24, 6 (2009), 573–587.

[49] Eugenia Rosca and Julia Bendul. 2015. Combining Frugal Engineering and Effectuation Theory : Insights for Frugal Product Development in Entrepreneurial Context. *R&D Management - (Fast?) Connecting R&D* (2015), 1–10.

[50] Saras D Sarasvathy. 2001. Causation and Effectuation: Toward a Theoretical Shift from Economic Inevitability to Entrepreneurial Contingency. *Academy of Management Review* 26, 2 (2001), 243–263.

[51] Saras D. Sarasvathy and Nicholas Dew. 2005. Entrepreneurial logics for a technology of foolishness. *Scandinavian Journal of Management* 21, 4 SPEC. ISS. (2005), 385–406.

[52] A Sarin, L Annala, and JL Green. 2016. Co-production of Frugal Innovation: Case of Low Cost Household Reverse Osmosis Filters in India. *Journal of Cleaner Production* (2016). http://www.sciencedirect.com/science/article/pii/S0959652616309532

[53] Ulrike Schultze. 2010. Embodiment and Presence in Virtual Worlds: A Review. *Journal of Information Technology* 25, 4 (2010), 434–449.

[54] G Seyfang and A Smith. 2007. Grassroots Innovations for Sustainable Development: Towards a New Research and Policy Agenda. *Environmental Politics* 4016, 4 (2007), 37–41.

[55] Pavan Soni and Rishikesha T. Krishnan. 2014. Frugal Innovation: Aligning Theory, Practice, and Public Policy. *Journal of Indian Business Research* 6, 1 (2014), 29–47.

[56] Mari Klara Stein, Robert D. Galliers, and M. Lynne Markus. 2013. Towards an Understanding of Identity and Technology in the Workplace. *Journal of Information Technology* 28, 3 (2013), 167–182.

[57] Rajnish Tiwari and Cornelius Herstatt. 2012. Frugal Innovation : A Global Networks ' Perspective. *Die Unternehmung* 66, 3 (2012), 245–274.

[58] Rajnish Tiwari, Katharina Kalogerakis, and Cornelius Herstatt. 2014. Frugal Innovation and Analogies: Some Propositions for Product Development in Emerging Economies. (2014). http://tubdok.tub.tuhh.de/handle/11420/1175

[59] Olga Volkoff and Diane M. Strong. 2013. Critical Realism and Affordances: Theorizing IT-Associated Organizational Change Processes. *MIS Quarterly* 37, 3 (2013), 819–834.

[60] Robert Wardrop, Bryan Zhang, Raghavendra Rau, and Mia Gray. 2015. *The European Alternative Finance Benchmarking Report*. Technical Report February. 44 pages. http://www.jbs.cam.ac.uk/index.php?id=6481

[61] Richard T. Watson, K. Niki Kunene, and M. Sirajul Islam. 2012. Frugal information systems (IS). *Information Technology for Development* 19, 2 (2012), 1–12.

[62] Chris Welter, René Mauer, and Robert J Wuebker. 2016. Bridging Behavioral Models and Theoretical Concepts: Effectuation and Bricolage in the Opportunity Creation Framework. *Strategic Entrepreneurship Journal* 10 (2016), 5–20.

[63] Marco B Zeschky, Bastian Widenmayer, and Oliver Gassmann. 2011. Frugal Innovation in Emerging Markets: the Case of Mettler Toledo. *Research Technology Management* 54, 4 (2011), 38–45.

[64] Bryan Zhang, Robert Wardrop, Tania Ziegler, Alexis Lui, John Burton, Alexander James, and Kieran Garvey. 2016. *Sustaining Momentum: The 2nd European Alternative Finance Industry Report*. Technical Report September.

Effects of Organization Insiders' Self-Control and Relevant Knowledge on Participation in Information Systems Security Deviant Behavior

Full Paper

Princely Ifinedo
Cape Breton University
1250 Grand Lake Road, Sydney, NS
Canada
princely_ifinedo@cbu.ca

ABSTRACT

[1] Disastrous consequences tend to befall organizations whose employees participate in information systems security deviant behavior (ISSDB) (e.g., connecting computers to the Internet through an insecure wireless network and opening emails from unverified senders). Although organizations recognize that ISSDB poses a serious problem, understanding what motivates its occurrence continues to be a key concern. While studies on information technology (IT) misuse abounds, research specifically focusing on the drivers of ISSDB remains scant in the literature. Using self-control theory, augmented with knowledge of relevant factors, this study examined the effects of employees' self-control, knowledge of computers/IT, and information systems (IS) security threats and risks on participation in ISSDB. A research model, including the aforementioned factors, was proposed and tested using the partial least squares technique. Data was collected from a survey of Canadian professionals. The results show that low self-control and lower levels of knowledge of computers/IT are related to employees' involvement in ISSDB. The data did not provide a meaningful relationship between employees' knowledge of IS security threats/risks and desire to participate in ISSDB.

CCS CONCEPTS

• Security and privacy →Human and societal aspects of security and privacy. Social and professional topics →Computing and business. Human-centered computing → Field studies.

SIGMIS-CPR '17, June 21-23, 2017, Bangalore, India
© 2017 Association for Computing Machinery.
ACM ISBN 978-1-4503-5037-2/17/06...$15.00
http://dx.doi.org/10.1145/3084381.3084384

KEYWORDS

Computer/IT knowledge; IS security threats knowledge; self-control; information systems security deviant behavior; employee

ACM Reference format:

P. Ifinedo. 2017. Effects of Organization Insiders' Self-Control and Relevant Knowledge on Participation in Information Systems Security Deviant Behavior. In Proceedings of SIGMIS-CPR '17: 2017 Computers and People Research Conference
Proceedings
DOI:

1 INTRODUCTION

Organizations advocate acceptable computing behaviors through a variety of policies (e.g., ethical computer use policy, acceptable use policy, email use policy, social media policy). In the context of this study, deviant behaviors would be any practices or acts engaged by organizational members that diverge from recommended guidelines and policies. Deviance relating to non-compliance with information systems (IS) security rules poses a serious risk to organizational data assets [1-3]. Oftentimes, organizations across the world spend millions of dollars to control IS security threats posed by employees who are seen as a major concern in the IS security chain [1-7]. To this end, research on employee IS security misbehavior is both topical and necessary.

Information systems security deviant behavior (ISSDB) refers to sanctioned practices related to the volitional use of computing technologies and general information systems security misbehaviors that are contrary to the legitimate interests of an organization. ISSDB encapsulates deviant computer-related misbehaviors with benign intentions (e.g., opening emails from unverified senders and using generic and unencrypted USBs on an organization's network) and does not include unintentional actions such as accidental data entry or intentional malicious computer security practices (e.g., data sabotage and theft) [1-4]. Academicians and practitioners agree that ISSDB poses a serious threat to organizations [6-12].

The role of human agents in enabling information security threats and risks to organizational digital assets has been widely recognized [7,8,11,12]. In fact, the human factor is considered the weakest link in terms of ensuring information systems (IS) security in organizations [7,8,12,13]. An exemplar of human agents is the organization insider who could pose a more dangerous threat to organizational information systems (IS) than outsiders' actions [8]. This is because insiders often have intimate knowledge of organizational informational assets because they use such systems for routine work activities [14]. Organization insiders are individuals (e.g., full-time and part-time employees) who have access to organizations' IS resources while fulfilling their duties [8]. While the IS security acts of organization insiders can be accidental or intentional [2,3], the impact of ill-advised practices or actions exert significant influence on the organizational IS security chain [8,10-12]. Others have discussed employees' malicious IS security behaviors [3]; however, the focus of this study is on benign deviant IS use misbehaviors.

Abundant information exists on organizational insiders engaging in ISSDB that place organizations' digital assets at risk [4-18]. For example, a survey of 443 IS/IT professionals reported that "twenty-five percent of respondents felt that over 60 percent of their organizations' financial losses were due to non-malicious actions by insiders" [11]. Inform Security Magazine [18] noted "58% information security incidents attributed to insider threat." These examples underscore the significance of the topic.

While several prior studies have focused mainly on employees' IS policy violations in organizations [7,13,14], misuse of IS resources [20,21], unethical IS use behavior [19], and illegal online computing behaviors [22], to date, not many have specifically examined the relationship between employees' self-control, knowledge of information technology (IT) resources, and IS security risks knowledge, on the one hand, and ISSDB, on the other. The current study is designed to fill this gap.

There is growing focus on ISSDB and related behavior [4-8,14] in the IS domain; some studies have used theories of crime and deviance. We accept that the use of theories likely to explain ISSDB and related behavior is welcome. One such theory pertinent to understanding and explaining deviant behaviors is Gottfredson and Hirschi's self-control theory [23]. The concept of self-control is popular among criminologists and recently, IS scholars researching IS security violations have drawn from it [14]. The premise of Gottfredson and Hirschi's theory is that deviant behaviors are likely to occur when individuals with low self-control are confronted with opportunities to participate in sanctioned activities [23-25]. Additionally, the literature indicates that individuals with low self-control were more likely to engage in ISSDB in work environments [22,25,26].

Intelligence and self-control are accepted by psychologists as two main traits that tend to produce a broad range of benefits [27]. By the same token, intelligence and knowledge are closely related concepts [28,29]. To add more insight to the discourse, employees' knowledge of relevant factors of value to this current inquiry is considered. Evidence suggests that individuals who possess adequate knowledge of computing, IT/IS resources [21,30-32], and IS security threats are less likely to facilitate security breaches in their organizations [33].

This current study contributes to the literature by modeling the influence of the aforementioned factors on employees' participation in ISSDB. To achieve our objective, self-control theory [23], which was complemented by knowledge of computer and IT resources as well as IS security threats, is used as the base of analysis. This study attempts to answer the following research questions: What is the effect of employees' self-control on participation in ISSDB? How does employees' knowledge of computers/IT and IS security threats influence desire to engage in ISSDB?

2 THEORY AND BACKGROUND INFORMATION

2.1 Self-control Theory

Gottfredson and Hirschi [23] developed a "general theory of crime" (also known as the self-control theory of crime) to explicate a wide range of criminal activities in society. This criminological theory posits that lack of individual self-control is the main factor behind criminal and deviance behavior. Self-control refers to an individually imposed ability to regulate a behavior. According to [23], low self-control is a characteristic that is established early in life and remains relatively stable throughout the lifetime of an individual. Gottfredson and Hirschi also suggested individuals with low self-control are likely to commit acts of deviance and crime-analogous behavior. On the other hand, individuals with high self-control tend to consider the long-term consequences of their behavior [23] and display good behavioral adjustment [34].

Longshore et al. [35] found that it is possible to create and obtain valid measures of an individual's self-control level using self-reported attitudinal measures. Drawing from Gottfredson and Hirschi's theory, Grasmick et al. [24] developed a six-factor attitudinal low self-control scale encapsulated by 24 items. These researchers found that the six dimensions, specifically, impulsivity, simple tasks, risk taking, physical activities, self-centeredness, and temper, constituted an invariant, multidimensional, low self-control trait. The 24 response categories used anchors of 1 = strongly disagree and 4 = strongly agree. The scale had a range of 24 to 96 with higher scores on the scale indicating lower self-control (this information is important in understanding the data analysis results).

Past researchers [e.g., 36] have employed selected elements of Grasmick et al.'s scale. This study will use 5 of their dimensions which are represented by 3 items that best capture the essence of each dimension. The component of physical activities on the scale was excluded as it was not deemed relevant for this study. Namely, participation in ISSDB requires a mental and not a physical effort. Grasmick et al.'s dimensions and items used for the study are shown in Table 1. Pratt and Cullen's [37] meta-analysis of past studies that used Gottfredson and Hirschi's theory demonstrated that regardless of the type of low self-control measure used, the theory explains considerable variation in criminal and deviant behaviors. Researchers across diverse disciplines found that low levels of self-control correlated with undesirable and deviant behaviors [14,37,38]. It is worth noting that self-control theory has been used to explain deviant behavior such as information security violations [14].

Table 1: Dimensions of attitudinal indicators of self-control

Dimension	Item	Description
Impulsivity	Imp1	I often act on impulse (spur of the moment) without stopping to think.
	Imp2	I often do whatever brings me pleasure here and now, even at the cost of some distant goal.
	Imp3	I'm more concerned with what happens to me in the short run than in the long run.
Simple tasks	Sim1	I frequently try to avoid projects that I know will be difficult.
	Sim2	The things in life that are easiest to do bring me the most pleasure.
	Sim3	I dislike really hard tasks that stretch my abilities to the limit.
Risk taking	Ris1	I like to test myself every now and then by doing something a little risky.
	Ris2	Sometimes I will take a risk just for the fun of it.
	Ris3	Excitement and adventure are more important to me than security.
Selfcentered ness	Sel1	I try to look out for myself first, even if it means making things difficult for other people.
	Sel2	I will try to get things I want even when I know it's causing problems for other people.
	Sel3	I'm not very sympathetic to other people, even when they are having problems.
Temper	Tem1	I lose my temper pretty easily.
	Tem2	When I am really angry, other people better stay away from me.
	Tem3	When I have a serious disagreement with someone, it's usually hard for me to talk calmly about it without getting upset.

2.2 Knowledge of Relevant Factors

Knowledge refers to facts and information acquired by an individual through education or experience. Attewell's [39] theory of IT diffusion and organizational learning suggests that organizations lacking internal IT knowledge resources will struggle with new technological ideas and products. In particular, research has shown that general knowledge of computers and IT is important for achieving success with complex systems (e.g., enterprise systems) [31] and computer skills correlated with technology misuse [21]. Similarly, knowledge of IS security threats and risks, which workers sometimes acquire from security awareness programs, boded well for organizational well-being [20,34]. For example, PCI Data Security Standard [40] noted that it is "vital that organizations have a security awareness program in place to ensure employees are aware of the importance of protecting sensitive information, what they should do to handle information securely, and the risks of mishandling information."

2.3 Information Systems Security Deviant Behavior (ISSDB)

Various taxonomies of individual IS security behaviors have been suggested [1-3,5-8]. This study draws mainly from Loch et al. [1] who identified sources of information security threats to an organization, and Stanton et al. [2] who proposed a taxonomy of end-user security risk behaviors. The latter categorized IS security threats as either malicious or non-malicious. As indicated, ISSDB excludes malicious end-user security risk behaviors. It compares with Weatherbee's counterproductive technology use behavior [22], Posey et al.'s protection-motivated behaviors [8], and Chu and Chau's information security deviant behavior [5]. For illustration purposes, this study utilizes a small list of commonly practiced ISSDB (Figure 1) sourced from practitioners' reports and academicians' studies [5,8-12,41,42]. Three IS professors' and four IS security experts' opinions were sought in selecting the ten items used for the study. Namely, items #1 to #7 came from [41]; #8 and #9 were taken from [42], and #10 was sourced from [5]. To a large degree, more recent practitioners' reports and academic studies in the area offer support for relevance of the selected ISSDB items [8,10,12].

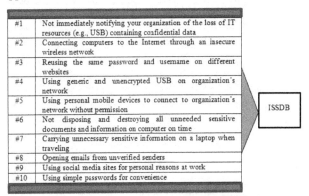

Figure 1: ISSDB Items Used for the Study.

3 RESEARCH MODEL AND HYPOTHESES

The study's research model, which includes relevant control variables, is shown in (Figure 2). Past studies show that variables such as age [21], gender [43], education [44], profession [45], and organization size [12,41] have effects on employees' counterproductive use of IT in work settings.

In any organization, deviant behavior is likely to occur when individuals with low self-control are presented with the opportunity to commit deviant behavior [35-38,46]. Contrastingly, employees with high self-control tend to avoid behaviors that are inconsistent with organizational aspirations and goals [34]. Gottfredson and Hirschi [23] found that individuals with low self-control have a tendency to respond to tangible stimuli in the immediate environment and are less likely to consider the long-term consequences of their actions. With respect to ISSDB, researchers have shown that individuals with low self-control were more likely to engage in the counterproductive use of information and communication technologies (ICT) at work [24,26,38]. Higgins et al. [38] and others [47] found that individuals with low self-control were more likely to engage in activities such as digital piracy and computer crime. Using techniques from cognitive neuroscience, Hu et al. [14] demonstrated that individuals with low self-control were more likely to violate IS security guidelines.

H1: Low self-control will be positively related to participation in ISSDB.

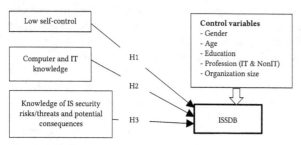

Figure 2: Research model.

Employees with adequate skills and knowledge of computing and IT resources may possess sufficient information regarding what to do or not do with such technologies in work environments. Knowledge of computing technologies, for those possessing such, would enable them to have general understanding of the sorts of problems that could arise when these tools are not used properly. Studies by Torkzadeh and Lee [32] and Ifinedo [30] indicated the existence of a positive relationship between employees' computer/IT knowledge and the effectiveness of enterprise-wide business applications. Research on employee misuse of IT technology resources that showed workers with lower levels of computer skills [21] and IT knowledge [48] were more likely to engage in such misbehavior. Thus, it is predicted that employees possessing low levels of computer/IT knowledge will be more likely to participate in ISSDB.

H2: Lower levels of computer and IT knowledge will be negatively related to participation in ISSDB.

Employees possessing a good knowledge of general IS security threats and risks are considered valuable assets in any organization [2,9-12]. Individuals with high levels of moral

values [49] and self-regulation [21] relating to acceptable IS security norms have a high degree of security compliance and knowledge. In most cases, workers are provided with competent knowledge of IS security risks and threats through enterprise-wide security education, training, and awareness (SETA) programs. In short, it is reasonable to believe that employees possessing sufficient know-how of IS security threats and risks are more likely to understand the consequences of their IS security actions and would be less likely to engage in ISSDB and similar misbehavior [20,50,51]. It is possible that workers with low levels of knowledge in such matters may knowingly or unknowingly engage in ISSDB. Past studies confirmed that individuals with high IS security capabilities and competence tend to follow organizational IS security guidelines and seem to understand the dangers of noncompliance [43,48,52]. It is argued that employees lacking knowledge of IS security risks and threats and their   potential consequences on organizational IS assets will more likely participate in ISSDB.

H3: Lower levels of knowledge of IS security risks and threats and their potential consequences will be negatively related to participation in ISSDB.

4   RESEARCH METHODOLOGY

4.1 Study Design and Procedure

To validate the research model, a field survey was used. Pre-test and pilot surveys were conducted to enhance the content and face validities of the measuring items used. This main study used the services of a market research firm to collect data from panelists. Other IS researchers [e.g., 48,53] used the same approach for data collection to circumvent difficulty in obtaining information-security information from organizations [54], among other reasons Full-time employees of organizations were targeted by the company. Panelists were notified of the purpose of the study and participation was voluntary. Information from the research company showed that 661 panelists were invited to participate in the study and 346 responded (52.3%). Poorly completed responses were excluded from subsequent data analysis. In all, 218 responses were used for the study to give an effective response rate of 32.9%. The sample size compares with those of similar studies [53].

4.2 Demographic Characteristics of the Sample

Both sexes are represented in the sample; 111 are males (51%) and 106 are females (49%) with many of them having bachelor (41%) and post-graduate degrees (12%). In the sample, 36%, 24%, and 17% of respondents were in the 21 to 30, 31 to 40, and 51 to 60 age ranges, respectively. The data has a few missing cases.

The participants' average years of computer use is 20.1 years (standard deviations [S.D.] = 7.9) and they have 3.1 years (S.D. = 1.3) tenure at their current organizations. The sample has 65 IT professionals (30%) and 147 non-IT professionals (67%). Some of the participants' job titles include distribution manager, operations manager, IT manager, and senior IT analyst. Diverse industries such as IT, manufacturing, retail, and healthcare were included in the sample. The data sample includes an even distribution of organization size and annual revenue. 76 (35%) respondents are from organizations with less than 100 employees and 53 (24%) participants are from organizations with 2500 workers and above.

Given the survey data collected both independent and dependent data from the same source, common method variance (CMV) cannot be ruled out. CMV refers to a bias in the dataset due to something external to the measures used in the study. Procedural remedies recommended by Podsakoff et al. [55] to reduce the effects of CMV were followed. CMV was not a problem for the collected data.

4.3 Study's Constructs

As already indicated, items used to represent the ISSDB construct (Table 2) were taken from the following sources: [5,8-12,41,42]. The study's participants were asked the question: "Please indicate how often you participate in the ISSDB listed [in Figure 1]." Their responses were assessed on a seven-point Likert scale ranging from "Almost never" (1) to "Almost always" (7). Items used to operationalize the attitudinal indicators of low self-control were taken from Grasmick et al.'s [24] scale. The measuring items were assessed on a seven-point Likert scale ranging from "Strongly disagree" (1) to "Strongly agree" (7).

To assess employees' knowledge of computers and IT, this study used a similar question asked in a prior study in the area [48], i.e., "How would you rate your knowledge of computers and information technologies (IT)?" Similarly, a single item adapted from [56] was used to assess employees' knowledge of IS security threats and risks, and their potential consequences. They were asked: "How would you rate your knowledge of IS security risks and threats and their potential consequences on organizational IS resources"? Participants provided responses on a seven-point Likert scale ranging from "Very low" (1) to "Very high" (7) for these two questions. Following recommendations in structural equation modeling studies for categorizing research constructs [57], the constructs of ISSDB and low self-control were modeled as formative constructs in this study. The other variables in the research model are single-item reflective constructs.

Table 2: ISSDB items, descriptive statistics, and validity tests

Item no.	Mean	SD	Weight	p-value	VIF
#1	1.950	1.669	0.134	0.022	1.888
#2	2.106	1.706	0.146	0.014	2.064
#3	3.593	2.115	0.134	0.022	1.667
#4	2.604	1.958	0.153	0.010	1.880
#5	3.157	2.235	0.128	0.027	1.610
#6	2.452	1.848	0.158	0.009	2.072
#7	2.088	1.700	0.152	0.011	2.150
#8	2.235	1.679	0.164	0.007	2.496
#9	2.851	2.061	0.127	0.029	1.520
#10	2.982	1.830	0.122	0.033	1.484

Note: Please see Figure 1 for description of item #s.

5 DATA ANALYSIS

The Partial Least Squares (PLS) technique, which utilizes a principle component-based for estimation, was used for analysis [58]. PLS was selected mainly because it has the capacity to accurately measure formative constructs. This study used WarpPLS 5.0 software to conduct PLS analysis; this software supports both linear and nonlinear relationships in an integrative manner and the software provides useful information needed to assess the validity of formative constructs [59]. In general, PLS recognizes two components of a casual model: the measurement and structural models.

5.1 Measurement Model

It is not customary to provide reliability and validity indicators for single-item constructs (recall some of the study's antecedents have one item). That noted, information on the study's main variables (i.e., the formative constructs) are provided. Due to the nature of formative constructs, their validity and reliability are assessed differently from reflective constructs' [57,60]. Among the tests recommended are examination of weights and the presence of multicollinearity. Items weights show how significantly linked item indicators are to their specified constructs. Excessive collinearity within formative scales is undesirable as it can make the construct unstable [60]. To assess multicollinearity among the variables, the variance inflation factors (VIF) are checked. VIFs below the conservative cutoff of 3.33 are considered adequate [57].

WarpPLS 5.0 provides information on VIF and item weights. Table 2 shows that VIFs and item weights used to capture ISSDB are satisfactory. All the VIFs are below 3.33 and the weights are significant at p <0.05 level. For the low self-control construct, we created a superordinate second order factor by using the factor scores of first order factors (e.g., impulsivity, simple tasks, risk taking). The results shown in Figure 3 reveal the weights of formative indicators are significantly linked with the low self-control construct and the VIFs are below the recommended 3.3 threshold as well. These tests show that items used to gauge the validity and reliability of the formative constructs are adequate.

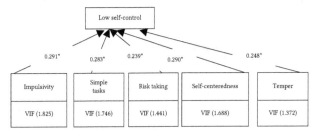

Figure 3. Formative nature of Low self-control.

Table 3: Inter-construct correlations.

Construct	ISSDB	Self-control	knowCIT	knowRisk
ISSDB	1	0.636	-0.093	0.077
Self-control	0.636	1	-0.185	-0.028
knowCIT	-0.093	-0.185	1	0.132
knowRisk	0.077	-0.028	0.132	1

Note: knowCIT = knowledge of computers and IT; knowRisk = knowledge of IS security risks and threats and their potential consequences

Furthermore, evidence of construct validity is provided via inter-construct correlations among the study's constructs (Table 3). The entries show that multicollinearity was not a problem for the model's formative and reflective constructs.

5.2 Structural Model

The standardized PLS path coefficients are shown in Figure 4. The results show that the main constructs and control variables explained 49% of the variance in the hypothesized model. Falk and Miller [58] recommended a minimum value of 0.10 (10%) and according to Chin [59], R2 of 0.20 (20%) implies substantive influence. The explained variance of the study is above the noted thresholds to indicate the proposed research model is of value.

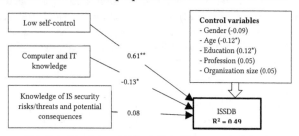

Note: * significant at p < 0.05 level; ** significant at p < 0.001 level

Figure 4. Results of PLS Analysis for the Model.

WarpPLS 5.0 also provides information on Goodness of Fit (GoF) and Predictive relevance (Q2). The former is a global fit measure that accounts for both measurement and structural model performance [60]. The GoF obtained for this study is 0.66, which is above the cut-off value of 0.36 for large effect sizes [61]. Predictive relevance (Q2) represents a synthesis of function fitting and cross-validation that determines the capacity of the model to predict. Q2 values greater than zero indicate that the observed values are appropriately reconstructed and have predictive relevance. Similarly, values below zero signify a lack of predictive relevance [62]. The Q2 of the independent variables on the dependent construct is 0.488.

Consistent with H1, low self-control was found to be positively related to participation in ISSDB (β = 0.61, p <0.001). Support was found for H2, which predicted that lower levels of computer

and IT knowledge would be negatively related to participation in ISSDB (β = -0.13, p <0.05). Lower levels of knowledge of IS security risks and threats and their potential consequences was not found to be negatively related to participation in ISSDB (β = 0.08, p = 0.10). The data also showed that younger workers (β = -0.12, p <0.05) and more educated employees (β = 0.12, p <0.05) are more likely to participate in ISSDB.

6 DISCUSSIONS AND CONCLUSION

The objective of this study was to examine the effects of employee self-control, knowledge of computers/IT, knowledge of IS security risks and threats, and their potential consequences on participation in ISSDB. It is important to stress that this study is not designed to establish a cause-and-effect relationships. The results show that low self-control has a significant positive effect on engagement in ISSDB. That is, employees with low self-control are more likely to participate in ISSDB. This result is consistent with established views suggesting that individuals with low self-control are more likely to commit deviant behavior [23,24], engage in digital piracy [38,63], and participate in ICT use misbehavior at work [25,26,47]. The result affirmed the prediction indicating that employees possessing lower levels of knowledge of computers and IT are more likely to engage in ISSDB. This result is in agreement with past research that showed that misuse of IT resources are higher among individuals with lower levels of computer skills and IT knowledge [21,48].

The data did not provide support for the prediction indicating that employees with lower levels of knowledge of IS security risks and threats and their potential consequences would have greater tendency to participate in ISSDB. A plausible explanation for the lack of support for this hypothesis might be due to extraneous influences. Evidence exists to show that very knowledgeable employees working in IT companies participate in ISSDB and similar misbehavior to suggest that an understanding of IS threats and risks may not be a sufficient factor that dissuades participation in such behavior. For example, a report by Cisco Systems [15,16] found that about 80% of their employees engage in inappropriate e-mail practices that could cost organizations dearly. Additionally, research has also shown that knowledgeable employees even use various neutralization mechanisms and techniques to flout compliance with IS security guidelines and rules [64].

6.1 Structural Model Study's Contributions and Implications

This study is the first of its kind to examine factors likely to motivate employees' participation in ISSDB with its use of self-control and relevant knowledge factors. Given that non-malicious IS-related counterproductive behaviors scarcely garner a mention in the literature [5,7,22] its contribution to the literature in this area is welcome. Unlike prior studies [e.g., 5,6,8] of ISSDB that offered taxonomies for classifying such behaviors, this study took one step further by examining factors that influence such behavior.

This study offers both theoretical and practical implications for understanding employees' urge to engage in ISSDB. It provides empirical support for Gottfredson and Hirschi's self-control theory of crime and lends support for its suitability in studying ICT misuse and deviant behavior [14,25,37,38,47]. By drawing from self-control theory, this study has contributed to the debate regarding what motivates employees to engage in ISSDB and similar behavior; something academicians and practitioners have vigorously questioned. Likewise, the results from this study offer support for Attewell's theory of IT diffusion and organizational learning insofar as our results suggest that organizational actors' knowledge of computers and IT help decrease desire to engage in ISSDB.

Other researchers could be enticed to further explore the phenomenon of ISSDB, either from our perspective or by incorporating other relevant concepts from theoretical frameworks pertinent to the topic. Deeper knowledge in the area may lead to the emergence of a process-oriented analysis (i.e., step-by-step courses of action to follow) of potential cognitive and attitudinal factors that could be understood in trying to curb such behaviors.

With respect to this study's practical benefits, managers could use the instrument or scale used for this study to screen employees' moral attitude and self-control. Those identified to have lower scores on the scale could be provided with reinforced SETA programs or offered incentives (i.e., monetary or otherwise) to help modify their behavior regarding acceptable measures and practices that protect organizational digital assets. Others have suggested that such measures could bear useful fruits [20,50,51]. At the same time, Hu et al. [14] commented that using a psychological instrument to screen employees for the purpose of job assignment is a sensitive matter. Given the critical importance of computer and IT knowledge, management could regularly promote company-wide training and sessions to improve employees' computer and IT competence, especially as it relates to acceptable ICT use behaviors.

Another important conclusion is that the control measures – gender, profession, and organization size - were insignificant in the research model. However, age and educational attainment mattered. More focused attention and special monitoring could be given to cohorts of workers likely to engage in ISSDB and similar unsanctioned computer security practices in work environments. The provision of psychological counselling and therapy, e.g., Employee Assistance Program (EAP), for employees could be explored for those found to be deficient in acceptable IS use behavior [66].

In general, the present study helps management understand more about employees' desires to participate in ISSDB. To reduce the occurrence of ISSDB in organizations, managers should develop policies and programs that can curb employees' desire to engage in ISSBD. This study has provided initial insights in that aspect. Security specialists and practitioners can also use the information provided in this study to develop specific technological innovations and applications that remind workers with low self-control and knowledge of computing risks about the potential dangers of ill-sanctioned practices to organizational IS assets and resources.

6.2 Study's Limitations and Future Research Avenues

Although this study's findings offer valuable information about what drives participation in ISSDB, the study still has limits. First, as the study employed only the views of employees, it is difficult to know whether the findings are generalizable to all human agents, e.g., part-time workers and consultants. Second, the number of measures used to represent some of the study's constructs could be increased. The use of single-item constructs is limiting. Third, the data came from a cross-sectional field survey; longitudinal data may facilitate more insight. Fourth, the data was obtained from practitioners based in a developed country; perceptions of IS security threats and control vary by nations. Despite the limitations reported, the study still offers benefits to research and practice.

Future studies should endeavor to overcome the shortcomings associated with this present study. Attention should be paid to other end-user security behaviors, such as malicious ISSDB, in future studies. Other theoretical perspectives (e.g., protection motivation theory) could be fused with self-control theory to deepen insight. Perceptions of IT/IS issues differ by organizational hierarchies. To that end, future studies could compare views across hierarchies to deepen understanding of what motivates ISSDB and related behaviors among workers.

ACKNOWLEDGMENTS

This study was supported by a research grant received from Cape Breton University, Canada. The author is grateful for helpful comments and suggestions provided by two anonymous reviewers of an earlier version of the paper.

REFERENCES

[1] Loch, K. D., Carr, H. H., and Warkentin, M. E. 1992. Threats to information systems: today's reality, yesterday's understanding. *MIS Quart.* 16, 2, 173-186. DOI= https://doi.org/10.2307/249574
[2] Stanton, J. M., Stam, K. R, Mastrangelo, P., and Jolton, J. 2005. Analysis of end user security behaviors. *Comput Secur.* 24, 2, 124-133. DOI= https://doi.org/10.1016/j.cose.2004.07.001
[3] Willison, R., and Warkentin, M. 2013. Beyond deterrence: an expanded view of employee computer abuse. *MIS Quart.* 37, 1, 1-20.
[4] Ifinedo, P. 2015. Effects of organizational citizenship behavior and social cognitive factors on employees' non-malicious counterproductive computer security behaviors: an empirical analysis. In *Proceedings of International Conference on Information Resources Management (Conf-IRM)*, May 18-20, 2015, Ottawa, Canada.
[5] Chu, A.M.Y., and Chau, P.Y.K. 2014. Development and validation of instruments of information security deviant behavior. *Decis Support Syst.* 66, 93-101. DOI= https://doi.org/10.1016/j.dss.2014.06.008
[6] Guo, K. H. 2013. Security-related behavior in using information systems in the workplace: a review and synthesis. *Comput Secur.* 32, 242-251. DOI= https://doi.org/10.1016/j.cose.2012.10.003
[7] Guo, K. H., Yufei, Y., Archer, N. P., and Connelly, C.E. 2011. Understanding nonmalicious security violations in the workplace: a composite behavior model. *J Manage Inform Syst.* 28, 2, 203–236. DOI= https://doi.org/10.2753/mis0742-1222280208
[8] Posey, C., Roberts, C. L., Lowry, P. B., Bennett, R. J., and Courtney, J. F. 2013. Insiders' protection of organizational information assets: development of a systematics-based taxonomy and theory of diversity for protection-motivated behaviors. *MIS Quart.* 37, 4, 1189-1210.
[9] Verizon Business Systems. 2011. *2011 Data Breach Investigations Report.* Verizon RISK Team Research Report, Verizon Communications, New York, NY.
[10] Verizon Business Systems. 2016. *2016 Data Breach Investigations Report.* Verizon RISK Team Research Report, Verizon Communications, New York, NY.
[11] Richardson, R. 2012. *CSI Computer Crime and Security Survey 2010/2011.* Computer Security Institute, New York. Http://gocsi.com/survey/, accessed 12 August 2014.
[12] Ponemon Institute 2014. *2013 Cost of Cyber Crime Study: United States.* http://media.scmagazine.com/documents/54/2013_us_ccc_report_final_6-1_13455.pdf, 2014.

[13] Ifinedo, P. 2014. Information systems security policy compliance: an empirical study of the effects of socialisation, influence, and cognition. *Inform Manage.* 51, 1, 69-79. DOI= http://dx.doi.org/10.1016/j.im.2013.10.001

[14] Hu, Q., West, R., and Smarandescu, L. 2015. The role of self-control in information security violations: insights from a cognitive neuroscience perspective. *J Manage Inform Syst.* 31, 4, 6-48. DOI=https://doi.org/10.1080/07421222.2014.1001255

[15] Cisco Systems. 2008a. *Cisco Study on Remote Workers Reveals Need for Greater Diligence Toward Security.* http://newsroom.cisco.com/dlls/2008/prod_020508.html, accessed June 22, 2015.

[16] Cisco Systems. 2008b. *Data Leakage Worldwide: Common Risks and Mistakes Employees Make.* Cisco Systems, Inc., San Jose, CA.

[17] Cisco Systems. 2011. Cisco Connected World Technology Report. Cisco Systems, Inc., San Jose, CA.

[18] Inform Security Magazine, 2013. News. *58% Information Security Incidents Attributed to Insider Threat.* http://www.infosecurity-magazine.com/view/32222/58-information-security-incidents-attributed-to-insider-threat-, accessed Dec. 24, 2016.

[19] Leonard, L. N. K., and Cronan, T. P. 2001. Illegal, inappropriate, and unethical behavior in an information technology context: a study to explain influences. *J Assoc Inf Syst.* 1, 1, Article 12. DOI= https://doi.org/10.1016/j.im.2003.12.008

[20] D'Arcy, J., Hovav, A., and Galletta, D. 2009. User awareness of security countermeasures and its impact on information systems misuse: a deterrence approach. *Inform Syst Res.* 20(1), 79-98. DOI= https://doi.org/10.1287/isre.1070.0160

[21] D'Arcy, J. P. and Devaraj, S. 2012. Employee misuse of information technology resources: testing a contemporary deterrence model. *Decision Sci.* 43, 6. 1091-1124. DOI= https://doi.org/10.1111/j.1540-5915.2012.00383.x

[22] Weatherbee, T.G. 2010. Counterproductive use of technology at work: information & communications technologies and cyberdeviancy. *Hum Resour Manage R.* 20, 1. 35-44. DOI= https://doi.org/10.1016/j.hrmr.2009.03.012

[23] Gottfredson, M., and Hirschi, T. (Eds.)1990. *A General Theory of Crime.* Stanford University Press, CA.

[24] Grasmick, H., Tittle, G., Bursik Jr., R., and Arneklev, B. 1993. Testing the core implications of Gettfredson and Hirschi's general theory of crime. *J Res Crime Delinq.* 30, 1 (1993), 5–29. DOI= https://doi.org/10.1177/0022427893030001002

[25] Yellowees, P., & Marks, S. (2007). problematic internet use or internet addiction. *Comput Hum Behav.* 23, 1447–1453. DOI= https://doi.org/10.1016/j.chb.2005.05.004

[26] Wang, J. Tian, J., and Shen, Z. 2013. The effects and moderators of cyber-loafing controls: an empirical study of Chinese public servants. *Inf. Technol. Manage.* 14, 269-282. DOI= 10.1007/s10799-013-0164-y.

[27] Kyeyune, S. 2015. *Devotional Journal Living: Nuggets of Wisdom for Practical Living; Scrolling Through Sermons from My Daily Posting.* AuthorHouse, Bloomington, IN.

[28] Rolfhus, E. L., and Ackerman, P. L. 1999. Assessing individual differences in knowledge: knowledge, intelligence, and related traits. *J Educ Psychol.* 91, 3 (Sep 1999), 511-526. DOI= https://doi.org/10.1037//0022-0663.91.3.511

[29] Muammar, O. M. 2015. Intelligence and Self-Control Predict Academic Performance of Gifted and Non-gifted Students. *Turkish J of Giftedness and Education.* 5, 1, 67-81.

[30] Ifinedo, P. 2011. Internal IT knowledge and expertise as antecedents of ERP system effectiveness: an empirical investigation. *J Org Comp Elect Com.* 21, 1, 1-23.

[31] Lazar, J., Jones, A., Hackley, M., Shneiderman, B., 2006. Severity and impact of computer user frustration: a comparison of student and workplace users. *Interact Comput.* 18, 2, 187–207. DOI= https://doi.org/10.1016/j.intcom.2005.06.001

[32] Torkzadeh, G., and Lee, J. W., 2003. Measures of perceived end-user's computing skills. *Inform Manage.* 40, 7, 607–615. DOI= https://doi.org/10.1016/s0378-7206(02)00090-3

[33] Whitman, M. E. 2004. In defense of the realm: Understanding the threats to information security. *Inform Manage.* 24, 1 43–57. DOI= https://doi.org/10.1016/j.ijinfomgt.2003.12.003

[34] Tangney, J. P., Baumeister, R. F., and Boone, A. L. 2004. High self-control predicts good adjustment, less pathology, better grades, and interpersonal success. *J Pers.* 271-324. DOI= https://doi.org/10.1111/j.0022-3506.2004.00263.x

[35] Longshore, Douglas and Susan Turner. 1998. Self-control and criminal opportunity: cross-sectional test of the general theory of crime. *Crim Justice Behav.* 25, 81-98. DOI= https://doi.org/10.1177/0093854898025001005

[36] Burton, V. S., T. Evans, T. D. Cullen, F. T., Olivares, K. M., and Dunaway, R. G. 1999. Age, self-control, and adults' offending behaviors: a research note assessing a general theory of crime. *J Crim Just.* 27, 45-54. DOI= https://doi.org/10.1016/s0047-2352(98)00035-x

[37] Pratt, T. C., and Cullen, F. T. 2000. The empirical status of Gottfredson and Hirschi's general theory of crime: a meta-analysis. *Criminology*, 38, 931-964. DOI= https://doi.org/10.1111/j.1745-9125.2000.tb00911.x

[38] Higgins, G., Wolfe, S., & Marcum, C. 2008. Digital piracy: an examination of three measurements of self-control. *Deviant Behav.* 29, 5, 440–460. DOI= https://doi.org/10.1080/01639620701598023

[39] Attewell, P., 1992. Technology diffusion and organizational learning: the case of business computing. *Organ Sci.* 3, 1, 1–19. DOI= https://doi.rg/10.1287/orsc.3.1.1

[40] PCI Data Security Standard. 2014. *Information Supplement: Best Practices for Implementing a Security Awareness Program.* https://www.pcisecuritystandards.org/documents/PCI_DSS_V1.0_Best_Practices_for_Implementing_Security_Awareness_Program.pdf, accessed Dec. 2, 2016.

[41] Ponemon Institute, 2012. *The Human Factor in Data Protection.* http://www.ponemon.org/local/upload/file/The_Human_Factor_in_data_Protection_WP_FINAL.pdf, accessed Dec. 14, 2016.

[42] Blue Coat Systems, Inc. (2015). *Research Shows Workers Ignoring Known Cyber Risks, Surfing Adult Content and Downloading Unapproved Apps.* https://www.bluecoat.com/company/press-releases/research-shows-workers-ignoring-known-cyber-risks-surfing-adult-content-and, accessed Nov 4, 2016.

[43] Herath, T., and Rao, H. R. 2009. Protection motivation and deterrence: a framework for security policy compliance in organizations. *Eur J Inform Syst.* 18, 2, 106-125. DOI= https://doi.org/10.1057/ejis.2009.6

[44] Zhang, Y. 2005. Age, gender, and Internet attitudes among employees in the business world. *Comput Hum Behav.* 21, 1–10. DOI= https://doi.org/10.1016/j.chb.2004.02.006

[45] Lee, Y., & Larsen, K. R. (2009). Threat or coping appraisal: determinants of SMB executives' decision to adopt anti-malware software. *Eur J Inform Syst.* 18, 2, 177-187. DOI= https://doi.org/10.1057/ejis.2009.11

[46] Vazsonyi, A. T., L. E. Pickering, M. Junger, and D. Hessing. 2001. An empirical test of a general theory of crime: a four-nation comparative study of self-control and the prediction of deviance. *J Res Crime Delinq.* 38, 91-131. DOI= https://doi.org/10.1177/0022427801038002001

[47] Zhang, L., Smith, W.W., and McDowell, W.C. 2009. Examining digital piracy: self-control, punishment, and self-efficacy. *Inform Resources Manage J.* 22, 1, 24–44. DOI= https://doi.org/10.4018/irmj.2009010102

[48] Bulgurcu, B., Cavusoglu, H., and Benbasat, I. 2010. Information security policy compliance: An empirical study of rationality-based beliefs and information security awareness. *MIS Quart.* 34, 3, 523-548.

[49] Boss, S. R., Kirsch, L. J., Angermeier, I., Shingler, R. A., and Boss, R. W. 2009. If someone is watching, I'll do what I'm asked: mandatoriness, control, and information security, *Eur J Inform Syst.*18, 2, 151-164. DOI= https://doi.org/10.1057/ejis.2009.8

[50] Hight. S. D. 2005. The importance of a security, education, training and awareness program. http://www.infosecwriters.com/Papers/SHight_SETA.pdf, accessed Dec. 12, 2016.

[51] Stephanou, T., and Dagada, R. 2009. The impact of information security awareness training on information security behaviour: the case of further research. In *Proceedings ISSA 2008 Conference* (Johannesburg, 2 - 4 July 2008). University of Johannesburg, South Africa.

[52] Ifinedo, P. 2012. Understanding information systems security policy compliance: an integration of the theory of planned behavior and the protection motivation theory. *Comput Secur.* 31, 1, 83-95. DOI= http://dx.doi.org/10.1016/j.cose.2011.10.007

[53] D'Arcy, J., Herath, T., and Shoss, M. K. 2014. Understanding employee responses to stressful information security requirements: a coping perspective. *J Manage Inform Syst.* 31, 2, 285–318. DOI= https://doi.org/10.2753/mis0742-1222310210

[54] Kotulic, A. G., and Clark J. G. 2004. Why there aren't more information security research studies. *Inform Manage.* 41, 5, 597-607. DOI= https://doi.org/10.1016/j.im.2003.08.001

[55] Podsakoff, P. M., MacKenzie, S. B., Lee, J. Y., and Podsakoff, N. P. 2003. Common method biases in behavioral research: a critical review of the literature and recommended remedies. *J Appl Psychol.* 88, 5, 879-903. DOI= https://doi.org/10.1037/0021-9010.88.5.879

[56] Blythe, J. M. Coventry, L., and Little, L. 2015. Unpacking security policy compliance: the motivators and barriers of employees' security behaviors. In *Proceedings of the Eleventh Symposium on Usable Privacy and Security (SOUPS 2015),* Carleton University, Ottawa, Canada.

[57] MacKenzie, S., Podsakoff, P., & Podsakoff, N. (2011). Construct measurement and validation procedures in mis and behavioral research: integrating new and existing techniques. *MIS Quart.* 35, 2, 293-334.

[58] Falk, R., and Miller, N. B. 1992. A Primer for Soft-Modeling. University of Akron, Ackron, Ohio.

[59] Chin, W. 1998. Issues and opinion on structural equation modeling. *MIS Quart.* 22, 1, vii-xvi.

[60] Tenenhaus, M., Vinzi V. E., Chatelin ,Y.-M., and Lauro C. 2005. PLS path modeling. *Comput Stat Data An.* 48 1, 159–205. DOI= https://doi.org/10.1016/j.csda.2004.03.005

[61] Wetzels, M., Odekerken-Schroder, M. G. and Van Oppen, C. 2009. Using PLS path modeling for assessing hierarchical construct models: guidelines and empirical illustration. *MIS Quart.* 33, 1, 177-196.

[62] Kock, N. (2014) Advanced mediating effects tests, multi-group analyses, and measurement model assessments in PLS-based SEM. ScriptWarp Systems, Laredo, TX.

[63] Higgins, G. E. 2007. Digital piracy, self-control theory, and rational choice: an examination of the role of value. *Int J Cyber Crim.* 1, 1, 33-55.

[64] Siponen, M., A., and Vance, A. 2010. Neutralization: new insights into the problem of employee information systems security policy violations. *MIS Quart.* 34, 3, 487-502.

Managing Security in Organizations:
Adoption of Information Security Solutions

Work In Progress[†]

Tejaswini C. Herath*
Department of Finance, Operations
and Information Systems,
Goodman School of Business,
322 Taro Hall, 500 Glenridge Avenue,
St. Catharines, Ontario, Canada L2S
3A1, therath@brocku.ca

Hemantha S. B. Herath
Department of Accounting,
Goodman School of Business,
240 Taro Hall, 500 Glenridge Avenue,

St. Catharines, Ontario, Canada L2S
3A1, hherath@brocku.ca

John D'Arcy
Department of Accounting & MIS
Alfred Lerner College of Business and
Economics
University of Delaware
jdarcy@udel.edu

ABSTRACT

We develop an integrative model grounded in two theoretical perspectives – the diffusion of innovation theory and the technology–organization–environment framework - to examine the diffusion of information security solutions (ISS) in organizations. We specify four innovation characteristics that are specific to ISS (compatibility, complexity, costs, and relative advantage), two organizational factors (organizational readiness and top management support), and two environmental factors (external pressure and visibility) as drivers of ISS diffusion.

The model will be tested using data collected through survey questionnaires. We hope to share the results at the workshop in June.

KEYWORDS

Information Security, Diffusion, Adoption, Assimilation, Diffusion of Innovation, Technology Organization Environment

1 INTRODUCTION

Information security has become a major concern for information and communication technology (ICT) applications utilized worldwide and across industries. Although organizations initially considered the implementation and adoption of ICTs to create and maintain a competitive advantage, ICTs soon became a necessity for organizations' day-to-day operations [1, 2]. Many cyber security experts argue that the need to be proactive and vigilant in protecting against cyber threats has never been

greater [3, 4]. Effective cyber security encompasses the three elements of the cyber ecosystem – people, technology and policy - and necessitates security practices that are understandable and usable [5]. These security best practices include use of security technologies and services, policies, and planning activities [6], which we collectively refer to in this paper as *Information Security Solutions* (ISS).

Although it is widely recognized that comprehensive security measures and best practices reduce information system vulnerabilities, the examination of adoption of ISS by organizations is just commencing. In this paper, we develop an integrative model of ISS diffusion grounded in two theoretical perspectives – the diffusion of innovation (DOI) theory [7], which emphasizes the characteristics of an innovation, and the technology–organization–environment (TOE) framework [8], which emphasizes the context of an innovation. We specify four innovation characteristics specific to ISS (compatibility, complexity, costs, and relative advantage), two organizational factors (organizational readiness and top management support) and two environmental factors (external pressure and visibility) as influences on the diffusion of ISS in organizations.

2 Theoretical Background

The classic theory of DOI [7, 9, 10] proposes relative advantage, compatibility, complexity, observability and trialability as five major characteristics that contribute to diffusion. Relative advantage is the degree to which an innovation can bring benefits to an organization; compatibility is the degree of consistency of the innovation with existing business processes, practices and value systems; complexity is the level of difficulty in using the innovation; observability is the extent of an innovation's visibility to others; and trialability is the degree to which an innovation may be experimented with. Moore and Benbasat [11] expanded this initial list to the IT context by generating eight factors (voluntariness, relative advantage, compatibility, image, ease of use, result demonstrability, visibility, and trialability) that impact the adoption of IT in organizations.

The TOE framework identifies three dimensions that influence organizational usage of a technological innovation: (1) technological context, which describes the existing technologies in use and relevant technical skills available in the organization; (2) organizational context, which refers to internal measures of the organization such as its size; and (3) environmental context, which is the external arena in which a company conducts its business – its industry, competitors and trading partners [8].

Our synthesis of the DOI theory and the TOE framework leads to the integrative model of ISS diffusion shown in Figure 1.

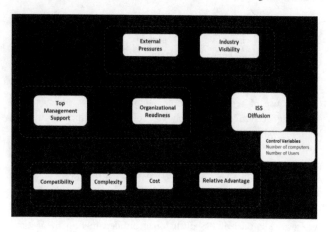

Figure 1: Theoretical Model of ISS Diffusion

3   Research Methodology

The data collection is in progress for empirical testing of the proposed model.

ACKNOWLEDGMENTS

This work was partially CGA Ontario Research Excellence Fund (CGAO REF) and CA Institute for International Issues in Accounting (IIIA).

REFERENCES

[1] Carr, N. G. IT doesn't matter. *Educause Review,* 38 (2003), 24-38.

[2] King, W. R. The "IT Deniers" Versus a Portfolio of IT Roles. *Information systems management,* 24, 2 (2007), 197-199.

[3] Paganini, P. *Cleaning up the Cyber Mess: Adopting Cyber Hygiene principles* SecurityAffairs, City, 2015.

[4] Center for Internet Security. City.

[5] Magnuson, S. *New Cyber Hygiene Campaign Seeks to Curtail Attacks.* City, 2014.

[6] Whitman, M. and Mattord, H. *Management of information security.* Cengage Learning, 2013.

[7] Rogers, E. M. Diffusion of innovations. *New York* (1995).

[8] Tornatzky, L. G., Fleischer, M. and Chakrabarti, A. K. *Processes of technological innovation.* Lexington Books, 1990.

[9] Rogers, E. M. Bibliography on the Diffusion of Innovations (1962).

[10] Zhu, K., Dong, S., Xu, S. X. and Kraemer, K. L. Innovation diffusion in global contexts: determinants of post-adoption digital transformation of European companies. *European journal of information systems,* 15, 6 (2006), 601-616.

[11] Moore, G. C. and Benbasat, I. Development of an instrument to measure the perceptions of adopting an information technology innovation. *Information Systems Research,* 2, 3 (1991), 192-222.

A Discursive Perspective on the Organizational Field Formation Process: Issues of Information Technology in Indian Healthcare

Full Paper

Mayank Kumar

Indian Institute of Management Tiruchirappalli

India-620015

mayank.f140203@iimtrichy.ac.in

ABSTRACT

This study examines the process through which a new organization field is formed around an issue and identifies the mechanism behind that process. Adopting a single case method and discourse analysis tool, it examines the field formation around an issue of Healthcare Information Technology (HIT) in the case of Indian healthcare. Based on the data collected from the secondary sources, the study finds that formation of a field around an issue follows the discursive process and organizational field is the discursive function of issue, power and subjectivity1.

KEYWORDS

Organizational field, HIT, Discourse, Indian healthcare

1 INTRODUCTION

Organizational field is the central construct of Institutional theory. An organizational field constitutes "*a recognized area of institutional life*" [1, p. 148] in which "*participants interact with one another more frequently and fatefully than with actors outside the field*" [2, p. 56]. Prior work on organizational field has focused on two aspects, formation of a new field [e.g. 3] and change of an established field [e.g. 4]. While the formation of new field means bringing together initially disparate organizations, change in a field means the change in the *composition* of the field [5]. Furthermore, while existing studies on both formation and change have been studied around industries and common technologies [4], attention has recently turned to study field dynamics around issues [6, 7]. Such changes in the study on organizational field draw attention to fields as arenas of struggle and conflict [8, 9] as they "become centers of debates in which competing interests negotiate over issue interpretation" [6, p.351]. [9] called such conceptualization of the field as the 'relational space' [10] and

advocated for the future study to look at "how do various disparate organizations come together to form a new field around an issue". This is the purpose of present study. The study examines the formation of field formation around an issue of Healthcare Information Technology (HIT) in Indian Healthcare to understand how did various disparate actors came together to form the field.

The study examines this field formation process and mechanisms behind this process using discourse analysis tool [11, 12] and finds that formation of field around an issue follows the discursive process. The study uses discourse analysis tool because the formation of a new field involves bringing together the actors which were initially disparate and so to understand the formation of field requires the understanding of *mechanism or dynamics* which led to formation of a particular field with a given set of actors and not others. Discourse analysis tool, proposed by [13], is appropriate for this purpose which helps in unveiling the mechanism behind the formation of one particular representation and not the others [11], organization field being one representation of the set of actors around an issue.

Balance of the paper has been organized as followings. Next section describes about organization field, and its various constituents. The section following that explains discourse analysis and the meaning of discursive process in detail. Then, the study explains empirically how the formation of a field around the issue of HIT in Indian healthcare follows the discursive process and unveils the mechanisms behind this process.

This study makes a number of contributions. Firstly, this is the unique study to examine the formation of new field around *an issue* using discourse analysis. Second, this study shows how various actors produce *discourses in practice* which is instrumental for the field formation. Though past studies have looked at discourse analysis to understand the dynamics of field-level activity, this study is unique in terms of analyzing the *discourse in practice2*.

2 ORGANIZATIONAL FIELD

Literature has seen three broad conceptualizations of organizational field [9]. First conceptualization considered it as

SIGMIS-CPR '17, June 21-23, 2017, Bangalore, India

© 2017 Association for Computing Machinery.

ACM ISBN 978-1-4503-5037-2/17/06...$15.00

http://dx.doi.org/10.1145/3084381.3084411

---

2 Section 3 explains the difference in detail.

static entity and defined it as the collection of organizations that produced similar services or products, suppliers, resources and product consumers, regulatory agencies, and others [1]. Behavior of organizations within the field was supposed to be guided by cultural-cognitive, normative, and regulatory 'structures' that provided stability and collective meaning [14]. These structures acted as 'social facts' which organizational actors took into account when determining appropriate action [15]. Once a social fact became institutionalized, it provided actors with the templates for action in an unconscious way [9] which leads to isomorphism [1] for the purpose of 'legitimacy' [15]. Second conceptualization condemned this homogeneity of organizational field and brought the concept of agency, change and politics. This new view conceptualized field as dynamic entity and capable of moving towards something other than isomorphism. [16] argued that an organization's willingness and ability to conform to an institutional pressure depended on *Why, Who, What* and *Where* of the pressure. From this perspective, all organizations didn't march quietly down the path towards homogeneity [9]. Third view conceptualized field as a 'Relational Space' [10] that "provides an organization with the opportunity to involve itself with other actors" [9, p.138]. Treating field in this way makes it possible to understand the *mechanism* which leads to formation of new field or change in an established field [9]. Following [9], the present study has adopted the third view that helps in not only understanding the process of new field formation but also the mechanisms behind this process. Following paragraph explains the constituents of such conceptualization of field that will be instrumental in understanding the formation of a new field.

An organizational field is made of three components: positions (or spaces), (shared) understandings, and rules [5, 17]. First, field is a "*relational spaces* - a structured space of positions [10] occupied by the actors that make up that field [18] and provide an opportunity to involve with other actors" [9, p.138]. Second, field is made of shared meaning systems [14]-"shared beliefs" [19, p.153] based on "shared conceptions that constitute the nature of social reality"[3, p.57]; these are taken-for-granted understandings which shape what is considered appropriate behavior [15] and give meaning to actions of the actors in that space [20]. Third, fields are characterized by formal rules such as various rules, laws and standards [21, 12] to which actors in the space must conform [6]. This study argues and empirically shows that formation of all three constituents of field is a discursive output. Following section explains the discourse analysis and discursive process in detail before moving to the empirical examination of field formation process.

3   DISCOURSE ANALYSIS

Foucault's work has been instrumental in unveiling the mechanisms through which discourses produce a permissible mode of being [11]. Discourses are, usually, defined as the "interrelated bodies of texts that define the 'normal', 'standard' and acceptable' and thereby helps in "institutionalizing practices"" [22, p.544]. Texts are generally symbolic expressions depicted in one or other way by various actors [23], to make them accessible to others [24]. Texts may include range of written documents; sometimes also may be verbal [25]. The production, distribution, and consumption of these discourses create a *discursive space* [11, 26]- a physical or virtual space in which actors discuss, debate and dispute about "issues they perceive to be of consequence to them" [27, p. 64]. A discursive space has been defined as sites of contestation in which various actors discuss about the issues, problems and how they should be addressed [11, 28]. This space is characterized by multiple voices as various actors engage in discursive struggle [29]. Thus, the discursive space creates an opportunity for the shared representation of the reality to be created [30].]. Discourse analysis creates the possibility of standing detached from those discourses, bracketing its familiarity, in order to analyze the theoretical and practical context with which it has been associated [11, 13].

Organization field formation- A discursive process
Organizational fields are held in place by structured, coherent discourses that produce widely shared, taken-for-granted meanings [31]. Discourse analysis is an established tool for examination of field configuration events to study change in an established field [5]. [5] argues that the process of a field change follows a discursive process. The present study makes an argument that not only change, but also the formation of a new field follows the discursive space. Appearance of an (important) issue in the environment may draw the attention of various (interested) actors to engage in the discourse. However, these discourses need not necessarily be produced through texts; it might also be produced through practice- what [11, p. 11] calls 'Discourse in Practice'- discourse applied in concrete practice and acting that produces certain reality.

Building on these arguments and borrowing the concepts from discourse analysis, this paper presents a conceptual model (Figure 1) that explains the discursive process of the formation of a reality. The study further empirically examines this process using discourse analysis around the issue of HIT in Indian Healthcare. While doing so, the study also identifies the mechanism behind this process. This study uses discourse analysis in a unique way by analyzing "*discourse through practice*". The reason behind adopting '*discourse through practice*' was that focus of this study was to identify the field formation process by examining the key HIT events (that included HIT implementation projects) which are produced only through practice.

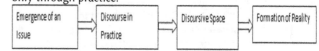

Figure 1: Discursive process

4   HEALTHCARE INFORMATION TECHNOLOGY (HIT)

HIT refers to the set of technologies used to deliver healthcare and managing information [32]. Broadly, HIT is of two types: (1) HIT for diagnosis/treatment (2) transactional HIT, such as Electronic Health Records (EHR). While the former is a task specific technology and focuses on the quality of medical services, the second is process specific and primarily improves the coordination and sharing of medical information across parties involved in the healthcare service chain [32]. This study has focused on the formation of a field around the second category of HIT. There are diverse set of users of this type of HIT including physicians, Administrators, Patients, Nurses etc., [33, 34]

"Health IT covers following areas[3]:
1. EMR/EHR/PHR all are one and same with little difference
2. Telemedicine
3. Digital health knowledge resource e.g. Digital Medical Library
4. Hospital Information management system
5. e-learning technologies and application in health Science
6. Biomedical informatics for biomedical research applications
7. Artificial Intelligence in clinical medicine and health management
8. Public health informatics
9. Medical Internet
10. Virtual Reality and Simulation for health"

5   METHODS

This study concerns the formulation of field around the issue of HIT in Indian healthcare. It uses a single exploratory case study [35] to provide a detailed, holistic understanding of the field-level mechanism in this context [5]. The study selects this case because information is largely in the public domain, as are official records and media accounts and it consists of all three components of an organizational fields, set of actors, standards rules to be followed by those actors and common understanding of EMR/EHR in Indian healthcare.

5.1   Case Study

Since 1990s, many of the healthcare organizations in India have started using HITs. Recognizing the potentials to improve the healthcare delivery, implementation of HIT has been on the government's radar. Ministry of Health and Family Welfare (MoHWF), regulatory body of Indian Healthcare, in 2013 announced the standards for the use of EHR in healthcare. This policy consists of set of rules regarding the use of EHR, actors who come under this policy and the common understanding of EHR by these actors. However, the formation of the policy and committee to decide the policy were not one-time events. It took close to 20 years since the introduction of HIT in India. Therefore, this study attempts to understand the dynamics during these years which led to the formation of this field.

5.2   Data Collection

Data for this study have been collected from the secondary sources. Secondary sources have been quite established source of data for understanding the field dynamics [7]. Looking at the large period of 20 years and quite unstructured secondary data, it was not possible to include all the possible events

around the issue of HIT in Indian Healthcare. However, it was also not good to collect any events as data sources for the analysis. Hence, while selecting the events care has been taken care to avoid two pitfalls: vulgar eclecticism and 'inbreeding'[36]. The former concerns the ad hoc selection of ideas – taking any events. The latter refers to focusing too narrowly on the small set of events. Hence, the study limits itself to the some of the key events in this case[4]. Source of these events are mentioned in the reports published by Federation of Indian Chambers of Commerce & Industry (FICCI) and MoHWF who are the key actors of this field. Moreover, the study also selects the events mentioned by a scholarly article on this issue [37]. List of the key events during 1990-2013 selected for the further analysis is given in table 1.

Table 1: Selected Events

Events	Source	Source reference site (If any)
(1) Tele-Cardiology, 1996 (2) Implementation of HIS Software at SGPGI and GTB hospital, New Delhi, 1997 (3) Apollo's Telemedicine in Andhra Pradesh, 1999 (4) GRAMSAT, 2000 (5) Teleopthomology, 2003 at Shankar Netralaya	Kalpa, 2012	http://citeseerx.ist.psu.edu/viewdoc/download?doi=10.1.1.476.7598&rep=rep1&type=pdf
(1) Tele-Healthcare, 2001 (2) Telemedicine for tropical disease, 2002 (3) Tele-Radiology, 2002 (4) Telemedicine in Karnataka, 2002 (5) Integrated Disease Surveillance Programme (IDSP), 2004		http://www.ficci.com/spdocument/20101/Status-Paper-Health-IT.PDF
Committee of Experts for development of an Information Technology (IT) based electronic medical records maintenance system for hospitals, 2010	Federation of Indian Chambers of Commerce & Industry (FICCI), MoHFW	http://clinicalestablishments.nic.in/WriteReadData/107.pdf http://www.itbhuglobal.org/chronicle/EMR-Standards-

---

[4] There could be several other events that are not included in the present study. But the purpose of this study was not to include all the possible events, instead to select a few exemplary events and examine the process and the mechanisms behind that process. Therefore, there was some aspect of subjectivity involved in selecting the events.

SIGMIS-CPR'17, June 21-23, 2017, Bangalore, India

		Committee-MoHFW-GoI.pdf http://www.readbag.com/itbhuglobal-chronicle-emr-standards-committee-mohfw-goi
Approval of the standard by Govt. of India (GoI)	MoHFW	http://ictpost.com/approved-ehr-standards-for-india/

5.3 Data Analysis -Discourse in practice, discursive space and field

To analyze the field formation process using discourse analysis in the spirit of figure 1 and to argue that the process is a discursive process, the study has performed the followings:
(1) Sorted the events in chronological order to provide the temporal dimension an essential component of process study [38].
(2) Coded the events in three categories: (a) Discourses in practice (b) Discursive process (c) Formulation of field. The coding for this purpose has been done according to the definition of these events explained in the earlier sections. While the definition of discourse in practice and discursive space have been taken from the discussion on discourse and discourse in practice of [11], formulation of field has been identified based on the identification of three components of field explained earlier.
(3) Identified the mechanism behind each event. Identification of mechanisms is useful in understanding the trigger that led to next event [39].
5.3.1 Sorting the events in chronological order. All the events selected during data collection level were sorted in their respective time order. Table 2 presents this chronological order.
5.3.2 Coding the events. Post identification of the chronological order, all the events were coded in three categories as explained above[5]. Events before "Committee of Experts for development of an Information Technology (IT) based electronic medical records maintenance system for hospitals" have been coded discourses (in practice) because these events generally included various disparate actors engaging into the implementation of HIT. Formulation of committee has been called as the formation of discursive space

---
[5] While the coding was done by only one author, the study believes that coding process is reliable as the definitions of all categories of coding (such as 'discourse in practice', 'discursive space', and the three components of field')were adopted from the literature and hence the coding involved very less subjectivity.

as it provides the opportunity for different actors to come together and develop a shared understanding about the HIT phenomenon. Approval of the suggestions by government in 2013 has been coded as the field formation as it brings all three components of a field together. Details of the events coded in each category have been given in table 2.

Table 2: Chronology of events and their respective categories

Events	Category
(1) Implementation of HIS Software at Sanjay Gandhi Postgraduate Institute of Medical Sciences and Guru Teg Bahadur Hospital, New Delhi, 1997.	Issue and Power
(2) Apollo's Telemedicine in Andhrapradesh, 1999	**Discourse in Practice**
(3) GRAMSAT, 2000	
(4) Tele-Healthcare, 2001	
(5) Telemedicine for tropical disease, 2002	
(6) Tele-Radiology, 2002	
(7) Telemedicine in Karnataka, 2002	
(8) Teleopthomology, 2003 at Shankar Netralaya	
(9) Integrated Disease Surveillance Programme (IDSP), 2004	
(10) Committee of Experts for development of an Information Technology (IT) based electronic medical records maintenance system for hospitals, 2010	**Discursive Space** Subjectivity Issue, Power, And subjectivity
(11) Approval of the standard by Govt of India (GoI)	**Formation of Field**

5.4 Findings: Identifying the Mechanisms

Since the recognition of the potential of HIT especially telemedicine, various healthcare organizations such as Apollo started their Implementation. Apollo is often credited to be the harbinger in bringer telemedicine in India [40]. During the same time other healthcare organizations such as GTB hospital and SGPGI started building HIS software for the medical purpose. GRAMSAT project was also one of the important initiatives of this duration. All of these events involved the implementation of HIT, which is *discourse in practice around the issue of HIT.* However, there was no shared understanding about the implementation of HIT and definition of various terms until MoHFW, regulatory body of healthcare in India, exercised its **power** to form a committee to discuss about the standards to follow in the HIT implementation. This committee is a discursive space- a physical or virtual space in which actors discuss, debate and dispute "issues they perceive to be of consequence to them and their group" [27, p. 64], where the chosen actors come to discuss and debate about what is normal and standard in the implementation of HIT In this committee various actors[6] came together to discuss about the meaning of what is normal and standard in HIT implementation. The selection of actors in this discursive space was done based on the exercise of power of by MoHFW. This shows the role of *'power'- an important factor* in discursive process [11]. The final decision by the actors on what is 'normal' regarding HIT was based the subjective interpretation of these members. This shows the aspect of *'subjectivity'* in the discursive process field formation, which [11] calls as one of the essential in a discursive process. The discussion among the actors in this discursive have resulted in the decision of following two:

(1) Various actors who will have to follow these standards formed by the committee. This is the 'relational space'-one component of organizational field. In other words, it defined the boundary of the field, which is the indication of the formation of a field [9].

(2) Identification of the shared norms and standards, which is the "shared conceptions that constitute the nature of social reality about HIT implementation", which is called taken-for-granted understandings that shape what is considered appropriate behavior [15]- second component of organizational field.

However, the formation of field requires the attainment of one more component- formal rules. The shared meaning of HIT implementation formulated by the members in the committee achieved formal status only after the **exercise of power** by MoHFW in 2013 to give the approval of those standards. This again shows the importance of power.

---

6 The actors included the representatives from the key hospitals, software vendors and from the government of India. Readers are advised to refer to http://clinicalestablishments.nic.in/WriteReadData/107.pdf for the full list of actors involved in the committee

Thus, the above findings indicate that: (1) Formation of a space to form each of the components of a field is the discursive function of "power and issue".

Space for HIT discussion= F (Issue, Power)

Where Issue is HIT and power is the regulatory power of MoHFW to form the committee.

And (2) the formation of a field with all three components is the discursive function of issue, power and subjectivity.

Organizational field = F (Issue, Power and Subjectivity)

Where Issue is HIT, subjectivity is the creation of the standards and meaning of various terms regarding HIT implementation, and Power is the regulatory power of MoHFW to approve the suggestions of the committee.

6   DISCUSSION

Power and Subjectivity in Field formation. Findings from the field formation process around HIT in Indian healthcare issue show that the field formation follows the discursive process. The study has identified the process and its mechanisms by (1) adopting discourse analysis tool which allows the analysis of a particular representation without being actually part of it, and (2) adding the temporal dimensions to the various events around the issue of HIT.

The study discovers that the discursive process of field formation involves the aspect of 'subjectivity' and 'exercise of power'. In this case, the reality of organizational field around HIT in Indian Healthcare was the result of subjectivity of various actors involved in the discursive space of committee and exercise of power by MoHFW- both in the selection of actors in the discursive space and approval of the formal rules of the field. These findings lead to propose the following:

P1: Formation of an organizational field around an issue follows a discursive process.

P2: Appearance of an issue brings together various disparate organizations to produce the discourse through the practices.

P3: Creation of the shared understanding about the issue requires the formulation of a space which is subject to the exercise of power.

P4: Formulation of an organization field is the discursive function of *issue, power and subjectivity.*

Figure 2: Organizational field

7   CONTRIBUTIONS

The study makes a number of contributions. This study investigates the process of field formation around an issue. While there have been several studies in past which have looked at the field formation in an industry, there is paucity of studies on field formation around an issue. This study is also unique to examine this process by using discourse analysis. While discourse analysis has been used to study field level dynamic in past, the present study is unique in two ways- first, unlike earlier studies that used discourse analysis to study *change* in the field this study examines the *formation* of a field. Second, unlike past studies which have focused on analyzing the discourse produced through texts, this study has focused on analyzing the discourse produced through the practice. These uniqueness of identifying the process of field formation using discourse in practice tool led to highlighting the role of power and subjectivity in a field formation

Along with the above mentioned academic relevant contributions, the study has contributions for the practitioners as well. More often than not, there are continuous changes in the business environment which have the bearing on organization in one or other way. By looking at the formation of field around an issue- which can be any environmental change such as the technological change- the study informs managers to focus on the various changes in the environment and get involved in the discourses through practice to be part of the field and develop the shared understanding. Mangers in such situation might need to consider the aspect of subjectivity and power which the study has found out.

8 CONCLUSION

The study has examined the formation of an organizational field around an issue of HIT in Indian healthcare. The study has used discourse analysis to understand the mechanism behind the formation of such field and has proposed that formation of an organizational field follows the discursive process. It finds that power and subjectivity have key roles to play in such a discursive formation of a filed. With its findings, the study hopes to contribute to both practitioners as well researchers interested in understanding the field formation process.

8 LIMITATIONS

While the study makes number of contributions, it does not claim to be void of limitations. Selection of data from secondary sources is the major limitation of this study. Though the study has taken sufficient care to ensure the selection of those events which can unveil the true mechanism behind the formation of field, it does not claim to be exhaustive selection. Second limitation is the generalizability. Like any process study, the generalizability of findings depends on the cross-case comparison. This study has looked at only one case of HIT in Indian Healthcare. Hence, the study does not claim the generalizability of its findings. Future studies may extend to few other cases to increase generalizability. The study also suffers from the inter coder reliability. Coding and classification of the events have been done by only one researcher. In future, the study plans to build on the current findings and include more than one researcher to perform the coding to ensure the inter-coder reliability.

However, notwithstanding with the aforementioned limitations, the study believes that the findings would be relevant for the practicing managers. The findings would also contribute to the literature discussing on the issues of field formation and change by extending the current understanding.

REFERNCES

[1] P. DiMaggio, and W. W. Powell. 1983. The iron cage revisited: Collective rationality and institutional isomorphism in organizational fields. *American Sociological Review 48,* 2 (1983), 147-160.

[2] R. Garud. 2008. Conferences as venues for the configuration of emerging organizational fields: The case of cochlear implants. *Journal of Management Studies 45,*6 (2008), 1061-1088

[3] W. R. Scott. (2001). *Institutions and organizations.* Thousand Oaks, CA: Sage.

[4] N. Anand, and R. M, Watson. 2004. Tournament rituals in the evolution of fields: The case of the Grammy Awards. *Academy of Management journal 47,* 1 (2004), 59-80.

[5] C. Hardy, and S. Maguire, 2010. Discourse, field-configuring events, and change in organizations and institutional fields: Narratives of DDT and the Stockholm Convention. *Academy of Management Journal 53,* 6 (2010), 1365-1392.

[6] J. A. Hoffman, 1999. Institutional evolution and change: Environmentalism and the US chemical industry. *Academy of management journal 42,*4 (1999), 351-371.

[7] T. Reay, and B. C. Hinings. 2005. The recomposition of an organizational field: Health care in Alberta. *Organization Studies 26,* 3 (2005), 351-384.

[8] S. Brint, and J. Karabel. 1991. Institutional origins and transformations: The case of American community colleges. *The new institutionalism in organizational analysis* (1991), *337,* 360.

[9] M. Wooten, and J. A. Hoffman. 2008. Organizational fields: Past, present and future. *The Sage handbook of organizational institutionalism* (2008), 130-147.

[10] P. Bourdieu. 1993. *Sociology in question* 18. Sage.

[11] A. Escobar. 2011. *Encountering development: The making and unmaking of the Third World* (2011) Princeton University Press.

[12] S. Maguire, S., and C. Hardy. 2009. Discourse and deinstitutionalization: The decline of DDT. *Academy of management journal 52,* 1, 148-178.

[13] M. Foucault. 1986. Disciplinary power and subjection. *Power,* (*1981),* 229-242.

[14] R. W. Scott. 1995. *Institutions and organizations* (1995) Thousand Oaks, CA: Sage.

[15] W. J. Meyer, and B. Rowan. 1977. Institutionalized organizations: Formal structure as myth and ceremony. *American journal of sociology* (1977)340-363.

[16] C. Oliver. 1991. Strategic responses to institutional processes. *Academy of management review 16,* 1 (1991), 145-179.

[17] C. Mazza, and S. J. Pedersen. 2004. From press to e-media? The transformation of an organizational field. *Organization Studies, 25,*6 (2004), 875-896.

[18] S. Maguire, C. Hardy, and B. T. Lawrence. 2004. Institutional entrepreneurship in emerging fields: HIV/AIDS treatment advocacy in Canada. *Academy of management journal 47,*5 (2004), 657-679.

[19] B. T. Zilber. 2008. The work of meanings in institutional processes. *The SAGE handbook of organizational institutionalism*

[20] R. Greenwood, C. Oliver, R. Suddaby, and K. Sahlin-Andersson. (Eds.). 2008. *The Sage handbook of organizational institutionalism.* (2008) Sage.

[21] R. Greenwood, and R. Suddaby. 2006. Institutional entrepreneurship in mature fields: The big five accounting firms. *Academy of Management journal 49,*1 (2006), 27-48.

[22] S. Meriläinen, J. Tienari, R. Thomas, and A. Davies. 2004. Management consultant talk: A cross-cultural comparison of normalizing discourse and resistance. *Organization, 11,* 4 (2004), 539-564.

[23] R. J. Taylor, and J. E. Van Every 1993. *The vulnerable fortress: Bureaucratic organization and management in the information age.* (1993) University of Toronto Press.

[24] R. J. Taylor, F. Cooren, F, N. Giroux, and D. Robichaud. 1996. The communicational basis of organization: Between the conversation and the text. *Communication theory*, *6*, 1 (1996), 1-39.

[25] N. Phillips, B. T. Lawrence, and C. Hardy. 2004. Discourse and institutions.*Academy of management review*, *29*, 4 (2004), 635-652.

[26] A. M. Hajer. 1995. *The politics of environmental discourse: ecological modernization and the policy process* (p. 40) (1995). Oxford: Clarendon Press.

[27] A. G. Hauser. 1999. *Vernacular voices: The rhetoric of publics and public spheres.* (1999) Univ of South Carolina Press.

[28] A. K. Jacobs, J. Kemeny, and T. Manzi. 2004. Social constructionism in housing research.

[29] O. Belova, I. King, and M. Sliwa. 2008. Introduction: Polyphony and organization studies: Mikhail Bakhtin and beyond. *Organization Studies*, *29*, 4 (2008), 493-500.

[30] K. J. Fletcher, L. Bailyn, and S. Blake-Beard. 2009. Practical pushing: Creating discursive space in organizational narratives. *Critical management studies at work: Multidisciplinary approaches to negotiating tensions between theory and practice*, (2009) 82-93.

[31] N. Phillips, B. T. Lawrence, and C. Hardy. 2004. Discourse and institutions.*Academy of management review*, *29*, 4 (2004), 635-652.

[32] G. Peng, D. Dey, and A. Lahiri. 2014. Healthcare IT Adoption: An Analysis of Knowledge Transfer in Socioeconomic Networks. *Journal of Management Information Systems*, *31*, 3 (2014), 7-34.

[33] M. McMullan. 2006. Patients using the Internet to obtain health information: how this affects the patient–health professional relationship. *Patient education and counseling*, *63*,1 (2006), 24-28.

[34] C. T. Rindfleisch. 1997. Privacy, information technology, and health care .*Communications of the ACM*, *40*, 8 (1997), 92-100.

[35] K. R. Yin. 2013. *Case study research: Design and methods.* (2013)Sage publications.

[36] C. Avgerou. 2007. Information Systems and Innovation Group London School of Economics and Political Science (2007).

[37] S. Kalpa. 2012. Health IT in Indian Healthcare System: A New Initiative. *Research Journal of Recent Sciences, 2277*, 2502.

[38] H. A. Van de Ven. 2007. *Engaged scholarship: a guide for organizational and social research: a guide for organizational and social research.* (2007) OUP Oxford.

[39] T. L. Huber, T. A. Dibbern and R. Hirschheim. 2013. A process model of complementarity and substitution of contractual and relational governance in IS outsourcing. Journal of Management Information Systems, 30, 3, (2013), 81-114.

[40] K. Ganapathy, and A. Ravindra. 2009. Telemedicine in India: the Apollo story. *Telemedicine and e-Health, 15*,6 (2009), 576-585.

Would Technology Obliterate Medical Transcription? The Antecedents and Consequences of Technology-driven Obsolescence Perceptions on Turnover Intentions of Medical Transcriptionists

Full Paper

S. Balaji
University of Wisconsin – Whitewater
Whitewater, WI
sankarab@uww.edu

Gary C. David
Bentley University
Waltham, MA
gdavid@bentley.edu

K. R. Vishwanath
University of Wisconsin-Whitewater
Whitewater, WI
vishwanaKR02@uww.edu

C. Ranganathan
University of Illinois-Chicago
Chicago, IL
ranga@uic.edu

ABSTRACT

Increasingly, the adoption of speech recognition technology (SRT[1]) by various hospitals has posed a threat to the medical transcription profession. As turnover intentions among medical transcriptionists are on the rise, understanding the role of technology in shaping turnover intentions requires attention, and yet is a significant gap in the literature. Drawing upon the theories of stress and turnover intentions, and prior work on professional obsolescence, we propose a new construct called technology-driven obsolescence perceptions in the medical transcription domain. We posit that technology-driven obsolescence perceptions positively impact turnover intentions, and antecedents such as work-family conflict, fairness of rewards, work excellence and job commitment have differential impacts on technology-driven obsolescence perceptions. Results indicate that all the hypotheses in the study are supported. Our study makes important contributions to the obsolescence and turnover intentions literature, and has important implications for research and practice alike.

KEYWORDS

Medical transcription; technology-driven obsolescence; stress; turnover intentions; work excellence; work-family conflict; job commitment.

SIGMIS-CPR '17, June 21-23, 2017, Bangalore, India
© 2017 Copyright is held by the owner/author(s). Publication rights licensed to ACM. ACM ISBN 978-1-4503-5037-2/17/06...$15.00
http://dx.doi.org/10.1145/3084381.3084414

1 INTRODUCTION

Healthcare providers are increasingly outsourcing their information technology as well as key back-office business process operations, including medical transcription services (MTS) to third-party providers. Medical transcription is the process by which physician dictated medical information is converted into a standardized text format for inclusion in a patient's electronic medical record. It involves a number of elements including understanding the technological components such as audio files and healthcare language and terminology, understanding physician's way of speaking and converting the dictation in an electronic text format. The job of medical transcriptionist entails labor intensive tasks with huge potential to save costs for healthcare organizations [3, 11]. According to a report by Transparency Market Research, global medical transcription services market which was valued at $41.4 billion in 2012, is estimated to reach $60.6 billion by 2019 [29].

In order to be effective, medical transcriptionists need to possess and apply both technical and healthcare-specific domain knowledge to accurately convert dictated medical information to texts that can be ported in health IT systems. A medical transcriptionist requires a wide variety of knowledge bases, including medical lexicon, anatomy, physiology, language, grammar, and word-processing, editing and associated software. According to US Bureau of Labor Statistics, the US medical transcription services industry employed over 70,000 professionals in 2014 with an annual median pay of $34000 [31].

There are three key factors that pose serious challenge to the medical transcription professionals. First, growth of various speech recognition technology (SRT), and automated voice-to-text applications have posed a threat to medical transcription profession [5]. Though automated voice recognition tools have been available for over a decade, they are prone to cause errors in health records, especially in complex medical terms. Hence the role of a transcriptionist has expanded to include editing and error-correction tasks. The role of a medical transcriptionist is no longer solely about mere transcribing, but expanding to edit voice recognition draft reports and proofread them. Second, the available of low cost, skilled labor in offshore destinations have propelled a rise in number of MTS firms outside USA [19]. Third, the changed regulatory guidelines for electronic health records, and rigid requirements regarding security and privacy of health information pose additional challenges to how MTs create, access and manage sensitive health data [7]. From a word-processed document, health data in EHRs are now stored and processed in a structured data format with in-built medical terms, codes and lexicon. MTs will need to adjust their roles and retrain in these newer developments. Given the uncertainty in the profession and aforementioned challenges, it becomes important to understand how medical transcriptionists view these changes and their continued services in the profession.

Despite the importance of medical transcription for the healthcare IT sector, there is a dearth of academic studies that have thrown light on key issues in the medical transcription sector, and the professionals working in this industry. Our study seeks to address this key research gap. The main purpose of the article is to examine the turnover intentions of medical transcriptionists. We specifically focus on how the transcriptionists view technology-driven obsolescence necessitated by advances in SRT and automation, and its association with their turnover intentions. Further, we also posit and examine how job-related and transcriptionist-related antecedents impact their perceptions regarding technology-driven obsolescence.

We address the following research questions in this study:

1. *How do medical transcriptionists view the technology-driven obsolescence? How do these perceptions impact their turnover intentions?*

2. *What are key job factors and transcriptionist factors that impact medical transcriptionists' perceptions pertaining to technology-driven obsolescence in their profession?*

2 THEORETICAL BACKGROUND

March & Simon (1958) in their seminal work on organizations were the first to identify turnover intentions as an organizational issue by focusing on employee decision to participate. Since then a plethora of scholarly work on turnover intention has appeared in the literature. Definitions of Turnover Intentions abound from employees' conscious and considered purposiveness to exit the organization [30] to employees' intent to find a new job within a year [22]. Regardless, the relationship between Turnover Intentions and Job Satisfaction and Work Engagement and Burnout is well established [4, 30]. Mobley (1977) concluded the path to Job Turnover originates with Turnover Intentions with

Job Satisfaction and Organizational Commitment each uniquely contributing to Turnover Intentions [23, 30].

A significant body of literature has considered the antecedents of turnover intentions among employees for example job burnout or work exhaustion. Researchers contend that a professionals' perceived fairness or rewards work overload significantly contribute to work exhaustion and consequently, work exhaustion plays a decisive role in the turnover of professionals [20]. Occupational stress expresses itself in other ways such as, modifications in the business environment and organizational restructuring among others triggering work exhaustion [20]. Work Exhaustion, being an emotional condition, has a profound impact on turnover intentions [16, 21]. Employees experience work exhaustion because of unmet job expectations and explicit characteristics of job occurrences leading to trepidations of technology change or a change in the business environment in general [16]. A principal antecedent of work exhaustion is work-family conflict - defined as an inter-role conflict leading to reciprocal incongruity - as a source of occupational stress [1]. Fairness of rewards has been found to have a direct bearing on employees' commitment to their organization [13] and directly act as a stimulus for Turnover. Furthermore, fairness of rewards may have a deep and undeviating impact on the organization as a reactionary manifestation of low organizational commitment [1].

While prior work has considered work exhaustion as a significant mediator of turnover intentions, recent research also points to skills obsolescence, the manifestation of a gap in knowledge and skill-set necessary for effective job performance, being a predictor of turnover intentions in IT workers [33]. Pazy (1994) states that two wide-ranging categories that are said to influence obsolescence are situational factors (including the work environment, organizational policy, work-family conflict, job commitment, managerial support etc.) and personal factors (including age, education and attitudinal variables) [27]. Zhang et al. (2012) maintain there is a direct relationship between obsolescence perceptions and turnover. These individual characteristics are important to consider when studying turnover models in different settings.

We adapt the perceived obsolescence perspective in our research, but contextualize the obsolescence concept to the medical transcription domain. In other words, these perceptions of obsolescence relate to the medical transcriptionists' perceptions of whether the technology will completely replace i.e. eliminate their job. The professional obsolescence literature [33] has focused primarily on the *needs for skills change* and its impacts, and has paid little attention to the antecedents and consequences of perceived obsolescence, related to how technology *replaces* work. Notably, the relationships between situational factors such as work-family conflict, job commitment, which are related to work exhaustion, have been understudied in the context of obsolescence. Situational factors become extremely important in this context. For instance, as medical transcriptionists perceive higher levels of fairness in rewards, they are more likely to believe that technology is actually helping them perform their work, rather than eliminating them. Therefore, our research study seeks to address a notable research gap in prior work by studying the situational factors as antecedents, and impacts of technology-driven obsolescence perceptions and turnover intentions in medical transcriptionists. We describe the research model and the hypotheses for our study in the next section.

3 RESEARCH MODEL AND HYPOTHESES DEVELOPMENT

3.1 Dependent Variable: Medical Transcriptionist Turnover Intentions

We define medical transcriptionist turnover intentions as the intentions of the medical transcriptionist to leave the medical transcription job in the near future. Prior research that have studied turnover in organizational settings have theorized or empirically validated turnover intentions as their dependent variable [1, 18, 20, 24].

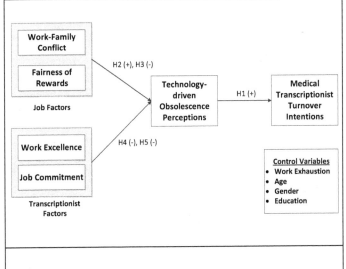

Figure 1 Research Model - Antecedents and Consequences of Technology-driven Obsolescence Perceptions

As our primary objective in this study is to study turnover issues in medical transcription domain, we utilize the "intentions" to turnover as our dependent variable. Consistent with prior research on turnover intentions in the HR and IT domains [18], we develop our construct of turnover intentions for the medical transcription domain.

3.2 Impact of Technology-driven Obsolescence Perceptions

In this study, technology-driven obsolescence perception is defined as the extent to which the medical transcriptionists

believe that technology (e.g. speech recognition technology, EHR systems) can eliminate their job. This new construct has parallels in the professional obsolescence literature [33], which argues for the extent to which skills and knowledge gaps need to be updated by the employee. Adapting theories on professional obsolescence [33], we postulate that technology-driven obsolescence perceptions will also lead to turnover intentions in medical transcriptionists. As employees perceive that the technology can effectively eliminate or replace their profession, they are likely to make future plans about leaving their profession, as reflected in their turnover intentions. Hence, we postulate that:

H1: Technology-driven obsolescence perceptions will have a positive impact on medical transcriptionist turnover intentions.

3.3 Job Factors

3.3.1 Work-Family Conflict. Work-family conflict is defined as the "inter-role conflict between demands of work and family" [12]. It is defined as the extent to which the work activities interfere with the family-oriented activities, creating an environment of work-life imbalance. Work-family conflict is found to be an important antecedent of turnover intention in a variety of settings [18]. As work-life balance gets affected, this can act as a stressor [2] which can alter the perceptions of the employee regarding the job, indirectly leading to turnover intentions. We posit that work-family conflict will have a positive impact on technology-driven obsolescence perceptions. As conflict increases, the employee is highly likely to attribute blame on the technology-related job stressors [2], which in this case, relates to technology-driven obsolescence. As the employee perceives more work-life balance issues, he/she is likely to believe that technology is either altering or can alter the perceived technology related changes in the organization. Therefore, we posit that:

H2: Work-family conflict will have a positive impact on technology-driven obsolescence perceptions.

3.3.2 Fairness of Rewards. Fairness of rewards is defined as the extent to which the employee perceives that the rewards provided are on par with their performance [24]. Fairness of rewards is found to be an important predictor of work exhaustion and other antecedent conditions in different settings [1, 18, 24]. We posit that fairness of rewards will have a negative impact on technology-driven obsolescence perceptions. Prior research posits that as employees perceive that the rewards are fairly distributed, they may perceive their work in a more favorable light [24]. On the contrary, lack of fairness in rewards can have a negative impact on their perceptions of their work. In the case of medical transcription, transcriptionists who are satisfied with their rewards may feel that technology is actually helping them conduct their work, rather than obliterating their work. Therefore, we postulate that:

H3: Fairness of rewards will have a negative impact on technology-driven obsolescence perceptions.

3.4 Transcriptionist Factors

3.4.1 Work Excellence. Work excellence is defined as the extent to which medical transcriptionists expect to perform their work without making errors. Prior research notes that medical transcription files do contain significant medical errors, and such errors could potentially cause downstream healthcare challenges [6]. Medical transcriptionists typically view their profession as maintaining the medical records meticulously. This work ethic is reflected in the work excellence of the medical transcriptionists. Higher levels of work excellence could mean that they have a favorable opinion of the job and the technology which allows them to perform their work. This means that their perceptions of technology-driven obsolescence will be lower. On the contrary, lower levels of work excellence could mean that their opinion of their job and technology will be lower, where they will attribute blame on the technology. Hence, we posit that:

H4: Work excellence will have a negative impact on technology-driven obsolescence perceptions.

3.4.2 Job Commitment. Job commitment is defined as the extent to which a medical transcriptionist "is involved in, and identifies with one's organization" [1, 25]. Job commitment reflects a sense of association with the current organization, and the willingness of the employee to go above and beyond the required norms of work. Higher levels of job commitment could mean that medical transcriptionists feel an emotional connect with the job and the associated aspects [25]. This would imply that transcriptionists with higher levels of job commitment would attribute less blame on the technology replacing their job. On the contrary, lower levels of job commitment would mean that medical transcriptionist's beliefs about the technology replacing their job would be less favorable. Hence, we postulate that:

H5: Job commitment will have a negative impact on technology-driven obsolescence perceptions.

4 METHOD

As part of a larger study, we conducted a survey of medical transcriptionists to understand their perceptions about a variety of issues including perceptions about their organization, job, technology and turnover intentions. A positivist survey was considered to be appropriate for our study, since the study focuses on theory-testing [32]. In this study, the measures for work-family conflict, job commitment, fairness of rewards, work exhaustion and turnover intentions were adopted from prior studies [1, 24]. New items for work excellence and technology-driven obsolescence were created. Prior research has established work exhaustion as a key mediator of antecedent conditions and turnover intentions. Since our focus in the study is on technology-driven obsolescence and turnover intentions, we model work exhaustion as a control variable. In addition, we also

model demographic variables such as age, gender and education as our control variables.

The online surveys were coordinated by the medical transcriptionist service organizations (MTSOs), and resulted in 1050 usable responses for this study, with a majority of respondents being women (typical for medical transcriptionists). The analysis and results are provided below.

5 ANALYSIS AND RESULTS

We utilized SmartPLS to validate the measurement model and structural model in our study. Following Gefen and Straub (2005) for validating measures using PLS, we establish the reliability and validity of the measures [9]. Cronbach's alpha and internal consistency reliability estimates for the measures were greater than 0.7 [26] indicating reliability of measures (Appendix B). The AVE for all the measures were greater than 0.5 indicating convergent validity (Table 1). Discriminant validity was verified by comparing the AVE with the correlations of constructs in Appendix A. The AVE values were found to be greater than the corresponding off-diagonal elements [8].

Figure 2 shows the structural model for our study with the significant results. Results show that technology-driven obsolescence is found to positively impact Turnover Intentions supporting lending support for H1 (b=0.225, p<0.001). Work-family conflict positively impacts technology-driven obsolescence (b=0.074, p<0.05), lending support for H2. Fairness of rewards is a significant positive predictor of technology-driven obsolescence (H3 supported, b=-0.182, p<0.001). Work excellence significantly predicts technology-driven obsolescence which supports H4 (b=-0.139, p<0.001), while job commitment significantly predicts technology-driven obsolescence (H5 supported, b=-0.163, p<0.001). The R2 for turnover intentions is found to be 0.226. Finally, Harmon's single factor test [28], indicates that common method variance may not be a significant concern in our study.

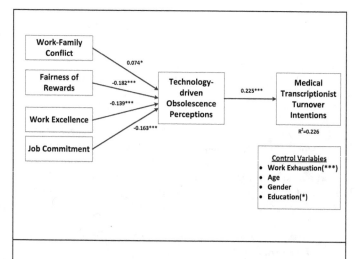

Figure 1 Antecedents and Consequences of Technology-driven Obsolescence Perceptions

6 DISCUSSION AND CONTRIBUTIONS

The primary purpose of this study is to introduce a new construct of technology-driven obsolescence perceptions and its antecedents and impacts in the medical transcription domain. We defined technology-driven obsolescence perceptions as the extent to which the medical transcriptionists believe their job will be eliminated due to the introduction of technology. We theorized that job factors and transcriptionist factors will influence the technology-driven obsolescence perceptions, and that technology-driven obsolescence perceptions will have a positive influence on turnover intentions of medical transcriptionists. Results indicate that all our hypotheses are supported, which validates our research model.

Our study makes three important research contributions to the prior research and literature. First, practitioner research and anecdotal evidence have pointed to a growing theme in the medical transcriptionist community regarding the introduction of speech recognition technology and other IT systems. As SRTs have become sophisticated, this has led to negative feelings about the impacts of the technology on the profession. While other studies have focused on professional obsolescence [33], our study conceptualizes a new contextually-embedded construct, while simultaneously operationalizing its measures, which are unique contributions to the literature on medical transcription.

Second, our study theorizes on the impacts of technology-driven obsolescence on turnover intentions in medical transcriptionists. Technology-driven obsolescence is shown as a key mediator of the link between antecedent factors and turnover intentions, even after controlling for work exhaustion. In essence, work exhaustion, which was once viewed as the one road to turnover [24], is being reconceptualized in the medical transcription context, by including technology-driven obsolescence as a key mediator. This extends prior literature on the antecedents of turnover intentions.

Third, by modeling and theorizing on specific antecedent conditions in the transcription domain (e.g. work excellence) and also building on prior work, we build the nomological network of antecedents and consequences of technology-driven obsolescence. This is an interesting contribution, as it provides the 'levers' that can be manipulated to change the perceptions of obsolescence in individuals. For example, exemplary employees are less prone to have perceptions of technology obsolescence. This can facilitate a gradual and deliberate acceptance of new technology that will garner positive responses. Further, to the extent higher levels of job commitment mitigates any perceptions of technology obsolescence, efforts to strengthen job commitment may result in employees embracing new technology. In summary, our study makes important theoretical contributions to the prior literature on turnover intentions, workplace studies and medical transcription domain.

7 LIMITATIONS AND IMPLICATIONS

Our study does have some limitations. We obtained all our responses from medical transcriptionists through MTSOs. Therefore, self-selection bias could be a limiting factor in our study. We also acknowledge that social desirability bias could have played a role in the medical transcriptionist responses on certain questions.

Our study has important implications for researchers and practitioners alike. Our study extends prior research in important directions and can be expanded in future studies to different contexts. For example, researchers could utilize the technology-driven obsolescence idea to new contexts such as situations where process automation is replacing workers. This research also opens possibilities for multiple roads to turnover intentions, which implies a fresh perspective in the IT context. Finally, our study also has important implications for practitioners. Our study shows that organizations need to pay attention to how employees feel about their job being replaced by technology. If retention is the goal, then organizations may need to invest in training and reassignment activities to boost the morale of their workforce. Such investments in human capital in addition to technology may be more beneficial to the companies in the long run.

REFERENCES

[1] M.K. Ahuja, K.M. Chudoba, C.J. Kacmar, D. H. McKnight and J.F. George. 2007. IT Road Warriors: Balancing Work-Family Conflict, Job Autonomy and Work Overload to Mitigate Turnover Intentions, MIS Quarterly, 31, 1, 1-17.

[2] R. Ayyagiri, V. Grover and R. Purvis. 2011. Technostress: Technological Antecedents and Implications, MIS Quarterly, 35, 4, 832-858.

[3] J. Bikman and S. Whiting. 2007. Medical transcription outsourcing greased lightning? Health. Fin. Mgmt., 61, 6, 94-98.

[4] C. F. Bothma and G. Roodt. 2013. The validation of the turnover intention scale. SA J. Human Res. Mgmt., 11, 1, 1-12.

[5] G. C. David, A.C. Garcia, A.W. Rawls and D. Chand. 2009. "Listening to what is said – transcribing what is heard: the impact of speech recognition technology (SRT) on the practice of medical transcription (MT)", Soc. of Health & Illness, 31, 6, 924-938.

[6] G. C. David, D. Chand and S. Balaji. 2014. Error rates in physician dictation: quality assurance and medical record production, International Journal of Health Care Quality Assurance, 27, 2, 99 – 110.

[7] M. Davino. 2004. Assessing privacy risk in outsourcing. Assessing Privacy Risk in Outsourcing/AHIMA, Amer. Health Info. Mgmt. Assoc.

[8] C. Fornell and D.F. Larcker. 1981. Evaluating Structural Equation Models with Unobservable Variables and Measurement Error, Journal of Marketing Research 18, 1, 39-50.

[9] D. Gefen and D. Straub. 2005. A Practical Guide to Factorial Validity using PLS-Graph: Tutorial and Annotated Example, Communications of the AIS, 16, 1, 91-109.

[10] S. A. Geurts, W. B. Schaufeli and C. G. Rutte. 1999. Absenteeism, turnover intention and inequity in the employment relationship. Work & Stress, 13, 3, 253-267.

[11] B. M. Ghodeswar and J. Vaidyanathan. 2008. Business Process Outsourcing: An Approach to Gain Access to World Class Capabilities, Bus. Process Mgmt. J. 14, 1, 23-38.

[12] B.A. Gutek, S. S. Searle and L. Klepa. 1991. Rational versus Gender Role Explanations for Work-family Conflict, Journal of Applied Psychology, 76, 4, 560-568.

[13] G. Harden, K. G. Boakye and S. Ryan. 2016. Turnover Intention of Technology Professionals: A Social Exchange Theory Perspective. J. of Comp. Info. Sys, 1-10.

[14] K.J. Harris, M. James, M, and R. Boonthanom. 2005. Perceptions of Organizational Politics and Cooperation as Moderators of the Relationship Between Job Strains and Intent to Turnover. J. of Manag. Issues, 17, 1, 26-42.

[15] P. W. Hom and A. J. Kinicki. 2001. Toward a greater understanding of how dissatisfaction drives employee turnover. Acad. Manag. Journal, 44, 5, 975-987.

[16] S. E. Jackson, R. L. Schwab, and R. S. Schuler. 1986. Toward an understanding of the burnout phenomenon. J. App. Psych, 71, 4, 630-645.

[17] O. Janssen. 2000. Job demands, perceptions of effort-reward fairness and innovative work behavior. Journal of Occupational and Organizational Psychology, 73, 3, 287-302.

[18] D. Joseph, K. Ng, C. Koh and S. Ang. 2007. Turnover of Information Technology Professionals: A Narrative Review, Meta-AnalyticStructural Equation Modeling, and Model Development, MIS Quarterly, 31, 3, 547-577.

[19] N. Kshetri and N. Dholakia. 2011. Offshoring of Healthcare Services: The Case of the Indian Medical Transcription Offshoring Industry, Journal of Health Org. and Mgmt. 25, 1, 1–20.

[20] M. Lacity, V. V. Iyer and P. S. Rudramuniyaiah. 2008. Turnover Intentions of Indian IS Professionals, Information Systems Frontiers, 10, 2, 225-241.

[21] C. Maslach and S. E. Jackson. 1981. The Measurement of Experienced Burnout, J. Org. Behavior, 2, 2, 99-113.

[22] E. Medina. 2012. Job satisfaction and employee turnover intention: what does organizational culture have to do with it? Master's Theses, Department of Quantitative Methods in the Social Sciences, Columbia University, New York.

[23] W. H. Mobley. 1977. Intermediate linkages in the relationship between job satisfaction and employee turnover. Journal of Applied Psychology, 62, 2, 237-240.

[24] J. E. Moore. 2000. One road to turnover: An examination of work exhaustion in technology professionals. MIS Quarterly, 24, 1, 141-168.

[25] R. T. Mowday, L. W. Porter and R. M. Steers. 1982. Employee–Organization Linkages: The Psychology of Commitment, Absenteeism, and Turnover, Academic Press, New York.

[26] Nunnally, J. "Psychometric Theory," McGraw-Hill, New York (2nd Ed.) 1978.

[27] A.Pazy. 1994. Trying to combat professional obsolescence: The experience of women in technical careers. Technological Innovation and Human Resources, 4, 1, 137-159.

[28] P.M. Podsakoff, S. B. MacKenzie, J.Y. Lee, N.P. Podsakoff. 2003. Common Method Biases in Behavioral Research: A Critical Review of the Literature and Recommended Remedies, Journal of Applied Psychology, 88, 1, 879-903.

[29] Transparency Market Research, Medical Transcription Services Market - Global Industry Analysis, Size, Share, Growth, Trends and Forecast: 2013 – 2019, available: http://www.transparencymarketresearch.com/medical-transcription-services.html

[30] R. P. Tett and J.P. Meyer. 1993. Job satisfaction, organizational commitment, turnover intention, and turnover: path analyses based on meta-analytic findings. Personnel Psychology, 46, 2, 259-293.

[31] US Bureau of Labor Statistics, https://www.bls.gov/ooh/healthcare/medical-transcriptionists.htm#tab-1

[32] R. K. Yin. 2013. Case Study Research - Design and Methods, 5th edition. Sage Publications, CA.

[33] X. Zhang, S. D. Ryan, V. R. Prybutok and L. Kappelman, L. 2012. Perceived Obsolescence, Organizational Embeddedness, and Turnover of IT workers: An Empirical Study. ACM SIGMIS Database, 43, 4, 12-32.

APPENDIX

Appendix A Measurement Model Validation

	Age	Commit	Edu.	Excel	Exhaust	Fairness	Gender	Tech. Obs.	Turnover	WF-Conflict
Age	**1.00**									
Commitment	-0.02	**0.86**								
Education	-0.04	0.04	**1.00**							
Work Excellence	0.02	0.18	0.00	**0.85**						
Work Exhaustion	0.00	-0.51	-0.04	-0.13	**0.85**					
Fairness	-0.03	0.62	0.03	0.09	-0.46	**0.87**				
Gender	0.06	-0.01	-0.10	-0.03	0.05	-0.02	**1.00**			
Tech. Obs.	0.03	-0.32	-0.03	-0.19	0.32	-0.32	0.04	**0.85**		
Turnover	-0.01	-0.62	0.04	-0.11	0.42	-0.50	-0.02	0.33	**0.89**	
WF-Conflict	-0.01	-0.32	0.05	-0.03	0.60	-0.31	0.03	0.19	0.32	**0.85**

Appendix B Constructs and Items

Items	Loadings
Work-family conflict	
The demands of my work interfere with my work and family life.	0.822
The amount of time my job takes up makes it difficult to fulfill family responsibilities.	0.920
Things I want to do at home get done because of the demands of my job are very reasonable (R).	0.760
My job produces strain in that it makes it difficult to fulfill family duties.	0.898
I have to make changes to my plans for family activities, due to work-related duties.	0.775
Fairness of Rewards	
My organization has processes that assure that all team members will be treated fairly and equitably.	0.897
I work in an environment that lacks good procedures to make things fair and impartial (R).	0.838
In my workplace, sound practices exist that help ensure fair and unbiased treatment of all team members.	0.885
Fairness to employees is not built into how issues are handled in my environment (R).	0.850
Work Excellence	
I am passionate about ensuring error-free records.	0.870
I feel like the 'guardian' of the accuracy of medical records.	0.786
I am responsible for ensuring minimal or no errors in my work.	0.853
Error-free medical records is my top priority.	0.883
Job Commitment	
I am willing to put in effort beyond the norms for the success of the organization.	0.705
My organization inspires the best in the way of job performance.	0.882
For me, this is the best of all possible organizations for which to work.	0.921
I am extremely glad to have chosen this organization to work for over other organizations.	0.923
Technology-driven Obsolescence Perceptions	
I expect that my job will benefit in the next few years due to technological advancement (R).	0.795
I expect that my job will be eliminated in the next few years as speech recognition technology (SRT) continues to improve.	0.881
I expect that my job will be eliminated in the next few years as doctors begin using electronic health records (EHRs).	0.874
Medical Transcriptionist Turnover Intentions	
I will most likely be working for the same company this time next year (R).	0.868
I will most likely take steps during the next year to secure a job at a different company.	0.928
I will not be with this company five years from now.	0.817
I will probably look for a job at a different company in the next year.	0.928

Understanding the Impact of Social Media on Marketing Strategies of Organizations in India

Short Paper

Deepali Bhardwaj
Banasthali Vidyapith
Vanasthali 304022
Rajasthan, India
deepali@ttmc.org.in

Sangeeta Shah Bharadwaj
Management Development Institute
Gurgaon 122001
Haryana, India
ssbharadwaj@mdi.ac.in

ABSTRACT

Social media empowered customers' are forcing organizations to adopt social media and engage their customers positively. This paper studies the Technology Acceptance Model, Users and Gratification Theory (U&G) and Technology – Organization – Environment (TOE) framework to identify key factors leading to adoption of social media by the organizations. The research also explores the impact of social media adoption on marketing strategies of the organizations.

KEYWORDS

Social Media; TAM; Users and Gratification; TOE framework; Marketing Strategies

ACM Reference format:
Deepali Bhardwaj, Sangeeta Shah Bharadwaj 2017. Understanding the Impact of Social Media on Marketing Strategies of Organizations in India. In Proceedings of SIGMIS-CPR '17, June 21-23, 2017, Bangalore, India.
DOI: http://dx.doi.org/10.1145/3084381.3084394

1 INTRODUCTION

With growing importance of social media, marketers are increasingly focusing on this medium to nurture consumer communities, create pull interactions, facilitate conversations, and listen to what people are saying about their brands, products and services [21]. This study is designed to identify factors leading to social media adoption by organizations in India. The study will also evaluate the impact of social media adoption on marketing strategies of these organizations.

In this study, social media managers, marketing managers using social media and senior leaders driving social media will collectively be termed as marketers. Customers will cover current and prospective external customers for marketing department.

2 LITERATURE REVIEW

Users can participate in social media by viewing, forwarding, commenting, creating, moderating discussions, and judging/ mediating conflicts [38]. This has empowered customers to create (detract) value for an organization through the sharing of positive (negative) news and opinions with others [29]. It has become important for organizations to engage with the customers positively and meaningfully [8, 19].

Empowered customer's involvement is forcing organizations to rethink their marketing strategies not only to integrate the use of social media for creating the customer experience and brand management [8] but also for opportunities of product co-creation [39]. Papasolomou et al. [37] recommend that to engage with their customers, marketers should invest in creating interesting content. Saxena et al.[46] in their research found marketers to be more successful in using social media when they provided functional information and also entertained their customers.

To realize its true potential, social media platforms should be selected carefully and should not only be aligned to each other but also with the traditional media [25].

3 RESEARCH GAP

Preliminary review showed that much of research on social media was from consumer's perspective of social media (e.g.[13, 49, 51]). There are studies on organizations evaluating and using social media with customer's perspective in view (e.g.,[34,26, 38]). There is limited research available on social media's role in an organization in innovation and customer co-creation of products (e.g.[35, 44, 42]). Current research will focus on studying the factors influencing organization's social media adoption and its impact on the marketing strategies of these organizations in India.

4 OBJECTIVES OF THE STUDY

The objectives and research questions of this research are as follows:

Objective 1: To understand the factors driving the usage of social media in organizations

Corresponding Research Question will be:

i. *What are the factors that drive the adoption of social media in an organization?*

Objective 2: To understand the depth and breadth of adoption of social media tools and how the adoption pattern changes with the size of the organization.

Corresponding Research Questions will be:

i. *What is the adoption of social media in terms of number of years of adoption?*

ii. *What is the adoption of social media based on presence of an organization on number of social media sites?*

iii. *Does adoption of social media varies among different organization: small vs. large?*

Objective 3: To assess the impact of factors driving usage of social media on marketing strategies.

Corresponding Research Question will be:

i. *What is the impact of the identified factors (that drive the adoption of Social media) on marketing strategies?*

ii. *What is the impact of social media adoption on marketing strategies?*

5 THEORETICAL FOUNDATION

5.1 Social Media Theories

Kaplan et al. [25] categorized different types of social media using the theories of Social Presence [47], Media Richness [7] and Social Processes [16]. In background of these theories, organizations need to select social media that are most relevant to their business.

5.2 Uses and Gratification Theory (U&G)

Uses and Gratifications (U&G) Theory looks to identify the psychological needs that motivate the individuals to seek out media that fulfill their needs and leads to ultimate gratification [28,30].

Though U&G theory was originally developed to examine traditional media [27,45], recent studies have explored U&G in non-traditional media [12, 15,33]. U&G makes a key distinction between gratifications obtained and gratifications sought[17,36]. And in cases where the gap between expected and obtained gratification remains large, users often become disappointed and cease utilizing the specific medium. Leveraging this concept of U&G, to maximize their customers' gratification and engagement, marketers should have their organization's present on multiple social media with each gratifying a certain need.

Whiting et al. [50], in their review of different frameworks of U&G and in studying why people use social media, identified themes of Social Interaction, Information Seeking, Pass Time, Entertainment, Relaxation, Communication, Convenience, Expression of opinions, Information sharing and Surveillance as the key U&G themes relevant for social media.

A marketer's use of themes of Social Interaction, Communication, and Surveillance will be further explored in this research through utilities of Social Media Interaction, Social Media Communication, and Social Media Surveillance.

5.2.1 Social media Interaction. Social Media Interactions (two-way) facilitated by organizations allow customers to express opinions, increase interactivity between organization and its customers and also between customers.

5.2.2 Social media Communication. Through this utility, marketers satisfy their need to communicate (one-way) with their customers regarding their brand and product and services.

5.2.3 Social media Surveillance. Extending the many different ways in which end users can use social media to watch over others [50], organizations can use social media for surveillance of their competition to know what they are doing on social media that gives them leverage in the market.

5.3 Technology Adoption Model (TAM)

TAM developed by Davis [9] as a study of user behavior acceptance patterns for computer information systems, is based on two key constructs: perceived usefulness (PU) and perceived ease of use (PE). Later TAM was applied in multiple technology contexts to predict usage of technology in both B2B and B2C environments [1,3,20]. And apart from PU and PE, Rauniar et al. [43] in their study of drivers of social media usage by end users, identified Critical Mass (CM), Social Media Capabilities (CP), Perceived Playfulness (PP) and Trustworthiness (TW), as critical determinants for social media adoption by individuals.

The current research will further explore the constructs of social media perceived usefulness (PU), social media critical mass (CM) and social media perceived playfulness (PP) to understand the organization's social media adoption decisions for its marketing activities.

5.3.1 Social Media Perceived Usefulness. Current study will explore whether marketers agree that there is a perceived usefulness in adopting social media.

5.3.2 Social Media Critical Mass. The theory of CM states that once a certain number of users (CM) have been reached, use and usage should spread rapidly throughout the community [5].

5.3.3 Social Media Perceived Playfulness. Davis et al.[10] found that enjoyment, and fun had a significant effect on computer acceptance and this is supported by other studies [24, 22, 32]. Current research will study whether marketers agree that incorporation of Playfulness into their social media engagement generates a pleasurable experience for their customers.

5.4 TOE Framework

Technology–Organization–Environment (TOE) framework, put forward by DePietro et al. [11] states that a decision to adopt a new technological innovation is affected by three aspects of an organization - Technological context, Organizational context and Environmental context [11].

In an organization, Top Management, can influence technology innovation adoption through its support and attitudes towards change [40,14] and by allocating sufficient resources [41, 2].

There are empirical studies that have noted the importance of competitive pressure in adoption of new technologies (e.g. [18,23,6]). In current context, knowledge of how competition is exploiting social media may play a significant role in defining social media strategy for marketing.

5.4.1 Social Media Leadership. 'Tiago et al. [48] in their study found "facilitation of top-down directives" to be one of the top three factors influencing effective utilization of digital media for marketing purposes.

5.4.2 Social Media Competitive Pressure. Current study will attempt to understand whether knowledge of what competition is doing on social media puts a pressure on the organization and whether it impacts the social media adoption of the organization.

6 CONCEPTUAL MODEL AND HYPOTHESES

Based on literature review and theoretical background, three input constructs namely Social Media Utility, Social Media Technology Acceptance and Social Media Organization and Environment are identified as factors impacting marketing strategies of an organization. Social Media Adoption is an intermediary construct that may influence the degree of impact of the input constructs on the marketing strategies.

Marketing Strategies

For this research, marketing strategies will refer to an organization's integrated decisions that go into creation, improvement and communication of products and services that offer value to customers and enable the organization to achieve its specific objectives.

New Product / Service Development

For the purpose of this study, new product or service will either be a new innovation, or acquisition of a product/service for which the organization has no previous experience.

Existing Product / Service Improvement

Product Improvement is defined as product that supplements an established product line (e.g. package sizes, flavors etc) or provide greater perceived value and replace existing product [4]. The same definition of Improvement will also be applied to Services offered by an organization.

Marketing Communication

An organization engages in a range of marketing communications to communicate with its suppliers, intermediaries, customers and various publics [31]. Marketing communication tools for this study would include Advertising, Direct Marketing and Sales Promotion.

6.1 Social Media Adoption

Kaplan et al. [25] defined social media as a group of Internet-based applications that build on the ideological and technological foundations of Web 2.0, and that allow the creation and exchange of User Generated Content. This research will adopt the same definition for Social Media.

H1: Social Media Adoption will positively impact the Marketing Strategies

H1 a: Social Media Adoption will positively impact the New Product / Service Development

H1 b: Social Media Adoption will positively impact the Existing Product / Service Improvement

H1 c: Social Media Adoption will positively impact the Marketing Communication

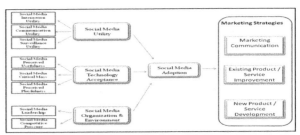

Figure 1: **Proposed Theoretical Model** (*Source: Researcher's own*)

6.2 Social Media Utility

As discussed earlier, Social Media Utility will be reviewed as the reflective index through the three utilities of Interaction, Communication and Surveillance.

H2: Social Media Utility will positively impact the adoption of Social Media

H2a: Social Interaction Utility will positively impact the adoption of Social Media

H2b: Communication Utility will positively impact the adoption of Social Media

H2c: Surveillance Utility will positively impact the adoption of Social Media

6.3 Social Media Technology Acceptance

This research would develop and validate previously identified and discussed constructs of PU, CM and PP from the point of view of the marketing activities of an organization.

H3: Social Media Technology Acceptance will positively impact the adoption of Social Media

H3 a: Social Media Perceived Usefulness will positively impact the adoption of Social Media

H3 b: Social Media Critical Mass will positively impact the adoption of Social Media

H3 c: Social Media Perceived Playfulness will positively impact the adoption of Social Media

6.4 Social Media Organization and Environment

Role of Leadership and Competitive Pressure will be evaluated through the constructs of Social Media Leadership and Social Media Competitive Pressure.

H4: Social Media Organization and Environment will positively impact the adoption of Social Media

H4 a: Social Media Leadership will positively impact the adoption of Social Media

H4 b: Social Media Competitive Pressure will positively impact the adoption of Social Media

7 RESEARCH METHODOLOGY

This is a *Quantitative research* study wherein the proposed model will be empirically tested using *questionnaire survey method*. A sample size of 200 of social media managers, digital managers and senior leaders driving social media will be targeted for the study. Unit of study will be the organization.

Understanding the Impact of Social Media on Marketing
Strategies of Organizations in India

.Bhardwaj and Bharadwaj

The depth and breadth of social media adoption will be analysed based on sectors (manufacturing vs. services), size of the organization (Large, medium, small), platform adopted and number of years of adoption.

Correlation, Regression and Factor analysis will be used to find out the relationship between independent and the dependent variables. Statistical Packages, Social Sciences (SPSS) version 20.0 and Analysis Moment of Structures Software (AMOS) version 20 will be used to perform the analysis.

8 PROPOSED CONTRIBUTION TO THEORY AND PRACTICE

Contribution of this research to theory would be in extending the U&G theory at the organization level and validating the constructs of interaction, information and surveillance from its perspective. This research will also contribute to the extension of TAM with respect to social media adoption at an organization level.

The findings of this research will help marketers to understand the factors that are important to consider while adopting social media for marketing functions. This can enable marketers to build social media strategies around the activities where the impact will be the highest.

REFERENCES

[1] Adams, D. A., Nelson, R. R., and Todd, P. A. 1992. Perceived usefulness, ease of use, and usage of information technology: a replication. MIS Quarterly. 16(2),
[2] Annukka, V. 2008. Organizational factors affecting IT innovation adoption in the Finnish early childhood education. Paper No. 133. In ECIS Proceedings of 16th European Conference on Information Systems (ECIS 2008). Galway. Ireland.
[4] Booz, Allen and Hamilton. 1982. New Product Management for the 1980s. New York. NY:Author
[5] Cameron, A.F. and Webster, J. 2005. Unintended consequences of emerging communication technologies: instant messaging in the workplace. Computers in Human Behavior. Vol. 21(1). 85-103.
[7] Daft,R. L. and Lengel, R. H. 1986. Organizational information requirements, media richness, and structural design. Management Science. 32(5). 554—571.
[8] Dateling, M. and Bick, G. 2013. The impact of social media on the marketing strategies of South African businesses. Global Science and Technology Forum.
[9] Davis, F.D. 1986. A technology acceptance model for empirically testing new end-user information systems: theory and results. Ph.D dissertation. MIT Sloan School of Management. Cambridge, MA.
[10] Davis, F.D. 1989. Perceived usefulness, perceived ease of use, and user acceptance of information technology. MIS Quarterly, Vol. 13(3). 319-340.
[11] DePietro, R, Wiarda, E and Fleischer, M. 1990. The context for change: organization, technology and environment .Tornatzky, L.G. and Fleischer, M. (Eds), The Process of Technological Innovation. Lexington Books. Lexington, MA.
[12] Dimmick, J, Kline, S. and Stafford, L. 2000. The gratification niches of personal e-mail and the telephone. Communications Research. Vol. 27. 227-48.
[13] Eagleman, A. N. 2013. Acceptance, motivations, and usage of social media as a marketing communications tool amongst employees of sport national governing bodies. Sport Management Review. Vol. 16(4). 488–497.
[14] Eder, L. and Igbaria, M. 2001. Determinants of intranet diffusion and infusion. Omega, Vol. 29(3). 233-242.
[15] Eighmey, J. 1997. Profiling user responses to commercial Websites. Journal of Advertising Research. May/June. 59-67.
[16] Goffman, E. 1959. The presentation of self in everyday life. New York: Doubleday Anchor Books.

[17] Greenberg, B. S. 1974. Gratifications of television viewing and their correlates for British children. Blumler J.G. & Katz E. (Eds.). The uses of mass communications: Current perspectives on gratifications research . 195-233. Beverly Hills, CA: SAGE.
[18] Grover, V. 1993. An empirically derived model for the adoption of customer-based Inter-organizational systems. Decision Sciences. Vol. 24(3). 603-640.
[19] Gruber, D.A, Smerek, R.E, Thomas-Hunt, M.C and James, E.H. 2015. The real-time power of Twitter: Crisis management and leadership in an age of social media. Business Horizons. 58. 163—172
[20] Ha, S, & Stoel, L. 2009. Consumer e-shopping acceptance: Antecedents in a technology acceptance mode", Journal of Business Research. 62(5). 565–571.
[21] Hipperson, T. 2010. The changing face of data insight – And its relationship to brand marketing. Database Marketing & Customer Strategy Management. Vol. 17. 2
[23] Iacovou, C., Benbasat, I. and Dexter, A. 1995. Electronic data interchange and small organizations: adoption and impact of technology. Management Information Systems Quarterly, Vol. 19(4). 465-485.
[24] Igbaria, M., Parasuraman, S. and Baroudi, J. 1996. A motivational model of microcomputer usage", Journal of Management Information Systems. Vol. 13(1).
[25] Kaplan, A.M., Haenlein, M. 2010. Users of the world, unite! The challenges and opportunities of social media. Business Horizons, 53(1). 59-68.
[26] Killian, G., MaManus, K. 2015. A marketing communications approach for the digital era: Managerial guidelines for social media integration.Business Horizons. 58.
[27] Kippax, S. and Murray, J. P. 1980. Using the mass media: Need gratification and perceived utility. Communication Research. Vol. 7.335-360.
[28] Ko, H., Cho, C.H. and Roberts, M.S. 2005. Internet uses and gratifications: a structural equation model of interactive advertising. Journal of Advertising. 34(2).
[29] Kumar, V., Aksoy, L., Donkers, B., Venkatesan, R., Wiesel, T. and Tillmanns, S. 2010. Undervalued or Overvalued Customers: Capturing Total Customer Engagement Value. Journal of Service Research. Vol 13(3). 297-310.
[30] Lariscy, R.W., Tinkham, S.F. and Sweetser, K.D. 2011. Kids these days: examining differences in political uses and gratifications, internet political participation, political information efficacy, and cynicism on the basis of age. American Behavioral Scientist, Vol. 55(6). 749-764.
[31] Lewis, B.R. 2014. Marketing Communication. in Wiley Encyclopedia of Management. Lee,n. and Farrell, A.M (Ed.). vol 9. 325 – 329.
[36] Palmgreen, P., Wenner, L. A. & Rayburn, J. D. 1980. Relations between gratifications sought and obtained: A study of television news. Communication Research. Vol 7. 161-192
[37] Papasolomou, I., & Melanthiou, Y. 2012. Social media: Marketing public relations' new best friend. Journal of Promotion Management. 18. 319–328.
[38] Parent, M., Plangger, K. and Bal, A. 2011. The new WTP: willingness to participate". Business Horizons. Vol. 54. 219-229.
[39] Piller, F.T., Walcher, D. 2006. Toolkits for idea competitions: A novel method to integrate users in new product development. R&D Management. 36(3).307 – 318
[40] Premkumar, G. and Michael, P. 1995. Adoption of computer aided software engineering (CASE) technology: an innovation adoption perspective. SIGMIS Database. Vol. 26 (2/3). 105-124.
[41] Premkumar, G. and Potter, M. 1995. Adoption of Computer Aided Software Engineering (CASE) Technology: An Innovation Adoption Perspective". ACM SIGMIS Database, Vol. 26(2/3). 105-124.
[42] Rathore, A.K., Ilavarasan, P.V. and Dwivedi, Y.K. 2016. Social media content and product co-creation: an emerging paradigm. Journal of Enterprise Information Management,. Vol. 29(1). 7 – 18.
[43] Rauniar, R., Rawski, G., Yang, J., and Johnson, B. 2014. Technology acceptance model (TAM) and social media usage: an empirical study on Facebook. Journal of Enterprise Information Management. Vol. 27(1). 6-30.
[44] Roberts, D.L., Piller, F.T. 2016. Finding the Right Role for Social Media in Innovation. MIT Sloan Management Review, Vol. 57(3). 41 – 47.
[45] Rubin, A. M. 1983. Television uses and gratifications: The interactions of viewing patterns and motivations. Journal of Broadcasting. 27(1). 37-51.
[46] Saxena,A., & Khanna, U. 2013. Advertising on social network sites: A structural equation modeling approach. Vision: The Journal of Business Perspective. 17.
[47] Short, J., Williams, E., & Christie, B. 1976. The social psychology of telecommunications. Hoboken. NJ: John Wiley & Sons, Ltd.
[48] Tiago, M.T.P.M.B. and Verissimo, J.M.C. 2014. Digital marketing and social media: why bother?. Kelly School of Business, Indiana University.
[49] Wang, J.-C. & Chang, C.-H. 2013. How online social ties and product-related risks influence purchase intentions: A Facebook experiment. Electronic Commerce Research and Applications. 12(5). 337–346.
[50] Whiting, A., Williams,D. 2013. Why people use social media: a uses and gratifications approach. Qualitative Market Research: An International Journal. Vol. 16(4). 362 – 369

Social Movements in the Age of Social Media: A Structural and Content-based Analysis

Short Paper

Pratik Tarafdar
Management Information Systems
IIM Calcutta
India
pratikt15@iimcal.ac.in

Priya Seetharaman
Management Information Systems
IIM Calcutta
India
priyas@iimcal.ac.in

ABSTRACT

A wave of protest movements in recent years leveraging the potential of social media reveals the evolution in the process of collective identity in social networks, including the radical shift in the content and semantics of protest identity. The interplay of social media with social movements needs to be studied not only by illuminating the structural notion of networks in digital activism but also the actual content that flows through the medium such as the discourses and the iconographies pertaining to the social movement. With an aim to achieve this understanding, we propose a generic framework for the study of social media movements focusing on structure and content of social networks specifically characteristics such as homophily, structural capital and media richness along with the process of resource mobilization. We suggest a mixed-method approach to help answer the proposed research questions and validate the framework. The paper also discusses possible implications for research and practice.

KEYWORDS

Social movement; social media; digital networks

ACM Reference format:

P. Tarafdar, P. Seetharaman 2017. Social Movements in the Age of Social Media: A Structural and Content-based Analysis. In *Proceedings of SIGMIS-CPR '17, Bangalore, India, June 2017 (SIGMIS-CPR '17), 4 pages.*
DOI: http://dx.doi.org/10.1145/3084381.3084406

1 INTRODUCTION

Computer-mediated social movements have been greatly fueled by the rapid proliferation of the internet. Social activists increasingly engage and organize people in pursuit of a social process through virtual petitions, online fundraising, forums, apart from the use of social media and email to recruit people [1]. In fact, social movements across the political spectrum utilize various computer-mediated communication (CMC) technologies to effect change and influence party politics [2]. Internet-mediated protests have impacted several policy changes bringing forth a plethora of opportunities to facilitate collective identity and solidarity. Some such protests have fueled high-impact movements, including the toppling of national governments, by creating channels to voice opinions and mobilize the mass towards the common objective.

The intriguing facet of the mass movements organized through the social media lies in its potential to bring rapid and significant changes in the realms of politics and governance. The gradual development of social media has strengthened the power of communication and affected the mobilizing structures and processes. The network of virtual relationships has enhanced the reach of social change beyond spatial and temporal constraints. Technology has brought openness and transparency to governance, empowered citizens allowing them to increasingly participate in institutional reform movements and has laid the foundation of a new form of political dynamics and governance model – open, consultative and inclusive [3].

More recent computing and software developments have provided us with quantitative tools to analyze the hidden dynamics of social movements as complex networks of social ties. Viewing the Internet as the mediator of mass movements will allow us the opportunity to perceive the subtleties in social ties, granularity, and interdependencies in the networks of relationships. We, therefore, formulated a research agenda surrounding three dominant themes in the context of social movements and social media: characteristics of social media; the spread of content and third, resource mobilization.

This paper attempts to present an overview of our research in progress. The paper is structured as follows. Section 2 develops the broad research framework articulating the theoretical background of each question and its position in the social media-social movement literature. The subsequent section delineates the methods to be used in this research. A plan for the research is presented in the concluding section along with possible implications for research and practice.

2 THEORETICAL BACKGROUND

Theoretical perspectives in the literature have explained social movements through lenses such as deprivation and mass-society in the earlier eras, subsequently through resource mobilization and more recently through political processes and cultural theories [4]. However, a significant volume of scholarly work explores the life cycle of social movements allowing researchers to explain the form, process, and forces that operate in and around such movements. A key assumption in such a life cycle approach is that a social movement develops through many stages of social processes with specific patterns[1] as they interact with the society in which they are embedded. These have been typified as five stages including incipiency, coalescence, institutionalization, fragmentation, and demise [5]. Although not all social movements strictly correspond to the stages, they are, for simplicity sake, generally abstracted to such an evolutionary trajectory. Sociologists also warn that the demarcations between the stages of the social movement processes are not very distinct, but are rather obscure in practicality. Interestingly, academic research has also examined how ideational linkages are formed across multiple social movements especially those that exhibit cultural similarity although such linking often results in changes in the prominence given to a particular issue [6]

2.1 Structure of Social Network

Social networks have been always regarded as major conduits for the spread of social movements. A social movement is considered a network of informal relationships that act as a centerpiece in the effort to mobilize resources for conflictual issues through collective action [7]. Like any network, social networks are seen as being composed of actors (often represented as nodes) connected by dyadic ties. The actors can be individuals or collectives, whereas ties represent any kind of social relationship between two actors. A path in the social network forms the mechanism for nodes to affect one another indirectly [8].

Contemporary research on social networks offers a diverse repertoire of conceptual frameworks encapsulating the behavior in such networks. Borgatti and Foster provided a grid to reflect on the fundamental conceptualization of social network research [9]. They identified that the social network studies differ from each other along two critical dimensions – structuralist and connectionist. The structuralist approach focuses on the topology of the network and hidden patterns in it, ignoring the

content of the ties. On the other hand, the connectionist approach focuses on the contents that flow through the social ties.

Studies along the dimension of structuralist approach are labeled "environmental shaping" and "structural capital." Environmental shaping refers to network environments which are similar due to structural equivalence thus influencing common attitudinal and behavioral characteristics of the members [9].

The literature on ecological phenomena, especially the principle of homophily has often been used as a reference domain to understand network processes in social networks and social movements. Homophily signifies the social phenomena where similarity breeds connection. Distance in social attributes translates into network distance [10]. Two types of homophily – status homophily and value homophily [11] have been widely used. Strong ties resulting from homophily, lead actors to conform with the perspective of the others [12]. Diffusion of social movements has been associated with homophily along dimensions of religious attitudes and beliefs [13]. However, homophily based on ascribed and acquired traits has been found to exhibit a mixed role in social mobilization [11]. We believe that the structural equivalence of actors in an online social network is influenced by dimensions such as status homophily and these influences vary through the different phases. Therefore, our first research question is

RQ1: How does status homophily of actors impact structural patterns of online social networks through the different phases of a social movement?

The structuralist approach also focuses on the network relations that assist actors' structural capital. It refers to the advantageous positions of certain actors in the network structure which allow them to readily access resources and influence networking behaviors. Traditionally, such actors have been named opinion leaders since they influence beliefs, attitudes, and behaviors of other actors. In the social media space, opinion leaders are termed social media influencers [14]. It is important to identify such influencers and their idiosyncrasies because these are the individuals who dominate the opinion sphere even though the network is comprised of thousands of individuals. They are the cohesive elements of the network that prevent its fragmentation [14]. Therefore, as the online social movement develops, the role of influencers in the social network becomes vital, and the study of network structure could provide insights on how the role of influencers transforms throughout the life cycle of the movement.

RQ2: How does structural capital of social media influencers in online social networks evolve through the different phases of social movements?

---

[1] Four Stages of Social Movements Essay by Jonathan Christiansen, M.A. EBSCO Research Starters® • Copyright © 2009 EBSCO Publishing Inc. • All Rights Reserved

2.2 Content of Social Network

The connectionist argument alludes to the interpersonal transmission process among those with pre-existing social ties. It refers to the perspective of flow of tangible and intangible contents between individuals through micro-mechanisms such as modeling (you use your iPhone when I interact with you, so I think of possessing one) and congruence (I like you, and you value social responsibility programs, so I value it too) [9]. The two types of connectionists approaches are labeled "contagion" and "social access to resources." Contagion implies inducing similarity amongst nodes based on interaction with similar content. Different types of network content flow through the social networks and affect the nodes that come in contact with it [8]. Contagion thus results in value homophily.

The feature in social media platforms that depicts the homogeneity of user behavior through digital content is expressed in the digital profile. Digital profile conveys the conscious and unconscious identity of individual [8] and tacitly captures the extent to which nodes influence or get influenced by the content contributed or contained in the network. Digital profiles help in establishing the digital presence of individuals through the social construction of meaning during information sharing [15]. Value homophily in social media network is thus likely to be influenced by richness, and depth of the digital content and the media itself [16]. The chat contents, event pages, groups, communities, photos, and videos reflect the richness of the social media. Therefore,

RQ3: How does the richness and depth of the digital media influence mechanisms of social homogeneity through the phases of social movements?

Individuals' access to valuable resource content flowing through their network connections improves his/her performance in the network [8]. Actors with high structural capital exploit ties to reach specific objectives. Their success depends on the quantity and quality of resources they can extract from his/her ties [9]. Similarly, social movement processes involve influential actors relentlessly exploiting their ties to mobilize resources and drive the movement forward. Ties in social networks have conventionally served as important recruitment channels for mobilization. In networks on social media, the patterns of digital information diffusion and recruitment and the social media tools have enhanced the access to social resources resulting in massive sharing of experiences and bringing about political change [17]. Activities such as recruitment, events, meetings or gatherings, online petitions, etc. are coordinated through social media platforms to mobilize resources for the movement. It is important to look at the process by which such mobilization is effected. Thus,

RQ4: How do people appropriate the digital content on the social media network to access resources and mobilize them during the course of social movements?

We present the overall theoretical framework in Figure 1.

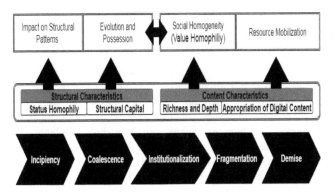

Figure 1: Framework for online social movement research (Adapted from Borgatti and Foster [9], Mauss [5])

3 PROPOSED RESEARCH METHODOLOGY

Extant literature on social networks and social movements firmly establish that the direction and intensity of their evolution are dependent on the structure and content of interaction amongst its members. Although several papers have argued for graph-theoretic and statistical methods of social network analysis, these fall short of sufficiently engaging with nuances and variations present in such networks, thereby necessitating the use of qualitative methods. A mixed-method strategy would comprehensively serve the purpose of online social movement study in the light of social network behavior [18].

In a mixed-design approach, quantitative and qualitative data, methods, techniques, concepts and/or languages are combined. On the one hand, it helps mathematicians fit a context to the phenomenon, and on the other hand, it helps sociologists appreciate patterns through mathematical tools [19].

We propose to employ quantitative methods to understand structural aspects of online social networks in organizing social movements. We will capture and analyze the network of connections based on standard metrics of social media network analysis [20]. Network connections are typically captured by "following" relationships, retweets, mentions, and replies on Twitter, and "following/friendship" relationships, likes, reactions, shares, and comments on Facebook. The socio-demographic attributes can be retrieved from actors' digital profiles. We plan to retrieve opinions on popular social movements during their course from Twitter and/or Facebook along with time stamps and location of the post. The phases of social movements can be corroborated with data from traditional media. Analysis of these using statistical algorithms, such as regression and time series analysis, Cox proportional hazard model, and other measures of centrality can help us answer RQ1 and RQ2.

In order to answer RQ3 and RQ4, we expect to use participant observation in online settings. 'Netnography' [21] or virtual ethnography [22] is a form of ethnographic research, espousing the perspectives of participant observation in online media. This will provide us access to actors' online interactions on specific social movements thus allowing us to collect and qualitatively analyze the data.

4 CONCLUSIONS

We expect this study to have two major implications. Given the lack of specific studies in the context of social movements and social media combining both content and structure, we believe our theoretical contribution will be that of bringing forth an understanding of homophily, structural capital, influence of media richness on homogeneity and resourcing mobilization. A practice-oriented implication is the possible guidelines on technology media mechanisms for activists and policy makers that we hope to suggest.

This paper presented a generic framework for the study of the interplay of social media and social movements using structure and content of social networks. It is our strong contention that given the widespread use of social media for social activism, the study has the potential to make significant contributions.

REFERENCES

[1] D. Rohlinger, A. Bunnage and J. Klein, "How Social Movements Are Using The Internet To Change Politics," *Scholars Strategy Network,* 2015

[2] M. Diani, "Social Movement Networks Virtual and Real," *Information, Communication & Society,* 2000.

[3] E. S. Madhavan, "Internet and Social Media's Social Movements Leading to New Forms of Governance and Policymaking : Cases from India," *Glocalism: Journal of Culture, Politics and Innovation,* 2016.

[4] S. Buechler, "New Social Movement Theories," *The Sociological Quarterly,* vol. 3, no. 36, pp. 441-464, 1995.

[5] A. Mauss, Social Problems as Social Movements, Philadelphia: J. B. Lippincott Co, 1975.

[6] J. Wooseok, B. King and S. Soule, "Issue bricolage: explaining the configuration of the social movement sector, 1960-1995.," *American Journal of Sociology,* vol. 1, no. 120, pp. 187-225, 2014.

[7] M. Diani, "The concept of social movement," *Sociological Review,* 1992

[8] G. C. Kane, M. Alavi, G. Labianca and S. Borgatti, "What's Different about Social Media Networks? A Framework and Research Agenda," *Management Information Systems Quarterly,* 2014

[9] S. Borgatti and P. Foster, "The Network Paradigm in Organizational Research: A Review and Typology," *Journal of Management,* 2003

[10] M. McPherson, L. Smith-Lovin and J. Cook, "Birds of a Feather: Homophily in Social Networks," *Annual Review of Sociology,* 2001.

[11] J. Alstott, S. Madnick and C. Velu, "Homophily and the Speed of Social Mobilization: The Effect of Acquired and Ascribed Traits," *PLOS ONE,* 2014.

[12] D. Strang and S. Soule, "Diffusion in Organizations and Social Movements: From Hybrid Corn to Poison Pills," *Annual Review of Sociology,* 1998.

[13] W. Bainbridge and R. Stark, "Friendship, religion and the occult: a network study," *Rev. Relig. Res.,* 1981

[14] M. Fresno García, A. J. Daly and S. Sánchez-Cabezudo, "Identifying the new Influencers in the Internet Era: Social Media and Social Network Analysis," *Revista Española de Investigaciones Sociológicas,* 2016.

[15] S. Miranda and C. Saunders, "The Social Construction of Meaning: An Alternative Perspective on Information Sharing," *Information Systems Research,* 2003

[16] R. Daft and R. Lengel, "Organizational information requirements, media richness and structural design," *Management Science,* 1986.

[17] E. Anduiza, C. Cristancho and J. Sabucedo, "Mobilization through online social networks: the political protest of the indignados in Spain," *Information, Communication & Society,* 2013

[18] J. Krinsky and N. Crossley, "Social Movements and Social Networks: Introduction," *Social Movement Studies,* 2014.

[19] I. Walsh, "Using quantitative data in mixed-design grounded theory studies: an enhanced path to formal grounded theory in information systems," *European Journal of Information Systems,* 2015.

[20] W. Nooy, A. Mrvar and V. Batagelj, Exploratory Network Analysis with Pajek, Cambridge University Press, 2005.

[21] R. Kozinets, Netnography: Doing Ethnographic Research Online, Sage, 2010

[22] C. Hine, Virtual Ethnography, Sage, 2000.

The Impact of Social Media as Technostress Inhibitor on Employee Productivity

Short Paper

Anupriya Khan
Indian Institute of Management Kozhikode
IIMK Campus P. O., 673570
India
anupriyak09fpm@iimk.ac.in

Monalisa Mahapatra
Indian Institute of Management Kozhikode
IIMK Campus P. O., 673570
India
monalisam09fpm@iimk.ac.in

ABSTRACT

The [1] positive and negative sides of information technology and systems are of interest to the researchers across different domains. Technostress, being a negative and unintended consequence rendered by the use of various information systems, has recently obtained significant attention in the information systems (IS) literature. It has been demonstrated in various studies how technostress affects the overall organizational performance by increasing role stress and reducing employees' job satisfaction, productivity, and performance. We extend the existing literature on technostress by reasoning that certain information technologies (IT) and systems may induce technostress that can be inhibited by certain other IT and systems such as social media. Drawing on coping theory, we explain the role of social media as technostress inhibitor. We thus provide the research model depicting the moderating role of social media, in which, we posit that the negative impact of technostress creators on employee productivity can be mitigated by the use of social media. We also provide the potential implications of the study and outline the research methodology that will be taken up in the next stage of our present research.

CCS CONCEPTS

• **Information systems** → Information systems applications → Collaborative and social computing systems and tools → Social networking sites

KEYWORDS

Social media; IT and systems use; Technostress; Coping theory; Employee productivity

SIGMIS-CPR '17, June 21-23, 2017, Bangalore, India
© 2017 Association for Computing Machinery.
ACM ISBN 978-1-4503-5037-2/17/06...$15.00
http://dx.doi.org/10.1145/3084381.3084407

1 INTRODUCTION

With the rapid evolution of information technology (IT) across the globe, individuals as well as organizations have started embracing new IT and systems (IT&S) to better their everyday practices. Such use of IT&S usually demonstrates its positive side, resulting into productivity efficiencies and effectiveness for organizations [41, 44-45]. However, there also exist negative sides of the use of IT&S in terms of creating stress and other issues which are counterproductive in nature [6]. We focus on one such important unintended consequence—technostress, the stress induced by the use of IT&S. While it is nearly impossible to run an organization without the implementation of necessary IT&S, at the same time we cannot ignore the negative impact of technostress on individual's job output. The phenomenon of technostress, its antecedents and consequences have recently received enormous attention in IS literature. However while observing closely, except a few, all other existing studies appear to analyze technostress creator as a second-order construct in an aggregated form without considering the individual impact of the five major dimensions—techno-overload, techno-invasion, techno-complexity, techno-insecurity and techno-uncertainty that constitute technostress creator—on different job outcomes [7]. We therefore intend to analyze the impact of each of those five first-order constructs on employee productivity. Besides, the literature indicates the need to curb the negative impact [3,29] that could be achieved by several coping mechanisms. Motivated by this, we aim to study the role of coping mechanisms in the form of technostress inhibitors. Social media technologies such as blogs, social networking sites, YouTube, and Wikis encourage communication, elevate new ideas, and foster supporting relationships among the employees to help them cope with the situation. Drawing on coping theory, we thus conceptualize social media to have the potential to reduce the effect of technostress. In essence, the questions that drive this study are as follows:

RQ1: How does each technostress creator individually influence employee productivity?

RQ2: Why does the usage of social media platforms moderate the relationship between individual technostress creators and employee productivity?

For scholars, the paper aims to strengthen the technostress literature by combining the views on technostress creator and technostress inhibitor in a single study, in which we consider social media technologies as technostress inhibitors and other IT&S as technostress creators.

2 LITERATAURE REVIEW

2.1 Technostress

The phenomenon of "Technostress" was introduced in 1984 by clinical psychologist Craig Brod, who defined it as "a modern disease of adaptation caused by an inability to cope with new computer technologies in a healthy manner" [46]. In information systems (IS) literature, the phenomenon of technostress and its impacts were initially studied and validated by Tarafdar et al. [1]. Based on the role theory and sociotechnical theory, they first introduced five important technostress creators namely Techno-overload, Techno-invasion, Techno-complexity, Techno-insecurity and Techno-uncertainty, and examined their impact on role stress and productivity. Other studies have also analyzed the consequences of technostress on end users' job satisfaction, organizational commitment, continuance commitment and performance [2-3]. However, such negative impact caused by technostress can also be moderated and mitigated in the presence of different other factors. Building on social cognitive theory [43], studies demonstrated that technology self-efficacy along with situational conditions, organizational support and computer self-efficacy can reduce the negative impact of technostress [5,8]. This is of practical significance to bring organizational effectiveness by reducing the unintended consequences of technostress. However, to our knowledge, most studies conceive any technology to be able to induce technostress. We accept such negative view of technology, but we also contend that certain technologies have the ability to inhibit technostress. Hence, we study the role of social media to realize its potency in this context.

2.2 Social Media

The last decade has witnessed the rise of social media technologies in our daily life. This led to a significant IS research area built around the impact of social media on individuals and organizations. Studying such impact appears to be essential as social media can serve as a tool to facilitate intra- and inter-organizational activities among peers, customers, business partners, and organizations. Social media helps in collaborative new product development [18-19], creation and use of knowledge sharing communities [20-22], implementation of corporate dialog at financial institutions [23], development of marketing strategies for brand management [24-25] and collaborative learning and creativity [26].

Beside its positive side, there also exist a dark side of social media platforms usage. Several studies indicate that social media usage leads to the creation of stress on end-users, development of negative emotions like guilt and fear, and incidents of cyberbullying and cybercrime [16-17,27-28,47]. Even in the context of technostress, social network is seen as a source of overload resulting into emotional exhaustion [42]. This paper acknowledges the negative side of social media, but perceives it as an opportunity because in practice, social media use by employees is usual and organizations can be benefitted if social media is put into use purposively and effectively.

3 RESEARCH MODEL

3.1 Technostress Creators and Employee Productivity

As stated earlier, individuals experience technostress as a result of their inability to cope with new technologies in their working environment. In an organization, several IT and systems are used by the employees at the same time and plausibly some, if not all, information systems create technostress [1,3,9,29]. In studying the impact on organizations of different phenomena, we have observed a number of dependent variables that are employed in technostress literature such as job satisfaction, performance, productivity, organizational commitment, job burnout and job engagement [2-3,10]. The present study thus considers employee productivity to measure the consequence of technostress [1].

The first technostress creator, techno-overload deals with overloaded information that human brain is incapable of processing during the execution of several information processing tasks necessitated by IT&S. When a lot of information becomes available and employees cannot identify the relevant ones, it leads to dissatisfaction and reduces their productivity [2]. Due to the wide use of mobile networks and connectivity, any employee can be reached out at any time at any place. Techno-invasion deals with this effect which essentially blurred the line between work-home balances, creates unnecessary disturbances and thus reduces their productivity [2]. Techno-complexity deals with the complexities associated with IT&S. Due to this employees may be unable to develop new skills frequently and their use of existing solutions to new IT&S may result in creating issues and errors thus decreasing the productivity [2]. Techno-insecurity creates a fear of job loss in employees as they perceive new IT&S may lead to automation or people with better skills and abilities to deal with IT&S will replace them in a long run [2]. Similarly, techno-uncertainty deals with the frequent and innovative changes in IT&S that makes workers uncertain about their work and job roles [2]. These two can induce negative emotions like anxiety, lower self-confidence in employees, thus reducing their productivity. Thus we hypothesize:

H1a: Techno-overload is negatively associated with employee productivity in organization.

H1b: Techno-invasion is negatively associated with employee productivity in organization.

H1c: Techno-complexity is negatively associated with employee productivity in organization.

H1d: Techno-insecurity is negatively associated with employee productivity in organization.

H1e: Techno-uncertainty is negatively associated with employee productivity in organization

3.2 Social media as Technostress Inhibitor

As stated by Tarafdar et al., technostress inhibitors are the organizational mechanisms that potentially reduce the effects of technostress [3]. When new technologies are introduced, employees require training, guidance and informal sessions with experts to understand how to effectively use the new technology. The lack of such supports is most likely to create stress and anxiety among the employees. Recently, in a study by Bucher et al., social media technologies are termed as technostress creators [38] and out of five, three factors [3] overload, invasion and uncertainty in the context of social media usage are found to create technostress in an individual. As opposed to this viewpoint of social media as technostress creators, we contend that social media technologies are technostress inhibitors by presenting those as effective coping mechanism.

According to coping theory, individuals when confronted with disruptive events and associated stressful situations, go through two cognitive processes, primary and secondary appraisal [11-12]. The primary appraisal deals with an individual's evaluation of the stressful event while the secondary appraisal is an assessment of the available coping resources and options. In the context of our study, we posit that employees faced with technostress perform problem-focused coping through the use of social media. The argument can be further evidenced by the benefits that social media platforms provide. Usage of social media platforms such as specific technical blogs, YouTube, Wikis, and social networking sites encourage communication, elevate new ideas, and provide technical support among the employees [13,14,15]. Technical support provision in terms of end-user support reduces the effects of technostress by solving users' IT&S related problems [3]. Additionally, we perceive social media technologies to be literacy facilitator since it fosters the sharing of IT&S related knowledge, and helps employees understand and cope with the demands of learning new technologies [8]. It is not the mere use of social media but the purposeful use of social media which is expected to reduce the effect of techno-stressors.

As new information systems get implemented in an organization, technostress is likely to be created because individual employees are unaware of how to cope with the systems. Now by using social media those employees will be able to better understand the new system by getting technical support, and relevant knowledge from the other employees [30-33,40]. This leads us to believe that social media users can apply the methods of active coping, seeking of instrumental social support and problem solving that are part of problem-focused coping mechanism. Apparently, this argument justifies our viewpoint that social media technologies do not always induce stress for an individual, but they play the role of technostress inhibitors, in presence of which the relationship between each of the technostress creators and employee productivity will be weakened. Thus we hypothesize:

H2a-e: Social media as a technostress inhibitor moderates the individual negative impact of Techno-overload, Techno-invasion, Techno-complexity, Techno-insecurity and Techno-

uncertainty on productivity, such that in the presence of social media the individual negative impact of technostress creators on employee productivity will decrease.

3.2 Control Variables

Existing literature suggests that the measure of dependent variables may be confounded by factors that are not considered in the hypothesized model. Therefore, in the research model we included suitable control variables such as age, gender, experience, computer self-efficacy, nature of the job and role stress.

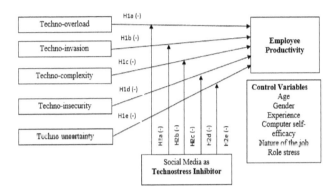

Figure 1: **Proposed Research Model**

4 RESEARCH METHODOLOGY

Since the aim of this study is to understand the impact of social media usage as a moderator on the relationship between technostress creators and employee productivity, a survey methodology will be implemented to collect the responses from the practitioners. The sampling frame consists of employees across different organizations where the use of social media platforms is allowed. We will also ensure that the respondents use social media technologies for their work. This would serve as a prerequisite for our survey.

The five technostress creators and employee productivity will be measured using the scale developed by Tarafdar et al. [1] and Torkzadeh and Doll [48] respectively. There is no existing scale to measure social media use as technostress inhibitor. Hence, we will develop the scale highlighting its purposeful use (e.g. literacy facilitation) guided by Ragu-Nathan et al. [3] and validate it subsequently. At the end, statistical analyses will be performed using structural equation modelling for hypotheses testing.

REFERENCES

[1]   Tarafdar, M., Tu, Q., Ragu-Nathan, B. S., & Ragu-Nathan, T. S. (2007). The impact of technostress on role stress and productivity. Journal of Management Information Systems, 24(1), 301-328.

[2]   Tarafdar, M., Tu, Q., & Ragu-Nathan, T. S. (2010). Impact of technostress on end-user satisfaction and performance. Journal of Management Information Systems, 27(3), 303-334

[3]   Ragu-Nathan, T. S., Tarafdar, M., Ragu-Nathan, B. S., & Tu, Q. (2008). The consequences of technostress for end users in organizations: Conceptual development and empirical validation. Information Systems Research, 19(4), 417-433.

[4]   Salanova, M., Llorens, S., & Cifre, E. (2013). The dark side of technologies:

technostress among users of information and communication technologies. International journal of psychology, 48(3), 422-436.

[5] Tarafdar, M., Pullins, E. B., & Ragu-Nathan, T. S. (2015). Technostress: negative effect on performance and possible mitigations. Information Systems Journal, 25(2), 103-132.

[6] Ayyagari, R., Grover, V., & Purvis, R. (2011). Technostress: technological antecedents and implications. MIS quarterly, 35(4), 831-858.

[7] Chandra, S., Srivastava, S. C., & Shirish, A. (2015). Do Technostress Creators Influence Employee Innovation?. In PACIS. 93.

[8] Shu, Q., Tu, Q., & Wang, K. (2011). The impact of computer self-efficacy and technology dependence on computer-related technostress: A social cognitive theory perspective. International Journal of Human Computer Interaction, 27(10), 923-939.

[9] Wang, K., Shu, Q., & Tu, Q. (2008). Technostress under different organizational environments: An empirical investigation. Computers in Human Behavior, 24(6), 3002-3013.

[10] Rajput, N., Gupta, M., Kesharwani, S., & Ralli, N. C. N. (2011). Impact of Technostress in Enhancing Human Productivity: An Econometric Study. Global Journal of Enterprise Information System, 3(3), 5- 13.

[11] Lazarus, R. S. (1966). Psychological stress and the coping process. New York: McGraw-Hill.

[12] Lazarus, R., and Folkman, S. (1984). Stress, Appraisal, and Coping, New York: Springer-Verlag

[13] Criado, J. I., Sandoval-Almazan, R., & Gil-Garcia, J. R. (2013). Government innovation through social media. Government Information Quarterly, 30(4), 319-326.

[14] Aral, S., Dellarocas, C., & Godes, D. (2013). Introduction to the special issue—social media and business transformation: a framework for research. Information Systems Research, 24(1), 3-13.

[15] Leonardi, P. M. (2014). Social media, knowledge sharing, and innovation: Toward a theory of communication visibility. Information systems research, 25(4), 796-816.

[16] Whittaker, E., & Kowalski, R. M. (2015). Cyberbullying via social media. Journal of School Violence, 14(1), 11-29.

[17] Dean, G., Bell, P., & Newman, J. (2012). The dark side of social media: review of online terrorism. Pakistan Journal of Criminology, 3(3), 103-122.

[18] Mangold, W. G., & Faulds, D. J. (2009). Social media: The new hybrid element of the promotion mix. Business horizons, 52(4), 357-365.

[19] Porter, C. E., & Donthu, N. (2008). Cultivating trust and harvesting value in virtual communities. Management Science, 54(1), 113-128.

[20] Fernando, I. (2010). Community creation by means of a social media paradigm. The learning organization, 17(6), 500-514.

[21] Kasavana, M. L., Nusair, K., & Teodosic, K. (2010). Online social networking: redefining the human web. Journal of Hospitality and Tourism Technology, 1(1), 68-82.

[22] Yates, D., & Paquette, S. (2011). Emergency knowledge management and social media technologies: A case study of the 2010 Haitian earthquake. International Journal of Information Management, 31(1), 6–13.

[23] Bonsón, E., & Flores, F. (2011). Social media and corporate dialogue: The response of global financial institutions. Online Information Review, 35(1), 34–49.

[24] Annie Jin, S. A. (2012). The potential of social media for luxury brand management. Marketing Intelligence & Planning, 30(7), 687–699.

[25] Laroche, M., Habibi, M. R., & Richard, M. O. (2013). To be or not to be in social media: How brand loyalty is affected by social media? International Journal of Information Management, 33(1), 76–82.

[26] Peppler, K. A., & Solomou, M. (2011). Building creativity: Collaborative learning and creativity in social media environments. On the Horizon, 19(1), 13–23.

[27] Maier, C., Laumer, S., Eckhardt, A., & Weitzel, T.(2015). Giving too much social support: social overload on social networking sites. European Journal of Information Systems, 24(5), 447–464.

[28] Maier, C., Laumer, S., Eckhardt, A., & Weitzel, T. (2012). Online social networks as a source and symbol of stress: an empirical analysis. In ICIS.

[29] Srivastava, S. C., Chandra, S., & Shirish, A. (2015). Technostress creators and job outcomes: theorising the moderating influence of personality traits. Information Systems Journal, 25(4), 355-401.

[30] Reagans, R., & McEvily, B.(2003). Network Structure and Knowledge Transfer: The Effects of Cohesion and Range. Administrative Science Quarterly, 48(2), 240-267.

[31] Sykes, T. A., Venkatesh, V., & Johnson, J. L. (2014). Enterprise system implementation and employee job performance: Understanding the role of advice networks. MIS quarterly, 38(1), 51-72.

[32] Sykes, T. A., Venkatesh, V., & Gosain, S. (2009). Model of acceptance with peer support: A social network perspective to understand employees' system use. MIS quarterly, 33(2), 371-393.

[33] Panahi, S., Watson, J., & Partridge, H. (2013). Towards tacit knowledge sharing over social web tools. Journal of Knowledge Management, 17(3), 379-397.

[34] Bharati, P., Zhang, W., & Chaudhury, A. (2015). Better knowledge with social media? Exploring the roles of social capital and organizational knowledge management. Journal of Knowledge Management, 19(3), 456-475.

[35] Islam, M. A., Agarwal, N. K., & Ikeda, M. (2014). Library adoption of knowledge management using Web 2.0 A new paradigm for libraries. IFLA journal, 40(4), 317-330.

[36] Jarrahi, M. H., & Sawyer, S. (2013). Social technologies, informal knowledge practices, and the enterprise. Journal of Organizational Computing and Electronic Commerce, 23(1-2), 110-137.

[37] Kahn, R. L., Wolfe, D. M., Quinn, R. P., Snoek, J. D., & Rosenthal, R. A. (1964). Organizational stress: Studies in role conflict and ambiguity. Oxford, England: John Wiley

[38] Bucher, E., Fieseler, C., & Suphan, A. (2013). The stress potential of social media in the workplace. Information, Communication & Society, 16(10), 1639-1667.

[39] Rosen, L. D., & Weil, M. M. (2000, February). Human-Ware, LLC. Retrieved from Humanware.com:http://www.technostress.com/busstudy2000.htm

[40] Beck, R., Pahlke, I., & Seebach, C. (2014). Knowledge Exchange and Symbolic Action in Social Media-Enabled Electronic Networks of Practice: A Multilevel Perspective on Knowledge Seekers and Contributors. MIS quarterly, 38(4), 1245-1270.

[41] Brynjolfsson, E., & Hitt, L.(1996). Productivity, Profitability and Consumer Surplus: Three Different Measures of Information Technology Value, MIS Quarterly, 20(2),121-142.

[42] Maier, C., Laumer, S., Eckhardt, A., & Weitzel, T. (2012). When social networking turns to social overload: Explaining the stress, emotional exhaustion, and quitting behavior from social networking sites' users. In 20th European Conference on Information System (ECIS), Barcelona, Spain.

[43] Bandura, A. (1982) Self-efficacy mechanism in human agency. American Psychologist, 37(2), 122– 147.

[44] Dos Santos, B., & Sussman, L. (2000). Improving the Return on IT Investment: The Productivity Paradox, International Journal of Information Management, 20(6), 429-431.

[45] Kudyba, S., & Diwan, R. (2002). The Impact of Information Technology on U.S. Industry, Japan and the World Economy, 14(3), 321-333.

[46] Brod, C. (1984). Technostress: the human cost of the computer revolution. Readings, MA: AddisonWesley

[47] Wall, D. S. (2008). Cybercrime and the culture of fear: Social science fiction (s) and the production of knowledge about cybercrime. Information, Communication & Society, 11(6), 861-884.

[48] Torkzadeh, G., & Doll, W.J. (1999). The development of a tool for measuring the perceived impact of information technology on work. OMEGA: The International Journal of Management Science, 27(3), 327–339.

License Choice and the Changing Structures of Work in Organization Owned Open Source Projects*

Full Paper

Poonacha K. Medappa
HEC Paris
1 Rue de la Libération
78350 Jouy en Josas Cedex
France
poonacha.medappa@hec.edu

Shirish C. Srivastava
HEC Paris
1 Rue de la Libération
78350 Jouy en Josas Cedex
France
srivastava@hec.fr

ABSTRACT

Digitally enabled transformations have allowed organizations and individuals to adopt open source as a viable mode of software development. In fact, organizations are increasingly moving away from traditional licenses in favor of open source licenses. However, extant literature reports conflicting findings regarding the impact of different open source licenses on the success of the project. Through this research, we attempt to reconcile the conflicting findings in literature by providing a more nuanced understanding of the mechanisms through which the type of license influences the success of the project. Using propensity score matching and ordinary least squares regression analysis on a sample of 2110 organization owned open source projects, we compare the structures of work across the two main types of licenses and study its relation to the success of the project. The results of our analysis indicate that different motivational mechanisms are at play under different licenses, which in turn has an influence on the optimal structures of work for a particular license. From these results we conclude that the success of the project depends on how well the structures of work are aligned to the motivational requirements created by the license. The findings provide significant insights for open source researchers and organizations as to how they can model the structures of work to facilitate the success of open source projects.

CCS CONCEPTS

•**Information systems** → **Open source software** •**Applied computing** → **Psychology** • **Applied computing** → **Economics**

KEYWORDS

Open source software; FLOSS; structures of work; open source license; motivation; copyleft; superposition

ACM Reference format:

P. K. Medappa, S. C. Srivastava. 2017. License Choice and the Changing Structures of Work in Organization Owned Open Source Projects. In *Proceedings of ACM SIGMIS-CPR'17, June 21-23, 2017, Bangalore, India.*
DOI: http://dx.doi.org/10.1145/3084381.3084410

1 INTRODUCTION

Digitally enabled transformations have led to profound changes in the way individuals and organizations view and structure work. Amongst them, the transformation of software development from being traditionally in-house to one that is open source is particularly noteworthy. Increasingly, both individuals and organizations are adopting free (libre) and open source software (FLOSS) as a viable mode of software development because of the multifarious advantages it offers with respect to evolved motivational mechanisms and structures of work. Further, organizations are discovering that FLOSS projects are often able to create software that surpasses proprietary software in terms of quality and functionality. For example, a recent study of 750 C/C++ FLOSS projects found that the quality of the FLOSS projects surpassed that of proprietary software [1]. This has led to a large-scale crossover of organizations from being just consumers to owners of FLOSS projects. For example, in November 2001, IBM embraced the open source approach by opening the source code for several of its software tools (estimated at $40 million) to the public domain [2]. This officially created the Eclipse open source project [3]. Another good example of a firm that has embraced the open source phenomenon is Google. To date, Google has released over 20 million lines of code and started over 900 FLOSS projects [4]. While this transformation has allowed organizations to tap into the vast reserves of programming skills spread across the globe, it has also created dilemmas in terms of motivating contributors and licensing the software. Despite the salience, research on these subjects especially from an organizational perspective is rather limited [5]. In recognition of this research need, we examine how license choice of organization owned FLOSS influences the success of the FLOSS project.

OSS licenses differ in the extent to which they restrict how users may use, modify and redistribute the software. At one extreme are restrictive licenses, such as the GNU general public license (GPL), and at the other extreme are permissive licenses, such as the Berkeley Software Distribution (BSD) license [6]. The choice of FLOSS license is one of the important decisions made by project owners [7], which has been found to affect the success of the project [8]. This salience has attracted researchers across many disciplines who have tried to understand the mechanisms involved in choosing a particular license (e.g. [9] [6] [10]) as well as the impact of the choice of license on the project (e.g. [8] [11] [12]). The research on the determinants of license choice has found that project characteristics [10], the nature of motivation [9] and social influence [6] all come together to help determine the choice of license. On the other hand, research on the impact of the choice of license has been less conclusive with conflicting findings across the two main types of licenses [5]. For example, Stewart et al. [8] found that projects with permissive licenses become more popular over time than restrictive licenses. On the other hand, Colazo et al. [11] found that the number of developers and productivity of developers were higher for projects under restrictive licenses as compared to permissive licenses.

With regards to the research on the impact of license choices, three gaps are noteworthy. First, the conflicting research findings accentuate the need for a complete explanation of how the choice of license impacts the success of the project. Second, Singh et. al. [6] find that the type of license chosen by a new project is influenced by the license type of existing projects that are socially closer to them. This raises concerns of self-selection bias and endogeneity related issues when studying the impacts of license choices. However, most previous researches on license choice do not adequately take into account these issues in their empirical models. Third, prior researches have largely concentrated on understanding the impact of license choice in community based FLOSS projects owned by individuals without much emphasis on understanding if the mechanisms involved holds through for organization owned FLOSS projects. Our research aims to address these research gaps by addressing the following research question: (i) How does the choice of licenses impact the success of organization owned FLOSS projects?

Through this research, we aim to make the following contributions to theory and practice. First, we advance the understanding of FLOSS licenses by teasing out the relationship between the choice of license and the success of the project. We do this by theorizing the impact of license choice on the motivation of contributors and consequently its impact on the structures of work. Second, by tying the impact of license choice with the structures of work, we provide insights for organization owners as to how best they can model the structures of work to facilitate the success of the FLOSS project.

2 THEORETICAL BACKGROUND

Traditional (proprietary) software developed by individuals or organizations are protected by copyright laws, which make the software a private good [10]. That is, the individuals or organizations that created the software own the source code, which is not made available to the customer for reuse and modification.

The Free Software Foundation (FSF, www.fsf.org) created by Richard Stallman in 1983 tried to create a legal basis which would allow collaboratively developed code to not only remain free to use, but also ensure the free availability of the source code [14]. This movement gave rise to software that followed the new copyleft (restrictive) licensing policy. Software that adopted restrictive licenses gave any user the right to copy, modify and redistribute the software. In addition to the above, any enhancement to code and even any proprietary software that made use of the source code would be bound by the same license and would be forced to remain open [5,15]. This copyleft feature of the license made sure that any offshoots of the restrictive licensed software would also remain free or open. The main idea behind the copyleft feature of the restrictive licenses was to prevent the collaboratively developed code from being commercialized and eventually closed.

In an effort the relax the copyleft feature of the restrictive licenses, permissive licenses emerged (e.g. BSD, ASF and MIT) which provided most of the open source features of the earlier restrictive license but also gave the developer the freedom to change the license policy of the software built. The Open Source Initiative (OSI; www.opensource.org) in 1997 spearheaded the creation of the permissive licenses in order to provide developers the freedom to use their code whichever way they choose. The creation of two distinct license regimes (restrictive and permissive) opened the doors towards new IS research that crossed boundaries between IS, public policy, economics and psychology.

Of particular interest for our current study are previous researches that have examined the impact of the choice of license on the success of the project. The results of these studies are often in-conflict with each other [5,16] with some favoring restrictive licenses while others (a larger set) favoring permissive licenses. The researches that favors permissive licenses include: Stewart et al. [8], who theorized a reduced level of perceived usefulness in projects adopting restrictive licenses since these licenses constrain the commercialization of the application. They found support for their hypothesis using an empirical study of 218 FLOSS projects hosted on Freshmeat (www.freecode.com), finding that projects with permissive licenses become more popular, thus attracting more users and developers over time than restrictive licenses. Similarly, based on a study of 71 FLOSS projects hosted on SourceForge, Fershtman and Gandal [7] found that the output per contributor in open source projects is much higher when licenses are less restrictive due to the greater commercial potential of permissive licenses. Based on a study of a large sample of OS projects hosted on SourceForge, Comino et. al. [17], found that projects distributed under highly restrictive licenses were less likely to reach an advanced stage of development.

On the other hand, researches that favors restrictive license include: Colazo et al. [11] who theorized that projects with restrictive licenses engender a stronger sense of social identity in contributors than permissive licenses. Based on an empirical study of 244 projects hosted on SourceForge the authors found that the number of developers and productivity of developers were higher for projects under restrictive licenses as compared to permissive licenses, supporting their hypothesis. Bonaccorsi and Rossi [18] surveyed Italian firms that use open source software and found that, on average, firms tend to adopt restrictive licenses in order to attract more contributions from the FLOSS community. Scotchmer [12] modeled firm level utility to understand the impact of a firm adopting restrictive open source licensing in-lieu of proprietary licenses. She found that if an industry as a whole can commit to a restrictive license before it is known which firm will be the first innovator then all of them would profit in expectation. In an effort to reconcile the conflicting findings regarding the impact of license choice and better understand its effect on project success we restrict the current study to the impact of the FLOSS license choice on the success of the project. To unearth the relationship between license choice and project success we look at how the choice of license impacts the motivation of the contributors and subsequently the structures of work.

The theory of collaboration through open superposition [19] provides a theoretical lens through which we can establish a link between motivation of contributors and the structures of work. Superposition is the process through which software development occurs in a sequential manner, with changes to the software added incrementally, one on top of another. Each change represents a task that is independently built by a contributor and that has its own functional payoff through the improvements it brings to the application [19]. The theory of superposition argues that in the case of FLOSS projects, superposition provides the most effective work breakdown structure that enhances motivation to contribute and at the same time allows for the creation of complex software. In order to build a case for this argument, the authors invoke theories of motivation and coordination. Specifically, they call upon the self-determination theory (SDT; [20]) and affective events theory (AET; [21]) to show that a superposed work breakdown structure satisfies the innate psychological needs of *autonomy*, *relatedness* and *competence* in the contributors which in turn lead contributors to expend greater task effort in FLOSS projects. Our research adopts this line of thought by studying the mechanisms through which the choice of license influences the motivations of contributors and in turn results in changes to the structures of work in FLOSS projects. This helps us establish a link between the choice of license, motivation of contributors, the structures of work and eventually the success of the project.

3 THEORY AND HYPOTHESIS

3.1 Relationship between License Type and the Structures of Work

To understand how the choice of license influences the structures of work, we invoke the theories of SDT, and superposition. SDT and its subtheories postulate the existence of three innate psychological needs: *autonomy*, *relatedness*, and

competence, which lead to enhanced self-motivation when satisfied and result in a positive affective state [20,22]. SDT also postulates that motivation is not a unitary or bipolar construct but rather a spectrum that varies from extrinsic to intrinsic motivation based on the extent to which the regulation is autonomous [20,22]. In specific, depending on how much autonomy is given, the spectrum of motivation comprises of external, introjected, identified, integrated, and intrinsic motivation; where intrinsically motivated behavior is observed when the regulation is fully autonomous [22].

Across the licenses types, we contend that based on the amount of restrictiveness of the license, the motivational mechanisms are altered along the spectrum of motivation. That is, projects with restrictive licenses predominantly attract intrinsically motivated contributors who seek high levels of autonomy while projects with permissive licenses attracts contributors who are not only intrinsically motivated but also motivated by the potential opportunity to commercialize their work. This is mainly because restrictive licenses include the copyleft clause, which prevents the commercialization of the contributions. Previous researches have also shown the differing motivational mechanisms across the license types: for example, Sen et. al. [9] found that intrinsically motivated individuals who are motivated by the challenge of the work prefer moderately restrictive over permissive licenses, while others who are extrinsically motivated by the opportunity for status, for instance, tend to prefer permissive licenses.

The theory of superposition helps us understand how the different motivational mechanisms and the need for autonomy influence the structure of work. In the case of projects that adopt a superposed structure of work, the software development occurs in a sequential manner, with changes to the software added incrementally, one on top of another. Howison and Crowston [19] proposed that superposition satisfies the innate psychological needs of autonomy, competence, and relatedness, creating a work breakdown structure that best motivates contributions in FLOSS environments. Superposed structure of work is found to be more effective than concurrent work when intrinsically motivated contributors are involved because concurrent work tends to create dependencies between contributors thereby reducing their autonomy [19]. However, we would expect that when the contributors are extrinsically motivated, they would be willing to swap some of their autonomy for concurrent work since concurrent work is more time efficient and can result in quicker completion of the task and provide quicker payoffs.

Thus we posit that projects with restrictive licenses will show higher degree of superposition since they attract intrinsically motivated contributors who seek higher levels of autonomy. Hence we hypothesize:

Hypothesis 1: *Projects that adopt restrictive licenses have a higher degree of superposition than those that adopt permissive licenses.*

3.2 Moderating Effect of License Type on the Relationship between the Degree of Superposition and the FLOSS Project Success

As a consequence of hypothesis 1, we study how the influence of superposition on the success of the project differs across the license types. Previous empirical research has shown that the decision to choose a particular license for a FLOSS project is important as it affects the success of the project [8]. Further, developers motivated to participate in a FLOSS project have to consider the fit between the FLOSS license and its ability to satisfy their motivational goals through the project, since the FLOSS license affects the freedom to use, modify, and redistribute the software [9]. That is, successful FLOSS projects are those that are more likely to create the right fit between the FLOSS license and the motivational goals of its contributors. The need for the optimal fit between license type and motivational mechanisms makes the relationship between license type and success of the project not direct but rather one of moderation where the license type interacts with the amount of autonomy offered (measured by the degree of superposition). This moderated relationship determined by the need for the right fit between FLOSS license type and the motivational mechanisms might also explain the conflicting findings found in prior research.

Thus, we posit that for restrictive licenses, projects that show higher degree of superposition should be in a better position to satisfy the high need for autonomy in the intrinsically motivated contributors creating a positive affective state in the contributors [19]. The positive affective state in contributors enhances the task effort that is expended by them [21] resulting in an increase in the functionality and quality of the software being built and eventually leading to the success of the project. Hence we hypothesize:

Hypothesis 2: *The type of license moderates the relation between the degree of superposition and the success of the project, such that, in the case of projects with restrictive licenses, the degree of superposition tends to have higher positive influence on the success of the project than in the case of projects with permissive licenses.*

4 METHOD

In order to understand the mechanisms through which the license types influence FLOSS projects, we conducted an empirical analysis of FLOSS projects hosted on GitHub. GitHub's popularity among programmers, its developer-focused environment, its integrated social features, and the availability of detailed metadata make it a popular environment for FLOSS research [23]. We restricted our study to a sample of 2110 public open source projects owned by organizations such as Google, Facebook, and Adobe. Our sample included both projects that adopted restrictive licenses (403 projects) and those that adopted permissive licenses (1707 projects).

4.1 Data collection

We employed Google's bigquery tool to query the archived project log data available in the GitHub Archive database [24]. Since this database is large (about 432 GB, with 134 million rows for the year 2014 alone [25]), we needed the bandwidth provided by a tool like Google's bigquery to run queries and export the results. In order to reduce the number and size of queries, we restricted our analysis to projects that were started during the first five months of 2014. Further, for each project, the task-level data collection was restricted to all development work that was undertaken in the year 2014. In all, we ran more than 30,000 queries over a period of 20 days.

While GitHub provides a rich dataset, care needs to be taken to overcome common perils in using the dataset (see Kalliamvakou et al. [23]). For example, care must be taken to avoid projects that do not involve software development, are too small, or are mirrors or personal stores. After addressing the perils, we were left with a sample of 2110 organization owned FLOSS projects that we considered for our analysis.

4.2 Measurement

GitHub offers a good environment in which to measure degrees of superposition and study their relationship with the license type and project's success. More specifically, two features of GitHub make it ideal for this research. First, the granularity of the data and the availability of time stamps for all events enabled us to clearly identify the versions of a project and the task order, which allowed us to operationalize the degree of superposition (see Medappa and Srivastava [26]). Second, the availability of detailed contributor- and project-specific data allowed us to measure the dependent variable and create a rich set of controls. The different variables that we used in this research are detailed in the following subsections.

4.2.1 Dependent variable.

Degree of superposition is the dependent variable of interest for testing hypothesis 1. Degree of superposition was operationalized taking into account Howison and Crowston's [19] characterization of superposition and measured as the ratio of the total number of versions of the project to the total number of tasks added to the project [26]. Based on this operationalization, the degree of superposition for a project takes a value between 0 and 1. If degree of superposition = 1, all of the project's tasks were added sequentially, with each task representing a new version of the project. The degree of superposition decreases as a project adopts a concurrent development approach and approaches 0 as more and more tasks are concurrently added to a single version of the project.

Success of the project is the dependent variable of interest for testing hypothesis 2. In order to measure the success of a project, we used the total number of stars that the project received. In GitHub, the term user includes all the individuals who use the software. This not only includes contributors who use and contribute to the project but also those who just make use of the software without making any project contributions. Each user can "star" projects in order to keep track of projects that they find interesting and also to show their appreciation for those projects [27]. Starring a project on GitHub is comparable to "liking" a page or content on social media outlets such as Facebook where a user can like any post or page that they find interesting. Thus, the number of stars a project has received approximately indicates the total number of people who are satisfied with and show support for that project. Moreover, stars can be seen as a multidimensional measure, because they capture not only the popularity of the project (since popular projects attract more users which in turn increases the number of stars it receives) but also user satisfaction with the project (users star a project only if they find it satisfactory), which have both been identified as measures of success for FLOSS projects [28]. As a consequence, the number of stars is a commonly used measure for identifying successful projects in the GitHub environment. For example, GitHub itself uses stars to identify trending projects and in its project rankings [27], Jarczyk et al. [29] use the log transformation of the number of stars as a measure of project quality and popularity of GitHub projects, and Tsay et al. [30] use the number of stars as a measure of popularity and project establishment.

4.2.2 Independent variable.

Our main objective is to study the mechanisms through which the different licenses motivate contribution and facilitate the success of the project. Consequently, the *restrictive license* flag is the main independent variable used in our analysis. This flag takes a value of "1" if the project is bound by a license that adopts the restrictive "copyleft" policy and is "0" otherwise.

Some of the researches tend to re-categorize the restrictive group of licenses as highly restrictive and moderately restrictive to create three classes of FLOSS licenses. For example, Lerner and Tirole [10] propose three classes of FLOSS licenses based on the restrictiveness of redistribution rights: highly restrictive, restrictive, and unrestrictive. Sen et. al. [9] classify licenses based on their restrictiveness as being either strong-copyleft, weak-copyleft or non-copyleft. However, in line with Stewart et. al. [13], we stick to the two-regime classification of licenses as being either restrictive (this includes moderately restrictive and highly restrictive classes of licenses) or permissive. We believe our results can be extrapolated to explain the mechanisms involved in moderately restrictive licenses.

4.2.3 Control variables.

GitHub maintains detailed project- and contributor-level data, which allows for the introduction of a rich set of control variables. Consequently, we identified two kinds of control variables for our analysis: contributor characteristics and project characteristics.

Contributor characteristics: We identified two measures to control the influence of contributor characteristics- the *total number of contributors* and the *average commits per contributor*. It is important to control for these two characteristics since they are expected to influence the success of the project by increasing the development activity within the project. Further, the number of contributors is expected to influence degree of superposition,

as there is a tendency for a project to adopt a more concurrent form of development as the numbers of contributors increase.

Project characteristics: We identified five measures to control for different project characteristics. The measures: *project size* and *number of programming languages* were included in our model to control the effects that project size and complexity have on the hypothesized relationships. We also included *average task size* because projects with larger tasks tend to differ in terms of degree of superposition when compared to projects with smaller tasks. Last, in order to control for the temporal effects of project start date and completion, we included *project completion flag*, and the fixed effects of *month of creation*.

5 RESULTS

5.1 Hypothesis Linking the Type of License and the Degree of Superposition of the Project

Table 1 provides the means, standard deviations, and correlation coefficients of the variables used in the analyses. Hypothesis 1 predicts that projects with restrictive licenses will display a higher degree of superposition than those with permissive licenses. To test this hypothesis, we check the impact of the restrictive license flag on the degree of superposition. Prior research on the determinants of FLOSS license choice find that the type of license chosen by a new project depends on the license types of existing projects that are socially closer to it in its inter-project social network [6]. This finding raises concerns of selection bias when we try to study the impact of license choice. That is, projects may not be randomly assigned to the treatment (restrictive license) and the control group (permissive license), but instead select into their own group. To overcome the potential bias arising from endogenously determined license choices for the projects, we use propensity score based matching [31].

Table 1. Mean, Standard Deviation, and Pairwise Correlation Coefficients of the Variables

	Variable	Mean	Std. Dev.	1	2	3	4	5	6	7	8
1	Stars	205.576	718.988								
2	Degree of superposition	0.676	0.172	-0.125**							
3	No. of programming languages	3.469	2.888	0.053*	-0.063**						
4	Total contributors	14.389	24.419	0.344**	-0.231**	0.273**					
5	Size of project in megabytes	3.017	24.530	-0.007	-0.011	0.345**	0.187**				
6	Average commits per contributor	60.031	126.041	-0.024	-0.059**	0.347**	0.054*	0.122**			
7	Average task size	2.676	7.526	-0.023	-0.009	0.102**	0.059**	0.039	0.059**		
8	Project completion flag	0.086	0.280	-0.066**	-0.028	-0.084	-0.114**	-0.026	-0.071**	-0.002	
9	Restrictive license Flag	0.191	0.393	-0.060**	0.038	0.259**	0.098**	0.119**	0.177**	0.061**	-0.007

$* p < 0.05.$ $** p < 0.01.$

The essence of the matching technique is to divide data into homogeneous groups on the basis of propensity scores by identifying a set of control projects (projects with permissive licenses) that are similar to the treated projects (projects with restrictive licenses) [32]. Each set should consist of projects that are homogenous in their attributes, but that differ in their adopted license regime. In propensity score matching method, we first obtain propensity scores of each project in the sample based on a set of contributor and project attributes using a probit model. In this probit model, the *restrictive license flag* is the dependent variable, which is regressed with two contributor attributes (*total number of contributors* and the *average commits per contributor*) and four project attributes (*number of programming languages, average task size, project completion flag* and the *log transformation of the number of stars*). The selection of these attributes was based on the consideration that they simultaneously influence the license choice and the outcome variable (the degree of superposition) [32].

Using the calculated propensity scores, we next identify a set of control projects (projects with permissive licenses) that is closest in terms of propensity scores to the treatment projects (projects with restrictive licenses)[2] (for details, see [33]). Finally, we obtain the treatment effect (effect of choosing a restrictive license) by computing the differences in degree of superposition between projects with restrictive licenses and their matched counterfactual projects with permissive licenses.

The results of the propensity score matching analysis support hypotheses 1. The average effect of the restrictive license choice on the degree of superposition is positive and significant (ATT = 0.036, t = 3.38, 95% Confidence interval: 0.014 to 0.058). Thus we can conclude that projects that adopt restrictive licenses tend to display a higher degree of superposition than those that adopt permissive licenses, albeit with a small effect size. This confirms that projects with restrictive licenses tend to provide a higher level of autonomy to the contributors than those with permissive licenses.

5.2 Hypothesis Linking License Type and Project Success

Hypothesis 2 predicts a moderating role of license type on the relationship between the degree of superposition and the success of a project. We test this hypothesis by using ordinary least squares (OLS) regression analysis with the number of stars as the dependent variable. Further, to correct for any potential heteroscedasticity in the error terms, we used heteroscedasticity consistent standard errors in our regression model [34]. To test the moderation effect, we included the interaction of license type with the degree of superposition term in the regression model. This moderation effect is expected to positively influence the relationship between degree of superposition and success of the project such that the coefficient of the interaction term (β_3) is positive and significant. From Table 2, we can see that β_3 is positive and significant (353.225, p < 0.05), confirming that projects that adopt restrictive licenses tends to positively increase the influence of degree of superposition on the success of the project.

Figure 1 depicts the relationship between degree of superposition and the success of the project for projects with restrictive and permissive licenses. We see that for projects that adopt restrictive licenses, the relationship between degree of superposition and success of the project is positive while its

effect is negative for projects with permissive licenses. The shift of the relationship between degree of superposition and success of the project from linearly decreasing for projects with permissive licenses to linearly increasing for projects with restrictive licenses has strong implications to theory and practice. We discuss some of these implications in the next subsection.

Table 2. Results of Moderated Regression Analysis Predicting Stars

Measure	Co-efficients of regression (*Significance*)	Full model Co-efficients of regression (*Significance*)
No. of programming languages	1.585 (*0.79*)	1.86 (*0.743*)
Total contributors	10.401 (*0.000*)**	10.413 (*0.000*)**
Size of project	-0.15 (*0.225*)	-1.878 (*0.051*)
Average commits per contributor	-0.15 (*0.225*)	-0.153 (*0.052*)
Average task size	-3.391 (*0.082*)	-3.396 (*0.174*)
Project completed flag	-74.1905 (*0.16*)	-68.935 (*0.001*)**
Degree of superposition (β1)	-251.337 (*0.01*)	-246.098 (*0.027*)*
Restrictive license flag (β2)	-388.105 (*0.009*)**	-390.161 (*0.005*)**
Degree of superposition X Restrictive license regime (β3)		353.225 (*0.049*)*
Fixed effects of month of creation	Yes	Yes
R²		0.137
N		2,110

* p < 0.05. ** p < 0.01.

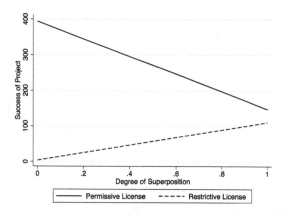

Figure 1. Plots of the Relationship between Degree of Superposition and Project Success for Restrictive and Permissive Licenses

6 DISCUSSION AND CONCLUSION

In view of the growing use of open source as a viable modality for organizational work, we sought to understand how the choice of licensing mechanism influences the structures of work and the success of the FLOSS projects. Two underlying motivations for this research were (i) a need to provide a more complete explanation for how the choice of license influences

---

[2] We match projects using the kernel-based matching method

the success of the project and (ii) a desire to reconcile the conflicting findings in previous researches concerning the impacts of choosing a particular license. To gain insights into these issues, we drew on the theory of superposition [19], SDT [20], and AET [21]. Our study yielded two overarching findings that inform us about the unique mechanisms that operate in organization owned FLOSS environments. First, the two license regimes (restrictive and permissive) invoke different motivational mechanisms in the contributors, which results in changes to the ideal structures of work. Second, success of the project is not directly related to the license choice as is often hypothesized but rather depends on how well the project is able to satisfy the differing motivational mechanisms invoked by the license.

Through this research, we advance the understanding of FLOSS licenses by providing a comprehensive theoretical model that explains the relationship between the type of license and the success of the software development project. In this model, we propose that depending on the restrictiveness of the license, the motivational mechanism of the contributors vary along a spectrum between intrinsic and extrinsic motivations. Our findings help reconcile the conflicting findings in extant literature by proposing that success of a project is not determined by the type of license but rather depends on how well the structures of work are aligned to best provide for the motivational mechanisms induced by the type of license. In light of these findings, organization owners looking to choose a particular license will be well advised to keep in mind that the choice of license determines the nature of contributors that the project attracts. And depending on the underlying motivational needs of the contributors that the license attracts, the structures of work need to be adapted in order to facilitate the success of the project.

7 REFERENCES

[1] Coverity Report. Coverity Scan: 2013 Open Source Report [Internet]. 2013. Available from: http://softwareintegrity.coverity.com/rs/coverity/images/2013-Coverity-Scan-Report.pdf

[2] Lohr S. Some I.B.M. tools to be put in public domain. *New York Times (November 5) [Internet].* 2001; Available from: http://www.nytimes.com/2001/11/05/technology/05OPEN.html?pagewanted=all

[3] Wagstrom PA. Vertical interaction in open software engineering communities. Carnegie Mellon University; 2009.

[4] Google. Open source projects released by *Google [Internet].* 2017. Available from: https://developers.google.com/open-source/projects

[5] Crowston K, Wei K, Howison J, Wiggins A. Free/Libre open-source software development. *ACM Comput Surv [Internet].* 2012;44(2):1–35. Available from: http://dl.acm.org/citation.cfm?doid=2089125.2089127

[6] Singh PV, Phelps C. Networks , Social Influence , and the Choice Among Competing Innovations: Insights from Open Source Software Licenses Networks , Social Influence , and the Choice Among Competing Innovations: Insights from Open Source Software Licenses. *Inf Syst Res.* 2013;24(August 2014):539–60.

[7] Fershtman C, Gandal N. Open source software: Motivation and restrictive licensing. *Int Econ Econ Policy.* 2007;4(2):209–25.

[8] Stewart KJ, Ammeter AP, Maruping LM. Impacts of license choice and organizational sponsorship on user interest and development activity in open source software projects. *Inf Syst Res.* 2006;17(2):126–44.

[9] Sen R, Subramaniam C, Nelson ML. Determinants of the Choice of Open Source Software License. *J Manag Inf Syst [Internet].* 2008;25(3):207–40. Available from:

[10] Lerner J, Tirole J. The scope of open source licensing. *J Law, Econ Organ.* 2005;21(1):20–56.

[11] Colazo JA, Fang Y, Neufeld D. Development Success in Open Source Software Projects: Exploring the Impact of Copylefted Licenses. In: *AMCIS 2005 Proceedings [Internet].* 2005. Available from: http://aisel.aisnet.org/amcis2005/432

[12] Scotchmer S. Openness, open source, and the veil of ignorance. *Am Econ Rev.* 2010;100(2):165–71.

[13] Stewart KJ, Ammeter AP, Maruping LM. A Preliminary Analysis of the Influences of Licensing and Organizational Sponsorship on Success in Open Source Projects. In: *38th Hawaii International Conference on System Sciences.* 2005.

[14] Stallman R. The GNU Operating System and the Free Software Movement. In: *Open Sources Voices from the Open Source Revolution [Internet].* 1999. p. 272. Available from: http://www.oreilly.com/catalog/opensources/book/stallman.html

[15] Lerner J, Tirole J. Some Simple Economics of Open Source. *J Ind Econ [Internet].* 2003;50(2):197–234. Available from: http://doi.wiley.com/10.1111/1467-6451.00174

[16] Colazo J a, Fang Y. Following the Sun: Temporal Dispersion and Performance in Open Source Software Project Teams. *J Assoc Inf Syst.* 2010;11(11):684–707.

[17] Comino S, Manenti FM, Parisi ML. From planning to mature: On the success of open source projects. *Res Policy.* 2007;36(10):1575–86.

[18] Bonaccorsi A, Rossi C. Licensing schemes in the production and distribution of Open Source software. An empirical investigation. :1–32. Available at SSRN:https://ssrn.com/abstract=432641 or http://dx.doi.org/10.2139/ssrn.432641

[19] Howison J, Crowston K. Collaboration Through Open Superposition: A Theory Of The Open Source Way. *MIS Q.* 2014;38(1):29–50.

[20] Ryan RM, Deci EL. Self-Determinaton Theory and the Facilitation of Intrinsic Motivation, Social Development, and Well-Being *Am Psychol.* 2000;55(February):68–78.

[21] Weiss HM, Cropanzo R. Affective Events Theory: A Theoretical Discussion of the Structure, Causes and Consequences of Affective Experiences at Work. *Res Organ Behav.* 1996;18:1–74.

[22] Ke W, Zhang P. The effects of extrinsic motivations and satisfaction in open source software development. *J Assoc Inf Syst.* 2010;11(12):784–808.

[23] Kalliamvakou E, Gousios G, Singer L, Blincoe K, German DM, Damian D. The promises and perils of mining GitHub. In: *Proceedings of the 11th Working Conference on Mining Software Repositories.* 2014. p. 92–101.

[24] Grigorik I. *The GitHub Archive [Internet].* 2012. Available from: https://www.githubarchive.org/

[25] Google. *Table details: 2014.* [Internet]. 2017. Available from: https://bigquery.cloud.google.com/table/githubarchive:year.2014?pli=1&tab=details

[26] Medappa PK, Srivastava SC. Does the Task Structure of Open Source Projects Matter? Superposition and Value Creation. In: *Thirty Seventh International Conference on Information Systems.* Dublin; 2016. p. 1–10.

[27] GitHub. *About Stars.* 2017; Available from: https://help.github.com/articles/about-stars/

[28] Crowston K, Howison J, Annabi H. Information systems success in free and open source software development: Theory and measures. *Softw Process Improv Pract.* 2006;11(2):123–48.

[29] Jarczyk O, Gruszka B, Jaroszewicz S, Bukowski L. GitHub Projects. Quality Analysis of Open-Source Software. In: SocInfo 2014: *The 6th International Conference on Social Informatics.* 2014. p. 80–94.

[30] Tsay J, Dabbish L, Herbsleb J. Influence of social and technical factors for evaluating contribution in GitHub. 36th *Int Conf Softw Eng.* 2014;356–66.

[31] Rosenbaum PR, Rubin DB. The Central Role of the Propensity Score in Observational Studies for Causal Effects. *Biometrika.* 1983;70(1):41–55.

[32] Caliendo M, Kopeinig S. Some Practical Guidance for the Implementation of Propensity Score Matching. *Discuss Pap Ser.* 2005;(1588).

[33] Heckman JJ, Ichimura H, Todd P. Matching As An Economic Evaluation Estimator. *Rev Econ Stud [Internet].* 1998;65(2):261–94. Available from: http://restud.oxfordjournals.org/content/65/2/261.short

[34] Hayes AF, Cai L. Using heteroskedasticity-consistent standard error estimators in OLS regression: An introduction and software implementation. *Behav Res Methods.* 2007;39(4):709–22.

[35] Bonaccorsi A, Giannangeli S, Rossi C, Rossi C. Entry Strategies Under Competing Standards: Hybrid Business Models in the Open Source Software Industry. *Manage Sci.* 2006;52(7):1085–1098.

[36] August T, Shin H, Tunca TI. Licensing and Competition for Services in Open Source Software. *Inf Syst Res.* 2013;24(4):1068–1086.

When Do Vendors Behave Opportunistically? An Empirical Study of Financial Market Impacts on Firms in IT Outsourcing Relationships

Full Paper

Rajiv Kishore
State University of New York at Buffalo,
Buffalo, NY, USA
rkishore@buffalo.edu

Akie Iriyama
Waseda Business School,
Tokyo, Japan
airiyama@gmail.com

Laxmi Gunupudi
Indian Institute of Management
Bangalore, India
laxmi.gunupudi@gmail.com

Background

Organization [1] specific knowledge is the most strategically important resource that provides a basis for sustainable competitive advantage [1]. However, when firms partner with one another, knowledge spillovers often taken place [2]. This can either be intended or unintended. When vendors work with multiple clients, knowledge transfer in an outsourcing relationship not only increases the supplier performance specific to that partnership, but the spillovers also result in increase in the ability of the supplier to redeploy competencies outside the learning dyad [3]. Firms in the same industry have similar knowledge applications. Though the level of competition or rivalry among these firms may not necessarily be high, applicability of knowledge across the firms is high. Leakage or spillover of such business process knowledge or specialized knowledge assets can fundamentally lead to holdup problems [4, 5]. These problems are exacerbated owing to vendor opportunism which causes misappropriation of specialized assets such as specialized and proprietary knowledge assets [6].

Extant literature has suggested several mechanisms by which firms may prevent knowledge spillovers to the vendor. For instance, one of the main foci of TCE is the design of appropriate governance structures to safeguard the specialized assets involved in the transaction thereby mitigating ex post holdup [7]. In addition, one of the most reasonable conditions to prevent knowledge spillover is the size of the firm. Larger firms are resource rich partners who provide vendors with greater knowledge. Owing to their size, they have a better bargaining position in crafting contracts so as to govern the relationship appropriately and prevent any such knowledge leakage. However, when the contract terminates and the firm is no longer in a relationship with the vendor, the issues of knowledge leakage and holdup by the vendor could become rather exacerbated for larger firms. This is because of the large amount of knowledge the vendor may have acquired from them and the fact that knowledge assets are inherently difficult to protect even with the use of various contracting provisions such as confidentiality and non-compete provisions. While the holdup problem is at the heart of TCE, the focus of the TCE literature has predominantly been on dyadic relationships between a buyer firm and a supplier firm, and on the holdup experienced by the buyer firm from the supplier firm. This literature, has to our knowledge, not examined the holdup that may be experienced by the rivals of a focal firm who enters into an alliance with a focal vendor and when the vendor in question also provided or currently provides services to rivals of the focal firm.

In this paper, we examine the nature of holdup due to knowledge spillovers experienced by rivals of a focal firm that are in a current relationship or have terminated their relationship with the vendor when the focal firm announces a new contractual relationship with the vendor. Announcement of such strategic decisions lead to market reactions about the value creation or destruction effects about the announcement. Knowledge leakage is very difficult to measure and can only be observed through proxies [8]. Therefore, we studied 510 contract announcements by various firms with vendors and the resulting CAR of their rival firms.

Research Study

Alliance announcements affect the wealth of the allying firms' rivals [9]. Research based on event studies shows that announcement of such strategic decisions lead to market reactions about the value creation or destruction effects [10, 11]. Any firm's announcements with respect to strategic decisions such as mergers, acquisitions, strategic alliances etc. impact the CAR of directly or indirectly competing firms [12]. Therefore in this study, we take the cumulative abnormal returns (CARs) of rival firms as the dependent variable that accrues to them in response to a focal firms' contract announcement with the

[1] All authors contributed equally to this paper and their names are in reverse alphabetical sequence of the last name.

common vendor. The resulting outcomes of knowledge spillovers are thus observed in terms of CARs of the rivals of a focal firm.

We examine the CAR of the rival firms when a focal firm announces a new contract with a focal vendor. We seek to understand the role of firm size in preventing or promoting knowledge leakage in such contracting networks. Synthesizing logics from the research based on knowledge leakage, TCE, and shadow of the future, we derive the following hypotheses.

H1: *A rival firm that has a current contractual relationship with a focal vendor will not experience any statistically significant loss or gain in terms of CAR around the date of announcement of a new contract between a focal firm and the focal vendor.*

H2: *A rival firm that has no current contractual relationship with a focal vendor will experience a loss in terms of negative CAR around the date of announcement of a new contract between a focal firm and the focal vendor.*

H3: *A rival firm that has a current contractual relationship with a focal vendor will experience a gain in terms of positive CAR around the date of announcement of a new contract between a focal firm and the focal vendor when the rival firm is larger in size relative to the focal firm.*

H4: *A rival firm that has no current contractual relationship with a focal vendor will experience a greater loss in terms of negative CAR around the date of announcement of a new contract between a focal firm and the focal vendor when the rival firm is larger in size relative to the focal firm.*

Using a sample of 510 IT outsourcing contract announcements, we observed losses and gains through cumulative abnormal returns (CARs) that accrue to rival firms around the date of announcement of a new IT outsourcing contract by a focal firm. Results support our hypotheses and show negative CARs for rivals that in the past had a relationship with the focal vendor but do not have a current relationship with the vendor. We also find that the rival firm size relative to the focal firm size plays an important role in vendor calculus and resulting knowledge spillovers.

Implications

The current study contributes to the extant research literature in the field of IT outsourcing and TCE by making two important contributions by extending the notion of vendor opportunism.

Upon the announcement of this new contract, the focal firm and the focal vendor are the two parties in a contractual relationship. However, we propose and show that a third party who is a rival of the focal firm in the same industry may experience gains or losses in financial markets upon announcement of a new contract by the focal firm due to potential knowledge spillovers from either the focal firm to the rival firm or from the rival firm to the focal firm depending upon two conditions: a) whether or not the rival firm has a current and/or had a prior contractual

relationship with the focal vendor; and b) the relative size of the focal and rival firms.

We also make another contribution to the literature on governance in IT outsourcing alliances by examining the role of firm size in knowledge spillovers in IT outsourcing networks. Current understanding suggests that client size can mitigate hold up *ex post* (after the signing of the contract but during the currency of the contract) due to asymmetric power over the vendor firm. Further, the literature suggests that vendors are bound by contractual agreements with the focal rival firm that will prevent knowledge leakage and mitigate holdup [4]. We provide a nuanced understanding about the role of firm size as a safeguard against knowledge appropriation by proposing and showing that the vendor will leak knowledge from a smaller to a larger firm only when the larger firm has a current ongoing relationship with the vendor. If the larger firm ceases its relationships with the vendor, it will in fact experience a loss of knowledge.

Our findings have implications for IT outsourcing alliance strategies for firms. Findings suggest that vendors are inherently opportunistic and firms must form alliances after very careful consideration. They must be cognizant of the knowledge leakage issues that can generate losses even after termination of their contracts with a vendor. Our results suggest that firms are advised to engage in only long term alliances to prevent issues of knowledge leakage and resulting losses in capital markets.

References:

[1] Oxley, J. and T. Wada, Alliance structure and the scope of knowledge transfer: Evidence from US-Japan agreements. Management Science, 2009. 55(4): p. 635-649.

[2] Inkpen, A.C., Learning and knowledge acquisition through international strategic alliances. The Academy of Management Executive, 1998. 12(4): p. 69-80.

[3] Mesquita, L.F., J. Anand, and T.H. Brush, Comparing the resource-based and relational views: knowledge transfer and spillover in vertical alliances. Strategic Management Journal, 2008. 29(9): p. 913-941.

[4] Susarla, A., R. Subramanyam, and P. Karhade, Contractual provisions to mitigate holdup: Evidence from information technology outsourcing. Information Systems Research, 2010. 21(1): p. 37-55.

[5] Klein, B., R.G. Crawford, and A.A. Alchian, Vertical integration, appropriable rents, and the competitive contracting process. The Journal of law & economics, 1978. 21(2): p. 297-326.

[6] Sampson, R.C., R&D alliances and firm performance: The impact of technological diversity and alliance organization on innovation. Academy of Management Journal, 2007. 50(2): p. 364-386.

[7] Rindfleisch, A. and J.B. Heide, Transaction cost analysis: Past, present, and future applications. The Journal of Marketing, 1997: p. 30-54.

[8] Mayer, K.J., Spillovers and governance: An analysis of knowledge and reputational spillovers in information technology. Academy of Management Journal, 2006. 49(1): p. 69-84.

[9] Han, K., et al., Value cocreation and wealth spillover in open innovation alliances. MIS Quarterly, 2012. 36(1): p. 291-325.

[10] Kalaignanam, K., et al., The effect of CRM outsourcing on shareholder value: a contingency perspective. Management Science, 2013. 59(3): p. 748-769.

[11] Tanriverdi, H. and V.B. Uysal, Cross-business information technology integration and acquirer value creation in corporate mergers and acquisitions. Information Systems Research, 2011. 22(4): p. 703-720.

[12] Lee, S.H., S.B. Bach, and Y.S. Baik, The impact of IPOs on the values of directly competing incumbents. Strategic Entrepreneurship Journal, 2011. 5(2): p. 158-177.

Framework for Alignment of Service Provider Value Drivers with Client Expectations in IT Services Outsourcing

Full-Paper

Arup K Das
Management Development Institute
Gurgaon 122001
Haryana, India
akdas_000@yahoo.com

Sangeeta Shah Bharadwaj
Management Development Institute
Gurgaon 122001
Haryana, India
ssbharadwaj@mdi.ac.in

ABSTRACT

In this competitive environment, service provider organizations are keen to create value for their client organizations and differentiate their services during delivery of IT services outsourcing projects. However, there are variations in value delivery as per client expectations. It is critical to understand how alignment can be achieved between B-to-B client and vendor organizations to minimize this variation. Through dyadic case studies, this research paper develops a framework of (mis)aligned practices at three levels of conceptualization- contractual alignment, knowledge alignment and business alignment. Further, a project alignment measurement framework has been developed along with propositions for future study. This research adopted a practice based analyses of organizations Findings from data collected through interviews and project documentations resulted in nineteen practices showing aligned behaviors and twenty-three practices showing mis-aligned behaviors at contractual alignment level; six practices showing aligned behaviors and eleven practices showing mis-aligned behaviors at knowledge alignment level; and fourteen practices showing aligned behaviors and eleven practices showing mis-aligned behaviors at business alignment level.

KEYWORDS

IT Outsourcing; Value Creation; Service Provider; Client Expectation; Alignment; Framework.

ACM Reference format:

SIGMIS-CPR '17, June 21-23, 2017, Bangalore, India
© 2017 Copyright is held by the owner/author(s). Publication rights licensed to ACM.
ACM ISBN 978-1-4503-5037-2/17/06...$15.00
http://dx.doi.org/10.1145/3084381.3084394

1 INTRODUCTION

The last two decades have witnessed an increase in activities centered on outsourcing as a source of competitiveness and value creation. In this competitive B-to-B environment (B-to-B is the

short form of Business-to-Business, where both seller & buyer are business enterprises), service provider organizations are keen to create value for their client organizations and differentiate their services during delivery of IT services outsourcing projects. However, variations in value quite common in an IT service outsourcing environment. Not only do such gaps exist between one project and another, but such differences exist within a project also. Hence it is critical to understand how alignment can be achieved between B-to-B organizations.

The research question addressed through this study is as follows:

1. *How do the service provider value drivers align with the client expectation value drivers in the context of IT services outsourcing in a B-to-B environment?*

An extensive literature study of extant literatures in outsourcing environment spread over more than two decades brought out the service provider and client value drivers that helped us to design a conceptual value driver alignment model. Case study based research methodology was adopted to get answer to this research question. The main purpose of the case study based research was to understand the nature of alignment between service provider value drivers and client expectations using the value driver alignment framework.

We used the concept of practice based analyses of organizations as the tool to identify how service provider practices are (mis)aligned with the client practices. Practice based analyses are becoming increasingly widespread in the management disciplines because of their special capacity to understand how organizational action is enabled and constrained by prevailing organizational and societal practices[9]. Value creation in buyer supplier relationship is not new. Sharing of knowledge, technology and resources between buyer and supplier takes place in-order to improve the competitive advantage of the two. This process is termed as value creation . Wilson and Jantrania [31] continued and proposed a model to measure value creation in such B-to-B relationships. Biggemann and Buttle [2] conceptualized B-to-B relationship value by conducting extensive case-based research and found that relationships deliver value in forms that go beyond simple financial considerations.

Through this research work, we develop an understanding of the client expectations. At a minimum, client expectation is limited to the commitments of delivery as defined in any outsourcing contractual agreement. The delivered value to this expectation is called contractual value. However, there is a lot beyond this level of client expectation – especially, client's hidden expectations that's never captured in any contractual agreement. The delivered value to this expectation is the surplus value that generates positive experience to a client in an outsourcing relationship. The first level of (mis)alignment starts as early as during the selling process. The second level (mis)alignment might exist with respect to capability and competency gaps in project teams, while the third level of (mis)alignment might be at the working level relationships between the project delivery teams at both ends (i.e. service provider end and as well as in the client end). We developed a framework of alignment to measure this (mis)alignment between client and service provider based on the outcome of research. A positive alignment leads to a successful B-to-B relationship, whereas negative alignment leads to a poor B-to-B relationship.

2   THE ALIGNMENT MODEL

An extensive literature survey of one hundred and twenty two research papers spread over more than two decades (1988–2013) resulted in identification of service provider and client value drivers that have form the basis of value driver alignment model. A rigorous process was adopted to identify the terminologies in the research journals that went through levels of iterations on most frequently used words / phrases. At the very initial stage, Agency Cost Theory seeks to explain the B-to-B relationships better in the context of establishing outsourcing relationships, while Transaction Cost Economics (TCE) theory seeks to explain the formation of this relationship by adopting largely a cost-efficiency oriented perspective ([28],[29],[30]). However, along with cost efficiency, clients also expect the outsourced IT project to be completed within schedule and as per delivery quality standards. Value is created only when the service provider services exceed the expectations of all the value driver attributes— cost, schedule and quality, we call this as Total Contract Value (TCV). As the services delivered are knowledge

intensive, there are many instances of mis-alignment w.r.t contractual value expected by clients, specially related to quality of the services. Service providers who are competent in domain knowledge and as well as related technology knowledge are able to address this gap through competent and capable resources.

As technology becomes obsolete very fast and technology not being the core-competence of clients, the client organizations rely heavily on the service provider's competency, experience and domain knowledge as explained by Resource Dependence Theory. This entices the service provider organizations to build resources, capabilities and knowledge as their key value offerings. They want to become the capable partner of the client by developing tangible resources as well as intangible capabilities that are unique and inimitable. Clients expect their service providers to be flexible in their approach in delivering project scope, which may not have been accurately captured in the contract. Consistent and reliable output of service provider's delivery is another expectation of the client. Thus, client expectations in terms of service provider capabilities, and flexibility and consistency in service delivery help in building a long-lasting B-to-B relationship between a service provider and a client.

At the third stage, as the relationship between the client and service provider matures, co-operation, interactions, interdependence and social and economic exchanges become important in creating value for the client. This level of mutual interdependence is aimed at achieving joint accomplishments leading to alignment at business level. Appendix A summarizes the service provider and client value drivers as identified through literature survey. The **Error! Reference source not found.** represents the Value Driver Alignment Model and Table 1 and 2 represents service provider and client value drivers.

An examination of the value driver alignment model shows that alignment between service provider value drivers and client expectations is key to generate satisfaction and surplus benefits to clients. This alignment was investigated using three levels of conceptualization based on the theoretical concepts by Saxena and Bharadwaj [23]:

1. **Contractual Alignment**: Contractual alignment measures the alignment between the client expectation value driver "Deliver within TCV" and the service provider value drivers "Technology Solution" and "Delivery Quality." The focus is at the operational aspects.

2. **Knowledge Alignment:** Knowledge alignment measures the alignment between the client expectation value driver "Flexibility and Consistency" and the service provider value driver "Service Delivery Capability." The focus is beyond the day-to-day operational aspects.

3. **Business Alignment**: Business alignment measures the alignment between the client expectation value driver "Strategic Partner" and the service provider value driver "Strategic Relationship." The focus is at the strategic level.

3. RESEARCH METHODOLOGY AND DATA ANALYSIS

The case study research methodology was used. The main purpose of the case study methodology was to understand the nature of alignment between service provider value drivers and client expectation value drivers using the value driver alignment model as represented in **Error! Reference source not found.**. Multiple case study design belonging to different types of projects was considered suitable for increasing the external validity of the findings ([32]). Pre-defined selection criteria for this study were three-folds:

- Project Complexity: This is measured by the total contract value of the project, size of the project team and project duration. We decided to select projects of total contract value between US$ 250,000 and US$ 5,000,000; project team size between ten and fifty people; and project duration between six months and two years;
- Nature of the Project: Although there were no major restrictions to the nature of the project, the focus here was on IT application services projects in consulting/development/testing/integration/operations and maintenance;

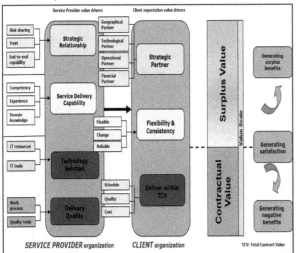

Figure 1: Value Driver Alignment Model

Client Value Drivers	Theoretical Argument	Theoretical Orientation	Value driver attributes	References
Deliver within TCV	'Deliver within TCV' refers to service provider's delivery against a working level agreement that defines a contractual agreement with clear scope, schedule, cost & quality.	Agency Theory,	Schedule, Quality, Cost	[26], [18]
Flexibility & Consistency	'Flexibility & consistency' is defined as a behavior that is repeatable and demonstrated through pro-activeness and	Relationship Theory, TQM for parties through contractual	Flexible, Change, Reliable	[7], [22]. [25]

	accommodating & adapting to client requirement changes in an IT service outsourcing project.	agreements.		
Strategic Partner	A strategic partner will achieve, enhance or maintain competitive advantage for each participant forming alliances	Relationship Theory, Strategic Partnering	Geographical Partner, Technological Partner, Operational Partner and Financial Partner	[17], [4], [24]

Table1: Service Provider Value Drivers

- Dyadic Case Study: Another important criterion was to ensure that we get access to interviewees from both service provider-end and client-end for dyadic case study analysis of the same IT services outsourcing projects. Access to such case studies was quite difficult and limited too.

Service Provider Value Drivers	Theoretical Argument	Theoretical Orientation	Value Driver Attributes	References
Delivery Quality	Delivery Quality is ability of service provider to create value in terms of quality related to processes and services.	Agency Theory, CMM	Work Process, Quality Tools	[10, [12]
Technology Solution	Technology solution is delivering superior technology solution both tangible and intangible (through skilled workforce) which is efficient.	Agency Theory, TCE, RBV	IT Resources, IT Tools	[27], [5]
Service Delivery Capability	Service Delivery Capability is the whole set of competency, experience and domain knowledge of the service provider's resources to deliver IT services.	RBV	Competency, Experience, Domain Knowledge	[8]
Strategic Relationship	Strategic Relationship is creating relational value which is beyond efficiency and effectiveness and is strategic in nature.	Relationship Theory	Risk Sharing, Trust, End-to-End Capability	[7], [22]. [25]

Table 2: Client Value Drivers

Case study interview scripts were studied to understand the nature of alignment between service provider value drivers and client expectation value drivers. The interview questions were framed to probe how each of the service provider and client value drivers have influenced in successful or un-successful project delivery thereby generating positive or negative experiences respectively. For example, in-order to assess the service provider's delivery capability- interview questions was prepared from both client-end and as well service provider-end perspectives. We asked the client- *'Did you find- your service provider had necessary service delivery capabilities (competency, experience, domaiCn knowledge) and technology (IT resources, tools) to deliver the project?'* Similarly, we asked the service provider – *'What was your service delivery capabilities required for this project? What all service delivery capabilities your team had and how did you build these capabilities?* Answers to these questions through dyadic interviews gave meaningful insights of how (mis)aligned are their views on the same context. Four case studies were conducted as part of this research work. The Table 3 gives a snapshot of the case study details.

Case Study Protocol	Case Study Characteristics
Unit of Analysis	IT Service Outsourcing Project
Case Design	Dyadic Interviews of both client & service provider end practitioners of the same IT service outsourcing project
Number of Case Study	4 Case Studies of IT service outsourcing projects
Primary Data	Interview
Secondary Data	Project Document (Proposal Document; Contract Document; Project Plan; Emails; etc.)
Number of Interviews	16 interviews Case-1: 2 service provider & 2 client practitioners Case-2: 2 service provider & 2 client practitioners Case-3: 2 service provider & 2 client practitioners Case-4: 2 service provider & 2 client practitioners
Profile of Interviewees	1 project manager and 1 technical leader from each end (i.e., service provider end and client end)
Mode of Interviews	Phone Conference Call or face-to-face interview
Average duration of interviews	60 minutes
Client Demographics	1 client based in Australia; 2 clients based in Europe and 1 client based in Africa
Service Provider Demographics	All 4 service providers based in India

Table 3: Case study details

The **Error! Reference source not found.** gives a brief snapshot of the project demographics along with the client's strategic business drivers. Each of the case study analyses (i.e. *Within Case Analysis*) was done using content analysis of the interview scripts. *Cross Case Analysis* was done at the end after content analysis code groups were summarized and consolidated through four stages for each of the service provider and client interviews. Findings from primary data collected through interviews were corroborated with secondary data collected through project documentations. Triangulation was done by conducting interviews of two project team members of the same IT services outsourcing project at either end- service provider-end or client-end. Multiple case studies strengthened the generalizability of this research work, while the answers to the interview questions were recorded in interview scripts against each and every question, thereby increasing the reliability of the research because the procedures can be repeated ([32]).

3.1   Data Analysis

We adopted practice based analyses of organizations, which are becoming increasingly widespread in the management disciplines because of their special capacity to understand how organizational action is enabled and constrained by prevailing organizational and societal practices ([9]). The label "practice" carries with it a double meaning: "practice" signals both an attempt to be close to the world of practitioners and a commitment to sociological theories of practice. The key insight of these practice based studies have been that strategy work ("strategizing") relies on organizational and other practices that significantly affect both the process and the outcome of resulting strategies. Thus, Strategy-as-Practice (SAP) research offers an alternative to the individualistic models of decision-making that still dominate the field of strategic management . Through the case studies, we identify practices that are seen as (mis)alignment practices, as observed and analyzed through the interviews of client-end and service provider-end practitioners.

In this context, we can take an analogy, where aligned practices are behaviors or actions which generates positive experiences to client as a result of service provider delivery; whereas mis-aligned practices are behaviors or actions which generates negative experiences. Through this process of data analysis – we identify eighty four (mis)aligned practices grouped into three groups- (a) Contractual Alignment, (b) Knowledge Alignment and (c) Business Alignment.

Case No	Project Team size (No. of people)	Duration (in months)	Contract size (approx. US$)	Telecom Client's Strategic Business Drivers
Case-1	40	10	650,000	Launch Mobile Broadband solution targeted towards gold and platinum customers
Case-2	25	14	600,000	Mobile number portability solution conforming to government regulations
Case-3	30	11	800,000	Next generation Telecom IT billing solution targeted towards new customer acquisition through faster and flexible offers
Case-4	20	8	600,000	Expansion of Telecom network solution in Africa

Table 4: Case study details

4. DYADIC ALIGNMNET FRAMEWORK AND PROPOSITION

Based on the eighty-four (mis)alignment practices, we introduce a dyadic alignment framework, which can be used by any researcher for any future research work. The dyadic alignment framework will allow performing dyadic alignment tests to determine the nature of alignment between a client organization and a service provider organization in the context of an IT services outsourcing project.

We built the dyadic alignment framework using a three-step process:

Step-1: Framework to capture absolute alignment analysis scores for each of the eighty-four practices as well as differential alignment analysis scores under the three alignment categories—Contractual, Knowledge and Business

Step-2: Framework to determine Contractual Alignment Index, Knowledge Alignment Index and Business Alignment Index for each of the three alignment categories—Contractual, Knowledge and Business and

Step-3: Framework to determine the overall Project Alignment Index of the IT Services Outsourcing Project based on the project alignment indices for each of the three alignment categories—Contractual, Knowledge and Business.

The framework captures the alignment indices (Low, Moderate, and High) from both client and service provider perspectives based on the absolute client and service provider alignment scores and as well the differential alignment scores between client and service provider. The differential scores bring-in the intensity of the difference in perception between client and service provider on the same practice that's being reviewed by both. A high alignment index is achieved only when absolute alignment score is >70% and the differential alignment score is <10%. Moderate contractual alignment index is achieved only when absolute alignment score is >70% and the differential alignment score is between 10-30% OR when absolute alignment score is between 30-70% and the differential alignment score is <10%. For all other scenarios, alignment index is considered low. Based on these client and service provider contractual, knowledge and business alignment indices, we capture the overall project alignment index. The three groups of absolute alignment scores (%) - '0-30', '30-70' and '70-100' were derived by equally dividing the scale of '1-100' into three equal parts and then adjusting the decimals to the nearest tens of digit. For example, the absolute alignment score (%) groups first identified were − '0-33.33', '33.33-66.66' and '66.66-100', which were later adjusted to '0-30', '30-70' and '70-100'.

On the differential scale, the range of '>30' was considered significant because both the lowest absolute score group ('0-30') and the highest absolute score group ('70-100') had a span of 30 and hence it was considered important to capture any deviation that's '>30'. The remaining part of the differential scale ('0-30') was again divided equally between two parts (since we already identified the differential group of '>30') − '0-15' and '15-30', which was later adjusted to the nearest tens of digit − i.e. '0-10'

and '10-30'. Thus, we identified three differential alignment (%) groups of '0-10', '10-30' and '>30'.

5. DISCUSSION AND CONCLUSION

5.1 Contribution to Knowledge

The focus of this research work was on client expectations and service provider value propositions, and alignment of the two during IT services outsourcing project delivery in a B-to-B environment. There is a threefold contribution from this research work:

1. Developing a comprehensive list of client expectation value drivers and service provider value drivers through literature study; Building a practice-based framework of (mis)alignment of service provider's value drivers with client expectations through dyadic case studies of B-to-B organizations; and

2. Proposing a measurement framework for measuring alignment of service provider value drivers and client expectation value drivers in the context of IT outsourcing at three levels— Contractual, Knowledge and Business

The research work has made significant contribution to the literature and theories. From the service provider perspective, our theoretical grounding is on Resource Based View (RBV) Theory resulting in capability based sourcing. Competency, Experience and Domain Knowledge are rare, valuable and un-imitable that helps create a strategic advantage to a service provider organization. We identify this set of capabilities as Knowledge, which is intrinsic to an organization and critical for its success. Client organizations look towards knowledge-based sourcing, since through this they also get access to these rare, valuable and un-imitable resources that put them, as well, in a strategic advantageous position against their competitors. Knowledge capability exists in three forms—firstly, basic knowledge about product or technology that's required to deliver a project as per contractual agreement; secondly, knowledge regarding the customer's business environment, technical / IT environment and overall solution domain; and thirdly, knowledge regarding customer relationship and client's hidden expectations that's key to deliver services beyond the contractual agreements. We have seen knowledge practices that have generated positive experiences to clients in IT outsourcing projects in all these three stages of knowledge capability sourcing. The central theme of this research work, i.e. value alignment, contributes to three new meta-theoretical concepts-Contractual Alignment, Knowledge Alignment and Business Alignment.

5.2 Contribution to Practice

The research work contributes significantly to the working practitioners in the client and service provider organizations. Organizations may design trainings for their team members to make them aware on (mis)aligned practices that can subsequently help team members practice aligned practices during project delivery. The dyadic alignment framework provides a platform for quantitative analysis of alignment of service provider value against client expectations in a B-to-B environment.

5.3 Limitations and Scope for Future Research

The scope of the case study research was limited to a micro level study of projects only. In other words, what came out of the study (practice-based alignment framework) was micro level B-to-B alignment through trust, work culture and relationships between project team members at both ends (client as well as service provider). Few attributes of B-to-B level alignment which focuses on financial, geographical etc. did not come clearly at project level. Further, it would be interesting to study the nature of alignment where the service provider is an internal IT organization. Such scenarios can exist in case of an Offshore Development Center (ODC) or Global Delivery Center (GDC) [in our context, service provider organization], who are responsible for providing IT services to their parent organizations [in our context, client organization]. Lastly, the practice-based alignment framework is generic and can capture more value drivers and (mis)alignment practices based on similar future research work.

REFERENCES

[1] Barney, J.B. 1991. Firm Resources and Sustained Competitive Advantage. *Journal of Management,vol.* 17, no. 3, 99-120.

[2] Biggemann, S. and Buttle, F. 2005. Conceptualizing Business-to-Business Relationship Value. *The IMP Journal.*

[3] Bowman, C. and Ambrosini, V. 2007. Firm value creation and levels of strategy. *Management Decision* , vol 45, no.3, 360-371.

[4] Clarke-Hill, C.M., Robinson, T.M. and Bailey, J. 1998. Skills and competence transfer in European retail alliances: A comparison between alliances and joint ventures. *European Business Review, vol.* 98, no. 6, 300-310.

[5] Click, R. and Duening, T.N. 2005. Business Process Outsourcing: The Competitive Advantage. *Wiley, Hoboken, NJ* .

[6] Coase, R.H. 1937. The Nature of the Firm. *Economica,* 4 no. November, 386-405.

[7] Dyer, J.H. and Singh, H. 1998. The Relational View: Cooperative Strategy and Sources of Interorganizational Competitive Advantage. *The Academy of Management Review* , vol 23, no. 4, 660-679.

[8] Edvinsson, L. and Sullivan, P 1996. Developing a model for managing intellectual capital. *European Management Journal* ,vol.14, no. 4, 356-364.

[9] Feldman, M.S. and Orlikowski, W.J 2011. Theorizing practice and practicing theory. *Organization Science* , vol.22, no. 5, 1240–1253.

[10] Hirvonen, P. and Hilander, N. 2001. Towards joint value creation processes in professional services. *The TQM Magazine* , vol.13 no. 4, 281-291.

[11] Jensen, M.C. and Meckling, W.H. 1976, "Theory of the Firm: Managerial Behavior, Agency Costs and Ownership Structure." *Journal of Financial Economics,* vol 3 , 305-360.

[12] Jiang, B. and Amer, Q 2006. Research on outsourcing results: current literature and future opportunities. *Management Decision* , vol.44 no. 1, 44-55.

[13] Kern, T 1997. The Gestalt of an Information Technology Outsourcing Relationship: an Exploratory Analysis. *Proceedings of the 18th International Conference on Information Systems Atlanta, Georgia.*

[14] Klepper, R 1995. The Management of Partnering Development in I/S Outsourcing. *Journal of Information Technology* , vol.10, 249-258.

[15] LaPlaca, Peter J. and Katrichis, Jerome M 2009. Relative Presence of Business-to-Business Research in the Marketing Literature. *Journal of Business to Business Marketing,* vol. 16 no. 1-2, 1-22.

[16] Lam, W. and Chua, A.Y.K 2009. Knowledge outsourcing: an alternative strategy for knowledge [28] Gruber, D.A, Smerek, R.E, Thomas-Hunt, M.C and James, E.H. 2015. The real-time power of Twitter: Crisis management and leadership in an age of social media. Business Horizons. 58.   163—172 management. *Journal of Knowledge Management* , vol.13, no. 3 , 28-43.

[17] Mohr, J. J. and Spekman, R. E. 1994. Characteristics of partnership success: Partnership attributes, communication behavior, and conflict resolution techniques. *Strategic Management Journal,* vol. 15, no. 2, 135-152.

[18] Ngwenyama, O.K. and Sullivan, W.E 2007. Outsourcing contracts as instruments of risk management: Insights from two successful public contracts. *Journal of Enterprise Information Management,* vol. 20, no. 6 , 615-640.

[19] Penrose, E.T 1959. The Theory of the Growth of the Firm. *New York: Blackwell.*

[20] Peters, L.D 1997. IT enabled marketing: a framework for value creation in customer relationships. *Journal of Marketing Practice Applied Marketing Science,* vol. 3, no. 4, 213-229.

[21] Pfeffer, J. and Salancik, G.R 1978. The External Control of Organizations: A Resource Dependence Perspective. *New York: Harper & Row.*

[22] Poppo, L. and Zenger, T 1998. Testing alternative theories of the firm: Transaction cost, knowledge-based, and measurement explanations for make-or-buy decisions in information services. *Strategic Management Journal, vol.*19, no. 9 , 853–877.

[23] Saxena, K.B.C. and Bharadwaj, S.S 2009. Managing business processes through outsourcing: a strategic partnering perspective. *Business Process Management* , vol.15, no. 5, 687-715.

[24] Spekman, R. E., Forbes, T. M. I., Isabella, L. A. & MacAvoy, T. C 1998. Alliance management: A view from the past and a look to the future. *The Journal of Management Studies,* vol. 35, no. 6, 747-772.

[25] Ulaga, W 2003. Capturing value creation in business relationships: A customer perspective. *Industrial Marketing Management* , vol.32, 677-693.

[26] Wang, E.T.G., Barron, T. and Seidmann, A 1997. Contracting Structures for Custom Software Development: The Impacts of Informational Rents and Uncertainty on Internal Development and Outsourcing. *Management Science,* vol. 43, no. 12, 1726-1744.

[27] Wernerfelt, B 1984. A Resource-based view of the firm. *Strategic Management Journal,* vol. 5, no. 2, 171-180.

[28] Williamson, O.E 1975. Markets and Hierarchies, Analysis and Antitrust Implications: A Study in the Economics of Internal Organization. *New York: Free Press* .

[29] Williamson, O.E 1981. The Economics of Organization: The Transaction Cost Approach. *American Journal of Sociology* , vol.87, no. 3, 548-577.

[30] Williamson, O.E 1985. The Economic Institutions of Capitalism: Firms, Markets, Relational Contracting. *New York, London Free Press, Collier Macmillan.*

[31] Wilson, D.T. and Jantrania, S 1993. Understanding the Value of a Relationship." *Asia - Australia Marketing Journal,* vol. 2, no. 1, 55-66.

[32] Yin, R.K 2013. Case Study Research Design and Methods. *Applied Social Research Methods Series,* vol.5 ,1-28.

Exploring Critical Issues of Technical Support in Contact Centers of the Philippines: Toward a Grounded Theory

Industry Case Paper

Meldie Apag
De La Salle University
Xavier University
Manila Philippines
meldie_apag@dlsu.edu.ph

Raymund Sison
De La Salle University
DLSU-Science and Tech Complex
Laguna Philippines
raymund.sison@delasalle.ph

ABSTRACT

The contact center industry in the Philippines, named by Deloitte as one of the two top contact center destinations in Asia, has been expanding rapidly in terms of technology, workforce size, and economic scope. This study aims to explore, using the Glaserian grounded theory method (GTM), the main concern of contact center agents, particularly inbound technical support representatives, in Northern Mindanao in the Philippines, and how they resolve their main concern, especially using information technology. GTM goes beyond the descriptive approach of most qualitative methods by generating from the data, a theory of the substantive area. The rationale for GTM reflects the source of the developed theory grounded in the behavior, words, and actions of those under study. The theory can inform the development of systems, processes, structures, and policies that will support the actors in the substantive area. Preliminary results suggest that staying at the organization or else seeking other employment opportunities is the main concern of the technical support representatives, who resolve this main concern using a cyclical process, each cycle of which has four stages: training, struggling, coping, and motivating. The application of technologies in contact center operations can play a key role in sustaining the technical support representatives' decision to stay longer in the industry.

KEYWORDS

Contact Center; Business Process Outsourcing (BPO); Inbound Technical Support; Glaserian Grounded Theory Method (GTM)

1 INTRODUCTION

The contact center, an Information Technology Enabled Services – Business Process Outsourcing (ITES-BPO) sector, has undergone an irreversible evolution over the last decade [1]. It has been rapidly expanding in terms of technology, workforce size, and economic scope [1,2]. Increasingly, it utilizes advanced

SIGMIS-CPR '17, June 21-23, 2017, Bangalore, India
© 2017 Association for Computing Machinery.
ACM ISBN 978-1-4503-5037-2/17/06...$15.00
http://dx.doi.org/10.1145/3084381.3084383

expertise through appropriate channels of communication that enable interactions to create value for the customer and organization [4]. The channels of communication may include one or more online call centers and other types of customer contacts such as voice calls and data applications including electronic mail, web-based chat, instant messaging, and dynamic web pages. The interactive service work of contact center representatives in technical support includes customer inquiries and technical assistance.

Situated at the customer-organization interface and representing the organization to customers, the concerns of the technical support representatives become critical for contact centers and the society as a whole [5]. This study explore the experiences of technical support representatives, using Glaserian Grounded Theory Method (GTM), to understand their main problem situation experienced and how they deal with this [6,7,8].

1.1 Contact Centers in the Philippines

In the Philippines, the call center industry first emerged in 1997. It is a major provider of front- and back-office support such as voice, electronic mail, order processing, shared services, and many more, to global businesses [9]. Over time, this ITES industry has grown into a US$13 billion industry in 2015 and tagged as the 'Sunshine Industry' because of its massive expansion over the last 10 years [9,2]. The 2016 IBM Global Location Trends Annual Report identifies the Philippines as one of Asia's global leader in business support functions in shared services and BPO and Deloitte (2015) named the Philippines as one of the two top contact center destinations in Asia.

In 2016, according to the Contact Center Association of the Philippines (CCAP), the Philippines have more than 600,000 contact center representatives. This is because of its less expensive operational and labor costs, highly skilled workforce proficient in American-style English and idioms, strong affinity with the United States and European cultures, and constant stream of college-educated graduates entering the workforce [12]. Moreover, there are 229 economic zones in the Philippines with 142 IT parks and more than 85 contact center companies distinguished between foreign-owned, in-sourced, and Filipino-owned contact centers [13].

Furthermore, the Mindanao Strategic Development Framework for 2010-2020 of the Philippine National Economic and Development Authority (NEDA) states that one of the employment generator and growth driver for Mindanao in Southern Philippines is its growing ITES industry, where Mindanao shall venture into positioning itself as the BPO Hub in the South. In 2010, Mindanao has 9 IT parks and continues to grow in number alongside the demands for BPO- and IT-related services. On the other hand, Cagayan de Oro City is the regional center and business hub of Northern Mindanao. It ranked fifth in the contact center offshore cities in the Philippines in its competitiveness as a contact center hub [15]. In 2010, it has more than 20 contact centers including major players in the contact center industry that employs thousands of contact center representatives [16].

1.2 Studies on Contact Center Representatives

The ITES-BPO sector finds interacting with customers using technologies as a significant challenge since while technology can potentially reduce costs on per-transaction basis, an appalling customer experience can damage customer satisfaction and long-term customer loyalty [17]. Hence, the people and technology used in ITES organizations that can greatly affect customer service warrants attention. Studies on the persons in an organization is essential, since by conducting research in its social context, researchers are able to obtain a good appreciation of the work of people as active builders of their own physical and social reality [18].

However, among the very few recent studies on contact centers [17], most involved infrastructure and facilities rather than people and work environment [4,17]. Most of these studies on contact center representatives are quantitative. For example, Barnes and Collier (2013) used structural equation modeling which studied factors that affect work engagement of frontline employees of contact centers, including service climate, job satisfaction, and affective commitment, as well as the effect of work engagement on career commitment and adaptability. Ishtiyaque and A Gera (2014) conducted a survey, the results of which suggested that the monotonous and stressful nature of work, disruption in social and family life, and lack of career growth in contact center jobs in India are major factors for low sustainability in call center jobs in the said country. Possibly, the only qualitative research on contact center agents is the study by Singh (2014) of what makes customer contact employees "tick." This study identified two themes: passion-to-serve and passion-to-solve.

Furthermore, in the Philippines, there are also a few recent studies conducted on contact center representatives. Hechanova (2013), using a mixed method approach, reported that organizational support moderates the relationship between work-life conflict and intent to leave. Ilagan, Gumasing, Estember and Carlos (2014) used multiple regression analysis to identify stress risk factors present in inbound call centers. Meanwhile, Reese and Soco-Carreon (2013) concluded that formative power and internalization of discourses of rules within individual life strategies are preventing the establishments of unions and other collective action structures. Ponce (2015) explored the notions of transnational subjectivity in the lifestyle practices of non-mobile Filipino call center agents and results

showed that the practices are inextricably connected with their non-mobile transnational habitués, agency, work structures, and the global occupational demands of the third party offshore call center.

2 RESEARCH DESIGN

To explore the experiences of technical support representatives in contact centers, a Glaserian Grounded Theory Method (GTM) is used. GTM is used to present directions for theoretically informed main concern of representatives influenced by the contact center industry and its customers, and how representatives resolve their main concern. Further, GTM is used on the ensemble view of the interaction between group of people and technology to stress the interpretive, contextual, and emergent nature of theory development pertinent for use in investigating social processes in information systems researches [7,25,26].

2.1 Data Collection

From the substantive area of inbound technical support in contact centers, twenty representatives from four contact centers in Northern Mindanao, Philippines were participants of the study. Of the twenty inbound technical support representatives, ten of them are males and ten are females. Five of the representatives had been in the contact center industry for two to six months, another five representatives had been working in the industry for seven to ten months, and the rest of the representatives had been with the industry for years. The purposive sampling technique was used in finding the research subjects that took advantage of identifying inbound technical support representatives to provide the potential participants in this study. A purposive sample is a non-probability sample that is selected based on the characteristics of a population and the objective of the study. A 30-minute to an hour of semi-structured interviews with open-ended questions based on the experiences of the inbound technical support representatives was done. Field notes of the interviews conducted to the representatives included not only the responses of the participants to questions, but also observations of their non-verbal behavior during the face-to-face interviews.

2.2 Glaserian Grounded Theory Method (GTM)

Grounded theory is a systematic and inductive approach to developing ground theory to help understand complex social processes [6,27,26]. Glaser (2001) originated the basic process of GTM described as the constant comparative method where the analyst begins analysis with the first data collected and constantly compares incidents, themes, and categories as the theory emerges. With this analysis, with emphasis on the ability to use theoretical sensitivity in discovering patterns of behavior in data, we define the basic properties of each category, identify relationships between categories, and facilitate the identification of patterns. This process continues until the identification of the core category that accounts for most of the variation in the patterns of behavior [25].

The identification of the core category is through an iterative process of coding (open coding, selective coding, and theoretical coding), generating memos, theoretical sampling, and theoretical sorting. Coding is a process aimed at identifying as many tentative categories and their properties as possible. Open coding highlight the data believed to be important beyond the description of the context of the data. In selective coding, as analysis proceeds, understanding must deepen and some characteristics must emerge and begin to selectively code for core categories, and in theoretical coding, we consider only those variables that relate to the core category in the parsimonious theory [8]. Further, embedded within the constant comparative method, theoretical sampling and theoretical sorting of data analysis is the iteration of the approach until theoretical saturation, as in Figure 1 [27,7,8,25,26,28].

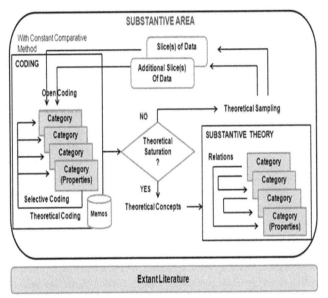

Figure 1: The grounded theory method (GTM).

The Glaserian method claims the dictum 'all is data' [25]. It is all about the data obtained from interviews, observational data or whatever comes the researcher's way while studying a substantive area that will be used in the comparative process as well as literature data from science or media or even fiction [25,26]. Thus, the method is not limited to the realm of qualitative research that is devoted to descriptive accuracy but it emphasizes conceptualization, abstract of time, place, and people.

On the other hand, in the context of Glaser's approach to grounded theory, emphasis on theoretical sensitivity in grounded theory studies is essential. It is the conceptual ability of the researcher to recognize the patterns of behavior discovered in data [8]. A researcher should develop the necessary theoretical sensitivity to discover substantive grounded categories that is a prerequisite in the process of transcending from description to conceptual theory [27,25,26].

As the process of analysis begin to yield a number of themes, concepts, and relationships, the researcher starts to compare these with the extant literature [8,25,26]. Enfolding the literature involved asking what it was similar to, what did it

contradict, and why [26]. A comparison should be made of the different themes that incorporated different grounded theory explanations with the already developed models or frameworks published particularly in the expansion literature of the substantive area [27,8].

3 FINDINGS

Immersion in the data, during the process of analysis in this study, helps gain insight into the inbound technical support representatives' experiences. This allows intuitive and interpretive capacities to identify themes, patterns, and categories to emerge from the data [8,25,26]. With this, preliminary results suggest that staying at the organization or else seeking other employment opportunities is the main concern of the technical support representatives, who resolve this main concern using a cyclical process, each cycle of which has four stages, namely training, struggling, coping, and motivating as in Figure 2.

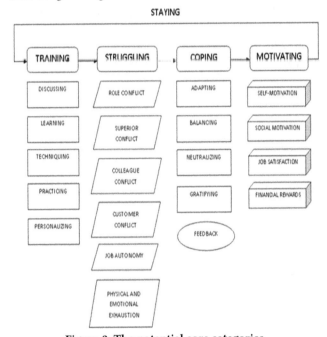

Figure 2: The potential core categories.

3.1 The Main Concern of Technical Support Representatives

This study identifies staying at the organization or else seeking other employment opportunities as the main concern of the technical support representatives. Many factors contribute to this concern such as when representatives are not satisfied with their jobs anymore they tend to leave the organization. Failure in acting on job-related responsibilities and an appalling job performance as shown in negative feedbacks and negative responses leads to think of quitting or leaving the organization. The contact center do not have trust in their representatives anymore, the intention towards turnover will be greater. Additionally, work and personal conflicts arising from the contact center environment provides great impact in the experiences of the representatives and may result to leaving and looking for other employment opportunities. With these factors, technical support representatives must take into account measures so that they may want to stay in the organization longer, while contact centers may influence the decision of technical support representatives through motivation from coping with the struggles of the representatives starting with the training.

3.2 Inbound Technical Support Training

Contact centers have become a major gateway linking customers to organizations. However, research shows that consumers have some dismal contact center experiences [29]. Contact center problems are not surprising considering that the turnover rate among contact center representative in the Philippines is very high [30]. This rate of turnover implies that contact centers must conduct trainings on the lookout for efficient and effective ways of training and retaining contact center representatives. In this study, The themes that had emerged for the training of inbound technical support representatives includes discussing, learning, techniquing, practicing and personalizing as in Figure 3.

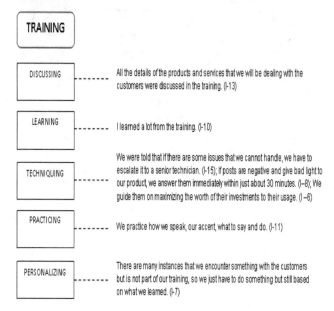

Figure 3: Sample incidents of the training category.

In trainings, technical support representatives are able to discuss the details of their products and services for its customers and the ways to improve verbal and social skills to facilitate effective and efficient communication. Learning also take place in the training where the representatives are able to learn the aspects of verbal communication, understanding of questioning and listening skills, learning effective ways to negotiate with the customers, and other important elements of the contact center environment. Moreover, training techniques for improving representative's performance are also essential. The techniques equip the representatives on how to handle customers through role-play training which has a theoretical base in behavioral modeling. However, the primary drawback of role-play training is that it is not individualized, not easily

scalable, and is susceptible to situational characteristics and variation in the quality of instruction [29]. With the techniques presented, the representatives must practice the techniques to enhance the necessary skills needed in a contact center. Finally, personalizing is also fundamental. The representatives must be able to realize the value of personalizing interactions and developing relationships, discover personalized techniques to manage individual and social issues, and enrich the importance of creating and delivering meaningful messages through personalization

3.3 Struggles of Inbound Technical Support Representatives

Contact center representatives perform an essential role in the implementation of customer contact strategies and in the delivery of frontline services. With these work demands comes corresponding struggles that may affect work performance, personal decisions, and individual characters [31]. On the category of struggling, the emerging themes include role conflict, superior conflict, colleague conflict, customer conflict, job autonomy, and physical and emotional exhaustion as in Figure 4.

Inbound technical support representatives may experience struggles in the form of role conflicts. Role conflict arises when expectations of the organization may clash with what the representative knows and does. In many instances, the technical skills of these representatives are at first not sufficient to do technical work and thus require the proper training to be able to deliver properly their work and satisfy its customers. Superior conflicts may also occur, supervisors and team leaders stressing operational efficiency using technology may not realize that a critical element of a representatives' performance is the level of satisfaction based on meeting customer expectations. The lack of supervisor support, poor supervisor and representative communication, and abusive supervision can greatly contribute to the struggles of technical support representatives. Furthermore, colleague conflicts also take place in working environments. Differences in personalities, capabilities and aspirations often times affect relationships. Customer conflicts are also very transparent in contact centers as this sector is customer-centric. While contact centers may encourage customer complaints in order to improve systems and promote customer satisfaction, dealing with disappointed, bad-tempered, enraged, and egotistical customers who have experienced a service failure adds to the struggles of the representatives. Another struggle of technical support representatives is job autonomy. The state of acting separately from others because of difference in work schedules, especially if the representative is in graveyard shift, affects the social and personal life of the representatives such as disregarded self, family, friends and societal obligations. Lastly, representatives often experiences physical and emotional exhaustion. Physically, the representatives' lack of sleep and rest affects their health conditions. Moreover, emotional stress can also greatly affect ones disposition in life.

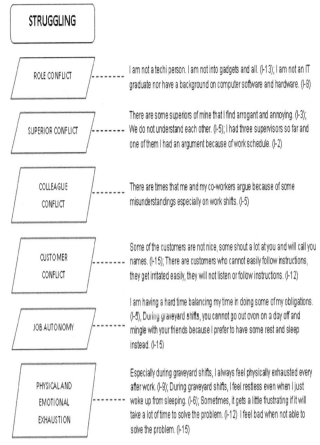

Figure 4: Sample incidents of the struggling category.

3.4 How Representatives Manage Struggles

As technical support representatives experiences struggles in their work and even in their personal lives, coping up with these instances is a challenge. The themes on the coping category include adapting, balancing, neutralizing, and gratifying as in Figure 5.

Work shift is an immense concern in contact centers [32]. Adapting to graveyard shifts and other rotating work shifts requires extensive adjustment plans. Adjustments on how to deal with supervisors, colleagues, customers, and even on personal activities and lifestyles is also important in the management of the struggles of the representatives. Balancing is also one of the means to cope up with struggles. Handling customers effectively meant that representatives had to interact with them politely regardless of the customer's reactions and own mood or frame of mind. Representatives should be able to demonstrate organizational value for customers while simultaneously completing contact requirements within a timeframe set by the contact center. Balancing time for work and for other personal activities is also a way of coping up with struggles. Another theme is neutralizing. Most of the representatives did not consider customer interaction as stressful. They maintained that they enjoyed their job even when experiencing some struggles. Appreciative customers who were grateful to the technical support representatives illustrated

that positive interactions are also present in this encounters and therefore neutralizes the struggles of the representatives. Additionally, gratifying is a coping mechanism for technical support representatives. As a service-oriented organization, contact centers aim at satisfying customers. The training given to technical support representatives is not just to give the customers what they need but also to consider the customer's reactions to create a personal and direct relationship that can satisfy customers.

On the other hand, with the coping mechanisms to be able to manage the struggles of the inbound technical support representatives, feedback is very essential. The supervisors and team leaders provide feedback on the representatives' technical and social performances. They guide the technical support representatives on how to improve their skills to provide good customer service while improving their lives.

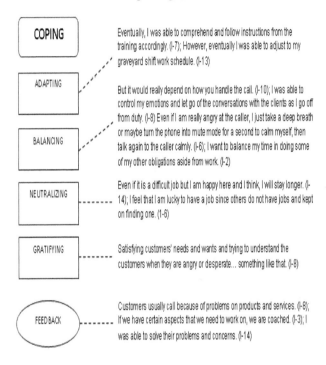

Figure 5: Sample incidents of the coping category.

3.5 Technical Support Representatives Motivation

Another challenging aspect in contact centers is increasing the technical support representatives' motivation. Work motivation is essential to retain successfully the human resource of an organization [33]. The category on motivating has themes that include self-motivation, social motivation, job satisfaction, and financial rewards as in Figure 6.

Industry Case Session 5.1   SIGMIS-CPR'17, June 21-23, 2017, Bangalore, India

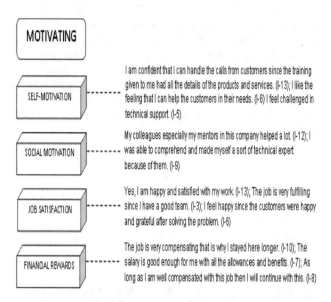

Figure 6: Sample incidents of the motivation category.

Motivation is a process that initiates, guides, and maintains goal-oriented behaviors. It is a reason for certain actions, desires, and needs [32]. There is a need to motivate technical support representatives in terms of respect, recognition, variety, and fair compensation for their efforts. Self-motivation is the ability to finish work, without influence from other people or situations [34]. Representatives with self-motivation can find a reason and strength to be able to complete the job even when challenges occurs and without giving up or needing another to encourage them. On the other hand, as representatives interact with colleagues, family, friends, and customers, it is also important to consider social motivation. The need for representatives to interact with their environment and accepted by them is important for their social and personal growth [35]. Representatives are motivated if their superiors approve of their work, if their colleagues believe in them, if their family understands them, if their friends are proud of them, and when customers appreciate them. More so, when a representative's work is having worth and feels happy and satisfied with their performance, there is job satisfaction. Finally, financial rewards are also a big factor in motivating technical support representatives. As much as their skills are required, a fair compensation is also important to give justification to their work. Financial rewards can inspire loyalty, increase productivity, stimulate work, enhance commitment, reshape behaviors, satisfy job, inculcate zeal and enthusiasm towards work, and get the maximum of the representatives' capabilities so that they are exploring and utilizing maximally [35]. Financial incentives may be in the form of security of service, recognition, suggestion schemes, job enrichment, or promotion opportunities [36].

3.6 Application of Technologies in Contact Center Operations

The application of technologies in contact center operations can play a key role in encouraging inbound technical support

representatives to stay longer in the industry. There are some considerations on alternative training methods using technology other than classroom training and role-playing. Computer-Based Training (CBT) and simulation trainings can improve customer service and satisfaction [29]. Simulation training in contact centers includes paced observations, modularized practice with feedback, and integrated practice with feedback. Furthermore, technology can facilitate management on the struggles of inbound technical support representatives. Simulated social interaction can determine possible conflicts and thus provide hints and possible coping mechanisms. It can also provide feedback on the struggles of the representatives and coping mechanisms to improve inbound technical support motivation.

4 IMPLICATIONS AND CONTRIBUTIONS

Influenced by the rapid development of information technology services, contact centers had expanded the service sector during this past decade [1]. The Philippines, particularly Cagayan de Oro City of Northern Mindanao, had invested much in contact centers for employment generation. As the result of the expansion of global outsourcers and providers, employment in contact centers grew remarkably [12].

In a contact center setting, the technical support representatives have to display emotions that comply with certain norms or standards of the organization to create a desired state of mind in the customer [36]. These representatives must appear happy to serve the customer in spite of some private misgivings, job stressors and other conflicts they may have. Thus, aside from the necessary computer skills and product knowledge acquired from the technical trainings in contact centers, they must possess social skills and coping mechanisms. They should possess the ability to remain calm under pressure, maintain a friendly and positive attitude, or disengaged in instances of discourteous, egotistical or ill-tempered customers. Motivation is also very important to each of the representatives. Customer satisfaction and good work performance are necessary to be able to provide successful customer-representative relationship and better customer service. With these, there can be a higher desire to stay in the contact center for a longer period as this is the main concern of inbound technical support representatives.

The themes and categories that had emerged as the results of this study are, however, not precise enough for decision-making or policy development, and so a further grounded theory inquiry is still recommended. Nevertheless, the preliminary results can play a key role in sustaining the technical support representatives' decision to stay longer in the industry.

In the use of GTM in this study, it can contribute to richer methodological understanding of grounded theory approach to research through the identification of useful theoretical conceptualizations based on a thorough methodical and comprehensive approach to data collection and analysis. This study will help improve the use of the method and to the quality and dissemination of grounded theory research outcomes as such that grounded theory studies have been used in information systems studies.

REFERENCES

[1] Association of Government Contact Center Professionals (AGCCP) (2016). http://www.agccp.org/.

[2] Contact Center Association of the Philippines (CCAP) (2016). Priorities Status Report November 2016. http://www.ccap.ph/index.php/about-ccap/.

[3] Association of Modern Technologies Professionals (AMTP) (2016). http://www.itinfo.am/eng/it-enabled-services/.

[4] Belfiore, B., Chatterley, J. and Petouhoff, N. (2012). Research Report the Impact of Technology on Contact Center Performance. Benchmark Portal.

[5] D'Cruz, P. and Noronha, E. (2008). "Doing Emotional Labour: The Experiences of Indian Call Centre Agents". Sage Publications. Vo. 9, No. 1: pp. 131-147.

[6] Glaser, B. and Strauss, A. (1967). The Discovery of Grounded Theory: Strategies for Qualitative Research. Chicago, IL: Aldine Atherton.

[7] Glaser, B. (1992). Basics of Grounded Theory Analysis: Emergency Versus Forcing. Mill Valley, CA: Sociology Press.

[8] Glaser, B. (1998). Doing Grounded Theory: Issues and Discussions. Mill Valley, CA: Sociology Press.

[9] Ecumenical Institute for Labor Education and Research, Inc. (EILER) (2016). Modern Day Sweatshops in the Service Sector: Business Process Outsourcing (BPO) in the Philippines.

[10] IBM Global Services (2016). 2016 Global Location Trends Annual Report. IBM Global Business Services, October 2016.

[11] Deloitte (2015). 2015 Global Contact Center Survey Executive Summary. Deloitte Development. June 2015.

[12] International Labour Organization (2015). "Employment Relationships in Telecommunications Services and in the Call Centre Industry". Sectoral Policies Department. Issues Paper Discussion at the Global Dialogue Forum on the Employment Relationships in the Telecommunications Services and in the Call Centre Industry. GDFERT/2015.

[13] Philippine's Department of Trade and Industry (DTI) (2015). http://dti.gov.pg/.

[14] Philippine's National Economic and Development Authority (NEDA) (2010). Mindanao Strategic Development Framework 2010-2020.

[15] NeoIT (2010). Outsourcing to the Philippines: Metro Manila and Beyond. Offshore Insights Market Report Series. Vo. 3, No. 9.

[16] Philippine Economic Zone Authority (PEZA) (2010). http://www.peza.gov.ph/.

[17] Barnes, D.C. and Collier, J.E. (2013). "Investigating Work Engagement in the Service Environment". Journal of Services Marketing. Vo. 27, No. 6: pp. 485-499.

[18] Orlikowski, W. and Iacono, S. (2001). "Research Commentary: Desperately Seeking the "IT" in IT Research-A Call to Theorizing the IT artifact". Information Systems Research. Vo. 12, No. 2: pp. 121-134.

[19] Ishtiyaque, M. and A Gera, R. (2014). "Economic and Social Implications and Sustainability of Call Center Jobs in India". Journal of Urban and Regional Sudies on Contemporary India. Vo. 1, No. 2: pp. 1-7.

[20] Singh, J. (2014). "Words That Make Customer Contact Employees Tick: A Grounded Study". Academy of Management Proceedings, 2014 (1), 11380. Academy of Management.

[21] Hechanova, M.R. (2013). "The Call Center as a Revolving Door: A Philippine Perspective". Personnel Review. Vo. 42, No. 3: pp. 349-365.

[22] Ilagan, J., Gumasing, M.J., Estember, R., and Carlos, M.C. (2014). "The Effects of Coping Mechanism, Gender and Shift to Stress Risk Levels of Inbound Call Center". Proceedings of the 2014 International Conference on Industrial Engineering and Operations Management. Bali, Indonesia. January 7-9, 2014.

[23] Reese, N. and Soco-Carreon, J. (2013). "No Call for Action? Why There is No Union (Yet) in Philippine Call Centers". ASEAS – Austrian Journal of South-East Asian Studies. Vo. 6, No. 1: pp. 140-159.

[24] Ponce, F. (2015). "Exploring the Transnational Subjectivity in the Lifestyle Practices of Filipino Call Center Agents". American Research Thoughts. Vo. 1, No. 10: pp. 2340-2366.

[25] Glaser, B. (2001). The Grounded Theory Perspective: Conceptualization Contrasted with Description. Sociology Press, Mill Valley, CA.

[26] Glaser, B. (2003). The Grounded Theory Perspective II: Descriptions Remodeling of Grounded Theory Methodology. Sociology Press, Mill Valley, CA.

[27] Glaser, B. (1978). Theoretical Sensitivity: Advances in the Methodology of Grounded Theory. Mill Valley, CA: Sociology Press.

[28] Fernandez, W. D. (2004). "The Grounded Theory Method and Case Study Data in IS Research: Issues and Design". In Information Systems Foundations Workshop: Constructing and Criticising. Vo. 1: pp. 43-59.

[29] Murthy, N., Challagalla, G., Vincent, L., and Shervani, T. (2008). "The Impact of Simulation Training on Call Center Agent Quality at Call Centers". International Journal of Management & Information Systems. Vo. 14, No. 3.

[30] Montalbo, A. (2016). The Burnout Level of Call Center Agents in Metro Manila, Philippines. June 2016.

[31] Thite, A., and Russell, B. (2010). "The Next Agent: Work Organisation in Indian Call Centres". New Technology, Work and Employment. Vo. 25, No. 1.

[32] Rod, M., and Ashill, N. (2013). The Impact of Call Centre Stressors on Inbound and Outbound Call-Centre Agent Burnout. Emerald Group Publishing, Limited.

[33] Cho, D.H., and Son, J.M. (2012). "Job Embeddedness and Turnover Intentions: An Empirical Investigation of Construction IT Industries". International Journal of Advanced Science and Technology. Vo. 40, March 2012.

[34] Labach, E. (2010). "Improving Customer Retention Through Service Performance: a Field-Based Investigation". Management Science. Vo. 54, No. 2: pp. 384-399.

[35] Saeed, I., Waseem, M., Sikander, S. And Rizwan, M. (2014). "The Relationship of Turnover Intention with Job Satisfaction, Job Performance, Leader Member Exchange, Emotional Intelligence and Organizational Commitment". International Journal of Learning & Development. Vo. 4, No. 2: 242-256.

[36] DeTienne, K.B., Agie, B., Phillips, J., and Ingerson, M.C. (2012). "The Impact of Moral Stress Compared to Other Stressors on Employee Fatigue, Job Satisfaction, and Turnover: An Empirical Investigation". Journal of Business Ethics. Springer Science-Business Media.

itihaasa History of Indian IT:
Case Study of a Unique Digital Museum

Industry Case Paper

N Dayasindhu

itihaasa Research and Digital

IIITB, 26/C Electronics City

Hosur Road, Bangalore 560100, India

dayasindhu@itihaasa.com

ABSTRACT

This industry case study describes the genesis and development of itihaasa history of Indian IT, a unique digital museum chronicling the evolution of Indian IT over six decades. itihaasa is a free mobile app that captures important milestones defining the history of Indian IT in the voice of key actors who shaped them. It has a rich repertoire of original oral history videos, digital documents, and photographs from personal archives and publications. Users can navigate the itihaasa app based on timeline, people or organization views. Or they can search tags to access specific content. It is unique because the evolution of Indian IT is captured as oral histories of multiple key actors who shaped important milestones, and business history is presented in an entirely digital format.

CCS CONCEPTS

• **Information systems** → **Information system applications** → **Digital libraries and archives**; • **Social and professional topics** → **Professional topics** → **History of Computing.**

KEYWORDS

Digital museum, digital oral history, digital archives, digital library, business history, history of Indian IT, IT services, software services

ACM Reference format:

N. Dayasindhu. 2017. itihaasa History of Indian IT: Case Study of a Unique Digital Museum. In *Proceedings of ACM SIGMIS-CPR conference, Bangalore, India June 21-23 2017 (SIGMIS-CPR'17)*, 6 pages.

http://dx.doi.org/10.1145/3084381.3084388

1 INTRODUCTION

Indian IT (Information Technology) industry is integral to the rise of modern industrial India. The IT and BPM (Business Process Management) industry in India employs 3.7 million people [1]. India is among the largest and most preferred destination for global IT work, and IT has redefined India's perception among other nations. From a single modern computer in all of India in the mid-1950s, the industry today generates USD 143 billion of revenues including USD 108 billion of exports [1]. How did Indian IT evolve? Unraveling and chronicling the evolution of Indian IT over six decades was the inspiration for itihaasa history of Indian IT – a digital museum mobile app. itihaasa in many Indian languages signifies history. It is downloadable free for iOS and Android mobile devices. itihaasa is unique in two aspects.

One, it is a definitive oral history of multiple key actors - important decision makers - who shaped Indian IT over six decades. This is different from a single insider's account or third-party outsider accounts. Michael S. Mahoney, a historian of IT, posits that insider oral histories of key actors in IT are important in the long run as they become primary sources of its history [2]. In fact, the first major formal IT history project in the world was a series of oral history recordings in the early 1970s of key actors in American computing from the 1950s sponsored by the American Federation of Information Processing Societies (AFIPS) in collaboration with the Smithsonian Institution [3]. Two, the presentation of itihaasa is entirely in a digital mobile app format that is tailor-made for experiencing business history. It provides users the ability to consume itihaasa's rich oral history content as they wish. There are multiple intuitive pre-defined views for users - timeline, people and organization. Or users can intuitively search tags to access content.

This industry case study describes the genesis and development of itihaasa. It describes how best to combine rich original content - especially oral history - and the mobile app format to create a digital museum to showcase business history.

2 GENESIS OF ITIHAASA

itihaasa is the brainchild of S. "Kris" Gopalakrishnan, co-founder of Infosys, one of India's iconic IT companies. In his own words [4],

"[After I stepped down from Infosys]... I was thinking of some way I can give back... there are books but no other documentation in the form of records of voices and videos of the leaders who created this industry. It occurred to me that it would be fun to create an app for this."

In early 2015, Kris wanted to chronicle the evolution of Indian IT in the voices of the key actors who nurtured different aspects of this evolution. This was the itihaasa project. Two main reasons motivated this project. One, Indian IT is perhaps the only global scale modern industry where India has built a leadership position. Two, lessons from the evolution of Indian IT can be applied to other contexts including the emerging startups in India. For example, the rapid scaling up of operations in Indian IT services companies in the late 90s and early 2000s is relevant for Indian startups in the Internet enabled services space.

Business history provides a lens to assess the current trajectories of business and industry in the context of their evolutionary path. Business historians are interested in building their practice by relying on empirical evidence to understand business and contexts [5]. The team that anchored the itihaasa research project decided to focus on the empirical evidence in the form of oral histories of key actors who shaped different milestones in the evolution of Indian IT. This was leaning on the rich tradition of business historians like Alfred D. Chandler Jr. to focus on the important milestones, the capabilities that nurtured these milestones, and the key actors who shaped these milestones [6].

3 IMPORTANT MILESTONES AND INFORMATION ARCHITECTURE

3.1 Important Milestones

The research to arrive at a list of important milestones in the evolution of Indian IT was made up of two iterative parts. The first part was an exhaustive literature survey. The second part was interviews with V. Rajaraman, a key actor associated with Indian IT from the mid-1950s - as a research student, as a faculty member in IIT (Indian Institute of Technology) Kanpur and Indian Institute of Science, and as an advisor to the Government of India. He is a founding father of programming and computer science education in India. The starting point for the secondary research was V. Rajaraman's monograph on the history of computing in India [7]. The itihaasa team then identified other books, papers, and articles on the evolution of Indian IT. Since the history of Indian IT goes back to the mid-1950s, the team also decided to access archives of newspapers. A couple of challenges bring out the practical difficulties when working on business history especially when the timelines predate the Internet publishing era.

A challenge for the Bangalore based itihaasa team during the secondary research was that none of the leading institutional libraries in Bangalore other than the High Court library had archives of newspapers from the 1950s. The High Court library had physical archives, and the initial assessment of the itihaasa team was that it was not very well organized and preserved. The

High Court also had an elaborate approval process to access the library. And the lead time for approvals was typically about three months. The team was working on an aggressive timeline, and thankfully the IIM (Indian Institute of Management) Bangalore library had the digital archives of one leading newspaper, and bound volumes of a few other leading publications that were relevant. The itihaasa team also realized at this point that it was difficult to obtain permissions to access the physical and electronics archives of newspapers and publications in India.

While it was easy to identify the keywords that matter in IT and Indian IT in the past three decades, identifying keywords in a rapidly evolving technology domain like IT in the 1950s was not easy. For example, the itihaasa team did not realize that "computer" could be spelled "computor" in the 1950s. The interactions with V. Rajaraman were useful to identify keywords that mattered in that early era. One of the earliest (or possibly the earliest) newspaper report on computers or IT in India, a news item in *The Times of India* dated Sep. 1, 1955 titled "Electronic Brain for India" never mentions a computer but only an electronic "computor". This news item was about the installation of the first modern computer in India that was installed in the ISI (Indian Statistical Institute), Kolkata.

Based on the secondary research, the team identified forty-four important milestones in the evolution of Indian IT, the capabilities and context for these milestones, impact of these milestones, and the key actors who defined these milestones. For example, the first formal course on computer programming and architecture in India was offered at IIT Kanpur in 1963 after an IBM 1620 computer was installed there. This was the first time IT capability building started in India. And was the genesis of creating one of the largest pools of IT talent in the world today. V. Rajaraman and H. N. Mahabala were the faculty associated with the computer center in IIT Kanpur during this time, and key actors for this milestone. Or for example, Tata Consultancy Services (TCS) – the first Indian IT company and now the largest Indian IT services company in India with over USD 16 billion in annual revenue - was established in 1968 as a division of Tata Sons. F. C. Kohli joined around that period as a General Manager of TCS and later went on to become the CEO and Vice Chairman. He was a key actor for this milestone.

3.2 Key Actors and Research Interviews

Based on milestones, the itihaasa team identified about fifty key actors who shaped these milestones. All the key actors enthusiastically supported itihaasa, and were generous with their time. There are always some disappointments in a business history project since some of the key actors are no more with us or not in a position to speak or recollect events of the past. For example, none of the significant key actors associated with the installation of India's first two computers in ISI Kolkata in the mid-1950s are with us today. The team completed the secondary research by mid-2015.This included identifying the milestones, and the key actors to interview.

When the itihaasa team interviewed key actors for the first time, it was for primary research. The team undertook the primary research for three reasons. One, corroborate and obtain the key actors' perspective of the key milestones identified. Second, identify additional key milestones that may have been missed. Third, to check if there were any interesting narratives or anecdotes missed in the existing published artifacts. While the team was progressing with the project and began interviewing key actors, the exact final presentation format was still not finalized.

3.3 Information Architecture

By mid-2015, the itihaasa team completed a few research interviews and transcribed them. The information architecture emerged from the analysis of these interviews. Six dimensions became important to describe the history of Indian IT. Time, people, and organizations are the obvious three. For example, what happened in Indian IT in the 1970s, what was the role of N Vittal in facilitating the growth of Indian IT services industry, or what was Wipro's role in the genesis of R&D (Research and Development) outsourcing. The team also realized that there is always a context to understanding history. Technical and business context was important in the history of Indian IT. It was impossible to fully appreciate the history of Indian IT unless one is aware of mainframes, minicomputers, outsourcing, global delivery model, etc. The technical and business context also included the "firsts". For example, Infosys was the first Indian IT company to list in a US stock exchange when it got listed in NASDAQ in 1999. Policies were important in the Indian context. Indian industry was highly regulated in the era prior to 1991 when Indian industry was liberalized. It was Government policies like the STPI (Software Technology Parks of India) that was instrumental in the rapid growth of the Indian IT export industry from the early 1990s. Finally, place emerged as an important factor, as if it was another person lending its unique characteristics to history. For example, in mid-1980s, Texas Instruments became the first IT MNC to set up an engineering center in Bangalore, and led to many other IT MNCs choose Bangalore for their engineering centers.

To summarize, the six dimensions of the information architecture for describing history of Indian IT were time, people, organizations, technical and business context, policies, and place. Figures 1 and 2 show how these dimensions are an integral part of the itihaasa app design.

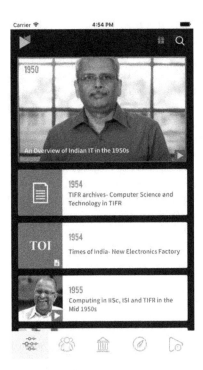

Figure 1: Timeline view of itihaasa with tabs for people and organization views.

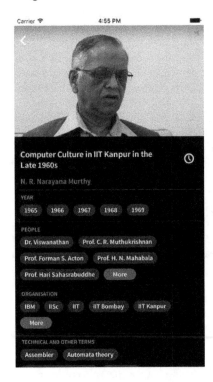

Figure 2: Clickable and searchable tags based on the information architecture in an itihaasa video artifact.

4 ITIHAASA MOBILE APP

After completing a few research interviews and identifying the information architecture, the team realized that the output of itihaasa could be entirely digital. And that it could be a mobile app. The initial contours of the app were brainstormed. The choice of the mobile app format was based on the fact that almost all of itihaasa's target audience segments - IT professional, policy maker, researcher, entrepreneur, student, etc. - both in India and elsewhere - owned a smartphone or a tablet or had access to one. In fact, the smart phone is becoming the predominant device to access the Internet in India. It is estimated by GSMA (GSM Association) that India had about 238 million smartphones in 2016 and that this number is likely to grow to over 600 million by 2020 [8]. A presentation layer for users to access digital artifacts in an intuitive way leveraging the information architecture was identified. Next, a robust and secure backend layer in the cloud to house video artifacts, scanned documents, scanned photographs, and tags was identified.

4.1 Presentation and artifacts

The opening screen for users – the timeline view (Figure 1) - self-selected itself since progress in time is most intuitive to experience history. Two other views were also intuitive in the context of history – people and organization. It was decided to extensively tag each of the video, document and photo artifacts. The team also decided to expose the tags so that it is easy for a user to access all relevant connected artifacts (Figure 2). It was also decided to store all artifacts on cloud platforms and make them accessible only from the itihaasa app. This was primarily to protect the copyright of artifacts, and does not prevent access in any way. The team obtained the copyrights to share the document and photo artifacts in itihaasa from a few publishing houses. The team also obtained document and photo artifacts from the personal archives of the key actors. The app is free to download, and provides free access to all the content. A design and IT partner team was identified by end of 2015, and they worked iteratively to design and develop the app.

The itihaasa team met the key actors for a second time from end of 2015 to video record a structured interview using professional videographers. The questions were identified based on the primary research interviews. The questions were shared in advance with the key actors so that they had time to prepare. The team also used the questions as a reference to break the video recording of interview into smaller self-complete segments of typically around five minutes for easy viewing. All videos were recorded in 1080p HD (High Definition) resolution. The ability to project on a bigger screen is helpful while using the itihaasa app as a presentation aid or using it as a teaching aid. All video, document, and photo artifacts were prepared to provide the best possible resolution in the app.

While the iOS development was easy, the itihaasa team realized that a few design elements were difficult to realize in Android. For example, the pinch and zoom feature in Android required the document or photo to be downloaded to the device. The team had to choose an alternate scaling button to zoom into document and photo artifacts for Android. This was because itihaasa's copyright agreements with publishing houses did not allow download of documents to the users' devices. Table 1 provides a measure of the artifacts in the itihaasa app in March 2017. Once the artifacts were ready they were associated with multiple tags that made it easy to search for relevant artifacts.

Table 1: Artifacts in the itihaasa app

Artifacts	Measure
Original HD video	37 hours and 28 minutes
Oral history of	44 key actors
No. of video segments	593
No. of documents and photos	378

4.2 Tags

The itihaasa team wanted a seamless experience for users to search the content they are interested to consume. Searching content - especially video content - using tags is intuitive thanks to popularity of existing video content platforms like YouTube. The tags in itihaasa were grouped based on the information architecture discussed earlier. An analyst who worked on the secondary research and immersed in the context, manually tagged the artifacts based on guidance from the team leaders. The quantity of different types of tags in March 2017 is provided in Table 2.

Table 2: Tags in the itihaasa app

Tags	Quantity
No. of total tags in the app	Over 12,000
No. of unique tags	4,867
No. of unique tags for technical and other terms	3,157
No. of unique tags for organization	967
No. of unique tags for people	512
No. of unique tags for place	171
No. of unique tags on policy	60

When about fifty video segments from the recordings of about five key actors processed and tagged, the itihaasa team decided to test the tag search feature. Off the shelf search algorithms were not very effective. For example, the top search results for IIT Kanpur would include those relevant to other IITs, while some of the IIT Kanpur tagged results would be lower down. The search algorithm was refined by experimenting with different models like the edit distance algorithm to make the tag search feature more robust and accurate [9].

Once the entire development and testing of the iOS and Android app was completed, all video, document and photo artifacts were uploaded to the cloud service platforms by early 2016.

5 CHALLENGES

There were four important challenges in the research stage. Three of them - access to the archives of newspapers, identifying keywords for the period 1950s and 1960s, and the fact that some of the key actors are no longer with us - were discussed in detail in the milestones section. The fourth challenge was the paucity of document, photo, and video archives with individuals and organizations. The itihaasa team realized that artifacts which capture important facets of the history of Indian IT over the past six decades are not systematically preserved. In hindsight, key actors and organizations felt that they should have preserved these artifacts in a more scientific manner. For example, the itihaasa team was unable find a copy of the reading material for the first course on computers and computer programming in India – a ten day course on computers in IIT Kanpur in 1963.

The two challenges during the development of the itihaasa app is discussed the sections on presentation and tags. First, realizing all the design elements were difficult in Android compared to iOS. Second, off the shelf search algorithms were not effective for tag search. A few iterations were required to make the tag search feature robust.

6 LESSONS LEARNT

The lessons learnt from itihaasa can be categorized into three perspectives - researching business history, presenting business history in an entirely digital format, and designing and developing the digital platform.

From a research method perspective, it is important to understand that there is no single truth in history, and key actors may have differing narratives of the same historical event [2]. Researchers from a management science or engineering background have to get used to this multiple truths paradigm [3]. From a tactical perspective, it is impossible to collect all the available literature before starting a business history project. An approach followed in itihasaa was to ask key actors for references to literature that they believed was important to the history of Indian IT.

While researching for prior art for a digital museum app for oral history, the itihaasa team realized that there was none close to what was being designed. Oral histories in business are traditionally preserved in private archives, and generally not easily accessible to all. The itihaasa team learnt how to design and develop the usability features of the itihaasa platform based on popular general purpose video platform apps. An important lesson learnt was how itihaasa specific requirements like how to protect copyright of the artifacts at the same time providing full and free access can be realized in a mobile app. Another important lesson learnt was identifying best format for presenting video, document, and photo artifacts that satisfies both user experience and copyright requirements.

Designing and developing the itihaasa platform was like an IT program. It required IT program management expertise, and an understanding of how IT systems are designed. The itihaasa team had more than two decades of prior collective experience in Infosys, a leading IT services company. It is essential for business historians considering an entirely digital presentation to include an IT expert in their team.

7 THE ROAD AHEAD

itihaasa was launched in April 2016, and has garnered close to 10,000 downloads on iOS and Android combined by the end of March 2017. itihaasa received favorable reviews across a spectrum of users - CEOs to students of IT. The average rating in Google's Play Store is 4.3 on 5 [10]. itihaasa was featured in the "Events and Sightings" section of *IEEE Annals of the History of Computing* [11]. Some Indian IT companies are planning to use itihaasa to provide a context in their induction program for fresh college recruits and experienced hires. The itihaasa team is also planning to socialize itihaasa in Indian business schools as a business history and industry evolution case study. A workshop elective course based on itihaasa for MBA students in IIM Indore was held in February 2017, and was well received. More workshops and elective courses in Indian business schools are planned.

itihaasa is an ongoing project, and the process for adding more content is currently underway. The number of artifacts and the number of tags will increase when new content is added. The objective is to make itihaasa the most definitive chronicle of the history of Indian IT, and a unique experiment in leveraging modern digital technology for showcasing business history. The itihaasa project led to creation of a company to study the evolution of Indian IT and its emerging trajectories. In the words of Kris, the patron of the itihaasa project [12],

"Based on the success of itihaasa: history of Indian IT research, I am establishing itihaasa Research and Digital, a Not for Profit Company, to research contemporary history of Indian IT and emerging IT trends in modern India. The objective of itihaasa's research is to enhance our understanding of the evolution of Indian IT, its impact, and future trajectories."

While itihaasa is an app chronicling history of Indian IT, it is also a platform - a digital museum for showcasing business history. It has all key elements specific to business history like time, people, organizations, contextual terms, and place. itihaasa also has a process framework for researching, archiving and processing video, document and photo artifacts.

To conclude, while there is definite merit is analyzing history chronicled in the words of the key actors to define the future [6], it is easier to do so if the lessons from history are instantaneously available in the palms of our hands. This is the uniqueness of itihaasa.

REFERENCES

[1] http://www.nasscom.in/indian-itbpo-industry

[2] M. S. Mahoney. 1988. The history of computing in the history of technology. *IEEE Annals of the History of Computing.* 10,2 (April-June 1988), 113-125. DOI: http://doi.ieeecomputersociety.org/10.1109/MAHC.1988.10011

[3] T. Haigh. 2004. The history of computing: An introduction to the computer scientist. In *Using History to Teach Computer Science and Related Disciplines,* A. Akera and W.Aspray (Eds.). Computing Research Association, Washington DC, 5-26.

[4] S. Desikan. 2016. From punch card to smart card. *The Hindu Metroplus.* 25 May. 2016.

[5] G. Jones, M. H. D.van Leeuwen, and S. Broadberry S. 2012. The Future of Economic, Business, and Social History. *Scandinavian Economic History Review.* 60, 3 (November2012), 225–253.DOI: http://dx.doi.org/10.1080/03585522.2012.727766

[6] A. D. Chandler Jr.2000. The information age in historical perspective: Introduction. In *A Nation Transformed by Information: How Information Has Shaped the United States from Colonial Times to the Present,* A. D.Chandler Jr. and J. W.Cortada, (Eds.). Oxford University Press, New York, 3-38.

[7] V. Rajaraman. 2012. *History of computing in India (1955-2010).* IEEE Computer Society. Bangalore, India.

[8] https://gsmintelligence.com/research/?file=134a1688cdaf49cfc73432e2f52b2dbe&download

[9] G. Navarro. 2001. A guided tour to approximate string matching. *ACM Computing Surveys.* 33, 1 (March 2001), 31-88. DOI: http://doi.acm.org/10.1145/375360.375365

[10] https://play.google.com/store/apps/details?id=com.itihasa.android&hl=en

[11] C. Kita. 2016. Events and Sightings (New App shares IT history in India) by V Rajaraman. *IEEE Annals of the History of Computing.* 38,3 (July-September 2016), 88. DOI: http://doi.ieeecomputersociety.org/10.1109/MAHC.2016.31

[12] http://businesswireindia.com/news/news-details/kris-gopalakrishnan-co-founder-infosys-launches-itihaasa-research-digital/49810

Institutional Isomorphism due to the Influence of Information Systems and Its Strategic Position

Full Paper

Abhipsa Pal
Indian Institute of Management Bangalore
PIN 560076
India
abhipsa.pal14@iimb.ernet.in

Abhoy Kumar Ojha
Indian Institute of Management Bangalore
PIN 560076
India
aojha@iimb.ernet.in

ABSTRACT

Institutional isomorphism is a concept at the core of institutional theory to explain the homogeneity of organizations in a field. DiMaggio and Powell (1983) developed a framework that presented the different mechanisms, including coercive, mimetic and normative, through which isomorphism occurs. Information systems (IS) have become a critical asset in the industry today, with firms heavily dependent on IS for either their day to day operational processes or to gain a strategic edge. This paper proposes that IS drives isomorphism in organizations. The IS impact affecting isomorphism is greater when the dependence of the firm on information technology is greater. McFarlan and McKenney's (1983) IS strategic grid identifies four kinds of IS dependence— strategic, turnaround, operational, and support. We propose a framework to understand the degree of isomorphism (through different mechanisms) that a firm is likely to experience under the influence of IS, based on the firm's position in the strategic grid. There has been studies linking institutional theory and strategic IT, and evidences of importance of such research, but none of the studies develops a framework observing the mechanisms of isomorphism due to IT impact. The paper analyses relevant cases from the industry using a framework that we developed. The framework has practical implications for firms to be prepared for the isomorphic changes they are expected to experience when their IS dependence places them in a particular strategic quadrant.

KEYWORDS

IS Strategic Grid; Institutional Theory; Isomorphism; Strategic Information Systems

SIGMIS-CPR '17, June 21-23, 2017, Bangalore, India
© 2017 Copyright is held by the owner/author(s). Publication rights licensed to ACM.
ACM ISBN 978-1-4503-5037-2/17/06...$15.00
http://dx.doi.org/10.1145/3084381.3084395

1 INTRODUCTION

Over the years, in most industries, information systems (IS) have become an essential weapon for a firm's survival in the competitive market (Bakos, 1986; Segars & Grover, 1995). Today information technology (IT) affects business success due to its impact on the mechanisms of business (Drnevich & Croson, 2013). However, IT implementation is influenced by isomorphic processes in an industrial context. Therefore, it is crucial to study the interactions between the two (Orlikowski & Barley, 2001). New conceptualizations of IS implementation can be built from understanding IS and how it shapes the industry or is shaped by it (Chiasson & Davidson, 2005). This paper attempts to build on two historically influential concepts– 'isomorphism' from institutional theory and 'strategic grid' from IS.

'Isomorphism' is what makes one entity similar to another. Organizations tend to undergo isomorphism and become homogeneous with other organizations in an industry when they are related through shared resources, consumers, and product type (DiMaggio & Powell, 1983; Meyer & Rowan, 1977). The institutionalized rules, defined processes, and rationalized activities get automatically implemented in the operations that the information systems (IS) support. Institutional theory suggests that once new models have been adopted by one organization and confirmed as successful (Bharadwaj, 2000), the model gets diffused across the entire industry, causing all the firms to grow similar to each other (Beckert, 2010). With the ease of replication and successful outcomes, IS-dependent organizational structures act as institutionalized models ready to be replicated by other firms. IS components are designed in such a way that the organizations using it are bound together through the homogeneous mechanisms of business and operational activities that the system makes its users follow, unquestioningly (Gosain, 2004). Therefore, all the three mechanisms of institutional isomorphism — coercive, mimetic and normative — are witnessed in IS-dependent industries.

IS performs different roles in the strategy of different firms (Bhatt, Grover & Grover, 2005). Some firms use IT strategically, while for others it can be just a cost-effective option or an additional support to the existing operations. The depth of influence of existing IS on the corporate business can be identified through McFarlan and McKenney's (1983) famous IS strategic grid. This framework places an organization on a quadrant in order to understand how important IT is for its business operations and sustenance. There are four such broad classifications to group firms based on the criticality of IS applications (Bakos, 1986), namely the factory, the strategic, the turnaround and the support quadrant. Empirical studies have supported the framework and its different quadrants (Raghunathan & Raghunathan, 1990). It is evident that the firms in different quadrants are impacted differently by IS and hence be subject to isomorphism to different levels.

Whenever firms make an effort to grow by replicating technology, it results in inevitable imitation (Kogut & Zander, 1992). The implications of isomorphism, as more firms adapt similar IT due to pressure from their supply chain partners, has been studied by Lai, Wong, and Chen (2005). Organizational change and alignment due to strategic IS has been observed in SMEs (Levy & Powell, 2000). The institutional pressure for IT outsourcing is resulting in homogenous systems (Ang & Cummings, 1997). Gosain's (2004) suggests that introduction of new enterprise IS carries institutional logic and offers systematization of the firm activities in a uniformly aligned fashion. On the other end, empirical tests to validate the strategic grid have been conducted with both private sector organizations (Raghunathan & Raghunathan, 1990) and government agencies (Tukana & Weber, 1996). The measures and constructs of the dimensions of strategic grid has been operationalized (Raghunathan, Raghunathan, & Tu, 1999). Firms have been using the strategic grid for their strategic IS planning and other future developmental activities (McBride, 1997) or shifting from traditional to intelligent IS applications (Yeon, 2007).Yet, there has been no previous research that develops a comprehensive framework to identify the extent of isomorphism depending on significance of IT and its operations.

The purpose of this paper is to investigate the interplay between each of the mechanisms of isomorphism, and the different degrees of IT criticality. For example, a firm where the role of IT is minimal and its use is not related to the basic operations, then the firm is likely not to undergo isomorphism as severely as compared to another firm that is heavily dependent on its IT systems. The three kinds of isomorphism will act differently for the firms in the various strategic positions. The framework developed would give the expected level of isomorphism when the firm's position in the strategic grid is known. The results would be useful for market analysis since IT is ubiquitous across industries today. A few relevant cases from the industry have been provided in the end of the article for an understanding of the practical implications.

2 ISOMORPHISM AND THE MECHANISMS

Meyer and Rowan (1977) suggests that organizations achieve legitimacy by adopting norms and regulation that the society prescribes, making them isomorphic. Bureaucratization and rationalization are two historic concepts that make individuals act rationally and shape all the organizations homogeneously (Dacin, 1997). This homogenization occurs when the

organizations in the field interact with or are dependent on each other through identical resources, consumers, and products, and the individuals make similar rational decisions, making the organizations react similarly to the environmental conditions. This process of this homogenization of an organization, from its inception to maturity, is referred to as 'institutional isomorphism'. According to DiMaggio and Powell (1983) the three mechanisms of institutional isomorphism are as follows:

Coercive Isomorphism. Coercive isomorphism can result due to pressure from the external environment. It could be from other organizations on which the firm is dependent, from the society and its cultural expectations, or from the government in form of regulations and policies.

Mimetic Isomorphism. In uncertain environmental conditions like ambiguity in defining goals, organizations tend to consciously or unintentionally imitate the models of other organizations that have been successful in the industry. This process results in mimetic isomorphism. This is most researched concept among the three in the academic journals (Mizruchi & Fein, 1999).

Normative Isomorphism. Professional occupation has predefined set of legitimized norms that the members are bound to. The system of formal education and training, and networks through which professionals of different firms are connected, has added to the universality. Professionalization is responsible for normative isomorphism, where the employees of different organizations share the same occupation.

Although the three concepts of isomorphism may overlap or blend on certain occasions, the environmental conditions affecting these are different (Frumkin & Galaskiewicz, 2004). Organizations have been influenced by mimetic and coercive isomorphism while developing their forthcoming business plans (Honig & Karlsson, 2004), whereas normative isomorphism has been noted in organizations with members belonging to professional associations (Frumkin & Galaskiewicz, 2004). The factors that impose coercive, mimetic and normative pressures on the firm include government policies, competitor behaviors, customer expectations, social worker group demands (Delmas & Toffel, 2004), and recently enterprise information systems and IT supply chains (Liang et al., 2007; Lai et al., 2005).

3 INFORMATION SYSTEMS AND INSTITUTIONAL ISOMORPHISM

Transparent and imitable IS components, pressure to digitize from firms in the supply chain, customer expectations of state-of-art digital systems, highly competitive market with stable market leaders, and similarly trained IT professionals (Granados & Gupta, 2013; Grover & Kohli, 2013;Markus & Loebbecke, 2013; Mata, Fuerst & Barney, 1995) causes coercive, mimetic and normative isomorphism.ERP systems have been subjected to all forms of institutional pressures in during the adoption and implementation phases (Liang et al., 2007). Technological innovations with respect to IS are based on rational organizational choices, and similar environmental conditions call for similar IT innovations (Swanson & Ramiller, 1997). Gosain's

(2004) study on enterprise IS found how IT components are carriers of institutional forces that cause isomorphism. Over the last two decades, organizations have been heavily outsourcing their IT needs to suppliers who typically follow similar business processes, and the products and services are identical in nature (Rivard & Aubart, 2015). When there is a demand for a firm to join an ecosystem of IS like inter-organizational systems or supply chains, the entire business community in the network heavily impacts the firm's IT decisions and forces firms to resemble one another (Hart and Saunders, 1998; Fichman, 2004).These evidences portray that IT use across firms and functionalities have become an inevitable expectation of the environment and this result in isomorphic change across the firms. However, different IS strategy will impact in isomorphism through different mechanisms and intensities.

4 STRATEGIC GRID: RELEVANCE OF INFORMATION SYSTEMS IN ORGANIZATIONS

IS plays different roles in different organizations based on its specific needs. Cash et al (1991) suggests that use of management tools is based on the context, and IS use and planning in an organization is dependent on multiple environmental factors. McFarlan and McKenney's (1983) strategic grid, further improved by McFarlan and Nolan (1995), is a framework that assesses a firm's IT strategic relevance based on two dimensions—how dependent the firm is presently on IS and IT artifacts, and the need for IS in the future for business operations. The two dimensions refer to very different kinds of payoffs for the firm concerning different individuals within. Refer to Figure 1 for the details.

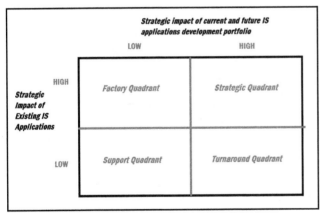

Figure-1: Information Systems Strategic Grid (Adopted from McFarlan & McKenney (1983), Ives & Learmonth (1984), and Raghunathan & Raghunathan (1990))

The four degrees of IS strategic position in an organization identified by the strategic grid framework (Raghunathan & Raghunathan, 1990) is given below.

Strategic Quadrant. Firms lying in this quadrant are critically dependent on their computer systems and IS applications currently for the firm performance and IS is integral in their future plans as well. Therefore, the management and planning for IS strategy and its alignment with core business is an important issue for the senior management.

Turnaround Quadrant. Organizations in this quadrant are primarily dependent on IS for only their operational support but not critical. The management has to do some amount of IS strategic planning mostly for opening up future strategic positioning opportunities.

Factory Quadrant. The operational functions of the firms lying in this quadrant are critically dependent on IS for its daily activities. A technical problem in the IS would cause major disruption in the functioning of the firm, and hence proper maintenance is vital. However, the firm does not use IS as a strategic weapon in the present, and neither does it have any plans for future.

Support Quadrant. The firms in this quadrant are neither dependent on IS for competitive advantage nor for its daily operations. There is no or minimal IS strategic planning. IS services are used mainly as an additional value-added support for the firms' business, and absence would not create any disruption.

Firms may move from one quadrant to another based on industry needs and evolving IT maturity (Ives & Learmonth, 1984). For example, banks moved from turnaround to strategic as a response to deregulation acts, and digitized processes as a competitive step. This framework is appropriate for understanding a firm's IS portfolio and to what extend IS impacts the firm's institutional behaviors.

5 ISOMORPHISM AND STRATEGIC INFORMATION SYSTEMS

In the following subsection, the interactions between isomorphic processes and quadrants of the IS strategic grid are examined.

5.1 Coercive Isomorphism and IS Impact

The Internet has brought all firms on a common transparent platform, causing data related to prices and products visible and comparable with the other firms (Zhu, 2002). Companies are now part of larger eco-complexes—a network of multiple other firms of the industry (Keen & Williams, 2013). Business processes are getting standardized and commoditized, forcing all organizations to use the same IT components to keep up with the trends and be a part of the larger ecosystem (Markus & Loebbecke, 2013). There is also a high amount of customer expectations for web-based business requirements (Bennis, 2013), and pressure from other firms in the supply chain to digitize the systems in order to include the firm into their business network (Lai et al., 2005). Thus the environment plays a very significant role. Coercive isomorphism expected for these firms due their heavy reliance on IS.

Firms in the strategic quadrant are heavily dependent on IT, and thereby the effect of IT is also highest for these firms. Motive of these firms is to generate irreplicable IS resources in order to both sustain its own strategic position in the market, as well as, create barriers to entry for new firms (Wade & Hulland,

2004). Even in the perfect information era, highly IS-strategy oriented firms will have the skill to selectively disclose information that would protect its advantage (Granados & Gupta, 2013). They have unique irreplicable IS assets. Coercive isomorphism, induced by external environment, hence will be low. There is an absence of stringent government regulations related to IT (Christmann & Taylor, 2001) and no isomorphic effects due to such regulations.

Hypothesis 1a (H1a): Coercive isomorphism will be low for firms in the strategic quadrant of IS strategic grid.

Organizations in the turnaround quadrant are somewhat dependent on IT for operational support but IT does not yet have any strategic role. The software applications used for support purposes are likely to be imitable. Without a strategic role, the budget for IT is low and imitating the applications from other firms or using standardized open applications is the lowest cost option. There will hence be influence of the environment like other firms' IT applications, standardized software, and competitors' IT planning leading to high coercive isomorphism. Yet, the isomorphism will be moderated by strategic IT goals since IT as a competitive weapon is an upcoming prospect.

Hypothesis 1b (H1b): Coercive isomorphism will be moderate for firms in the turnaround quadrant of IS strategic grid.

Factory quadrant has firms that critically dependent on IS for their daily operations and any IT failure leads to disruption in business processes. To avoid any risk of failure, these firms will tend to imitate the successful IT processes of other firms, and also use well-known standardized openly available software applications. Thus the impact of the environment including the IT artifacts used by other firms, IT requirements to be connected to other firms in its supply chain, the open software components available in the market, and the popular proprietary applications, is high. Hence, coercive isomorphism will be high.

Hypothesis 1c (H1c): Coercive isomorphism will be high for firms in the factory quadrant of IS strategic grid.

The firms in the support quadrant are not dependent on IT for its operations or strategic planning, and the presence of IT is only as an additional support. These firms will not undergo isomorphism due to IS influence.

Hypothesis 1d (H1d): Coercive isomorphism will be absent for firms in the support quadrant of IS strategic grid.

5.2   Mimetic Isomorphism and IS Impact

The Internet has made the environment for most industries both uncertain and highly competitive (Drnevich & Croson, 2013). Hundreds of online startups have boomed post the year 2000 Internet boom, and another hundred have failed and have been pushed out of the game (Mahajan, Srinivasan & Wind, 2002). There is no definite business procedure to guide companies to success owing to the rapid IT developments. Such an uncertain indecisive environment forms the basis of mimetic isomorphism. Additionally, common IS platforms makes the business processes transparent and visible, thus susceptible to imitation by other firms (Granados & Gupta, 2013; Grover & Kohli, 2013). This has resulted in standardized business processes that more

than one firm in a business community follow (Markus & Loebbecke, 2013). Usually at the epicenter of such a business community is the stable orchestrator firm. The unpredictability of success and ease of IT replication would automatically persuade younger firms to follow the footsteps of this orchestrator.

The strategic quadrant would have firms that are able to convert their distinctive IT assets into valuable inimitable strategic applications through their capacity of IT-based innovations (Sambamurthy, Bharadwaj & Grover, 2003). These firms do not imitate others, and it is difficult for others to replicate their IS since they have designed their innovations as inimitable and valuable. Thus mimetic isomorphism is low for these firms.

Hypothesis 2a (H2a): Mimetic isomorphism will be low for firms in the strategic quadrant of IS strategic grid.

Same computer technologies for operational purposes can be used across business and functions like storing, retrieving, transmitting data using different digitized information of identical formats (Brynjolfsson & Hitt, 2000). Using IS only as an operational support is likely to cause failure. Firms in the turnaround quadrant will be highly affected by the uncertainty in the absence of proper IT capabilities, and in the desperation to turnaround in the future with strategic IT, will imitate the stable or successful firms in the industry. This is a common phenomenon where ecosystems are led by an orchestrator firm who provides basic IS guidelines and standard process for others to follow (Markus & Loebbecke, 2013). This would inevitably lead to mimetic isomorphism.

Hypothesis 2b (H2b): Mimetic isomorphism will be high for firms in the turnaround quadrant of IS strategic grid.

Factory quadrant firms would have an incentive to reduce uncertainty and ensure proper functioning of their critical IT applications. These firms do not need to innovate, but be updated with the latest IS for most efficient operations of their business. These firms would imitate the IS applications of other matured firms to guarantee stability and smooth functioning, therefore influenced by high mimetic forces.

Hypothesis 2c (H2c): Mimetic isomorphism will be high for firms in the factory quadrant of IS strategic grid.

The organizations in the support quadrant today have chosen 'defensive denial' to the changing IT environments and continued with their traditional business processes (Granados & Gupta, 2013). While most firms have migrated to an IS-based infrastructure, the firms in the support quadrant show that they have decided to neither learn from nor copy the others' IT components, hence have no IS influence.

Hypothesis 2d (H2d): Mimetic isomorphism will be absent for firms in the support quadrant of IS strategic grid.

5.3   Normative Isomorphism and IS Impact

Professionalization results in normative isomorphism. Software engineering is a highly professional career, with universally standardized education and training globally. The curriculum design for IT is based on the industry requirement and curriculum of other universities and institutions (Reichgelt, Zhang & Price, 2011). Software development teams consists of members from various firms across the globe (Townsend, DeMarie & Hendrickson, 1998), there is automatically a call for standardized work practices. The information infrastructures used by most firms are homogeneous (Monteiro & Hanseth, 1996), forcing both users and developers to work identically. With attrition rate of software companies as high as 20 percent, the mobilization of software processionals across firms is high (Rajkumar & Mani, 2001). Advanced communication and networking systems like social networks are also enabling interactions and professional relationships across fellow IT professionals. Therefore, normative isomorphism is expected to be high for IT dependent organizations.

Firms in the strategic quadrant have qualified professionals to head and operate their IT planning and functions. Since firms that adopt innovations employ skilled labors (Bresnahan, Brynjolfsson & Hitt, 1999), the employees of these firms are likely to have been educated from esteemed engineering colleges, which follow standardized curriculum (Topi et al., 2010). With experience as an appraised measurement for qualification above most other factors, all experienced employees are likely to have had similar prior work experience (Salanova, Peiró & Schaufeli, 2002). To enrich their skills, the IT professionals would attend conferences and seminars, where they would meet and build network with other fellow practitioners. All these imply heavy impact of normative forces.

Hypothesis 3a (H3a): Normative isomorphism will be high for firms in the strategic quadrant of IS strategic grid.

The turnaround grid firms' IT employees may not all be computer professionals. For daily operational support through IS, individuals with basic working knowledge of computer is sufficient. Experienced professionals are relatively few in number responsible for future IS strategic planning. Thus, the mimetic isomorphism will be moderate for these organizations since the bulk of the IS department employees are not professionals but a few higher level strategic planners are.

Hypothesis 3b (H3b): Normative isomorphism will be medium for firms in the turnaround quadrant of IS strategic grid.

Firms in the factory quadrant essentially need a team of IT employees for the daily operations and smooth functioning of their business processes with minimal failure. The employees of the IT support department are professionals with identical training and experience. With regular operational tasks and negligble amount of intellectually challenging work, the attrition would be high for these employees. High mobility of the IT workers requires uniform work practices and similar background of replacement employee. This results in high normative isomorphism.

Hypothesis 3c (H3c): Normative isomorphism will be high for firms in the factory quadrant of IS strategic grid.

Support quadrant firms, with no current or future IS requirement, have minimal employees who are professionals in IT. Hence, like the other isomorphism mechanisms, normative effect due to the IS will be negligible for these firms.

Hypothesis 3d (H3d): Normative isomorphism will be absent for firms in the support quadrant of IS strategic grid.

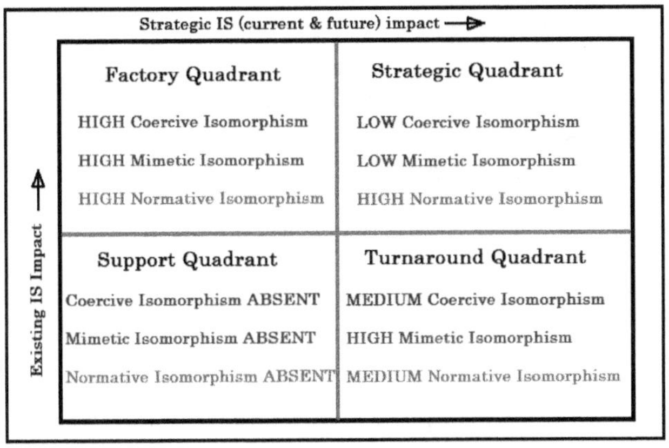

Figure-2: Isomorphic mechanisms and IS strategic quadrants

Please note, the isomorphism mechanisms may not hold when a firm is in a transitory stage with respect to IS strategic quadrants. For example, firms in the turnaround quadrant might already have built a team of IT experts as a readiness to transit to the strategic quadrant soon. In such a case, the normative isomorphism will be high instead of moderate due to the presence of skilled IT professionals. Refer to Figure-2 below for an overview of the isomorphic mechanisms on firms in various IS strategic quadrants.

6   PROPOSED METHODOLOGY

First, we would shortlist firms in India whose senior management and IS executives can be contacted via email. Once the firms are shortlisted, in order to classify the firms into the respective strategic grids, the senior IS executives of the firms will be sent a survey questionnaire as designed by Raghunathan, Raghunathan & Tu (1998) in their paper defining the contructs and measurements for the IS strategic grid. We also send out another survey questionnaire (adopted from the questionnaire designed by Ashworth, Boyne, & Delbridge (2009) to measure organizational change due to isomorphism) to the major function/unit heads, managers, and chief executives to understand the levels of normative, coercive, and mimetic isomorphism and thus verify the hypotheses.

When we receive the responses, the firms where more number of individuals has responded to the questionnaires will be chosen for further study. In case there are conflicts (same firm's exectives have evaluated the firm's strategic position differently), that firm will be excluded from the study. The remaining firms will be studied to verify the proposed hypotheses. The hypotheses related to each of the strategic quadrants would be tested on the same most generic functions/units of the firms, as suggested by Frumkin & Galaskiewicz (2004). For example, to test hypotheses 3a, 3b, and 3c, we may select the sales unit of all the firms in strategic grid for analysis, and thus use the responses of isomorphism survey of the sales unit managers and senior executives.

7 PRACTICAL CASES

The following are some examples from the industry that illustrate the intuition behind hypotheses and the framework.

Case 1. Lenskart is an online store specialized in eye-glasses and related products like contact lenses, sunglasses, eye-glass frames, lenses, and accessories. Currently its sales unit lies in the strategic quadrant of the IS strategic grid with highly innovative online store. Shoppers are able to three-dimensionally graphically see how a particular eye-frame looks on them, and online book for free eye-checkup, etc. It did not replicate the cliché ecommerce websites, thus implying low coercive isomorphism. Most ecommerce firms offer low-cost products (Eg.: Eye-frames on Snapdeal). Lenskart is clearly a differentiator in the industry without much replication need in the uncertain online environment, thus implying low mimetic isomorphism. The hiring advertisement of Lenskart reads "3 to 9 years solid experience in developing web applications utilizing Web 2.0 technologies... Responsible for the over-all systems development life cycle..." (Website: www.hackerearth.com). This is not different from most other IT jobs, and is likely to attract software engineers with similar training and background. This shows a high normative isomorphic effect due to Lenskart's dependence on IT. (Hypotheses H1a, H2a, and H3a).

Case 2. Nationalized banks like State Bank of India (SBI), Bank of Baroda (BoB), Punjab National Bank (PNB), and others, lie in the factory quadrant of the IS strategic grid. They essentially need IS their daily operations like customer account maintenance, transaction details, market share related data, etc (Bhattacherjee, 2001). Since all firms have moved to the online banking platform, the IS connecting the banks and its customers do not aid in building any competitive advantage. All the banks use identical web-based online banking services available as products developed by IT firms (Vatanasombut et al., 2008). This shows that these banks align their IT based on the available software components and other banks' business techniques, implying a high coercive isomorphism. Mimetic isomorphism is also high since the other banks replicated the internet banking as soon as ICICI bank proved to be stable and successful after the early launch of online banking on 1998 (Website: www.mckinsey.com). The IT employees of these banks support smooth functioning of the system, solve minor issues, and escalate the problems to the outsource firm. Such workers are required to have computer skills and software engineering background, and all banks would hire similar employees. Thus, normative isomorphism is high for the IT department of the banks. (Hypotheses H1c, H2c, and H3c).

Case 3. Indian hospitals use IT for support based operations like maintaining patient records, generating medical bills, and replenishing their drugs store and are subsequently investing on new medical expert systems that could perform specialized functions like automated diagnosis of diseases using artificial intelligence (Kandaswamy & Kumar, 2013; Smith, 1992; Arora, 2010). This puts the hospitals in the turnaround quadrant. The competitive advantage of the hospitals are not reliant on IT but on other features like expertise of doctors, and other medical facilities. However if competing hospitals start adopting expert systems, the others will also anticipate similar systems, implying moderate coercive isomorphism. The expert systems would require some IT support employees and some qualified doctors and nurses for supervision and database enrichment. With a combination of IT professionals and medical staff, the effect of normative forces due to introduction of the expert systems would only be moderate. When a particular expert system installed by a renowned hospital runs successfully, others will start adopting the system too, resulting in mimetic isomorphism. (Hypotheses H1b, H2b, and H3b).

All firms might not be following the framework precisely because the industry and the market create a complex environment where more than one factor impact organization structure, behavior, and changes. Also, the firms might be in transition phases across strategic quadrants while changing their IT plans. This makes the behavior of the firms unpredictable. It is also difficult to place firms in the turnaround quadrant since the future strategic plans are usually undisclosed by the management. With the assumption that available information is correct, the framework should be good to understand isomorphism influenced by the current IT trends in industries.

8 IMPLICATIONS

The benefit of the framework that brings together the two concepts — Isomorphism and Strategic Grid — is preparedness of a firm through industry prediction. A firm would know its position in the strategic grid from its IS dependency and could be able to predict the isomorphic changes that it would witness. Coercive isomorphism also results in invitation to join other firms in collusion (O Brien & Slack, 2004). If an organization would want to sustain independently, it should be careful about its position in the factory quadrant that leads to high coercive isomorphism. When smaller firms need to adopt IT to compete with the market trend, they will be forced to learn from or copy from the dominant leader, and result in mimetic isomorphism (Lai, Wong & Chen, 2006), leading to loss of their competitive advantage. Small firms in the turnaround and factory quadrant should be cautious of their IT moves. Strategic quadrant firms would want to reduce normative isomorphism this by recruiting specialized professionals who have expertise in specific areas of software.

Institutional theory has been historically used to understand IT adoption (Oliveira & Martins, 2011; Sherer, 2010). Current IS literature shows a significant number of studies on isomorphic changes due to use and implementations of various kinds of IS infrastructure (Currie, 2012; Cavusoglu et al., 2015; Zorn et al. 2011). This paper provides a framework for understanding how the IS strategic positions of firms will result in the isomorphic changes, adding to the literature that uses institutional theory for IS adoption and use.

9 CONCLUSION & FUTURE SCOPE

This paper uses two historic concepts—Institutional Isomorphism and its mechanisms formulated by DiMaggio and Powell, in the field of Organizational Theory, and IS Strategic Grid designed by McFarlan and McKenney in the field of Information Systems—and designs a framework to understand the effect of IT in isomorphic change, adding to the vast existing literature that uses institutional theory to analyze IS adoptions by organizations.

The practical examples towards the end of the article explain how the framework can be placed in the industrial context and and the proposed methodology offers a future research plan. The selection of the sample should be in way such that the effects of other major external forces, like sudden change in government regulations, change in market structure, or entry of strong competitors, is minimized, and the industry should have significant IS dependence.

REFERENCES

[1] Ang, Soon, and Larry L. Cummings. 1997. "Strategic response to institutional influences on information systems outsourcing." Organization science 8.3: 235-256.

[2] Arora, Payal (2010). "Digital gods: The making of a medical fact for rural diagnostic software." The Information Society 26.1: 70-79.

[3] Ashworth, R., Boyne, G., & Delbridge, R. 2009. Escape from the iron cage? Organizational change and isomorphic pressures in the public sector. Journal of Public Administration Research and Theory, 19(1), 165-187.

[4] Bakos, J. Yannis, and Michael E. Treacy. 1986. "Information technology and corporate strategy: a research perspective." MIS quarterly: 107-119.

[5] Beckert, Jens. 2010. "Institutional isomorphism revisited: Convergence and divergence in institutional change*." Sociological Theory 28.2: ¬¬¬¬¬¬150-166.

[6] Bennis, Warren. 2013. "Leadership in a digital world: embracing transparency and adaptive capacity." Mis Quarterly 37.2: 635-636.

[7] Bharadwaj, Anandhi S. 2000. "A resource-based perspective on information technology capability and firm performance: an empirical investigation." MIS quarterly: 169-196.

[8] Bhatt, Ganesh D., Varun Grover, and VARUN GROVER. 2005. "Types of information technology capabilities and their role in competitive advantage: An empirical study." Journal of management information systems 22.2: 253-277.

[9] Bhattacherjee, Anol. 2001. "Understanding information systems continuance: an expectation-confirmation model." MIS quarterly: 351-370.

[10] Bresnahan, Timothy F., Erik Brynjolfsson, and Lorin M. Hitt. 1999. Information technology, workplace organization and the demand for skilled labor: Firm-level evidence. No. w7136. National Bureau of Economic Research.

[11] Brien, Danny, and Trevor Slack. 2004. "The emergence of a professional logic in English Rugby Union: The role of isomorphic and diffusion processes."Journal of Sport Management 18: 13-39.

[12] Brynjolfsson, Erik, and Lorin M. Hitt. 2000. "Beyond computation: Information technology, organizational transformation and business performance." The Journal of Economic Perspectives: 23-48.

[13] Cash Jr, J. I., McKenney, J. L., McFarlan, F. W., & Glinert, S. 1991. Corporate information systems management: the issues facing senior executives. McGraw-Hill, Inc..

[14] Cavusoglu, H., Cavusoglu, H., Son, J. Y., & Benbasat, I. 2015. Institutional pressures in security management: Direct and indirect influences on organizational investment in information security control resources. Information & Management, 52(4), 385-400.

[15] Chiasson, Mike W., and Elizabeth Davidson. 2005. "Taking industry seriously in information systems research." Mis Quarterly: 591-605.

[16] Christmann, Petra, and Glen Taylor. 2001. "Globalization and the environment: Determinants of firm self-regulation in China." Journal of international business studies: 439-458.

[17] Currie, W. L. 2012. Institutional isomorphism and change: the national programme for IT–10 years on. Journal of Information Technology, 27(3), 236-248.

[18] Dacin, M. Tina. 1997. "Isomorphism in context: The power and prescription of institutional norms." Academy of management journal 40.1: 46-81.

[19] Delmas, Magali, and Michael W. Toffel. 2004. "Stakeholders and environmental management practices: an institutional framework." Business strategy and the Environment 13.4: 209-222.

[20] DiMaggio, Paul, and Walter Powell. 1991. "The Iron Cahe Revisited-Institutional Isomorphism and Collective Rationality." The new institutionalism in organizational analysis: 63-82.

[21] Drnevich, Paul L., and David C. Croson. 2013. "Information technology and business-level strategy: toward an integrated theoretical perspective." Mis Quarterly 37.2: 483-509.

[22] Fichman, Robert G. 2004. "Going beyond the dominant paradigm for information technology innovation research: Emerging concepts and methods." Journal of the association for information systems 5.8: 11.

[23] Florkowski, Gary W., and Miguel R. Olivas-Luján. 2006. "The diffusion of human-resource information-technology innovations in US and non-US firms."Personnel Review 35.6: 684-710.

[24] Frumkin, P., & Galaskiewicz, J. 2004. Institutional isomorphism and public sector organizations. Journal of public administration research and theory, 14(3), 283-307.

[25] Frumkin, Peter, and Joseph Galaskiewicz. 2004. "Institutional isomorphism and public sector organizations." Journal of public administration research and theory 14.3: 283-307.

[26] Gorgone, John T., et al. 2006. "MSIS 2006: model curriculum and guidelines for graduate degree programs in information systems." ACM SIGCSE Bulletin38.2: 121-196.

[27] Gosain, Sanjay (2004). "Enterprise information systems as objects and carriers of institutional forces: the new iron cage?." Journal of the Association for Information Systems 5.4: 6.

[28] Granados, Nelson, and Alok Gupta. 2013. "Transparency strategy: competing with information in a digital world." Mis Quarterly 37.2: 637-642.

[29] Grover, Varun, and Rajiv Kohli. 2013. "Revealing your hand: caveats in implementing digital business strategy." Mis Quarterly 37.2: 655-662.

[30] Hackerearth. Accessed on 21-Dec-2015. https://www.hackerearth.com/lenskart-hiring-challenge/

[31] Hart, Paul J., and Carol S. Saunders. 1998. "Emerging electronic partnerships: antecedents and dimensions of EDI use from the supplier's perspective."Journal of Management Information Systems: 87-111.

[32] Honig, Benson, and Tomas Karlsson. 2004. "Institutional forces and the written business plan." Journal of Management 30.1: 29-48.

[33] Ives, Blake, and Gerard P. Learmonth. 1984. "The information system as a competitive weapon." Communications of the ACM 27.12: 1193-1201.

[34] Kandaswamy, A., and A. Sukesh Kumar. 2013. "Role of medical expert systems in health care in the Indian context." Defence Science Journal 47.4: 499-504.

[35] Keen, Peter, and Ronald Williams. 2013. "Value architectures for digital business: beyond the business model." Mis Quarterly 37.2: 642-647.

[36] Kogut, Bruce, and Udo Zander. 1992. "Knowledge of the firm, combinative capabilities, and the replication of technology." Organization science 3.3: 383-397.

[37] Lai, Kee-hung, Christina WY Wong, and TC Edwin Cheng. 2006. "Institutional isomorphism and the adoption of information technology for supply chain management." Computers in Industry 57.1: 93-98.

[38] Levy, Margi, and Philip Powell. 2000. "Information systems strategy for small and medium sized enterprises: an organisational perspective." The Journal of Strategic Information Systems 9.1: 63-84.

[39] Liang, Huigang, et al. 2007. "Assimilation of enterprise systems: the effect of institutional pressures and the mediating role of top management." MIS quarterly: 59-87.

[40] Mahajan, Vijay, Raji Srinivasan, and Jerry Wind. 2002. "The dot. com retail failures of 2000: were there any winners?." Journal of the Academy of Marketing Science 30.4: 474-486.

[41] Markus, M. Lynne, and Claudia Loebbecke. 2013. "Commoditized digital processes and business community platforms: new opportunities and challenges for digital business strategies." Mis Quarterly 37.2: 649-654.

[42] Mata, Francisco J., William L. Fuerst, and Jay B. Barney. 1995. "Information technology and sustained competitive advantage: A resource-based analysis." MIS quarterly: 487-505.

[43] McBride, Neil (1997). "Business use of the Internet: Strategic decision or another bandwagon?." European Management Journal 15.1: 58-67.

[44] McFarlan, F. Warren, and Richard L. Nolan. 1995. "How to manage an IT outsourcing alliance." MIT Sloan Management Review 36.2: 9.

[45] McFarlan, Franklin Warren, and James L. McKenney. 1983. Corporate information systems management: The issues facing senior executives. Irwin Professional Publishing.

[46] McKinsey&Company. Accessed on 23-Dec-2015. http://www.mckinsey.com/clientservice/bto/pointofview/pdf/MoIT11_ICICInterview_F.pdf.

[47] Meyer, John W., and Brian Rowan (1977). "Institutionalized organizations: Formal structure as myth and ceremony." American journal of sociology: 340-363.

[48] Mizruchi, Mark S., and Lisa C. Fein. 1999. "The social construction of organizational knowledge: A study of the uses of coercive, mimetic, and normative isomorphism." Administrative science quarterly 44.4: 653-683.

[49] Monteiro, Eric, and Ole Hanseth. 1996. "Social shaping of information infrastructure: on being specific about the technology." Information technology and changes in organizational work: 325-343.

[50] Oliveira, T., & Martins, M. F. 2011. Literature review of information technology adoption models at firm level. The Electronic Journal Information Systems Evaluation, 14(1), 110-121.

[51] Orlikowski, Wanda J., and Stephen R. Barley. 2001. "Technology and institutions: What can research on information technology and research on organizations learn from each other?." MIS quarterly 25.2: 145-165.

[52] Raghunathan, B., Raghunathan, T. S., & Tu, Q. 1999. Dimensionality of the strategic grid framework: the construct and its measurement. Information Systems Research, 10(4), 343-355.

[53] Raghunathan, Bhanu, and T. S. Raghunathan. 1990. "Planning implications of the information systems strategic grid: an empirical investigation." Decision Sciences 21.2: 287-300.

[54] Raghunathan, Bhanu, T. S. Raghunathan, and Qiang Tu. 1999. "Dimensionality of the strategic grid framework: the construct and its measurement."Information Systems Research 10.4: 343-355.

[55] Rajkumar, T. M., and R. V. S. Mani. 2001. "Offshore software development."Information Systems Management 18.2: 63-74.

[56] Reichgelt, Han, Aimao Zhang, and Barbara Price. 2002. "Designing an information technology curriculum: The Georgia Southern University experience." Journal of Information Technology Education: Research 1.1: 213-221.

[57] Rivard, Suzanne, and Benoit A. Aubert (2015). Information technology outsourcing. Routledge.

[58] Salanova, Marisa, José M. Peiró, and Wilmar B. Schaufeli. 2002. "Self-efficacy specificity and burnout among information technology workers: An extension of the job demand-control model." European Journal of work and organizational psychology 11.1: 1-25.

[59] Sambamurthy, Vallabh, Anandhi Bharadwaj, and Varun Grover. 2003. "Shaping agility through digital options: Reconceptualizing the role of information technology in contemporary firms." MIS quarterly: 237-263.

[60] Segars, Albert H., and Varun Grover. 1995. "The Industry-Level Impact of Information Technology: An Empirical Analysis of Three Industries*."Decision Sciences 26.3: 337-368.

[61] Sherer, S. A. 2010. Information systems and healthcare XXXIII: An institutional theory perspective on physician adoption of electronic health records. Communications of the Association for Information Systems, 26(1), 7.

[62] Smith, David E. 1992. "Expert systems for medical diagnosis: a study in technology transfer." The Journal of Technology Transfer 17.4: 45-53.

[63] Swanson, E. Burton, and Neil C. Ramiller. 1997. "The organizing vision in information systems innovation." Organization science 8.5: 458-474.

[64] Topi, Heikki, et al. 2010. "Curriculum guidelines for undergraduate degree programs in information systems." ACM/AIS task force.

[65] Townsend, Anthony M., Samuel M. DeMarie, and Anthony R. Hendrickson. 1998. "Virtual teams: Technology and the workplace of the future." The Academy of Management Executive 12.3: 17-29.

[66] Tukana, Semi, and Ron Weber. 1996. "An empirical test of the strategic-grid model of information systems planning." Decision Sciences 27.4: 735.

[67] Vatanasombut, Banphot, et al. 2008. "Information systems continuance intention of web-based applications customers: The case of online banking."Information & Management 45.7: 419-428.

[68] Wade, Michael, and John Hulland. 2004. "Review: The resource-based view and information systems research: Review, extension, and suggestions for future research." MIS quarterly 28.1: 107-142.

[69] Yeon, Seung-Jun. 2007. "A strategic grid for implementing ubiquitous computing."ETRI journal 29.2: 252-254.

[70] Zhu, Kevin. 2002. "Information transparency in electronic marketplaces: Why data transparency may hinder the adoption of B2B exchanges." Electronic markets 12.2: 92-99.

[71] Zorn, T. E., Flanagin, A. J., & Shoham, M. D. 2011. Institutional and noninstitutional influences on information and communication technology adoption and use among nonprofit organizations. Human Communication Research, 37(1), 1-33.

Executive Pay Before and After Technology IPOs: Who Receives More?

Full Paper

Tenace Kwaku Setor
Nanyang Technology University
Singapore
tenacekw001@e.ntu.edu.sg

Damien Joseph
Nanyang Technology University
Singapore
adjoseph@ntu.edu.sg

ABSTRACT

Technology IPOs expose Information Technology (IT) firms to significant challenges that are fundamentally different from those faced during the founding or startup stage. To tackle the post-IPO challenges, IT firms pay premium wages to hire professional executives from the external labor market rather than from within. Yet, how the executive pay of external hires compares to that of internal hires when IT firms mark significant milestones in their lifecycle remain understudied. The current study therefore examines the pay of internal and external hires and place it within the context of the IPO timeline i.e. pre- and post-IPO. By analyzing data from multiple sources using a linear mixed effects modelling technique, we find that IT firms pay internal hires significantly higher than external hires in the pre-IPO stage. In the post-IPO stage, IT firms pay external hires significantly higher than internal hires. We discuss the implications of the findings on theory and practice.

CCS CONCEPTS

• **Social and professional topics → Computing profession →** Employment issues; Computing occupations

KEYWORDS

Executive pay, Internal hires, External hires, Technology initial public offering, Human capital

ACM Reference format:

Tenace K. Setor, Damien Joseph. 2017. Executive Pay Before and After Technology IPOs: Who Receives More? *ACM SIGMIS CPR*, Article 25 (March 2010), 9 pages.
DOI: http://dx.doi.org/10.1145/3084381.3084397

1 INTRODUCTION

Initial Public Offerings (IPOs) continue to remain a rite of passage for Information Technology (IT) startups. Often, the popular press portrays technology IPOs as alluring exit stories. The reality, however, is that IPOs expose recently publicly-traded (young) IT firms to significant challenges that are fundamentally different from those faced at the pre-IPO or founding stage [1,2]. Overnight, young IT firms become the subject of bureaucratic and public scrutiny regarding their fiscal growth (or decline), management practices and corporate social responsibilities.

Ordinarily young IT firms consist of founding members "who are more interested in the initial development of a product or market but have very limited managerial interests or capacities" [3]. The normative strategy therefore is to turn to the external labor market for requisite managerial expertise rather than from within immediately after IPO; a practice referred to as firm professionalization [3–5]. Pointcast, Razorfish and eBay are a few examples of IT startups that were professionalized when it became apparent that the founding executives were ill-equipped, skills-wise, to administer the evolving firms [6]. But firm professionalization is a costly undertaking. In many instances, young post-IPO firms pay premiums to induce a switch or lure professional executives from the external labor market [7]. This is corroborated by empirical evidence emanating from the top management and pay literature which finds that external hires receive significantly higher compensation, salaries or wages than internal hires [7–9].

But this evidence, which implicitly suggest firms value the skills of external hires more than internal hires, run counter to the prescription flowing from the fundamental human capital literature. According to the human capital literature [10], internal hires are argued to be well-endowed with firm-specific skills – skills unique to the incumbent firm, and hence can be productively utilized to meet organizational goals .

External hires possess relatively less firm-specific skills but are endowed with general skills – skills that are readily transferable across firms. Such skills are abundant, less localized and hence less useful in meeting the organization's goals. Following this thesis, firms should value firm-specific skills more [10,11]. And by logic firms would reward internal hires with higher wages, setting up a conflict with the findings of the research on top management and pay earlier articulated. We contend that this conflict in the literature could be reconciled by taking a contextual view of the executive pay of internal and external hires. Indeed, entrepreneurship research that subscribe to the lifecycle view of firms provide a hint in resolving the conflict. As firms progress through the various firm lifecycle stages, different kinds of skills may be required to tackle the unique challenges accompanying each stage [5].

Executives who possess the requisite skills needed to surmount the challenges of each lifecycle stage would have a higher performance, which plays a role in determining pay [12]. It is therefore incumbent to investigate how firms discriminate pay, based on the distinct skills of internal and external hires, as the firms transition from one lifecycle stage to another. The outcome of such an investigation could bring nuance to the broader human capital literature by identifying the different kinds of human capital or skills that are valued at the different lifecycle stages. Accordingly, the current study examines the pay of internal and external hires and place it within the context of the lifecycle of IT firms. Specifically, we examine how technology IPO timelines (i.e. pre vs post-IPO) influence the pay of internal and external hires at the executive level.

2 THEORY AND HYPOTHESES DEVELOPMENT

In this section, we hypothesize the links between the stages of IT firm lifecycle and the executive pay of internal and external hires. For purposes of this study, we categorize firm lifecycle into pre-IPO and post-IPO timelines. The current study uses the terms "pre-IPO IT firms" and "technology startups" interchangeably. Our theoretical model is presented in Fig. 1.

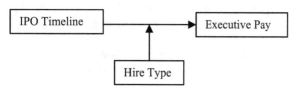

Fig. 1. Theoretical Model

2.1 Pre-IPO Timeline: Internal vs External Hires and Executive Pay

Technology startups take a relatively lean approach towards organizing [13]. They organize around the delivery of technology products and less the structure of the firm. The responsibilities of startup executives are forged towards improving the performance of line functions such as product development, project planning and technical reviews [13]. They must have the technical expertise and the ability to control and oversee the daily operations of the firm.

To be able to effectively execute their central roles as daily custodians of firm operations, startup executives must have detailed knowledge about core firm processes. Hence, internal candidates are more skillfully qualified to take up executive positions in startups rather than external candidates. According to the human capital literature [10], startups are compelled to

compensate internal hires at premiums because of their firm-specific skills and the productivity implication these skills have on line functions.

External hires, in contrast, are not well-endowed with firm-specific skills pertaining to their current firm. But the extant literature suggests firms would rather pay premiums to external hires for foregoing the value of firm-specific skills acquired in their old firms [7]. We contend however that in the pre-IPO stage, line functions are central to the organizing aspect of technology startups. Therefore, we expect startups to value the human capital attributes (e.g. firm-specific skills) that enable line function productivity and performance. Accordingly, we posit

Hypothesis 1: The executive pay of internal hires is higher than external hires in the pre-IPO stage.

2.2 Post-IPO Timeline: Internal vs External Hires and Executive Pay

As IT startups evolve to become public firms the core responsibilities of executives shift from direct oversight of technical operations to an expanded set of responsibilities including strategic planning [5,14]. Executives of young IT firms in the post-IPO stage require "knowledge, experience and social networks that are fundamentally different from those required during the founding phase" [5,14]. Managerial abilities at the executive level must evolve to meet the new set of challenges facing IT firms post IPO.

Young IT firms tend to respond to post-IPO challenges by hiring executives from the external labor market [3]. This is due to the lack of qualified internal candidates [15]. External candidates are more likely to have worked at firms that may have faced challenges pertinent to larger or public firms [3]. They therefore are well-equipped with the relevant professional knowledge and experience that can be readily transferred to the incumbent firm.

To attract external candidates, young post-IPO firms would pay premium wages [7]. In addition, external hires may be compensated for foregoing the future value of the firm-specific skills acquired in their old firm [7]. In sum, young IT firms value the relevant professional skills that are more useful in navigating the unchartered waters of the early post-IPO stage than the firm-specific skills of internal hires; which are relatively useful in the pre-IPO or startup stages.

Accordingly, we posit

Hypothesis 2: The executive pay of external hires is higher than internal hires in the post-IPO stage.

3 METHODOLOGY

3.1 Data Collection and Sample Description.

We collected data from multiple sources: the COMPUSTAT – available via the Wharton Research Data Services (WRDS) and Electron Data Gathering, Analysis and Retrieval (EDGAR) databases, NASDAQ and NYSE web portals. We constructed our sample as follows.

First, we downloaded the list of all technology companies on the NYSE and NASDAQ exchanges. We restricted our sample to

Information Technology firms based on the Industry Classification Benchmark (ICB) system. ICB is a classification system adopted by NASDAQ that segments firms into sub sectors by considering the business areas of the firm that generates the most revenue. For purposes of our study IT firms fall under the following sub sectors of the ICB system: Electron Data Processing (EDP) Services, Computer Software – Pre-packaged software and Computer Software – Programming, Data processing.

Next, we constructed our sample of IT firms that went public (IPO) between 1999 – 2013. Our choice of the range of IPO years is based on practical reasons. In 1999 the dotcom bubble was at its highest peak, with the IT industry recording high-growth rates and increased labor market activity. We ended our search in 2013 as this afforded us the opportunity to collect adequate post-IPO data for our analysis. Our firm sample consists of 71 IT firms.

For each IT firm we retrieved executive compensation data via the EDGAR database. The EDGAR database is a publicly available database that stores electronic reports of the U.S. Security and Exchange Commission (SEC) filings of all publicly listed companies in the U.S. We extracted pre-IPO compensation data of IT executives using form S-1 reports and 10-K annual filings for post-IPO compensation data.

We considered a maximum of 9 years of compensation data; 3 years pre-IPO, the year of the IPO and 5 years post-IPO. The reasons are two-fold. One, form S-1 provides annual compensation data as far back as the third year prior to the firm's IPO. Prior to that, compensation data is unavailable via the EDGAR database. Two, we considered a shorter window for our study so we could effectively distinguish between external and internal hires. Firms sometimes hire external candidates into lower positions in anticipation of promoting them into execution positions later [7].

In light of this, prior research defines external hires as those who have limited firm tenure and by extension internal hires have greater firm tenure. A wider window would confound external hires with internal hires as both groups would have accumulated enough firm experience to be considered as internal hires. The constructed sample of 71 IT firms yielded a total of 406 observations. In the next section, we describe in details the variables used in the current study.

3.1.1 Variable Description.

Dependent Variable. Our dependent variable is real executive pay. Real executive pay is measured as the annual basic (non-contingent) salaries, in USD million, of IT executives of the sample firms. We adjusted for inflation using the U.S. Consumer Price Index (CPI) deflator with 2015 as the baseline year.

Interaction Variables. Our interaction variables are IPO timeline and IT Executive Type. IPO timeline is a recoded continuous variable which represents the number of years before and after a firm's IPO. We designated the year of a firm's IPO as Year '0'. We used Year '0' as a reference point to situate prior and subsequent years. For example, Year '-1' denotes one year before the IPO year and Year '+1' denotes a year after the IPO year. Fig. 2. presents the IPO timeline used for the study.

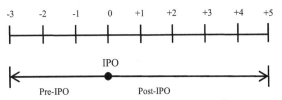

Figure 1: IPO Timeline

Executive Type is a dichotomous variable (0 = *Internal Hire* and 1 = *External Hire*). Guided by prior research we operationalize external hires as executives from the external labor market who have spent 0-5 years with the incumbent firm [7]. Internal hires have more than 5 years of firm tenure [7]. We coded Executive Type using information on forms S-1 and 10-K. Forms S-1 and 10-K provide a summary of the employment history of firm executives, including the year the executive was hired as well as the founding status of the executive.

Control Variables. Guided by prior research we include a series of control variables at the executive and firm levels.

Executive-level Controls. Education credentials attained by executives might influence pay [16]. We accounted for the level of education by using a four-level categorical variable (1 = "*Bachelor's degree*", 2 = "*Masters of Business Administration* (MBA) *degree*", 3 = "*Master's Degree*" and 0 = "*Others*" including doctoral degrees). Studies have shown that the founding status of executives influences compensation. We included a dummy variable measuring the founding status of executives (1 = "*founding member*" and 0 = "*non-founding member*").

Our results may be because of the differences in executive positions. We account for the possible effect of executive position by using a four level categorical variable (1 = "*Chief Executive Officer*" (CEO); 2 = "*Chief Technology and Engineering Executive* (CTEE)" including Chief Technology Officer, Chief Software Officer, Chief Technical Officer, Executive VP Engineering, Executive VP Operations and Engineering and Senior VP Engineering; 0 = "*Chief Product Executive* (CPE)" including Chief Product officer, Vice President (VP) Product Development, Senior VP Product Development.

We control for gender effects. Gender is a dichotomous variable (1 = "*Male*" and 0 = "*Female*"). Age is a logged measure used to proxy individual work experience. We logged age to aid the interpretation of the results. We included logged squared values of age to account for curvilinear effects of experience on compensation.

Firm-level Controls. Executive pay levels may be determined by firm size [17]. Firm Size is a lagged measure of the value of the total assets of the firm. Firm Size is lagged by one year to increase the predictive strength of Firm Size in determining executive pay and reduce simultaneity bias. Extant research has found a relationship between prior firm performance and executive compensation. Prior firm performance is usually operationalized as return on firm assets (ROA) of the previous year. We decided against using ROA as a proxy for prior firm performance because of collinearity concerns between ROA and Firm Size. We measured prior firm performance as the firm's profit margin i.e. the ratio of net income to sales recorded by a firm in the previous year. Firm Age is a measure of the firm's current age in years. Firm Service Type is a categorical variable measuring the type of technological service provided by the firm (1 = "*Electron Data Processing* (EDP)", 2 = "*Computer Software: Pre-packaged Software* (PS)" and 0 = "*Computer Software: Programming, Data Processing* (PDP)").

3.2 Data Analytical Technique.

The sample firms have multiple observations and thus there exist the possibility of non-independence of observation. Failure to account for non-independence of observations could yield biased estimates. Accordingly, we adopted a linear mixed effects modelling technique to analyze the data. Linear mixed effect modelling accounts for within and between group variation of observational data. And it enables the researcher to the error covariance structure of the specified model. Equation 1 denotes the relationships between Executive IT pay of executive i of firm j and the predictors. We estimated equation 1 by allowing the intercept β_0 to vary across firms.

Equation (1):

$$
\begin{aligned}
\text{Real Executive IT Pay}_{ij} &= \beta_0 + \beta_1 \text{IPOTimeline}_{ij} \\
&+ \beta_2 \text{ExecutiveType}_{ij} \\
&+ \beta_{3-5} \text{EducationLevel}_{ij} \\
&+ \beta_6 \text{FoundingExecutive}_{ij} \\
&+ \beta_{7-9} \text{ExecutivePosition}_{ij} + \beta_{10} \text{Gender}_{ij} \\
&+ \beta_{11} \ln \text{Age}_{ij} + \beta_{12} \ln \text{Age}^2{}_{ij} \\
&+ \beta_{13} \text{PriorFirmPerformance}_{ij} \\
&+ \beta_{14} \text{FirmSize} + \beta_{15} \text{FirmAge}_{ij} \\
&+ \beta_{16-17} \text{FirmServiceType}_{ij} \\
&+ \beta_{18} \text{IPOTimeline}_{ij} \times \text{ExecutiveType}_{ij}
\end{aligned}
$$

4 RESULTS

Table 1 presents the means, standard deviations and correlations. The results of the linear mixed effects model are presented in Table 2. Model I presents the coefficients of all the control variables. Model II presents the coefficients of the full model. To test hypotheses 1 and 2 we graphed the interaction between IPO Timeline (Pre-IPO Stage Vs Post-IPO Stage) and Executive Type (Internal Hire Vs External Hire).

Table 1: Descriptive Statistics and Correlations

		Means	SD	1	2	3	4	5	6
1	Real Executive Pay	373805.100	138622.100						
2	IPO Timeline	1.884	1.695	0.316					
3	Executive Type: External	0.254	0.436	0.103	0.093				
4	Education Level: Bachelors	0.402	0.491	0.027	0.044	-0.073			
5	Education Level: Masters	0.229	0.421	-0.087	0.006	0.059	-0.446		
6	Education Level: MBA	0.202	0.402	0.093	-0.027	-0.011	-0.412	-0.274	
7	Founding Executive	0.443	0.497	-0.216	-0.094	-0.475	-0.013	-0.156	0.045
8	Execution Position: CEO	0.759	0.429	0.323	0.057	-0.174	-0.090	-0.076	0.112
9	Executive Position: CTEE	0.175	0.380	-0.294	-0.034	0.045	0.139	0.027	-0.102
10	Executive Position: CPE	0.034	0.183	-0.093	-0.043	0.138	-0.045	-0.039	0.039
11	Gender: Male	0.980	0.139	-0.050	-0.041	-0.202	0.116	0.035	-0.238
12	Age	48.416	9.432	0.331	0.053	0.019	-0.088	0.037	0.023
13	Prior Firm Performance	-0.692	5.644	0.125	0.080	0.032	0.072	0.043	0.052
14	Firm Size	582.722	2455.087	0.251	0.086	0.042	-0.040	0.144	-0.041
15	Firm Age	13.074	8.126	0.251	0.211	-0.152	0.176	0.061	-0.070
16	Firm Service Type: EDP	0.431	0.496	-0.084	-0.049	0.155	-0.023	-0.037	0.070
17	Firm Service Type: PPS	0.414	0.493	0.016	0.060	-0.214	0.016	0.113	-0.074

Table 1 (continued)

		7	8	9	10	11	12	13	14	15	16
1	Real Executive IT Pay										
2	IPO Timeline										
3	Executive Type: External Hires										
4	Education Level : Bachelors										
5	Education Level : Masters										
6	Education Level : MBA										
7	Founding Executive										
8	Executive Position: CEO	-0.006									
9	Executive Position: CTEE	0.111	-0.816								
10	Executive Position: CPE	-0.060	-0.335	-0.087							
11	Gender: Male	0.091	-0.080	0.065	0.027						
12	Age	-0.177	0.275	-0.250	-0.056	-0.039					
13	Prior Firm Performance	-0.100	0.054	-0.078	0.023	-0.009	0.007				
14	Firm Size	-0.119	-0.138	0.121	0.012	0.020	-0.056	0.030			
15	Firm Age	-0.227	0.126	-0.114	-0.027	0.106	0.272	0.109	-0.009		
16	Firm Service Type: EDP	-0.106	0.084	-0.034	-0.164	-0.127	-0.024	0.089	-0.117	-0.023	
17	Firm Service Type: PPS	0.196	-0.064	0.087	0.115	0.083	0.172	-0.105	-0.062	0.026	-0.731

Hypothesis 1 predicted that executive pay of internal hires is higher than external hires in the pre-IPO stage. Fig. 3. indicates that the pay of internal hires is greater than external hires in the pre-IPO stage and difference in pay is significantly different than zero ($\Delta\beta_{Year(-3)}$ = USD 97207.9, t = 2.533; $\Delta\beta_{Year(-2)}$ = USD 75098.9, t = 2.178; $\Delta\beta_{Year(-1)}$ = USD 52412.6, t = 1.988). Hypothesis 1 is therefore supported.

Hypothesis 2 predicted that executive pay of external hires is higher than internal hires in the post-IPO stage. Fig. 3. indicates that the pay of external hires is greater than internal hires in the post-IPO stage. However, the difference in pay is significantly different than zero from the third to fifth year post IPO. ($\Delta\beta_{Year(+3)}$ = USD 38332.5, t = 1.966; $\Delta\beta_{Year(+4)}$ = USD 61018.8, t = 2.266; $\Delta\beta_{Year(+5)}$ = USD 83705.1, t = 2.833). Hypothesis 2 is therefore partially supported.

Table 2: Results of Linear Mixed Model

		Model I		Model II	
		beta	se	beta	se
Intercept	β_0	-1.835	1.778	-1.548	1.721
IPO Timeline	β_1			0.007*	0.003
Executive Type : External Hire	β_2			-0.030	0.020
Education Level : Bachelors	β_3	-0.081***	0.022	-0.081***	0.021
Education Level : MBA	β_4	-0.077**	0.022	-0.088***	0.022
Education Level : Masters	β_5	-0.096***	0.021	-0.105***	0.021
Founding Executive	β_6	-0.036**	0.014	-0.023	0.017
Execution Position : Chief Executive Officer	β_7	0.166***	0.029	0.142***	0.028
Executive Position : Chief Technology & Engineering Executive	β_8	0.087**	0.031	0.079**	0.030
Gender: Male	β_{10}	-0.035	0.036	-0.010	0.035
ln Age	β_{11}	1.112	0.916	0.945	0.886
ln Age^2	β_{12}	-0.149	0.119	-0.122	0.115
Prior Firm Performance	β_{13}	0.000	0.001	0.000	0.001
Firm Size	β_{14}	0.000***	0.000	0.000***	0.000
Firm Age	β_{15}	0.010***	0.002	0.005**	0.002
Firm Service Type: Electronic Data Processing	β_{16}	-0.059	0.045	-0.042	0.041
Firm Service Type: Computer Software - Pre-Packaged Software	β_{17}	-0.029	0.032	-0.024	0.029
IPO Timeline x External Executive	β_{18}			0.023***	0.005
Log Likelihood		443.639		453.312	
df		18		21	
Pseudo R-Square		0.269		0.284	

*** $p < 0.001$; ** $p < 0.01$ *$p < 0.05$

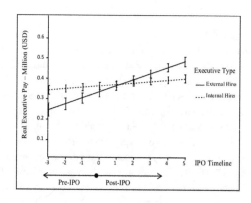

Fig. 3. Executive Pay of Internal vs External Hires

6   DISCUSSION

This research examined executive pay of internal and external hires contingent on the lifecycle stage of IT firms. Drawing largely on the human capital and firm professionalization literatures [3,10], we argued that startups or firms in the pre-IPO stage value firm-specific skills. Firm-specific skills enable line function productivity and performance, which is the central operational metric of startups or firms in the pre-IPO stage unlike post-IPO firms.

However, firms in the post-IPO stage, firms value relevant professional managerial skills required to overcome post-IPO challenges. In most instances, internal candidates of young IT firms are not endowed with such skills [3]. IT firms would therefore pay higher wages to lure external candidates to fill executive positions in the post-IPO stage.

Our findings are as follows. First, consistent with our theoretical prediction we found that the pay of internal hires is higher than external hires in the pre-IPO stage. The difference in pay is substantial in all three years prior to IPO. This finding is indicative of IT startups penchant for internally developed human capital [18]. Beside their valuable firm-specific skills, internal hires are more loyal and committed to the goals of the startup [15,19].

In addition, startups need managerial stability to achieve high levels of success. Compared with external hires, internal hires have a relatively higher fit with the startup's culture and values and are less likely to turnover [20]; thus providing the much needed stability that facilitates startups success. Startups therefore place more value on internal hires and reward them for the firm-specific human capital endowment.

Second, our finding that external hires of post-IPO firms are paid higher than internal hires, is consistent with the literature on firm professionalization (Auletta, 1998). Technology IPO marks the beginning of significant structural and managerial overhaul for IT firms. Young IT firms have the additional responsibility of accounting to external shareholders and ensuring that all post-IPO regulatory compliances are met. Meeting these responsibilities require that young IT firm executives have the requisite post-IPO skills, knowledge and managerial abilities. Considering that managing a firm post IPO is a novel concept to pre-IPO firms, often external candidates are brought in to steer the firm – a process referred to as professionalization. Post-IPO firms will therefore pay external hires higher than internal hires because of the relevant professional knowledge and skills.

7   CONCLUSION

This study examines the influence of internal and external hires on executive pay at different stages of firm lifecycle. We found that in the startup or pre-IPO stage, internal hires receive higher salaries than external hires. The post-IPO stage sees IT firms paying external hires higher salaries than internal hires. The difference in executive pay between internal and external hires highlights the differential value firms place on firm-specific and professional managerial skills at the pre-IPO and post-IPO stages respectively.

8   CONTRIBUTION TO THEORY

Our study contributes to the literature in the following ways. First, our study seeks to resolve the conflict between the arguments of the fundamental human capital literature and the findings of the top management and pay literature. On the one hand, the top management and pay literature suggests that firms value general managerial skills over firm-specific human capital. Proponents of this thesis draw on the firm professionalization literature and argue that firms rely on the professional managerial skills of external hires as firms evolve from an entrepreneurial focus to an established business.

The reason for professionalization lies in the notion that as firms transition through the different lifecycle stages, the capabilities and abilities of founding executives or internal hires, who have the natural proclivity of developing the product or service, may not be aligned with the evolving firm challenges and managerial responsibilities [3]. Accordingly, firms tend to hire executives from the external labor market to manage the affairs of the firm by enticing them with higher salaries or pay premium.

On the other hand, the human capital literature [10] emphasizes the value of firm-specific human capital over general human capital. Firm-specific human capital encompasses the accumulated experience and skills required to effectively perform assigned roles and tasks. This makes firm-specific human capital an enabler of firm productivity and performance. Firms value productivity and according to human capital literature firms would pay employees with high firm-specific human capital endowment higher wages or salaries.

Our study therefore bridges the conflicting views proffered by the two streams of literature by introducing the contextual influence of firm lifecycle stages. Prior literature hints that firms may require different human capital endowments or managerial skills to be able to cope with the evolving challenges accompanying firm life cycle transitions [5]. We argue that in the startup or pre-IPO stage firms value firm-specific human capital over general human capital and vice versa in the post-IPO stage.

Second, analyzing the pay of internal and external hires on the continuum of relative pre-and post-IPO years has the potential of informing temporal human capital and executive compensation theories. How and why firms compensate executives at specific periods is theoretically important but remain largely understudied. We contend that our findings provide a starting point to consider the conceptual and empirical implications of introducing a temporal component in human capital theorizing.

9   CONTRIBUTION TO PRACTICE

For practice, our study sets the benchmark for executive compensation of internal and external hires at the pre-and post-IPO stages of a firm's lifecycle. Candidates being considered for executive positions can rely on our results when assessing the relative compensation options available to them. This in turn could play an important role in deciding which career mobility paths to traverse if objective career success (measured by compensation) is the anticipated career goal.

Firms could rely on our results in setting competitive compensation guidelines for executives. Information about market competitive salaries of IT executives enables firms to craft internal human resource policies that serve to attract or retain IT talents.

10   LIMITATIONS AND FUTURE RESEARCH

The use of the S-1 form in constructing the executive IT salary dataset constrained us in constructing a sample that captures compensation data over extended periods prior to IPO. The S-1 form contains executive compensation data that spans at most three years before IPO. Information on executive compensation prior to the years declared on the S-1 form is usually proprietary and undisclosed to the public. We call on future research to explore other available options in collecting pre-IPO data that would contribute to constructing relatively larger datasets and thereby reducing any potential biases caused by sampling error.

In addition, we acknowledge that the pre-and post-IPO conceptualization of firm lifecycle is simplistic and may not adequately capture other firm lifecycle stages identified by the entrepreneurship literature. There is no general consensus on the number of firm lifecycle stages. The entrepreneurship literature identifies other distinct lifecycle models typically ranging from two to ten stages [21]. However, we settled on pre-and post-IPO conceptualization for reasons related to data limitation and theoretical significance. As earlier articulated, we are limited in constructing datasets spanning longer periods because of the proprietary restrictions of obtaining data of startup or pre-IPO firms. We could not effectively consider the intermediary lifecycle stages that firms transition through in the pre-IPO stages.

REFERENCES

[1] Bach, S. B., and Smith, A. D., 2007, "Are Powerful CEOs Beneficial to Post-IPO Survival in High Technology Industries?: An Empirical Investigation," J. High Technol. Manag. Res., 18(1), pp. 31–42.

[2] Carpenter, M. A., Pollock, T. G., and Leary, M. M., 2003, "Testing a Model of Reasoned Risk-Taking: Governance, the Experience of Principals and Agents, and Global Strategy in High-Technology IPO Firms," Strateg. Manag. J., 24(9), pp. 803–820.

[3] Boeker, W., and Karichalil, R., 2002, "Entrepreneurial Transitions: Factors Influencing Founder Departure," Acad. Manage. J., 45(4), pp. 818–826.

[4] Hellmann, T., and Puri, M., 2002, "Venture Capital and the Professionalization of Start-up Firms: Empirical Evidence," J. Finance, 57(1), pp. 169–197.

[5] Jain, B. A., and Tabak, F., 2008, "Factors Influencing the Choice between Founder versus Non-Founder CEOs for IPO Firms," J. Bus. Ventur., 23(1), pp. 21–45.

[6] Auletta, K., 1998, "The Last Sure Thing: PointCast Was Supposed to Become an Internet Legend, but Turned into a Silicon Valley Parable," NEW YORKER-NEW YORKER Mag. Inc.-, pp. 40–47.

[7] Harris, D., and Helfat, C., 1997, "Specificity of CEO Human Capital and Compensation," Strateg. Manag. J., 18(11), pp. 895–920.

[8] Bidwell, M., 2011, "Paying More to Get Less: The Effects of External Hiring versus Internal Mobility," Adm. Sci. Q., p. 1839211433562.

[9] Murphy, K. J., and Zabojnik, J., 2004, "CEO Pay and Appointments: A Market-Based Explanation for Recent Trends," Am. Econ. Rev., 94(2), pp. 192–196.

[10] Becker, G. S., 1975, "Front Matter, Human Capital: A Theoretical and Empirical Analysis, with Special Reference to Education," Human Capital: A Theoretical and Empirical Analysis, with Special Reference to Education, Second Edition, NBER, p. 22-0.

[11] Hashimoto, M., 1981, "Firm-Specific Human Capital as a Shared Investment," Am. Econ. Rev., 71(3), pp. 475–482.

[12] Rutherford, M. W., Buller, P. F., and McMullen, P. R., 2003, "Human Resource Management Problems over the Life Cycle of Small to Medium-Sized Firms," Hum. Resour. Manage., 42(4), pp. 321–335.

[13] Ries, E., 2011, The Lean Startup: How Today's Entrepreneurs Use Continuous Innovation to Create Radically Successful Businesses, Crown Books.

[14] Willard, G. E., Krueger, D. A., and Feeser, H. R., 1992, "In Order to Grow, Must the Founder Go: A Comparison of Performance between Founder and Non-Founder Managed High-Growth Manufacturing Firms," J. Bus. Ventur., 7(3), pp. 181–194.

[15] Howard, A., 2001, "Identifying, Assessing, and Selecting Senior Leaders," Nat. Organ. Leadersh. Underst. Perform. Imperatives Confronting Todays Lead., pp. 305–346.

[16] Falato, A., Li, D., and Milbourn, T., 2015, "Which Skills Matter in the Market for CEOs? Evidence from Pay for CEO Credentials," Manag. Sci., 61(12), pp. 2845–2869.

[17] Kostiuk, P. F., 1990, "Firm Size and Executive Compensation," J. Hum. Resour., pp. 90–105.

[18] Allison, P. D., and Long, J. S., 1990, "Departmental Effects on Scientific Productivity," Am. Sociol. Rev., pp. 469–478.

[19] Zhang, Y., and Rajagopalan, N., 2003, "Explaining New CEO Origin: Firm versus Industry Antecedents," Acad. Manage. J., 46(3), pp. 327–338.

[20] Chatman, J. A., 1989, "Matching People and Organizations: Selection and Socialization in Public Accounting Firms.," Academy of Management Proceedings, Academy of Management, pp. 199–203.

[21] Hanks, S. H., Watson, C. J., Jansen, E., and Chandler, G. N., 1993, "Tightening the Life-Cycle Construct: A Taxonomic Study of Growth Stage Configurations in High-Technology Organizations," Entrep. Theory Pract., 18(2), pp. 5–30.

Influence of R&D and IPR Regulations on the Performance of IT Firms in India: An Empirical Analysis using Tobin's Q Approach

Full Paper

Senthilkumar Thangavelu
Ph.D. Scholar, Amrita School of Business
Amrita Vishwa Vidyapeetham (University)
Bangalore, India
senmalkisasb@gmail.com

Amalendu Jyotishi
Professor, Amrita School of Business
Amrita Vishwa Vidyapeetham (University)
Bangalore, India
amalendu.jyotishi@gmail.com

ABSTRACT

Influence of Research and Development (R&D), as well as regulation on the performance of the industry, is known. However, in a stronger property regime R&D activities become more focused, and innovation-oriented that result in better performance in the organization. Information Technology (IT) industry being the front runner of the knowledge economy is driven by innovation, which in turn reflects on its performance. This quest led us to not only understand the separate influence of R&D and intellectual property rights regulations but also the interaction of both on the performance of IT firms. This paper, in the context of India, investigates the effects of R&D intensity, implementation of WTO-TRIPS agreement and their interaction, on the performance of Information Technology (IT) firms in India. We included some firm-specific controls to reduce their effects on the performance. The performance is measured using Tobin's Q. Firm-level data from Centre for Monitoring Indian Economy Pvt. Ltd (CMIE) Prowess database for the period 2000-2016 are used. An empirical study is conducted using unbalanced time series data and Random-effects GLS regression method with and without controls and interaction. Our results suggest that the IT firm's performance increases with increase in the R&D intensity when interacted with World Trade Organization - Trade-Related Aspects of Intellectual Property Rights (WTO-TRIPS).

Keywords

Intellectual Property Rights; firm performance; Innovation appropriability; Tobin's Q; IndustryQ; Information Technology; WTO-TRIPS; Research and Development

SIGMIS-CPR '17, June 21-23, 2017, Bangalore, India
© 2017 Association for Computing Machinery.
ACM ISBN 978-1-4503-5037-2/17/06...$15.00
http://dx.doi.org/10.1145/3084381.3084400

1. INTRODUCTION

The IT firms in India have made an investment in R&D to foster innovation in order to remain competitive in the business. They also deploy various strategies alongside R&D investment to enhance their innovative capabilities. Acquiring innovative firms aligned to their business, functioning like an angel investor or venture capitalist in promoting innovation by individuals or small firms, providing autonomy and ecosystem to the employees to innovate, are some of these strategies.

In this context, the paper attempts to understand the influence of R&D, IPR regulation and their interaction on the performance of the firm. R&D is an innovation enabler, whereas IPR regulation helps to commercialize the innovation. These two being the indicators of the innovation we attempt to understand their influence on the firm performance and its variance.

2. PREMISE OF THE RESEARCH: REVIEW AND FORMULATION OF HYPOTHESES

The innovativeness of a firm can be explained using Resource Based View (RBV) [7]. The knowledge base assets are the key sources of innovative ideas and the sources of innovation. Enabling these resources will lead to increased innovation in the IT firms. Ahuja and Katila [3] studied the innovation activities in the U. S. Chemical firms and found that the technically skilled resources and the availability of research supporting environment, can boost the innovation of a firm.

The appropriability of the innovation is explained by the Property Rights Theory (PRT) [18]. The role of governance in the planning and implementing governance mechanisms enhances the innovation activities in the IT firms. Laplume et al., [31] studied the role of IPR in determining the protection of entrepreneurs. The Property rights (PR) constrain the human behaviors and provide the right to use resources [29]. Kim and Mahoney [29] used the PRT to explain the oil field utilization in their study and also compare PRT with transaction cost theory and agency theory. PRT explains various rights of different actors in the innovation activities including the co-innovation and the joint ventures. The Grossman-Hart-Moore (GHM) model defined by [26] and [27] explains the contractual specific rights, residual rights, and ownerships. A firm owns many assets either tangible or non-tangible and the ownership can be transferred or traded to other firms. The innovations can be transferred to other parties in order to diffuse the innovations. The implementation of IPR through governance helps to bring many benefits to the innovators. These two theories help to explain the influence of combined effect of WTO-TRIPS and innovation.

2.1. Tobin's Q as a measure of firm performance

The Tobin's Q ratio, developed by James Tobin can be approached using different methods. One method is the ratio of the total market value of the firm to the total asset value. If Tobin's Q value of a firm is less than 1, then it means the cost to replace its assets is higher than the total value of its stocks. This implies its stock value is undervalued. If it is higher than 1, then its stock is more expensive to the replacement cost of its assets. This means the firm is overvalued. Larry and Stulz [32] used Tobin's Q to study the impact of the diversification of the firm on the performance. They concluded that more diversified firms have lower Q value compared to pure-play firms. Wernerfelt and Montgomery [43] used Tobin's Q to measure the firm's performance on the effect of diversification on firm's performance. Arora, et al., [4] used Tobin's Q to analyze the impact of R & D investment on the firm's performance using the US and Japanese listed IT firms. Bharadwaj et al., [9] studied the effects of IT assets on the firm's performance using Tobin's Q. In many earlier studies, Tobin's Q is used as a measure of firm's intangible value. In this paper, we advocate the use of Tobin's Q as an outcome measure as it reflects the contribution of IT to the firm and also its advantages over accounting measures. The Tobin's Q is theoretically a good and reliable measure compared to accounting measures like profit after tax, and revenue. One of the advantages of Tobin's Q is that it assimilates the capitalized value of benefits from the diversification of the firm. Tobin's Q corrects biases like the use of the risk-adjusted discount rates and it minimizes distortion due to tax and accounting conversions.

2.2. R&D: Performance on a Premise of Innovation

There are many factors which influence the innovation in a firm including, the number of highly skilled resources, access to high technology and tools, interaction and relationship with research institutes and organizations, research culture of the organization, and support from the management. A firm which allocates more funding to its research initiatives would create a better environment and favorable conditions for the innovations. Higher funding will lead to more innovations and development of advanced products. This leads to better sales and improvement in its market share. As per Dierickx and Cool [19], critical assets are accumulated rather than acquired. Greater commitments to R&D spending by a firm would lead to the greater internal development of resources and critical assets to enhance its innovative capabilities. Several studies looked at the relationship between R&D spending, productivity, and firm performance and they concluded conflicting results. A study conducted by Mcevily and

Chakravarthy [37] on biotechnology firms concludes that R&D spending on developing innovative capabilities shows a significant positive rate of return. Lin et al., [35] investigated how the technology based firm's performance is impacted by the R&D intensity. They defined R&D intensity as R&D expenditure divided by total assets, which is a proxy measure for R&D activities. R&D intensity signifies the strategic importance of innovation capabilities for a sustained competitive advantage of a firm. As per O'Brien [39], although the high level of investment of a firm in the R&D intensity does not guarantee innovation, the firm tries to compete and build capabilities to create a stronger workforce and resources for the innovation breakthrough. The IT firms create value to their customers through continuous innovation and improving R&D intensity. This leads to positive improvement in the firm's performance; hence we propose the hypothesis.

Hypothesis1 (h1): The R&D intensity of the Information Technology firms positively influences their performance

2.3. Property Rights Protection: Performance through Commercialization of Innovation

Property rights define the nature of human behaviors, which are sanctioned and provide the right to use resources. Kim and Mahoney[29] used the PRT to explain the oil field utilization in their study and compared the property rights theory, the transaction cost theory (TCE), and the agency theory. The GHM model defined by Grossman & Hart [26] and Hart & Moore [27] explains the contractual, specific, residual rights, and the ownership. The innovations or the technical know-how can be transferred to other parties in order to diffuse the innovations. The implementation of IPR through governance helps to bring many benefits to the innovators. Azevedo et al., [6] studied the impact of IPR on innovation and argue that the tightening of IPR will reduce the economic growth rate and suggested considering not only the IPR laws but also how they are enforced.

Many innovators fail to get the rent of their innovation [13]. Falvey and Foster [41] studied the impact of stronger implementation of IPR and its impact on the innovation and economic growth. They concluded that for the developing countries, implementation of TRIPS agreement should be based on their level of development and should be flexible in order to get the maximum benefit. Woo et al., [45] studied the impact of stronger IPR on the innovation and concluded that the tightening IPR in complex industries like electronics reflects a negative effect on excessive IPR. Williams [44] in her study on human genome provides evidence on the excessive IPR could hinder sequential innovations by imposing additional transaction costs. Sweet and Maggio [42] study confirms that stronger IPR protection has a positive impact on the country's ability to increase its innovation activities, but this is negative for the developing countries. Arora et al., [5] studied the effect on patenting on R &D using the U.S. manufacturing data and estimated that the innovation value is increased by patenting in selected industries. A survey conducted by Nordic Innovation Centre shows that larger service companies fail to recognize IPR as part of their strategic management [10].

There are shocks to firm-level performance, which are common to all the firms across the IT industry due to effects of any policy changes. As we use the panel data of the IT firms, the estimates reflect both within-firm and within-industry changes. Due to the uncertain nature of the formal process of IPR changes in India, we designate the formal full compliant year of 2005 as the IPR policy shock year. We construct a year control variable ReformYear indicating all the years after 2004 for the impact of the TRIPS as defined by Dutta and Sharma [21] in their studies. Branstetter et al.,[12] defined a year dummy variable for reform year which takes value 1 for the year of reform and 0 for other years. In our study, we extend this approach to define the independent variable ReformYear. India signed the TRIPS agreement in 1994 to tighten the IPR implementation by following the standards defined in the TRIPS and by amending its domestic laws within ten years. By January 1, 2005, India became fully TRIPS compliant by enforcing product patents in all fields of technology. Enforcing the TRIPS agreement encourages the firms to find suitable opportunities and invest in the R&D.

Many foreign companies started R&D activities in India either through a collaboration or own India R&D centers. A study on the US multinational firms by Branstetter et al., [12] reveals that more technology transfer payments are made during the IPR reforms period. One of the potential benefits of tightening the IPR is foreign firms transfer technologies to reforming countries and they produce and sell goods locally.

In the service sector, innovations play a major role in the economic development, by creating new opportunities and increasing the employment opportunities. The TRIPS agreement under the WTO developed minimum standards for many forms of intellectual property (IP) including computer programs as literary work under copyright. The TRIPS enforces a strict implementation of the IPR among WTO members. In the Global Innovation Index (GII) Report [23] India is ranked 81 among 141 global economies in 2015 and 76th in 2014 [22]. In India, a persistent contradiction exists between commercializing and catering to the social needs. This results in weaker IPRs, as the policies and patent laws are crafted to balance commercialization and social needs.

The protection of IPR and the rents from the innovations encourage the innovators to create new or enhance products. This protection encourages the commercialization, technology transfer and also promotes the international trade. Bouet [11] studied the impact of the TRIPS on innovation using pharmaceutical export data and concluded that there is an increase in the trade after the TRIPS agreement. In recent times IP protection has created more attention among countries with different levels of economic development. It is a point of discussion that the stronger IPR increases economic growth against, IPR has a weak and negative relationship with the innovation and economic growth.

The current IPR regime in India, after the WTO-TRIPS agreement is strengthened and it is moving towards a stronger environment. The countries with stronger IPR regimes showed more development compared to countries with an absence of robust IPR protections. Basant and Srinivasan [8] studied the implications of IPR in health innovation and how the health care companies were impacted by IPRs and the government

policies. Dutta and Sharma [21] studied the impact of IPR reforms and the innovation output in Indian industries and concluded that there is an increase in the patenting after the TRIPS agreement. This paper analyzes the impact of IPR on IT innovation activities by studying the performance of Indian IT firms using a panel data from CMIE database. We propose the following hypothesis.

Hypothesis2 (h2): India's WTO-TRIPS agreement compliance positively influences the performance of the Indian Information Technology firms

2.4. R&D with Regulation: A proper platform for Performance

The R&D expenditure of IT firms and stronger implementation of WTO-TRIPS agreement create a positive environment among the IT firms. IT firms are thus encouraged to spend more on innovation activities to develop innovative products and services. The new or enhanced innovations are protected by the IPR and to realize the expected rents. The government's support to reduce or to remove completely any effort by imitators to copy the innovative products and encourages IT firms to allocate more funds to the R&D activities and other related activities. This also encourages IT firms to form a partnership with foreign IT firms and to perform new technology transfers. From the study of Lee [12], it is evident that stronger implementation of IPR would lead to improved technology transfers. Nandkumar and Srikanth [38] provided evidence that after India signed the WTO-TRIPS agreement, the more foreign firms started their offshore R&D development centers in India. In light of the R&D intensity and WTO-TRIPS, we propose the following hypothesis.

Hypothesis3 (h3): Interaction of the R&DIntensity and India's agreement of WTO-TRIPS positively influences the performance of the Indian Information Technology firms

2.5. Firm Specific Effects

2.5.1. Size

The relationship between the innovation capabilities and firm size has long been discussed and debated by many research studies such as Freeman and Soete [25], Acs and Audretsch [2]. Some studies show the R&D productivity declines with the size of the firm. The study conducted by Cohen & Klepper [16] concludes that the R&D rises with the firm size, hence the R&D and the firm size are positively related. The number of innovations generated per dollar of R&D declines with the firm size. It has been argued that large firms are better positioned to create and sustain competitive advantages Perez-Cano [40]. The firm size is used as either an independent variable or as a control variable by these studies. Some studies construct firm size variable using the number of employees which, is used as control or independent variable Acs et al., [1], Crepon et al., [17], Nandkumar and Srikanth [38], and some studies O'Brien [39] use the total assets to construct the firm size variable. This variable reduces the possible variances due to firm size since our sample draws on IT firms of different sizes. In our study, we use the firm size as a control variable and construct it by using the number of employees.

2.5.2. Age

Does the age of the firm really influence the innovation capacity of the firm? It is perceived that most of the innovation will be done by the older and experienced firms. But the current trend is different as new firms are innovating to a larger extent, backed by large investors. Lin et al., [36] studied the moderating effects of the firm's age on alliance partnership and its performance. Kalaignanam et al., [28] used the age of the firm as a control variable to study the alliance and the new product development. In our study, we control the effect of the firm's age on its performance. The age of a firm is measured as the number of years since its inception to till 2016.

2.5.3. Listed (Ownership type)

The ownership of IT firms can be mainly classified as public and private. If a firm is listed on a stock exchange, it means that it is a public firm. Joseph et al., [24] included listed companies in their study on R&D spillover and how the publically available information on R&D is reducing the manager's pressure. Dan et al., [34] defined the status of a firm based on whether it is listed on a stock exchange or not. In this research, we study the influence of ownership on the innovation activities of the IT firm. It is an important variable as the public firms are subject to shareholders' scrutiny.

2.5.4. Conglomerate group

If a firm is part of a business group, which is diversified across many industries, it has advantages including the shared resources, the best practices, and the corporate support. Such a firm has a wider network of resources and has an advantage over a stand-alone firm. Rishikesha and Srivardhini [30] studied the innovation strategies of market leaders and Conglomerate groups in emerging markets. In this study, we use this variable to control the influence of conglomerate on the IT firm's performance.

2.5.5. IndustryQ

Since we have the relevant information required for this paper for a limited number of IT firms, we have created an industry level variable IndustryQ, which will control the industry level impact. We have considered years 2000 to 2016 in our analysis. As we are studying only the firms in the IT industry, the industry level heterogeneity is not considered. Dushnitsky and Lenox [20] studied how the industry level heterogeneity helps to identify suitable industry and to invest to get maximum returns. The impact of WTO-TRIPS varies based on the primary function of the firms. As per Chadha's study [14], the patenting activities of firms increased after India signed the WTO-TRIPS in pharmaceutical industry. The majority of the firms in the IT industry provide software services and protecting services under patents is not yet well established as like the product patenting.

3. THE CONCEPTUAL MODEL

The conceptual model in Figure 1 shows the dependent variable (DV), independent variables (IV), and control variables (CV) and their interaction. A change in the R&D intensity (IV) would impact the innovation activities within a firm, which in turn impact its performance. The variables ReformYear and the interaction term R&DIntensityXReformYear are two more independent variables which would also impact the firm's performance. The other variables mentioned in the conceptual model are used as control variables.

Figure 1: The Conceptual Model

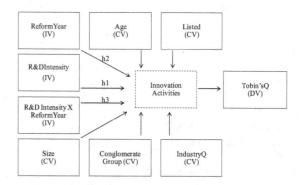

4. METHODOLOGY

4.1. Data Source

This study uses the Centre for Monitoring Indian Economy Pvt. Ltd (CMIE) Prowess database. This study includes IT firms with the national industrial classification (NIC) codes 620 (computer programming, consultancy, and related activities), 639 (other information service activities), and 829 (business support services). It is an unbalanced time series (2000-2016) panel data. The current study has the limitation on the availability of relevant data in the CMIE database. Based on the G2SLS random effects Instrument Variables (IV) regression testing there is no evidence of endogeneity effect among the variables.

4.2. Variables and Measures

4.2.1. Tobin's Q: A measure of performance

As a reference to earlier studies (Wernerfelt & Montgomery [43]; Larry & Stulz [32]; Arora et al., [4]), we use Tobin's Q as a measure of performance. We use the approach followed by Chatterjee [15] to calculate Tobin's Q.

Tobin's Q for the firm is constructed using the following steps:

Tobin's Q= Market Value / Replacement Cost of the Assets

Market Value = Market value of equity + Market value of debt

Market value of equity = Market value of common and preference shares

Market value of common stocks = Outstanding stocks multiplied by closing price at BSE on Year end (Last day of March)

Market value of preference stock = Paid up preference capital

Market value of the debt = Borrowings + Current liabilities & provisions

Replacement Cost = Total assets - Miscellaneous expenditure - Intangible assets.

4.2.2. R&D intensity: A measure of Innovation

This study uses the construct RD intensity which is calculated using R&D expenditure and sales of the firm for the year. To standardize the measure, the R&D expenditure is divided by yearly sales of the firm to get RD intensity, which will be a better measure of innovation input.

4.2.3. Reform Year: A dummy variable for property rights

India signed the TRIPS agreement in 1994 and became fully TRIPS compliant on January 2005 by enforcing product patents regulations. The ReformYear variable is created as an independent dummy variable. It takes 1 for 2005 onwards and 0 for previous years.

4.2.4. R&D Intensity X Reform Year: Innovation in action

To study the combined effect of R&D Intensity and WTO-TRIPS reforms, the R&DIntensityXReformYear variable is constructed by multiplying RDIntensity and ReformYear.

4.2.5. Control variables

As discussed earlier, the following variables are considered as control variables.

Size: Our study considers size to control the size effects. The number of employees is used as a measure of the size of the firm. When more employees are dedicated to R&D activities, this will lead to more innovation activities and new products and services to the market.

Age: To control the effect due to age. The age is calculated as the number of years starting from the year of incorporation up to the year 2016. The experience gained by an IT firm would lead to improved planning and effective utilization of its financial and human resources.

Conglomerate group (Conglo): If a firm is part or member of a business group (1) which has diversified business across many industries, it has many advantages. It has a wider network of resources over stand-alone firm (0).

Listed: whether the firm is listed on Indian stock exchanges (Bombay Stock Exchange or National Stock Exchange). If listed then this variable gets 1 else 0. This helps to control any impact due to public ownership.

IndustryQ: IndustryQ variable controls the industry level variation in a year. We have followed the method used by Chatterjee [15] to develop IndustryQ variable. This is computed as average Tobin's Q values of all the firms for a particular year to get that year's IndustryQ. IndustryQ is computed based on the information of 7218 observations over 17 years. Approximately 425 observations are included in computing IndustryQ for every year which is a fairly representative average of the IT industry.

4.3. Descriptive Statistics of the Variables

Table 1 provides the descriptive statistics of the study variables.

Table 1: Descriptive Statistics

Variable	Obs	Mean	Std. Dev.	Min	Max
Tobin's Q	178	3.95	5.88	0.13	61.85
RDIntensity	178	0.06	0.13	0.00	1.02
ReformYear	178	0.74	0.44	0	1
RDIntensity X ReformYear	178	0.05	0.13	0	1.02
Size (no. of employees)	178	22319	54534	35	355843
Age	178	26.47	5.36	5	40
Listed	178	0.98	0.13	0	1
Conglo	178	0.43	0.50	0	1
IndustryQ	7218	1.24	4.03	-94.25	72.80

4.4. Correlation Matrix of the Variables

Table 2 gives the correlation between the study variables.

Table 2: Correlation Matrix

	1	2	3	4	5	6	7	8	9
Tobin's Q	1.0								
RDIntensity	0.1	1.0							
Reform Year	-0.1	0.1	1.0						
RDIntensity X Reform Year	0.1	1.0	0.2	1.0					
Size	0.2	-0.1	0.2	-0.1	1.0				
Age	0.1	-0.1	-0.1	-0.1	-0.1	1.0			
Listed	0.1	0.0	0.0	0.0	0.1	0.2	1.0		
Conglo	0.1	-0.3	-0.1	-0.3	0.2	-0.1	0.1	1.0	
IndustryQ	0.5	0.0	0.1	0.0	0.1	-0.1	0.0	0.0	1

4.5. Method of Analysis

This study uses the OLS regression for the estimation. To decide fixed effect or random effect model of regression, the Hausman's specification test was performed. Since the probability is not less than 0.05, we used the random effect model for this study.

The generic form of the regression equation (1) is given below:

Regression Equation is $Y_i = f(X_{1i}, X_{2i}..., X_{ki}) + u_i$ (1)

Where Y_i is the dependent variable (DV), X_{1i} is the independent variable (IV) and X_{2i}, X_{3i} are control variables (CV) and u_i is the error term of Year $_i$ of firms 1, 2 etc.

5. RESULTS

The results of the models for the relationships of Tobin's Q, R&DIntensity, ReformYear, the interaction of R&DIntensity and ReformYear, size, age, conglomerate group, listed, and IndustryQ are tabulated in Table 3.

Table 3: Regression results

Tobin's Q	Without Control		With Control	
	Model 1w/o X	Model2 with X	Model3 w/o X	Model4 with X
Intercept Coeff (SErr)	4.79*** (0.87)	5.93*** (0.99)	-8.84*** (3.11)	-8.05** (3.12)
RDIntensity Coeff (SErr)	4.95 (3.34)	-33.53 (17.18)	7.77** (2.76)	-17.36 (13.81)
ReformYear Coeff (SErr)	-1.50 (1.01)	-2.74* (1.13)	-2.75** (0.83)	-3.57*** (0.93)
RDIntensityX ReformYear Coeff (SErr)		39.95* (17.50)		25.96* (13.98)
Size Coeff (SErr)			0.00002** (6.78e-06)	0.00002*** (6.74e-06)
Age (SErr)			0.20** (0.07)	0.19** (0.07)
Listed (SErr)			0.98 (2.77)	1.28 (2.75)
Conglo(SErr)			0.82 (0.76)	0.68 (0.76)
IndustryQ (SErr)			6.12*** (0.64)	6.00*** (0.64)

Note: *p <0.05, **p<0.01, ***p<0.001
w/o X – without interaction; with X – with interaction
Coeff: the coefficient of the estimate
(SErr): the standard error of the estimate

Applying the equation (1) we get the regression equations for the model1 (2), model2 (3), model3 (4), and model4 (5) respectively.

Tobin's Q = 4.79 + 4.95 RDIntensity - 1.50 ReformYear   (2)

Tobin's Q = 5.93 - 33.53 RDIntensity - 2.74 ReformYear + 39.95 RDIntensityXReformYear   (3)

Tobin's Q = -8.84 + 7.77 RDIntensity - 2.75 ReformYear + 0.00002 Size + 0.20 Age + 0.98 Listed + 0.82 Conglo + 6.12 IndustryQ   (4)

Tobin's Q = -8.05 - 17.36 RDIntensity - 3.57 ReformYear + 25.96 RDIntensityXReformYear + 0.00002 Size + 0.19 Age + 1.28 Listed + 0.68 Conglo + 6.00 IndustryQ   (5)

The Model1 equation (2) shows the results of STATA GLS regression test with random effect and Tobin'sQ as the dependent variable, R&D intensity and ReformYear as independent variables without control or interaction. There is no significant impact of both RDIntensity and ReformYear on Tobin's Q. The Model2 equation (3) includes the interaction term along with two independent variables used in Model1 without control variables. The ReformYear shows a negative significance and the interaction term RDIntensityXReformYear shows a positive and significant influence on Tobin's Q.

Model3 equation (4) shows the results of the regression testing with random effects in which all the independent variables and control variables without interaction between RDIntensity and ReformYear. The RDIntensity shows a positive and significant influence on Tobin's Q and ReformYear shows a negative and significant influence on Tobin's Q. The control variables Size, Age, and IndustryQ show significant influence on Tobin's Q.

The Model4 equation (5) shows the result of regression testing with all independent variables, control variables and interaction of RDIntensity and ReformYear. ReformYear shows a negative and significant impact on the performance. The interaction term shows a positive and significant influence on Tobin's Q. The control variables Size, Age, and IndustryQ also show a positive and significant influence on Tobin's Q.

In the Model4, the variable R&DIntensity has a negative but significant impact on the firm's performance (Tobin's Q). This study did not find sufficient evidence to support the h1. This result is not consistent with the findings of Bharadwaj et al., [9] spending on IT assets contribute to the firm's performance. The ReformYear variable has a significant but negative impact on the firm's performance. This result did not find significant evidence to support the h2, which says the WTO-TRIPS compliance will positively influence the performance of the IT firms. This empirical result is consistent with the study of Bouet [11] which concludes that TRIPS may be a necessary condition but not sufficient enough to positively influence the firm's performance.

In the Model4 equation (5) the interaction term RDIntensityXReformYear has an interesting result. The interaction effects RDIntensity and ReformYear on IT firms' performance are positive and significant which supports h3. This result highlights the importance of the role of the R&D expenditure and WTO-TRIPS implementation. The IT firms which increase the R&D expenditure along with the stricter implementation of WTO-TRIPS show a positive impact on their performance. IndustryQ shows a positive and statistically significant impact on the firm's performance. In Model4 the Age and the Size show positive and significant influence on the performance of the firm. The Listed and the Conglomerate group did not show any influence on the firm's performance.

6. DISCUSSION

Lee et al., [33] studied the internal capabilities and external network on firm performance. Our study explores various characteristics of the IT firms like R&D expenditure, age, size, and conglomerate group along with governance of IPR. Our study highlights the interaction of governance policy specifically WTO-TRIPS implementation and R &D intensity. Lin et al., [36] analyzed the interaction of firms and their alliance with other firms and institutions and its impact on firm's performance, but our research study is on the interaction of internal R&D spending with the external governance policies. Our finding suggests that the interaction of R&D with policy reforms has a stable, strong, and positive influence on firm's performance. However, policy reforms alone have a stable but negative impact on firm's performance. The firm size, age, and industry average performance have a significant influence on firm's performance. This study is unique in this perspective and contributes to the academic research and highlights the important of IPR governance. As the IT firms mature and get more experience, they channelize their resources in more productive ways to get maximum benefit from the resources.

7. CONCLUSIONS

Our findings extend the understanding of the role of R&D intensity, WTO-TRIPS implementation and their interaction in the IT firm's performance. We developed a conceptual framework with three hypotheses, conducted an empirical study of Indian IT firms using the CMIE Prowess data. Our findings shed light on the role of R&DIntensity, the WTO-TRIPS agreement reform shock, the interaction between R&DIntensity and ReformYear, Size, Age, Conglomerate group, Listed and, IndustryQ on the IT firm's performance using Tobin's Q. When a firm increases its R&D expenditure, it supports more innovation activities within the firm, by adding more skilled resources, training resources in advanced technologies, or initiating a relationship with a new partner for latest know-how. IT firms might not enhance their competitive advantage solely by just increasing their R&D expenditure. The R&D expenditure has a positive effect on performance when it is considered with the stronger implementation of WTO-TRIPS. The firm's age and the firm's size also play a positive role in improving its performance. This study is limited by the availability of data in CMIE database on IT firms. This study can further be extended by collecting additional innovation-related information like the patents, copyrights, and IPR related reforms to measure their impacts on IT firms' performance.

ACKNOWLEDGEMENTS

We thank Prof. Sai Yayavaram of IIMB, India and the reviewers of SIGMIS for their valuable comments. We also thank NSTMIS division of Dept. of Science and Technology, Govt. of India for the funding support.

REFERENCES

[1] Acs, Z.J.. et al. 1994. R & D Spillovers and Recipient Firm Size. The Review of Economics and Statistics. 76, 2 (1994), 336–340.

[2] Acs, Z.J. and Audretsch, D.B. 1988. Innovation in Large and Small Firms: An Empirical Analysis. American Economic Review. 78, 4 (1988), 678–690.

[3] Ahuja, G. and Katila, R. 2004. Where do resources come from? The role of idiosyncratic situations. Strategic Management Journal. 25, 8–9 (2004), 887–907.

[4] Arora, A. et al. 2013. Going Soft: How the Rise of Software-Based Innovation Led To the Decline of Japan'S IT Industry and the Resurgence of Silicon Valley. The Review of Economics and Statistics. 95, (2013), 757–775.

[5] Arora, A. et al. 2008. R&D and the patent premium. International Journal of Industrial Organization. 26, 5 (2008), 1153–1179.

[6] Azevedo, M.L. et al. 2014. Endogenous growth and intellectual property rights: A north-south modeling proposal. Economic Modelling. 38, (2014), 112–120.

[7] Barney, J. 1991. Firm Resources and Sustained Competitive Advantage. Journal of Management. 17, 1 (1991), 99–120.

[8] Basant Rakesh and Srinivasan Shruchi 2015. Intellectual Property Protection in India and Implications for Health Innovation: Emerging Perspectives. Indian Institute of Management Ahmedabad. (2015), 1–26.

[9] Bharadwaj, A.S. et al. 1999. Information Technology Effects on Firm Performance as Measured by Tobin's q. Management Science. 45, 6 (1999), 1008–1024.

[10] Birk, F. 2006. The Use of Intellectual Property Rights among Nordic Service Companies. Nordic Innovation Centre. March (2006).

[11] Bouet, D. 2015. A study of intellectual property protection policies and innovation in the Indian pharmaceutical industry and beyond. Technovation. 38, (2015), 31–41.

[12] Branstetter, L.G. et al. 2006. DO STRONGER INTELLECTUAL PROPERTY RIGHTS INCREASE INTERNATIONAL TECHNOLOGY TRANSFER? EMPIRICAL EVIDENCE FROM U . S . FIRM-LEVEL PANEL DATA. The Quarterly Journal of Economics. (2006), 321–349.

[13] Ceccagnoli, M. and Rothaermel, F.T. 2008. Appropriating the returns from innovation. Advances in the Study of Entrepreneurship, Innovation, and Economic Growth. 18, 7 (2008), 11–34.

[14] Chadha, A. 2009. TRIPs and patenting activity: Evidence from the Indian pharmaceutical industry. Economic Modelling. 26, 2 (2009), 499–505.

[15] Chatterjee, C. 2011. Title: Intellectual Property , Incentives for Innovation and Intellectual Property , Incentives for Innovation and Welfare: Evidence from the Global Pharmaceutical Industry. Dissertation Carnegie Mellon University. (2011).

[16] Cohen, W.M. and Klepper, S. 1996. A Reprise of Size and R & D. The Economic Journal. 106, (1996), 925–951.

[17] Crepon, B. et al. 1998. Research,Innovation and Productivity - an econometric analysis at the firm level. NBER WORKING PAPER SERIES. Working Pa, (1998).

[18] Demsetz, H. 1967. Toward a Theory of Property Rights. American Economic Review. 57, 2 (1967), 347–359.

[19] Dierickx, I. and Cool, K. ASSET STOCK ACCUMULATION AND SUSTAINABILITY OF COMPETITIVE ADVANTAGE. INSEAD.

[20] Dushnitsky, G. and Lenox, M.J. 2005. When do firms undertake R&D by investing in new ventures? Strategic Management Journal. 26, 10 (2005), 947–965.

[21] Dutta, A. and Sharma, S. 2008. Intellectual property rights and innovation in developing countries: Evidence from India. Working Paper. (2008), 2–51.

[22] Dutta, S. et al. 2014. The Global Innovation Index 2014: The Human Factor in Innovation.

[23] Dutta, S. et al. 2015. The Global Innovation Index 2015.

[24] Fan, J.P.H. et al. 2013. Innovation or imitation? The role of intellectual property rights protections. Journal of Multinational Financial Management. 23, 3 (2013), 208–234.

[25] Freeman, C. and Soete, L. 1997. The Economics of Industrial Innovation 3rd Ed. MIT Press.

[26] Grossman, S.J. and Hart, O.D. 1986. The Costs and Benefits of Ownership: A Theory of Vertical and Lateral Integration. Journal of Political Economy. 94, 4 (1986), 691.

[27] Hart, O. and Moore, J. 1990. Property Rights and the Nature of the Firm. The Journal of Political Economy. 98, 6 (1990), 1119.

[28] Kalaignanam, K. et al. 2007. Asymmetric New Product Development Alliances: Win-Win or Win-Lose Partnerships? Management Science. 53, 3 (2007), 357–374.

[29] Kim, J. and Mahoney, J.T. 2005. Property rights theory, transaction costs theory, and agency theory: An organizational economics approach to strategic management. Managerial and Decision Economics. 26, 4 (2005), 223–242.

[30] Krishnan, R.T. and Jha, S.K. 2011. Innovation Strategies in Emerging Markets: What Can We Learn from Indian Market Leaders. ASCI Journal of Management. 41, 1 (2011), 21–45.

[31] Laplume, A.O. et al. 2014. The politics of intellectual property rights regimes: An empirical study of new technology use in entrepreneurship. Technovation. 34, 12 (2014), 807–816.

[32] Larry, H.P.L. and Stulz, R.M. 1994. Tobin's q, Corporate Diversification, and Firm Performance. Journal of Political Economy.

[33] Lee, C. and Pennings, J. 2001. Internal Capabilities , External Networks , and Performance: A Study on Technology- Based Ventures. Strategic Management Journal. 22, (2001), 615–640.

[34] Li, D. et al. 2008. Friends, acquaintances, or strangers? Partner selection in R&D alliances. Academy of Management Journal. 51, 2 (2008), 315–334.

[35] Lin, B.W. et al. 2006. R&D intensity and commercialization orientation effects on financial performance. Journal of Business Research. 59, 6 (2006), 679–685.

[36] Lin, Z. et al. 2009. Alliance partners and firm performance: Resource complementarity and status association. Strategic Management Journal. 30, 9 (2009), 921–940.

[37] Mcevily, S.K. and Chakravarthy, B. 1999. RESOURCE CONTEXT AND THE RETURNS TO INVESTMENTS IN R&D. Academy of Management Proceedings. (1999).

[38] Nandkumar, A. and Srikanth, K. 2011. Patently different? How does IPR influence globalization of R & D? Evidence from Indian patent reforms. AoM 71st Annual Meeting. (2011).

[39] O'Brien, J.P. 2003. The capital structure implications of pursuing a strategy of innovation. Strategic Management Journal. 24, 5 (2003), 415–431.

[40] Perez-Cano, C. 2013. Firm size and appropriability of the results of innovation. Journal of Engineering and Technology Management - JET-M. 30, 3 (2013), 209–226.

[41] Rod, F. and Neil, F. 2006. The Role of Intellectual Property Rights in Technology Transfer and Economic Growth: Theory and Evidence. UNIDO. (2006), 1–14.

[42] Sweet, C.M. and Eterovic Maggio, D.S. 2015. Do stronger intellectual property rights increase innovation? World Development. 66, (2015), 665–677.

[43] Wernerfelt, B. and Montgomery, C.A. 1988. Tobin's q and the Importance of Focus in Firm Performance. The American Economic Review. 78, 1 (1988), 246–250.

[44] Williams, H.L. 2010. Intellectual Property Rights and Innovation: Evidence from the Human Genome. NBER WORKING PAPER SERIES. 121, (2010), 1–58.

[45] Woo, S. et al. 2015. Effects of intellectual property rights and patented knowledge in innovation and industry value added: A multinational empirical analysis of different industries. Technovation. 43–44, (2015), 49–63.

Job-Seekers and Social Networking in the "Networked" Age[1]

Poster Abstract

Michael L. Faulkner
DeVry University
630 U.S. Highway One
North Brunswick, NJ 08902
01-732- 729-3913
mfaulkner@devry.edu

Bruce C. Herniter
Louisiana Tech University
502 W. Texas, P.O.B 10318
Ruston, LA 71272
01-318-257-3264
herniter@latech.edu

Thomas F. Stafford
Louisiana Tech University
502 W. Texas, P.O.B 10318
Ruston, LA 71272
01-318-257-3886
stafford@latech.edu

ABSTRACT

This paper discusses the influence social networks have upon job search successes, with implications for technologically facilitated networking in leveraged social network searches for employment by job seekers.

CCS Concepts

• Human-centered computing→ Collaborative and social computing→ Collaborative and social computing theory, concepts and paradigms→ Social networks.

Keywords

Networking; social networking; job search.

1. INTRODUCTION

In this paper, we cover the historical and cultural context, the relationship among economics, information and networks, and social constructs.

2. HISTORIC & CULTURAL CONTEXT

2.1 Evolution

Fukuyama [10] discusses how the active engagement of one's contacts is evolutionary in nature, including the favoring family and friends as we had to rely on "favored others" for survival, and out of this arose an evolutionary tendency toward what we now call social networking.

Research in areas such as computer networks, neurological brain functions, and sociological aspects of *homophilic* communities (i.e., groupings of similarity) have increased contemporary understanding of social networking. Christakis and Fowler [7] argue that an individual's optimum social network is defined mostly by genetic evolution. In this view, the human neocortex (the outer thinking part of the human brain) allows humans to manage a social network of about 150 individuals successfully, known as Dunbar's number, which specifies the expected size of social groups based upon the brain structure.

2.2 Strong and Weak Networks

The emergence of the notion of the "Strength of Weak Ties" [11] suggested that "weak" connections between socially homogeneous groups whose members ordinarily do not interact with one another often lead to useful information transfers.

Most of the research has settled on subjective indicators of the closeness of a relationship. The term *weak tie* can be understood as indicating a relationship with someone *not yet met* [18, p. 483].

In Silliker's [23] study, nearly 70 percent of the social contacts of the persons surveyed were family members, friends, and friends of friends (strong ties). Strong networks are composed of individuals and the connections between them, with no traditional hierarchies. Such strong networks evolve from the natural tendency of individuals to seek others like themselves and work in personable environments, known as "the homophilic tendency" [7, p.13]. Damarin [8] suggests that in the flexible, high-mobility, heterogeneous labor markets of the postindustrial era, strong ties are more useful in general than they were in the sample of professionals that Granovetter examined in prior decades.

3. ECONOMICS, INFORMATION, & NETWORKS

Networking has an economic aspect. As Granovetter [12] posits, individual networking is a microeconomic event formed between job seekers and the greater movement of workers at large. From a pure economic perspective, the job discovery through social networking is more efficient and more productive, entailing lower costs and better offers.

Notable researchers in social mobility [2, 9, 13] hypothesized that there was an obstacle to the normal economic balance of supply and demand in the job search and filling mechanism because of the lack of perfect information. In this view, employers resorted to their informal networks because the economic effort required in determining the difference between the best available candidate and an acceptable candidate is expensive and leads to diminishing returns in recruitment [20].

In the traditional view, workers have a paucity of information regarding the existence of job openings and conditions among employers [21, 22]. Additional information came from strong tie networks (in-groups, to coin a term), and these strong affiliations often led to discovery of employment opportunities [11, 25]. In large homophilic groupings, complexity, size and

SIGMIS-CPR '17, June 21-23, 2017, Bangalore, India
© 2017 Copyright is held by the owner/author(s).
ACM ISBN 978-1-4503-5037-2/17/06.
http://dx.doi.org/10.1145/3084381.3084416

richness of available information tend to yield successful search more so than in smaller, less rich, networks [26].

3.1 Strong and Weak Tie Networks

Other factors may limit the effectiveness of the job search [20]. For example, there exist in job markets certain "non-competitive" networking practices in both *strong* (in-group) and *weak* (out-group) ties on both the demand and supply sides of the labor market. These include gentlemen's agreements, restrictive preferences, biases, and preferences [20]. Workers have similar anti-competitive inclinations. Leicht and Marx [14] suggest that there is a persistent physical, social and symbolic gender gap in American business with regard to social networking efficacy.

Because these weak tie links are with individuals less well-known than strong ties links, they can lead to more unique knowledge and less redundant job information, hence also providing more influence according to Granovetter [11, 12]. Bian and Yakubovich both agree with Granovetter that weak ties are more likely than strong ties to *serve as the bridge* to out-group contacts that will lead to job opportunities [1, 27].

Research has suggested that weak tie contacts are advantageous because more people, with more unique job and industry information, can be reached through them [20]. Other research [3, 17], however, suggested that weak-ties theory could not prove a broad and general connection between social access and increased job prestige in subsequent appointments. The classic evidence of the strength of weak ties arose from studies of job searches by white-collar college professors and other scientific professionals who were much more likely to find jobs through their weak tie contacts. In such studies, there has been a reliable positive relationship between the prestige of the job applicant's institution and the use of informal weak ties networks in obtaining an academic position [15], and the vast majority of academic professionals appear to learn about their current jobs through their weak ties network [4, 5].

4. SOCIAL CONSTRUCTS

4.1 Social Capital

Social capital is frequently framed in terms of civic participation, which ties individuals together for reasons of common, mutual, or public interest. A body of theoretical and empirical work links personal networks with the issue of social capital [11, 16, 24].

Granovetter [12] suggested networking is a social capital contribution because it is an observable characteristic of human capabilities linked to the improvement of the community and therefore a public good, thus enhancing social capital. Lin [16] sees social capital as a network-related resource that an actor could access through his or her direct or indirect ties.

4.2 Socioeconomic Status

It appears that the higher the socioeconomic level of the job seeker, the more likely he or she would be using a strong ties network (i.e., in-group) [6]. However, Granovetter's classic observation [11] suggests job seekers' opportunities are determined on the basis of their weak ties prestige. In a merger of the two views, another study concludes [19] that there is a strong correlation between the socioeconomic status of weak tie contacts and the prestige of subsequently obtained job opportunities. In fact, it seems likely that few social networks include total self-contained cliques [11, 20], suggesting that heterophilic spanning is an important capability.

5. CONCLUDING THOUGHTS

The central strand that has emerged in this review is that social capital, economics, and information all come together to favor social networking as an efficient tool for job search. Social networks provide information from trusted sources.

6. REFERENCES

[1] Bian, Y. 1997. Bringing strong ties back in: indirect ties, network bridges, and job searches in China. *American Sociological Review* 62(3), 365-385.

[2] Blau, P. M., and Duncan, O. D. 1969. The American occupational structure. *American Journal of Sociology* 75(3), 416-418.

[3] Bridges, W.P., and Villamez, W. 1986. Informal hiring and income in the labor market. *American Sociological Review* 51, 574-582.

[4] Brown, R. 1965. *Social Psychology*. Free Press, New York, NY.

[5] Brown, D.G. 1967. The mobile professors. *The American Council on Education*, Washington, D.C.

[6] Burt, R. S. 1978. Cohesion versus structural equivalence as a basis for network subgroups. *Sociological Methods & Research* 7(2), 189-212.

[7] Christakis, N., and Fowler, J.H. 2010. Social network sensors for early detection of contagious outbreaks, *PLoS ONE* 5(9), 2010, e12948. doi:10.1371/journal.pone.

[8] Damarin, A.K, 2004. Strong ties in flexible labor markets: Findings from New York City's new media industry. *Annual Meeting of American Sociological Association Meeting*.

[9] Featherman, D. L., and Hauser, R. M. 1987. Opportunity and Change. Academic Press, New York, NY.

[10] Fukuyama, F. 2010. The end of history, 20 years later. *New Perspectives Quarterly* 27(1), 7–10.

[11] Granovetter, M. 1973. Strength of weak ties. *American Journal of Sociology* 78(6), 1360-1380

[12] Granovetter, M.1995. *Getting a Job: A Study of Contacts and Careers*. University of Chicago Press, Chicago IL.

[13] Jencks, C., Smith, M., Ackland, H., Bane, M., Cohen, D., Gintis, H., Heyns, B., and Michaelson, S. 1972. *Inequality*. Basic Books, New York, NY.

[14] Leicht, K.T., and Marx, J. 2002. The consequences of informal job finding for men and women. *Academy of Management Journal* 40, 1179-1190.

[15] Light, D.W., Jr., et al. 1973. *The Impact of the Academic Revolution on Faculty Careers*. National Institute of Education, Washington, DC.

[16] Lin, N. 1999. Social networks and status attainment. *Annual Review of Sociology* 25, 467-487.

[17] Lin, N., Ensel, W., and Vaughn, J. 1981. Social resources and strength of ties: Structural factors in occupational status attainment. *American Sociological Review* 46, 393-405.

[18] Marsden P.V., and Campbell, K.E. 1984. Measuring tie strength. *Social Forces* 63(2), 482-501.

[19] Marsden, P.V., and Hurlbert, J.S. 1968. Social resources and mobility outcomes: A replication and extension. *Social Forces* 66, 1038-1056.

[20] Murray, S.O., Rankin, J.H., and Magill, D.W. 1981. Strong ties and job information. *Sociology of Work and Occupations* 8(1), 119–135.

[21] Palmer, G.L. 1954. *Labor Mobility in Six Cities: A Report on the Survey of Patterns and Factors in Labor Mobility*. Social Science Research Council, New York, NY.

[22] Parnes, H.S., Miljus, R.C.; Spitz, R.S., et al. 1969. *Career Thresholds: A Longitudinal Study of the Educational and Labor: Market Experience of Male Youth 14 to 24 Years of Age* U.S. Department of Labor Manpower Research Monograph, Washington, DC.

[23] Silliker, A.S. 1993. The role of social contacts in the successful job search. Journal of Employment Counseling 30(1), 25-34.

[24] Smith T.W. 1999. *Measuring Inter-Racial Friendships: Experimental Comparisons*. National Opinion Reproach Center, Chicago, IL.

[25] Spector, P.E., Method variance as an artifact in self-reported affect and perceptions at work: Myth or significant problem? *Journal of Applied Psychology* 72, 438-443.

[26] Van Hoye, G., Van Hooft, E.A.J., and Lievens, F. 2009. Networking as a job search behavior: A social network perspective. *Journal of Occupational and Organizational Psychology* 82, 661-182.

[27] Yakubovich, V. 2005. Weak ties, information, and influence: How workers find jobs in a local Russian labor market. *American Sociological Review* 70(3), 408-442

Use of Gamified Social Media with Home Telemonitoring for Patient Self-Management in Poorly Controlled Medicaid Diabetics: A Pilot Study of Health Outcomes, Social Influences, and Habit Formation*

Poster Abstract

Ramanpreet Khinda
Open Garden, USA
rkhinda@buffalo.edu

Srikanth Parameswaran
Management Science and Systems
SUNY at Buffalo, USA
sparames@buffalo.edu

Gourab Mitra
Computer Science and Engineering
SUNY at Buffalo, USA
gourabmi@buffalo.edu

Xiaolin Lin
Texas A&M University-Corpus Christi
xiaolin.lin@tamucc.edu

Christine Verni
Primary Care Research Institute
SUNY at Buffalo, USA
cmverni@buffalo.edu

Rajiv Kishore
Management Science and Systems
SUNY at Buffalo, USA
rkishore@buffalo.edu

Anthony Billittier
Millennium Collaborative Care, USA
Erie Country Medical Center, USA
abillittier@millenniumcc.org

1 MOTIVATION AND PROBLEM STATEMENT

Diabetes mellitus is a chronic disease characterized by persistent hyperglycemia. It is the seventh leading cause of death in the United States [1]. AHRQ [2] reports that patient compliance with medication and disease management protocols is, in fact, a major barrier to diabetes treatment goals. To motivate patients, enhance patient self-care of diabetes and improve health outcomes, we propose to conduct a study to evaluate the effectiveness of a gamified social media app with a competitive game element in conjunction with home remote patient monitoring (the proposed technology intervention) in a sample of Medicaid diabetic patients with poorly controlled diabetes.

*Research reported in this poster was supported by the Agency for Healthcare Research and Quality under award number 1R03HS023672-01A1. The content is solely the responsibility of the authors and does not necessarily represent the official views of the Agency for Healthcare Research and Quality.

SIGMIS-CPR '17, June 21-23, 2017, Bangalore, India
© 2017 Copyright is held by the owner/author(s).
ACM ISBN 978-1-4503-5037-2/17/06.
http://dx.doi.org/10.1145/3084381.3084417

2 BACKGROUND LITERATURE

We reviewed literature on patient motivation, diabetes self-management and gamification in health. Health belief Model posits that cue to action and an informed, activated patient yield positive health outcomes [3]. Studies in self-management of diabetes with home telemonitoring have yielded mixed effect sizes of health outcomes [4]. Use of gamification in social media is being used with good outcomes in the fitness industry, and has demonstrated good initial promise in self-management of diabetes in adolescent patients [5].

3 METHODS

Our strategy is to conduct an eight-month pilot study in which the proposed technology intervention will be used by a sample of 60 qualifying patients who will be randomized equally to control and intervention groups. During the first two months, remote telemonitoring will establish baseline compliance with daily blood glucose testing and fasting blood glucose levels for individual patients in both groups. During the next three-month intervention period, an app will be introduced to both groups. The gamified app introduced to the intervention patients will display daily information anonymously comparing the individual patient's compliance and fasting blood glucose level from the previous day to all other intervention group patients. The app for the control group will display daily information only for the individual patient's compliance and fasting blood glucose level from the previous day. The apps will then be withdrawn from both groups while remote telemonitoring continues during the last three-month period to explore whether anticipated improved health behaviors continue to impact self-management of diabetes and blood glucose control.

3.1 Design

Our app sends two daily notifications to the patients to check their previous day's compliance and fasting blood glucose level. Once opened, the control group app shows a screen with two tabs with the information from the first tab appearing first - showing the individual patient's compliance i.e. whether or not they checked their blood glucose the previous day. After a ten second delay the app automatically shows the second tab - showing whether the patient's blood glucose level the previous day was high, low or normal or it says that the patient did not their check their glucose. While using the app the patient can toggle between the two tabs. Similarly, the game app also shows two tabs with the first tab being shown first and the second one after a delay of 10 seconds. The first tab shows the percentage of patients who checked and percentage of patients who did not check their blood glucose the previous day. This information is presented graphically in two zones with the percentage converted to stick figures. This screen also indicates the zone the patient belongs to. Similarly, the second tab shows four zones with stick figures indicating the percentage of patients who had high, low and normal blood sugar levels, and the percentage of patients who did not check their blood glucose yesterday. This screen also indicates the zone the patient belongs to with the percentage converted to stick figures. Every Monday the game app announces as weekly winners those patients who complied the maximum number days the previous week and those patients who had normal glucose the most number of days. Other patients get a message encouraging them to play better and win the next week. Our app sends daily reports to the study team listing the patients with dangerously high\low glucose levels. A clinical research coordinator will immediately inform the patient and the primary care practitioner of the patient's condition. The daily report will also include the list of patients who did not comply and/or use the app for two days in order to monitor potential study withdrawal. The user interface of the app was designed in consultation with our study team consisting of experts in information systems, human factors, computer science, public health, and physicians who treat diabetics. Visual cues like color and language of the presentation of results and notification, aural cues like game sounds, and glucose ranges for results, notification and daily reports were built into the app based on literature and the inputs from this interdisciplinary team.

3.2 Development

The app was developed using Android version Lollipop (5.x). The app is targeted for the Samsung SM-T377P tablet in terms of display, size and resolution. Our frontend is an android application written in Java and the backend is a Django based web framework written in Python. The app is hosted on a backed server - an Amazon EC2 Instance. Our web server follows the HTTPS protocol – the widely used protocol for secure communication over a computer network.

3.3 Testing

The App underwent rigorous alpha and beta testing with an eight-member testing team. The control and intervention groups were assigned four members each. The test subjects received a glucometer kit and a tablet with the glucometry app and the game app. Test subjects were asked to randomly adhere in order simulate actual patient behavior. Subjects were asked to log their adherence and the performance of app features such as daily notifications to study team, daily notifications to patients, daily results to control and intervention group, and weekly results. Using this data, we resolved issues in app design during the testing phase. We did another round of testing by reversing the control and intervention group assignment in order to verify that the issues were resolved.

4 EXPECTED RESULTS

One, the proposed technology intervention should improve three specific patient outcomes: a) compliance with disease self-management tasks (behavioral outcome); b) diabetes control in terms of reduced HgbA1C levels (health outcome); and c) diabetes self-efficacy (psychological outcome). Two, positive social influence from patients' social networks around their diabetes would act as an antecedent of usage of the proposed technology intervention, and act as a moderator of the relationship between the proposed technology intervention and patient outcomes. Three, disease self-management habits (measured after removing the intervention) are formed as a result of usage of the proposed technology during the three-month intervention period.

5 IMPLICATIONS

If positive results are subsequently validated, then the proposed technology intervention focused on promoting good health behaviors and motivation for self- management of diabetes through cue-for-action, fun, and competition could significantly enhance the standard of care for diabetes particularly with respect to self-care. This change in clinical practice may also have broader implications for the self-management of other chronic diseases as well.

6 REFERENCES

[1] Murphy, S. L., Xu, J. and Kochanek, K. D. National Vital Statistics Report: Deaths: Final Data for 2010.
[2] AHRQ. Improving Care for Diabetes Patients Through Intensive Therapy and a Team Approach: Research in Action. Agency for Healthcare Research and Quality, City, 2001.
[3] Rosenstock, I. M., Strecher, V. J. and Becker, M. H. Social learning theory and the health belief model. *Health Education & Behavior*, 15, 2 (1988), 175-183.
[4] Jaana, M. and Paré, G. Home telemonitoring of patients with diabetes: a systematic assessment of observed effects. *Journal of evaluation in clinical practice*, 13, 2 (2007), 242-253.
[5] Kankanhalli, A., Taher, M., Cavusoglu, H., Kim, S.: Gamification: A New Paradigm for Online User Engagement. In: Thirty Third International Conference on Information Systems, Orlando, pp. 1–10 (2012).

Organizational Agility:
Leveraging Organizational Structure in Times of Digitalization

Poster Abstract

Hanna Kirchherr
Frankfurt School of Finance & Management
Frankfurt, Germany
hanna.kirchherr@fs-students.de

Friedrich Holotiuk
Frankfurt School of Finance & Management
Frankfurt, Germany
f.holotiuk@fs.de

KEYWORDS

Organizational Agility; Organizational Structure; Digital Innovation; Project Success

ACM Reference format:

H. Kirchherr, F. Holotiuk. 2017. Organizational Agility: Leveraging Organizational Structure in Times of Digitalization. In *Proceedings of ACM SIGMIS Computers and People Research 2017 conference, Bengaluru, India, June 2017)*, 2 pages.[1]

1 PROBLEM STATEMENT

Due to the increasing digitalization of the business environment and resulting changes in the market structure, firms are questioning if their current organizational structures align to the upcoming challenges [9]. Organizational structures have to align to the firm's strategy [2] and provide the needed flexibility as well as adaptability to changes. Research has put forward the concept of organizational agility which can provide a more adaptable organizational structure [3]. However, research on this matter is still scare and in its infancy. With our research, we want to analyze how organizational agility can mediate the effects of organizational structure on project success and digital innovation.

2 INTRODUCTION

Due to environmental changes that can be characterized as complex, unpredictable and instable, firms nowadays struggle to find an organizational structure that provides efficiency and is at the same time flexible enough to adapt to the changing environmental demands [8]. Based on the management

literature, the ability of a firm to cope with changes and to be flexible as well as adaptable in its organizational structure leads to 'organizational agility' [3]. Organizational agility is the capability of "every organization in sensation, perception, and prediction of available changes in the business environment" [6, pg. 100].

One major effect that causes tremendous need for adaption is digitalization. Digitalization is operationalized in our research as the development of digital innovations. They can be defined as the "redesign [of] processes and even entire business models to transform innovative information technology (IT) options and digitization opportunities into strategic advantages" [4, pg. 2].

Digital innovations do not only effect manufacturing or IT firms but also service firms such as consulting firms. Consulting firms provide services on various levels for their clients and are confronted with intense changes and turbulence in the business environment.

Hence, the needed level of agility is comparable high. Consulting firms benefit from digitalization as many firms engage with them to support the digital transformation but it is not evident how consulting firms themselves deal with digitalization and change [7]. In particular, organizational agility can help the consulting industry to stay competitive in times of digitalization [5]. However, the concept has not been applied in an empirical study with consulting firms and to the question how they can become more agile to cope with and profit from digitalization. By answering this question, we gain insights into the design of organizational structures and the effect of organizational agility on the development of digital innovation. We hope that our findings are generalizable to the entire service industry, which will yield avenues for further research.

3 RESEARCH QUESTIONS

Building on organizational structure as our first construct, we are going to measure and evaluate the influence of organizational structure on agility by focusing on a set of characteristics needed for innovation. The underlying assumption is that some characteristics of organizational structure foster agility more strongly than others. Based on existing literature in organization science a set of characteristics will be developed. Some of such characteristics have been

SIGMIS-CPR '17, June 21-23, 2017, Bangalore, India
© 2017 Copyright is held by the owner/author(s).
ACM ISBN 978-1-4503-5037-2/17/06.
http://dx.doi.org/10.1145/3084381.3084420

analyzed in the context of organizational structure and knowledge management.

RQ1: Which and how do organizational structure characteristics influence organizational agility?

An objective of every firm is to have an organizational structure that supports innovation because innovation provides competitive advantages and helps to keep up with the industry [9].

Many firms have already taken actions, but an overview of the possible adjustment screws does not exist. Hence, the aim of this research is not the evaluation of already taken actions but to explore possible options towards adjustments of the organizational structure to cope with the challenges of digitalization. Hence, the core of our research will be how organizational agility mediates the organizational structure effects and fosters digital innovation.

RQ2: What organizational structure characteristics drive a firm's organizational agility and thus digital innovation?

In the end, the agile organizational structure is required to also form a stable basis for daily operations. This stability can be achieved with continuous project success. Successful projects increase the ability to gain and/or sustain competitive advantages for all firms, including consulting firms. Hence, the aim is to evaluate whether the agile organizational structure allows to explore new business models and innovative ways to create value while also maintaining project success for daily business [5].

RQ3: How can organizational agility increase digital innovation while maintaining project success?

4 INTENDED RESEARCH

First, we will develop a research model which encapsulates the described constructs and illustrates the hypothesized relationships. Second, the items that measure which characteristics of the organizational structure foster the organizational agility will be derived from the existing literature. Organizational agility items will be developed with existing items along with items from the software project agility literature. Finally, we will conduct a survey for data collection.

The survey will take place in the course of this year and target employees of consulting firms on all levels to gain a well-rounded insight. Hence, we will have to control for a number of variables, e.g. the level of each employee or the firm size. The goal is to address more than 3.000 consultants across different firms and receive around 200 valid responses. Subsequently, the data analysis will also take place this year and focus on the outlined research questions.

5 EXPECTED OUTCOME AND IMPLICATION

The literature shows that the concept of agility is already applied to industries like manufacturing, e. g. workforce agility [1]. Workforce agility addresses the degree to which extent employees can deal with a changing environment. In addition, there are also other agility-related concepts that support an adaptable organization design, for instance structural flexibility, shared power, information transparency, development orientation, and flexible rewards [8].

From our research, we want to explain the influences of organizational structure on organizational agility. Furthermore, the effect of organizational agility on project success and digital innovation will be analyzed. Our research yields implications for practitioners by providing guidelines for firms regarding an organizational structure that enables the development of digital innovation. Next, we aim to extend the literature on organizational agility by providing a better understanding of needed adjustments of the organizational structure. Finally, we want to contribute to the concept of organizational agility by identifying the leveraging organizational structure characteristics and synthesize them in a framework for new organizational designs. Hence, our results can also yield as a research agenda for further research on organizational agility and digital innovation.

REFERENCES

[1] Alavi, S. et al. 2014. Organic Structure and Organisational Learning as the Main Antecedents of Workforce Agility. International Journal of Production Research. 52, 21 (2014), 6273–6295.
[2] Chandler, A.D. 1962. Strategy and Structure: Chapters in the History of the Industrial Enterprise. MIT Press.
[3] Crocitto, M. and Youssef, M. 2003. The Human Side of Organizational Agility. Industrial Management & Data Systems. 103, 6 (2003), 388–397.
[4] Leischnig, A. et al. 2016. When Does Digital Business Strategy Matter to Market Performance? Proceedings of ICIS2016 (2016).
[5] Mason, A. 2010. Inside the Black Box: Investigating Agility as a Dynamic Capability for Sustaining a Competitive Advantage within Consulting Firms. Capella University Dissertation.
[6] Razmi, B. and Ghasemi, H.M. 2015. Designing a Model of Organizational Agility: A Case Study of Ardabil Gas Company. International Journal of Organizational Leadership. 4, 2 (2015), 100–117.
[7] Werth, D. et al. 2015. Consulting 4.0 – Die Digitalisierung der Unternehmensberatung. HMD Praxis der Wirtschaftsinformatik. 53, 1 (2015), 55–70.
[8] Worley, C.G. and Lawler, E.E. 2010. Agility and Organization Design: A Diagnostic Framework. Organizational Dynamics. 39, 2 (2010), 194–204.
[9] Yoo, Y. et al. 2012. Organizing for Innovation in the Digitized World. Organization Science. 23, 5 (2012), 1398–1408.

Consulting Firms Under the Influence of Digitalization: The Need for Greater Organizational Agility

Poster Abstract

Javen Kohlen
Frankfurt School of Finance & Management
Frankfurt, Germany
javen.kohlen@fs-students.de

Friedrich Holotiuk
Frankfurt School of Finance & Management
Frankfurt, Germany
f.holotiuk@fs.de

KEYWORDS

Consulting Firms; Digitalization, Organizational Structure; Organizational Agility; Digital Innovation

ACM Reference format:

J. Kohlen, F. Holotiuk. 2017. Consulting Firms Under the Influence of Digitalization: The Need for Greater Organizational Agility. In *Proceedings of ACM SIGMIS Computers and People Research 2017 conference, Bengaluru, India, June 2017), 2 pages.*[1]

1 PROBLEM STATEMENT

Due to digitalization a number of industries are undergoing fundamental and far-reaching changes [2]. As consulting firms are advising clients on how to tackle these challenges, they are on the forefront of these changes. However, they are also affected by the changes themselves and have to, among other, rethink their organizational structure. Organizational structure has been identified as a leverage for complex change and innovations in times of high uncertainty [13]. We aim to test, if organizational agility can help consulting firms to develop digital innovation. Hence, our study sets out to explore the potential of new organizational structures in the consulting industry and to analyze the effect of organizational agility on digital innovation.

2 MOTIVATION AND RESEARCH QUESTIONS

The megatrend of digitalization influences all industries and leads to faster changing environments. The consulting industry shifts due to digitalization towards a highly competitive professional market and an increasing turbulent business environment. Hence, the focus of consultancies is to critically rethink their business model and culture [3].

SIGMIS-CPR '17, June 21-23, 2017, Bangalore, India
© 2017 Copyright is held by the owner/author(s).
ACM ISBN 978-1-4503-5037-2/17/06.
http://dx.doi.org/10.1145/3084381.3084421

There are different ideas of which organizational characteristics are enablers for the digital transformation. Agility is often named as an capability that supports digitalization [10]. Agility can be defined as "an effective integration of response ability and knowledge management in order to rapidly, efficiently and accurately adapt to any unexpected (or unpredictable) change in both proactive and reactive business/ customer needs and opportunities without compromising with the cost or the quality of the product/ process" [5 pg. 411]. Most research focused on agile manufacturing processes [6, 11, 12] and its definition or how Information Technology (IT) structure can support agility or digitalization [10]. However, a corresponding framework and understanding of organizational agility in service firms like consulting agencies is missing.

RQ1: What is the influence of organizational agility in the consulting industry?

Agility cannot easily be forced by managers, so the influencing characteristics are essential. Organizational agility can be separated in, for example, market capitalizing agility and operational adjustment agility [8]. Different sets of characteristics that can influence organizational agility are: intelligence, competencies, collaboration, culture, and information system [1] or integration, competence, team building, technology, quality, change, partnership, market, education, and welfare [7].

It is not clear in the academic literature how agile service firms are. The structure of consulting firms is interesting to look at because their primary asset is human capital and they have a minimum of fixed investments which should make them able to adapt faster than other firms [3]. Therefore, it seems fitting to use consulting firms as an industry to analyze how organizational agility can also enhance daily business, e.g. project success in consulting.

RQ2: How does organizational agility effects the project success of consulting firms?

The ultimate goal of consulting firms and also other firms is to have a structure that supports the development of innovation [9]. Furthermore, in times of digitalization, it is also important to understand the impact of organizational agility on the capability to develop digital innovation [4]. Therefore, we are analyzing organizational agility in consulting firms and its influence on digital innovation.

RQ3: How can organizational agility enable consulting firms to develop digital innovation?

With this research, we aim to understand the complex organizational characteristics that provide an organizational structure best suited for digital innovation. Furthermore, this knowledge may enable us to transfer the interdependence between organizational agility and digital innovation from the consulting industry to other industries.

3 METHODOLOGY

The core of our research will be an empirical study based on a survey. First, we will develop a research model that will be able to capture and measure the organizational agility in consulting firms. Second, we will operationalize the different constructs (namely organizational agility, organizational structure, project success, and digital innovation) and develop items from existing literature.

The goal is to examine and describe organization agility and its influence on digital innovation. The structure of the survey will be similar to the research approach used by Leischnig et al. [6].

Finally, we will design the survey and address more than 2.000 consultants through private contacts, firm contacts, and an alumni distribution list. The responses of the study will then be analyzed with a regression method, like the Partial Least Squares Regression method. We specifically aim to disentangle effects of organizational structure and organizational agility on digital innovation.

4 EXPECTED OUTCOME AND IMPLICATION

We want to be able to explain the potential of organizational agility in consulting firms which are under the influence of digitalization. A better understanding of how organizational agility can positively affect the development of digital innovation can support the design of new organizational structures well suited of the challenges of digitalization.

Also, our research is expected explain the influence of organizational agility on the capability to develop digital innovation in consulting firms. These insights can then be transferred to other industries afterwards. Therefore, the goal is not only to find the influential organizational characteristics of organizational agility, but also to develop a conceptual framework of organizational structure for future research regarding organizational agility and digital innovation in other industries.

REFERENCES

[1] Breu, K. et al. 2002. Workforce Agility: The New Employee Strategy for the Knowledge Economy. *Journal of Information Technology.* 17, 1 (2002), 21–31.
[2] Brynjolfsson, E. and McAfee, A. 2014. *The Second Machine Age: Work, Progress, and Prosperity in a Time of Brilliant Technologies.* W. W. Norton & Company.
[3] Christensen, C.M. et al. 2013. Consulting on the Cusp of Disruption. *Harvard Business Review.* 91, 10 (2013), 106–114.
[4] Fichman, R.G. et al. 2014. Digital Innovation As a Fundamental and Powerful Concept in the Information Systems Curriculum. *MIS Quarterly.* 38, 2 (2014), 329-A15.
[5] Ganguly, A. et al. 2009. Evaluating Agility in Corporate Enterprises. *International Journal of Production Economics.* 118, 2 (2009), 410–423.
[6] Hoyt, J. et al. 2007. Measuring organizational responsiveness: the development of a validated survey instrument. *Management Decision.* 45, 10 (2007), 1573–1594.
[7] Lin, C.-T. et al. 2006. Agility evaluation using fuzzy logic. *International Journal of Production Economics.* 101, (2006), 353–368.
[8] Lu, Y. and Ramamurthy, K.R. 2011. Understanding the Link Between Information Technology Capability and Organizational Agility: An Empirical Examination. *MIS Quarterly.* 35, 4 (2011), 931–954.
[9] Read, A. 2000. Determinants of Successful Organisational Innovation: A Review of Current Research. *Journal of Management Practice.* 3, 1 (2000), 95–119.
[10] Sambamurthy, V. et al. 2003. Shaping Agility through Digital Options: Reconceptualizing the Role of Information Technology in Contemporary Firms. *MIS Quarterly.* 27, 2 (2003), 237–263.
[11] Sharifi, H. and Zhang, Z. 1999. Methodology for achieving agility in manufacturing organisations: an introduction. *International Journal of Production Economics.* 62, 1 (1999), 7–22.
[12] Vázquez-Bustelo, D. et al. 2007. Agility drivers, enablers and outcomes: Empirical test of an integrated agile manufacturing model. *International Journal of Operations & Production Management.* 27, 12 (2007), 1303–1332.
[13] Yoo, Y. et al. 2012. Organizing for Innovation in the Digitized World. *Organization Science.* 23, 5 (2012), 1398–1408.

Systematic Literature Review of Big Data Analytics[*]

Poster Abstract[†]

Prajwal Eachempati
FPM, IT & Systems
Indian Institute of Management
Rohtak
P.O. Box 124001
India
fpm03.007@iimrohtak.ac.in

Praveen Ranjan Srivastava
Faculty, IT & Systems
Indian Institute of Management
Rohtak
P.O. Box 124001
India
praveen.ranjan@iimrohtak.ac.in

1 MOTIVATION

The aim of this paper[1]is to explore and empirically analyze the extent and quality of research work in business analytics worldwide and in India and present the most emerging domains that have a wide scope for research based on the existing work done at the global and national level.

2 BACKGROUND LITERATURE

2.1 "Big" Data

Big data [1] can be defined as the term used for data sets large and complicated and difficult to process using traditional data management tools or processing applications like relational databases and data warehouses.

2.2 "Big" Data Analytics

The millennial decade i.e., the 2000s paved the way for the transition to "Big" data, and led to the birth of what is now known as "big data" analytics due to the magnification of the "4 Vs" of data and can be categorized into: Visual, Predictive, Social Media and Descriptive Analytics

ACM Reference format:
P. Eachempati, P. R. Srivastava,2017. SIG Proceedings Paper in word Format. In Proceedings of ACM SIGMIS-CPR'17 conference June 21-23, 2017, Bangalore, India 2 pages.
DOI: 10.1145/3084381.3084422

3 METHODS

Figure 1: Research process for the study

As depicted in Fig. 1, a systematic literature review was conducted by capturing the existing work done in this subject area by academicians and industry experts worldwide and specifically in India backed by a domain-wise, nation-wise and within India, an institute-wise analysis of the contributions made. Based on the existing work, the need for applying analytics in emerging sectors is emphasized through the paper.

4 RESULTS AND IMPLICATIONS

The results that emerged out of this study are:

4.1 Global Domain-wise Analysis

The analysis on emerging countries domain-wise is presented below:

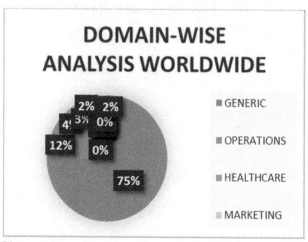

Figure 2: Domain-wise analysis worldwide (%)

From Fig. 2 it can be inferred that the domain of Operations, Healthcare, Marketing & Ecommerce are leading while Finance is an emerging domain.

On performing the institute-wise analysis in India, the following results emerged as follows:

4.2   Institute-wide analysis in India

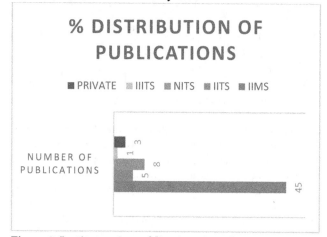

Figure 3: Institute-wise publications in India

IIMs constitute the major chunk followed by NITs (including IIITs) and IITs and private institutes are emerging as illustrated in Fig. 3.

Of all the emerging, untapped domains with scope for research in big data analytics, considering the specific interest of the stakeholder, the domain of banking and finance has been chosen for discussion.

One of the most important sectors today which offers one of the most critical services for any country is the banking and finance sector.

This domain has very wide scope for analytics particularly predictive analytics since there is a need to be able to forecast business scenarios that will help in taking managerial decisions, for instance, predicting stock market and exchange rate fluctuations is important to take decision regarding trade and investment and in the long run helps in determining the financial position of companies [2].

Other scenarios such as predicting investor sentiment and forensics like credit card defaults and fraud detections on a large scale cannot be accomplished unless analytics tools are harnessed to be able to handle the unstructured and structured data.

REFERENCES

[1] Larson, D., & Chang, V. (2016). A review and future direction of agile, business intelligence, analytics and data science. International Journal of Information Management, 36, 700-710.

[2] Das.S.(2016)."How Indian brokers use analytics to predict the stock market". The CIO. Retrieved from: http://www.cio.in/feature/how-indian-brokers-use-analytics-predict-stock-market.

The Impact of Individual Information Privacy and Personalization on Online Buying Behavior: An Experimental Study

Poster Abstract

Kanishka Priyadharshini A
Research Scholar
Department of Management Studies
Indian Institute of Technology Madras
India
kanish.dharshini@gmail.com

Saji K Mathew
Associate Professor
Department of Management Studies
Indian Institute of Technology Madras
India
saji@iitm.ac.in

ABSTRACT

We study the relationship between web personalization and individual information privacy on the customer's online buying behavior. Following a laboratory experiment we tested the differences for number of clicks and number of products added to cart with respect to two factors, namely Web Personalization and Information privacy related to a product. Our results show significant mean differences with respect to clicks and number of products added to the cart for privacy and non privacy products.

Keywords

Online Buying behavior; e-commerce; individual online privacy concern; web personalization.

1. INTRODUCTION

With recent technological advancements and the growth of online market place, personal information that concern user privacy has become a double edged sword. In an online commerce market, the users give-out their personal information to gain personalized offers or services and the firms use personalization as a tool to indirectly bolster their financial performance. As E-Commerce based businesses reduce the face-to-face interactions between the customers and the salespersons, one way to increase the value of the service and subsequently enhance customer loyalty is by effective personalization. This view-point is however marred by the fact that collecting user personal information involves infringing into a customer's privacy. The personal information of all the users of an E-Commerce market place are collected either by voluntary sharing of the data through surveys or involuntary collection of information through events like mouse clicks and keyboard inputs. A lot of studies have been done to study have been done to analysis and measure individual privacy (Smith. 1996, Malhotra. 2004) and web personalization (Chellapa, 2005, Tam

&Ko, 2006). The objective of the paper is to find the impact of individual information privacy concern and web personalization on customer's online buying behavior.

2. METHODOLOGY

In a laboratory experiment setup, multiple E-commerce portals were operated with respect to three factors - goal specificity, web personalization and information privacy concern. Personalization for a customer is deployed in terms of content relevance by displaying either relevant or irrelevant content banners. The model is grounded on social cognition and consumer research theories. We expect that customers are more likely to buy or browse products that are related to the pervious search or purchase history. Individual information privacy concern for a customer in the E-commerce portal is deployed in means of products that are considered in to two levels namely highly privacy concern products (example: intimate products) and not highly privacy concern products (example: pen, pencil). Categorization of both highly and non- highly concern products were done with the help of an online survey in which each product are ranked in the scale of one to five, where one represent strongly highly concern and five represent strongly non- highly concern. Further, goal specificity is implemented by requesting users either to just browse or to add specified number of products to the cart. Our study are based on experimental setup where we collected click stream data to study user behavior. We tested the differences for number of clicks, number of products added to cart and time spend by the consumers in the website.

3. PRELIMINARY RESULTS

Our findings show that customer buying decisions are influenced by both the product information privacy concern and web personalization. We found significant mean differences with respect to number of clicks and number of products added to the cart for highly privacy concern and non- highly privacy concern products. Online users' decision making process is significantly different when they are privacy conscious and when web content is personalized for the user and also with respect to set goals.

4. IMPLICATIONS

The findings have implications for design of recommender systems as E-commerce product categories also evoke different degrees of privacy concern to the users, which helps the E-commerce to offers personalized contents for the users according to the degree of privacy related to the corresponding products.

SIGMIS-CPR '17, June 21-23, 2017, Bangalore, India
© 2017 Copyright is held by the owner/author(s).
ACM ISBN 978-1-4503-5037-2/17/06.
http://dx.doi.org/10.1145/3084381.3084423

Further research could be carried out to validate these findings across different standard methods like Multiple Regression and Structural Equation Modeling(SEM) with larger and diverse samples.

5. REFERENCES

[1] Chellappa, R. K., & Sin, R. G. 2005. Personalization versus privacy: An empirical examination of the online consumer's dilemma. *Information technology and management.* 6(2), 181-202.

[2] Malhotra, N. K., Kim, S. S., & Agarwal, J. 2004. Internet users' information privacy concerns (IUIPC): The construct, the scale, and a causal model. *Information systems research.* 15(4), 336-355.

[3] Tam, K., & Ho, S. 2006. Understanding the impact of web personalization on user information processing and decision outcomes. *MisQuarterly.* 865-890.

Privacy Protection Dashboard: A Study of Individual Cloud-Storage Users Information Privacy Protection Responses

Poster Abstract

Surya Karunagaran
Indian Institute of Technology Madras
IIT P.O., Chennai 600 036
India
ms13d201@smail.iitm.ac.in

Saji K Mathew
Indian Institute of Technology Madras
IIT P.O., Chennai 600 036
India
saji@iitm.ac.in

Franz Lehner
University of Passau
Room 261-262 P.O., Passau 94032
Germany
Fraz.Lehner@uni-passau.de

ABSTRACT

Cloud computing[1] services have gained a lot of attraction in the recent years, but the shift of data from user-owned desktops and laptops to cloud storage systems has led to serious data privacy implications for the users. Even though privacy notices supplied by the cloud vendors details the data practices and options to protect their privacy, the lengthy and free-flowing textual format of the notices are often difficult to comprehend by the users. Thus we propose a simplified presentation format for privacy practices and choices termed as "Privacy-Dashboard" based on Protection Motivation Theory (PMT) and we intend to test the effectiveness of presentation format using cognitive-fit theory. Also, we indirectly model the cloud privacy concerns using Item-Response Theory (IRT) model. We contribute to the information privacy literature by addressing the literature gap to develop privacy protection artifacts in order to improve the privacy protection behaviors of individual users. The proposed "privacy dashboard" would provide an easy-to-use choice mechanisms that allow consumers to control how their data is collected and used.

1 INTRODUCTION

Information privacy in its simplest form refers to the concept of controlling how one's personal information is acquired and used [1]. Privacy notices and privacy seals are introduced to inform users about the collection and choices they have in order to protect their information privacy. However, there is a general notion that the length of the notices has led to information asymmetry resulting in an adverse selection and unawareness of privacy choices [4]. In order to improve the privacy protection behaviour of the consumers, a greater control over the collection and use of personal data through simplified choices and

increased transparency are some of the best practices proposed by FTC (Federal Trade Commission) in the recent years.

Cloud storage is a service model in which the user data are stored and accessed over the internet. This service delivery model of the cloud has led to the transmission and storage of data across borders giving rise to security and privacy concerns. Thus in our study, we propose a privacy protection artifact called "Privacy Dashboard" for the protection and control of information privacy based on Protection Motivation Theory (PMT). We test how the proposed privacy dashboard influences the privacy protection behaviour of cloud storage user and also measure cloud users individual privacy concerns.

2 LITERATURE REVIEW

Information privacy literature in the recent years emphasizes researchers to build actual implementable tools to protect individual's information privacy. Protection Motivation Theory (PMT) is one such theory that explains and promotes individual protection behaviors [6].Central to PMT concept is that, an individual considering a potential threat assesses the likelihood of falling victim to the threat (Threat Susceptibility), the potential severity of the outcome (Threat Severity) and effectiveness of threat coping mechanism motivates individuals protection behavior[3]. There has been recent call for in research for effective presentation of threat and coping mechanism[1,3]. To address this gap we developed a privacy artifact called "Privacy-Dashboard" where the data practices in the privacy notices are equivalent to the threat susceptibility and threat severity. While the privacy choice options in the form of opt-in/outs are equivalent to that of the coping mechanisms of PMT.

In order to test the effectiveness of the privacy artifact, we use cognitive fit theory as the theoretical framework. It suggests that when both information format and the task emphasize the same type of information, a cognitive fit occurs which leads to faster and more accurate performance in decision making [7]. Specifically we investigate how the fit between Privacy-Dashboard format and tasks such as search time and recall of privacy information.

3 METHODOLOGY

Privacy policies of 15 different cloud service providers were analyzed using NLP techniques. From the policies, the "information types "or" data items, which are noun phrases associated with collection practice, were compared against all possible information types found in Information Type Lexicon [2]. Also, the opt-out choices and data practices were also extracted and compared with the existing opt-out choices lexicons. Privacy-Dashboard was designed using the results from the extraction techniques.

A 2^1 factorial design is proposed to be used with two presentation format; a free-flowing text format is compared with Privacy-Dashboard format in order to test and validate its effectiveness on the individual protection behaviour. Accuracy and time to decide on privacy choices were identified as dependent variables and the presentation formats are the independent variable in this study. Also, results from the list of attributes/choices set by users are intended to model the cloud privacy concern at an individual level using item response theory/latent trait model. Following Liu and Terzi work [5], we evaluated score for subjects' privacy concern based on the privacy control settings made by the users.

4 PRELIMINARY RESULTS

From this study, new data practices related to cloud services were identified and termed as "content information" apart from the exiting information type entities such as financial, personal, contact and technical information found in the literature. A small group was made to interact with the developed interface. Based on their feedback with minor modifications the design was retained as such. We found evidence that people generally do not understand the information presented in free flowing privacy policies and also do not enjoy reading them. Almost all the participants expressed interest to read privacy policy when shown in the dashboard format and also said they would use the controls to protect their privacy when offered in a collated form. The results would be further validated for statistical significance from a full-scale experimental study.

5 CONCLUSIONS

The goal of this study was to determine whether the availability and accessibility of privacy information and choices affects individuals' protection behaviour. This study has implemented a modified version of privacy policy grounded on the theoretical basis of PMT, thus attempting to bridge the long standing divide between theories and practice in the IS field of research. The results from our study will add to the existing knowledge base of studies dealing with effective information representation and privacy concern measurement. Existing research has focused on the effectiveness of presentation format and intentions to use protective choices. This study goes a step further to investigate the actual behaviour as opposed to intentions there by addressing the need to design theoretically based IS artifacts that can be used for privacy protection. The results from this study would also benefit cloud vendors, where highly privacy concerned user could be profiled and premium privacy controls could be offered to improve the trust and usage of cloud services.

REFERENCES

[1] France Bélanger and Robert E Crossler. 2011. Privacy in the Digital Age: A Review of Information Privacy Research in Information Systems. *MIS Quarterly* 35, 4: 1017–1041. DOI: https://doi.org/10.1159/000360196

[2] Jaspreet Bhatia and Travis D. Breaux. 2015. Towards an information type lexicon for privacy policies. In *8th International Workshop on Requirements Engineering and Law, RELAW 2015 – Proceedings*, 19–24. DOI: https://doi.org/10.1109/RELAW.2015.7330207

[3] R.E. Crossler. 2010. Protection Motivation Theory: Understanding Determinants to Backing Up Personal Data. In *System Sciences (HICSS), 2010 43rd Hawaii International Conference on*. DOI: https://doi.org/10.1109/HICSS.2010.311

[4] Kai-Lung Hui, Hock HaiTeo, and Sang-Yong Tom Lee. 2007. The Value of Privacy Assurance: An Exploratory Field Experiment. *MIS Quarterly* 31, 1: 19–33. DOI: https://doi.org/10.2307/25148779

[5] Kun Liu and EvimariaTerzi. 2009. A framework for computing the privacy scores of users in online social networks. In *Proceedings - IEEE International Conference on Data Mining, ICDM*, 288–297. DOI: https://doi.org/10.1109/ICDM.2009.21

[6] Ronald W. Rogers. 1975. A Protection Motivation Theory of Fear Appeals and Attitude Change. *The Journal of Psychology* 91, 1: 93–114. DOI: https://doi.org/10.1080/00223980.1975.9915803

[7] I Vessey and D Galletta. 1991. Cognitive fit: An empirical study of information acquisition. *Information Systems Research* 2, 1: 63–84. DOI: https://doi.org/10.1287/isre.2.1.63

Real-Time Decision-Making to Serve the Unbanked Poor in the Developing World

Poster Abstract

Lakshmi Mohan

University at Albany, State University of New York
Albany, NY, 12222, USA
lmohan@albany.edu

Devendra Potnis

University of Tennessee at Knoxville
1345 Circle Park Drive, Suite 451, Knoxville, TN, 37996, USA
dpotnis@utk.edu

ABSTRACT

The World Bank estimated in 2015 that 60% of the world's poor earning less than USD2.00 a day do not have a bank account or are unbanked. A major impediment to serve the unbanked poor is the high cost of the process of distributing small loans and collecting repayments from barely literate borrowers. This process requires loan officers to meet the poor at their door step, making it a people-intensive process requiring frequent face-to-face interaction. Real-time decision-making is a solution to address the key challenge experienced by banks when serving the unbanked poor in the developing word. Our poster is drawn from two case examples: Banco Azteca, a bank in Mexico, and Equitas Holdings Limited that makes small amounts of loans to unbanked poor in India. We focus on an Azteca's automated decision support system to serve low income people ignored by banks in Mexico, and a real-time performance dashboard custom-built by Equitas to improve the productivity of loan officers. Our analysis suggests that real-time decision making cannot enable banks to scale their operations for achieving significant social impact unless the following conditions are met: process, application of real time data, user friendly interfaces, and leadership by top management.

CCS CONCEPTS

• **Information systems** → Information systems applications → Decision support systems → Expert systems • **Social and professional topics** → Computing and business → Economic Impact

KEYWORDS

Real-time decision-making; Unbanked poor; Developing world

1 MOTIVATION & PROBLEM STATEMENT

Access to formal finance is essential to graduate out of poverty [1]. The World Bank estimated in 2015 that 60% of the world's poor earning less than USD2.00 a day do not have a bank account, or are unbanked [2]. Around 90 percent of the unbanked adult population in the world live in developing countries, where there are only eight bank branches per 100,000 adults compared to twenty-four in developed countries.

SIGMIS-CPR'17, June 21-23, 2017, Bangalore, India.
© 2017 Copyright is held by the owner/author(s).
ACM ISBN 978-1-4503-5037-2/17/06.
http://dx.doi.org/10.1145/3084381.3084425

For instance, in India, the country with the fourth-largest banking network in the world, 47% of the adult population did not have a bank account in 2015, resulting in 233 million unbanked households [3].

2 BACKGROUND LITERATURE

A major impediment to serving the unbanked poor is the high cost of the process of distributing small loans and collecting repayments from barely literate borrowers. This process requires loan officers to meet the poor at their doorstep, making it a people-intensive process requiring frequent face-to-face interaction. Banks cannot scale their operations to serve the unbanked poor in the developing world. The tiny profits from small loans or savings accounts with small balances, also make it unprofitable to serve the poor [4].

3 METHODS

Our research is based on two case examples: Banco Azteca, a bank in Mexico, and Equitas Holdings Limited, that makes small amounts of loans to unbanked poor in India. We focus on Azteca's automated decision support system to serve low income people ignored by banks in Mexico, and a real-time performance dashboard custom-built by Equitas to improve the productivity of loan officers. We collected data through field visits and face-to-face interviews with CEOs, CTOs, and other team members of Banco Azteca and Equitas. We triangulated secondary data in English and Spanish from multiple sources including, but not limited to, annual reports, business case studies, and organizational websites.

3.1 Banco Azteca, Mexico

Banco Azteca was the first bank to target the 70 million people not served by banks in Mexico. Azteca's retail banking business model involves the deployment of loan officers in the field, who use an automated decision support system that has enabled it to rapidly scale its operations. As of April 2016, the bank had over 4,000 branches, 20,000 employees, and 18 million customers [5].

Loan officers visit potential borrowers at their doorstep. Borrowers complete a simple application for credit and have to furnish only proof of address and proof of income to get the credit approved. If proof of income is not available, the bank's loan officer makes a home visit within 24 hours of the application to ascertain information to determine the borrower's eligibility for credit.

The interactive rules-based engine of the automated decision support system residing in Azteca's corporate operations center in Mexico City prompts the loan officer to ask a series of questions. These questions include the specific assets owned by the borrowers, such as stereos, DVD players, TV, and refrigerators, which serve as collateral for the loan. The answers to the questions are entered by the loan officer into his handheld computer, which transmits the information to the corporate system. The system calculates the total resale value of the assets and determines the loan amount, which should be less than half the resale value, and the weekly repayment schedule. This information is transmitted to the mobile device of the loan officer who conveys it to the borrower. If the borrower accepts the offer, he can pick up the check at a local store. The loan officer also records the serial numbers of the assets like the stereo, DVD player, etc. on his handheld computer.

3.2 Equitas, India

Equitas provides small amounts of loans, usually less than USD100, so that the unbanked poor in India can generate income and improve their livelihoods. This young financial institution launched in December 2007 and rapidly scaled its outreach to serve 2.3 million customers by March 2015. Equitas built a customized real-time performance monitoring dashboard that was designed to satisfy the requirements of management for actionable, readily available information [6]. The core of the custom-designed system was a dashboard to alert corporate and branch management about problems in the efficiency of the loan officers' meetings with customers at their doorstep. The dashboard displayed three key metrics—meeting attendance in the customers' villages, loan collections, and the ending time of the meeting- all based on data sent by loan officers. Loan officers sent the data for these metrics within fifteen minutes after the meeting by using text messages on their mobile phones. Exception reports by branches with regard to attendance rates, collection problems, and timely management of meetings alerted management to problems in the field for timely corrective action.

The CEO periodically checked the corporate dashboard screen and sent SMS messages to branches and loan officers if he noticed problems in the field operations, especially with regard to collections. The rationale for the real-time feature of the performance dashboard, analogous to the real-time system used by stockbrokers, is the action taken by the CEO within fifteen minutes of the close of a meeting. Corrective action could be taken without any delay in the meetings scheduled for the rest of the day. The fact that the CEO was himself using the dashboard sent a strong signal to branch management, as well as the frontlines, that Equitas was a company that used analysis of data to inform its decisions [6].

4 RESULTS

Our data analysis suggests that real-time decision-making is a solution to address the key challenge experienced by banks when serving the unbanked poor in the developing word. Real-time decision making cannot enable banks to scale their operations for achieving significant social impact unless the following conditions are met: process, application of real time data, user friendly interfaces, and leadership by top management.

4.1 Process

Banks should design a customer-centric business process wherein financial services are offered to the unbanked poor at their doorstep. "Door-step banking" is a high-touch and, hence, a high-cost delivery channel which circumvents the difficulty of the poor having to travel to a bank for financial services [6]. With a door-step bank, the bank comes to the customer through the bank's loan officers, who travel to villages in order to disburse the initial

loan to customers and collect repayments in periodic installments, usually weekly or biweekly. Banks should recruit and train loan officers from the areas they would serve, which could keep the turn-over rate of loan officers low. Local loan officers could also build trust among potential customers for "outside" banks.

4.2 Application of Real-Time Data

Banks should invest in real-time decision making only if their business process requires them to make decisions in real time. If decisions are not made in real time, investments in related information systems for capturing and processing real-time data cannot create desired business value. It is important to note that real-time decisions do not necessarily have to be financial. Real-time operational decisions can also help banks rapidly scale their operations as Equitas did. The use of a real-time performance dashboard was instrumental in changing the management process of Equitas to that of a data-driven company.

4.3 User-Friendly Interfaces for Loan Officers

Banks can deploy mobile technologies like PDAs with user-friendly interfaces and pre-populated fields, which are easy even for semi-literate loan officers to use. The ability to use pre-populated fields could save time of loan officers when entering data, as well as reduce data entry errors.

4.4 Leadership by Top Management

The top management of banks should use systems for real-time decision-making to signal the importance of such systems to their employees like the CEO of Equitas did. In addition, the Chief Technology Officer was a member of the board of directors, which attests to the importance that the CEO placed on analytical systems and the alignment of analytical systems with corporate strategy.

5 IMPLICATIONS

Analytical systems like automated decision support system and real-time performance monitoring dashboard can provide a competitive advantage in the form of real-time decision-making. Real-time decision-making has the potential to help businesses mitigate operational inefficiency, a major impediment to serving the unbanked poor in the developing world. The analytical systems can be instrumental for achieving rapid scaling.

REFERENCES

[1] P. Honohan. 2006. Household financial assets in the process of development. Policy, World Bank Policy Research Working Paper No. WPS 3965. Washington, DC: World Bank.

[2] World Bank. 2015. Massive drop in number of unbanked. (April 15, 2015). Retrieved from http://www.worldbank.org/en/news/press-release/2015/04/15/massive-drop-in-number-of-unbanked-says-new-report.

[3] The Hindu. 2015. 175 million new bank a/c in India in three years: World Bank. (April 16, 2015). Retrieved from http://www.thehindu.com/business/Industry/175-million-new-bank-ac-in-india-in-three-years-world-bank/article7109166.ece.

[4] S. Khavul. 2010. Microfinance: Creating opportunities for the poor? ACAD MANAGE PERSPECT 24, 3 (Aug. 2010), 57-71.

[5] Banco Azteca. 2016. Banco Azteca website. Retrieved February 2016 from http://www.bancoazteca.com.mx.

[6] L. Mohan, D. Potnis, and S. Alter. 2013. Information systems to support "door-step banking": Enabling scalability of microfinance to serve more of the poor at the bottom of the pyramid. Communications of the AIS 33 (2013), 423-442. Retrieved from http://aisel.aisnet.org/cais/vol33/iss1/25/.

A Public-Private-Social Ecosystem: An Interdisciplinary Framework for Cybersecurity Capacity Building[*]

Poster Abstract

Rajni Goel
School of Business, Howard University
2600 6th St., Washington DC, USA
rgoel@howard.edu

Vineet Kumar
Cyber Peace Foundation
Ranchi Jharkhand, India
president@cyberpeacefoundation.org

[1]KEYWORDS

Cyber Safety; Cybersecurity; Interdisciplinary

1 MOTIVATION

"Cyberspace" has become a common language term societies today. This infrastructure, which provides global interconnectivity of digital information and communications, is now woven into the daily lives of members of modern society. As the technology has transformed the global economy, provided ease of functionality and seamlessly connected people, so have the cybersecurity threats and risks it has posed. The focus must now be on creating a secure and safe digital society. We claim that this is not just a technical problem, but rather multi-pronged beast: it is an integrated issue requiring solutions spanning management, organization, cultural and technology. We believe that cultivating a safe, secure and prosperous cyberspace requires creating a complete ecosystem involving collaboration and synergy among the four main pillars of society: Academia, Government, Industry and Social Civil Societies. One approach and recommendation for Cybersecurity capacity buildings in India involved a Public-Private-Social Partnership; this is the key pillar for Cybersecurity Development in India.

2 PROPOSED FRAMEWORK

2.1 Background

To better understand the current state of Cybersecurity in India, we engaged in a wide range activities to gather data on and better understand the current state and need in the capacity building of cyber security education in India. This included a multitude of interviews, seminar attendances, lectures, and events involving Cyber Industry leaders, Intelligence and Technology officials in Indian Government, Academia, Think Tanks and Social Service groups.

During the 6 months of intense research, it became apparent that India is optimally positioned for creating cyber-security talent. It has the young force ripe to be the cyber saviors of this nation. India has experienced tremendous opportunities, progression and growth in the technology sector. The country continues to provide much of the global Information Technology (IT) sourcing, has a newly government established "Digital India" and "Smart City" initiatives and is experiencing an increasing amount of growth of smartphone usage and e-commerce business.

For example, we know that India's vision of innovation and indigenous IP for shared prosperity includes the new 300,000 smart phones, which are forecasted to enter the market in next 2 years. To prevent malicious and improper usage of these phones requires a holistic campaign for Cybersecurity awareness and a strategic plan for what should correctly be promoted as a "Secure Digital India." The cybersecurity skills shortage and lack of public awareness is impacting organizations throughout India, with employers reporting difficulties hiring skilled candidates and preparing for cybersecurity threats.

2.2 Methods

Our proposed cyber ecosystem model centers on creating societal cyber security clusters that build cyber capacity, cyber-awareness, cyber-innovation and cyber-safety by implementing a multi-dimensional concept. This involves creating partnerships between Industry/Academia and Government and introducing them to analyzing Cyber Security Risk as a cross-functional, collective strategy (including policy). Public and private sector entities must develop a strategic, legal, policy and technological platforms that mandate participation from all 4 pillars to assist in building capacity in all areas of cybersecurity; this includes promoting cyber safety and security though an awareness campaign. We have developed a prototype of this ecosystem; an implementable holistic interdisciplinary framework for India.

Below, we describe a theoretical framework of the people, processes and organizational structure necessary to institutionalize a interdisciplinary cybersecurity capacity building agenda.

2.2 Cyber Cluster Ecosystem

The notion is to create a *Cyber Cluster ecosystem per state* where all 4 pillars of society collaborate in a multi-dimensional framework with a common central strategic, legal and policy governance oversight. The mission is to create a set of Best Practices in which each pillar seamlessly contributes to the cyber awareness, education, safety and advances of all citizens within their society.

1. Civil Service Societies (NGO): responsible for cyber-security awareness within the local communities. This includes seminars and programs creating a culture of cyber-hygiene (such as responsible use of mobile technologies, digital payments, privacy, cyber bullying, cyber victimization, etc.)

2. Government: responsible for communication with the federal authorities to influence adequate and proper funding of cyber innovation and education programs that align with the local cultural climate and for the creation of cyber policy and national cyber defense strategies. Local police and law authorities will be trained, using resources within the Cluster organizations (Academia and Industry), to respond to cyber crime and conduct proper cyber forensics.

3. Academia: responsible of creating a cyber-enabled workforce. Will train future leaders to be better security managers, will train and educate local law enforcement and government officials to detect and prevent cyber crime and incidences. Academia will work with industry to train the trainers and innovate the leading security products.

4. Industry: responsible for serving the consumers in society by developing the secure and safe technology, products, processes and services. This includes reducing the data breach and cyber crime risks to customers healthcare and financial data, to securing digital payments and providing human rights of privacy of customers records.

3 PROTOTYPES

To exemplify the framework, we have outlined a prototype for E-Raksha Research Center in India and Cyber-Security Curriculum building initiatives (including experiential learning and awareness strategies) as components of the *Public-Private-Social Ecosystem*.

The Cyber Peace Foundation has collaborated to set up e-Raksha Research Centers that will train students and local citizens on cybersecurity. The e-Raksha Center has four sections of operation – cybersecurity, cyber forensics, innovation and incubation. Cybersecurity will seek to create awareness about the cyber world and will provide people will the tools to practice cybersecurity in their daily lives. Cyber forensics will help various investigative agencies combat cyber-crime in an efficient and innovative manner. The Innovation lab will research on areas like robotics, artificial intelligence and upcoming technologies. The Incubation department will provide support and mentorship to different startups on Cyber Security. The lab will also aid in training school children, who are tech savvy but stray on the wrong path, on the correct uses of the Internet. The lab is an effort to tackle incidents of rising cyber-crimes.

Also, a helpline will be set up which will aid callers in tackling cyber-crimes. Through this effort, small children will also be educated on the cyber-space, cyber-threats and cybersecurity. Children as young as eight will be taught lessons on cybersecurity and ethical hacking. A majority of ethical hackers and Bug Bounty Hunters in the country learn their skills at a very young age, and some renowned ethical hackers are still teenagers. So, the idea is to nurture kids and prepare them to strengthen the country's network of cyber experts.

4 CONCLUSIONS

Collectively, the four agencies could increase cyber capacity of local communities by helping collect data by administering digital literacy surveys and cyber-hygiene surveys. Also, they could develop business models for cyber education and cyber awareness programs and reduce corruption in funding by holding one and another responsible for their actions.

Inbound Technical Support in Contact Centers of Northern Mindanao, Philippines: Toward a Grounded Theory

Doctoral Consortium

Meldie Apag
College of Computer Studies
De La Salle University
Manila Philippines
meldie_apag@dlsu.edu.ph

ABSTRACT

The contact center industry is a vast and rapidly expanding information technology-enabled services (ITES) industry. Deloitte has identified the Philippines together with India as the top contact center destinations of Asia. IBM Global Services has also singled out the Philippines as one of Asia's global leader in business process outsourcing (BPO), the biggest revenue-earning subsector of which is the contact center subsector. This study aim to explore, using the Glaserian or classic grounded theory method (GTM), the main concern of the ITES workforce in contact centers, particularly inbound technical support representatives, and how they resolve their main concern. GTM goes beyond the descriptive approach of most qualitative methods by generating from data a theory of the substantive area. The theory that will be generated by this research can be used to inform the development of systems, processes, structures, and policies that will support inbound technical support representatives.

CCS CONCEPTS

• **Social and professional topics**~Computing profession • **Social and professional topics**~Employment issues • **Social and professional topics**~Computing occupations

KEYWORDS

Contact Center; Business Process Outsourcing (BPO); Inbound Technical Support; Glaserian Grounded Theory Method (GTM)

1 MOTIVATION AND PROBLEM STATEMENT

Today, the contact center industry, an information technology-enabled services (ITES) industry, is vast and rapidly expanding in

Permission to make digital or hard copies of part or all of this work for personal or classroom use is granted without fee provided that copies are not made or distributed for profit or commercial advantage and that copies bear this notice and the full citation on the first page. Copyrights for third-party components of this work must be honored. For all other uses, contact the Owner/Author.

SIGMIS-CPR '17, June 21-23, 2017, Bangalore, India
© 2017 Copyright is held by the owner/author(s).
ACM ISBN 978-1-4503-5037-2/17/06.
http://dx.doi.org/10.1145/3084381.3084432

terms of technology, workforce, and economic scope [1,2]. This industry is finding that interacting with their customers via technology can be a significant challenge [3]. Hence, the people and technology used in ITES organizations, which can greatly affect customer service, warrant attention. It is important to study the persons in an organization since by conducting research in its social and historical context researchers are able to obtain a good appreciation of the work of people as active builders of their own physical and social reality [4]. Thereby, this study aim to explore on the main concern of inbound technical support representatives of contact centers in Northern Mindanao, Philippines, and how they resolve their main concern.

2 BACKGROUND LITERATURE

A contact center is a coordinated system of people, processes, technologies, and strategies that provides access to information, resources and expertise through appropriate channels of communication that enable interactions to create value for the customer and organization. It may include one or more online call centers and other types of customer contacts, such as voice calls and data applications like electronic mail, web-based chat, instant messaging, and web pages, among others.

The Philippines is a major provider of front- and back-office support such as voice, electronic mail, order processing, shared services, and many more, to global businesses. Its ITES industry is the 'Sunshine Industry' of the country because of its massive expansion over the last ten years [5]. The 2016 IBM Global Location Trends Annual Report situates the Philippines as one of Asia's global leader in business support functions in shared services and BPO [6]. Deloitte (2016) has also identified the Philippines together with India as the top contact center destinations of Asia [7]. According to Contact Center Association of the Philippines (CCAP), the Philippines is Asia's contact center capital, having more than 600,000 contact center workers in more than 85 contact center companies distinguished between foreign-owned, in-sourced, and Filipino-owned contact centers [2]. Further, Cagayan de Oro City is the regional center and business hub of Northern Mindanao, where Mindanao, one of the main islands of the Philippines, shall venture into positioning itself as the BPO Hub in the South [5,8]. It has more than 20 contact centers including major players in the contact center industry that employs thousands of contact center representatives [8].

3 METHODS

The Glaserian or classic grounded theory method (GTM) will be used to generate a theory for the substantive area of inbound technical support that deals with customer inquiries and technical assistance [9]. A theory is a set of relationships that offers a plausible explanation of the phenomenon that will provide a comprehensive, coherent, and simplest model for linking diverse and unrelated facts in a useful and pragmatic way [10].

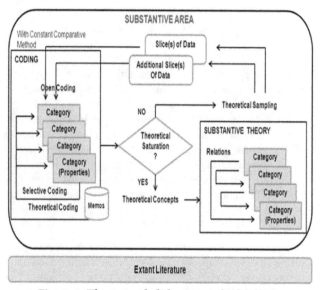

Figure 1: The grounded theory method (GTM).

In GTM, data collection will use theoretical sampling to determine where to go for information and who next to talk to, and only when no new patterns or possible categories emerging from the data could be found or the point of theoretical saturation, is the process of theoretical sampling ceased and sample size completed [11,12]. The constant comparative method will be used to explore the similarities and differences within the data collected and offer a guide for collecting other data. With this analysis, the basic properties of each category will be defined, relationships between categories will be identified, and the identification of patterns will be facilitated. The process continues until the core category is identified that which accounts for most of the variation in the patterns of behavior [11]. Further, coding is the process of breaking down the data into distinct units of meaning for analysis and systematically re-evaluating them for their inter-relationships enabling the researcher to move the data to a higher level of abstraction [11,12]. Memos will be used to record the analysis of data that maps emerging categories, properties and theory. Theoretical sorting is the key to formulating the theory, where it is the act of arranging a huge pile of memos into an integrated theory. Finally, as the analysis process undertaken began to yield a number of themes, concepts, and relationships, the researcher will compare these with the extant literature, asking what it is similar to, what did it contradict, and why [11]. The relevant literature will be woven in to put the theory in a scholarly context.

4 EXPECTED RESULTS

This study will provide new insights into the experiences, interactions, and outcomes of the emotional, cognitive, and behavioral relation between the individual inbound technical support representative and customer during and after service encounters and between representatives as well. In the process, this study is expected to present directions for theoretically informed main concern of representatives influenced by the contact center industry and its customers, and address how representatives resolve their main concern.

5 IMPLICATIONS

In the use of GTM in this study, it can contribute to richer methodological understanding of grounded theory approach to research through the identification of useful theoretical conceptualizations based on a thorough methodical and comprehensive approach to data collection and analysis. This study will help improve the use of the method and to the quality and dissemination of grounded theory research outcomes as such that grounded theory studies have been used in information systems studies. Moreover, the theory that will be generated by this research can be used to inform the development of systems, processes, structures, and policies. And because grounded theories are not tied to any preexisting theory, the grounded theory that will be generated is a novelty and has the potential for innovative discoveries in areas of research.

REFERENCES

[1] Association of Government Contact Center Professionals (AGCCP) (2016). http://www.agccp.org/.
[2] Contact Center Association of the Philippines (CCAP) (2016). Serving the World. http://www.ccap.ph/index.php/about-ccap/.
[3] Zeithaml, V.A., Parasuraman, A., and Malhotra, A. (2002). Service Quality Delivery Through Websites: A Critical Review of Extant Knowledge. Journal of the Academy of Marketing Science. 30 (4), 362-375.
[4] Orlikowski, W. and Iacono, S. (2001). Research Commentary: Desperately Seeking the 'IT' in IT Research- A Call to Theorizing the IT Artifact. Information Systems Research. 12 (2), 121-134.
[5] Ecumenical Institute of Labor Education and Research, Inc. (EILER) (2016). Modern Day Sweatshops in the Service Sector: Business Process Outsourcing (BPO) in the Philippines.
[6] IBM Global Services (2016). 2016 Global Location Trends Annual Report. IBM Global Business Services. October 2016.
[7] Deloitte (2016). Global Contact Center Survey Executive Summary. Deloitte Development. June 2016.
[8] Philippine Economic Zone Authority (PEZA) (2010). http://peza.gov.ph/.
[9] Glaser, B. and Strauss, A. (1967). The Discovery of Grounded Theory: Strategies for Qualitative Research. Chicago, IL: Aldine Atherton.
[10] Yin, R.K. (2010). Qualitative Research From Start to Finish. Guilford Press, 2010.
[11] Glaser, B. (2003). The Grounded Theory Perspective II: Descriptions Remodeling of Grounded Theory Methodology. Sociology Press, Mill Valley, CA.
[12] Fernandez, W. D. (2004). "The Grounded Theory Method and Case Study Data in IS Research: Issues and Design". In Information Systems Foundations Workshop: Constructing and Criticising. Vo. 1: pp. 43-59.

Impact of Product Review Summarization and Personalization on Online Consumers' Decisions: An Experimental Study

Doctoral Consortium Proposal

Mahesh Balan U

Department of Management Studies,
Indian Institute of Technology Madras,
Chennai, Tamil Nadu – 600036, India
u.maheshbalan@gmail.com

ABSTRACT

E-commerce platforms have a plethora of information available online in the form of online product reviews and product ratings. Although these product reviews are very helpful to consumers for making their buying decisions, it becomes very difficult to extract relevant information pertaining to product features. In this study, we extend personalization to online product reviews by integrating literature from information systems, computer science and social psychology to understand how task complexity varies in different information environments. In a controlled laboratory experiment users took buying decisions in three different information environments: unstructured voluminous reviews, structured with aspect level summarization of reviews and personalized information by providing personalization based on the stated preferences of the user.

Keywords

Online word of mouth, summarized reviews, personalization, e-commerce, cognitive efforts, consumer behavior

1. MOTIVATION AND RESEARCH PROBLEM

The effect of online product reviews on buying decisions and sales has been extensively studied in prior studies (Ghose & Ipeirotis., 2007; Archak, Ghose, & Ipeirotis, 2011). However, the multitude of alternatives, the dynamic nature of reviews and the degree of uncertainty associated with the review information have made the task of buying online a challenging task. Based on this context, we ask the following questions –

1)   How could we present online product reviews in a format that would enable the consumers to make their buying decision with ease?

2)   How would manipulating the format of review information presentation impact the decision process of the consumers?

2. BACKGROUND LITERATURE

Our research can be considered as an extension of (Archak, Ghose, & Ipeirotis, 2011) who study the pricing power of product reviews, (Tam & Ho, 2006) who studied the effect of personalization on consumers' buying decision process and, (Jiang & Benbasat, 2007) who evaluated the impact of different presentation formats on buying task complexity.

3. METHODS

This study adopts a mixed-methods approach which involve a laboratory controlled multi-factor experiment followed by a focus group discussion. The experiment involved three different e-commerce websites. First, the unstructured information environment which has voluminous product reviews in an unstructured format; second, the structured information environment that has an aspect level summarization of the reviews with average sentiment scores extracted from the review for every product feature and third, personalized information which has personalized product listing based on consumers' stated preferences and review information. Before the experiment, product features were extracted from more than 11,000 reviews provided by an online retailer and an aspect level summarization was developed based on average sentiment scores of every product feature. The clickstream data for the entire duration of the experiment was recorded and the cognitive efforts of the user were captured using three variables: product clicks, number of changes in product cart and time.

4. RESULTS

Our analyses showed that the cognitive efforts of the users and hence, the complexity of the buying task were significantly related to the information presentation format. The personalized information environment had the lowest cognitive effort. However, the group that had structured reviews in the form of a review summarization had higher cognitive efforts than the group which had unstructured raw textual reviews, which went against our hypothesis. Our focus group discussion provided an explanation to this behavior by observing that users when exposed to information overload simplify the decision process by adopting some heuristic to make their buying decision due to the limited information processing capacity of the working memory (Kahneman, 1973; Payne, 1976). This study contributes to information systems literature by proposing a product review based personalization strategy in e-commerce.

5. REFERENCES

[1] Archak, N., Ghose, A., & Ipeirotis, P. 2011. Deriving the pricing power of product features by mining consumer reviews. *Management Science* 57, 8 (2011), 1485-1509.

[2] Ghose, A., & Ipeirotis., P. 2007. Designing novel review ranking systems: predicting the usefulness and impact of reviews. *International Conference on Electronic Commerce 2007 (Minneapolis, MN, USA, 2007),* 303-310.

[3] Jiang, Z., & Benbasat, I. 2007. The effects of presentation formats and task complexity on online consumers' product understanding. *Mis Quarterly* (2007), 475-500.

[4] Kahneman, D. 1973. *Attention and effort.* Englewood Cliffs, NJ: Prentice-Hall.

[5] Payne, J. 1976. Task complexity and contingent processing in decision making: An information search and protocol analysis. *Organizational behavior and human performance* (1976), 366-387.

[6] Tam, K., & Ho, S. 2006. Understanding the impact of web personalization on user information processing and decision outcomes. *Mis Quarterly* (2006), 865-890.

2

Virtual Communities and User Participation

Doctoral Consortium Proposal

Ruochen Liao
State University of New York at Buffalo
rliao2@buffalo.edu

1 MOTIVATION AND PROBLEM STATEMENT

Information system is the extension of human society in the digital world. Technology is largely defined by the person using it, and this revelation rapidly grew alongside with the proliferation of personal computers in our daily life. Information system has long exceeded the function as a point-to-point communication tool, and becomes a vibrant social platform that carries contents created by individual users and facilitates sophisticated social interactions between large groups of people. The ability for users to mold and shape this process to customize their virtual experience also affects other users [1, 2]. A fundamental assumption of contemporary group research is that individual attitudes and behavior is affected by group context influences, even though other members may not be physically present [3].

Therefore, the defining characteristic of this new era is that user participation becomes a major determinant of quality of information, and UGCs can have much far-reaching rippling effect in the virtual community than any message designated at a specific recipient [4, 5]. Using the example of an online forum, a user may not be actively participating in any of the threads, but the number of participating users, the quality of the discussions, and the friendliness of the community would all influence the perceived informational value of the forum to the user. Similar to the way that social context can affect an individual, the internet has become a virtual community where the user is being influenced by other users both directly and indirectly.

We identify three critical ways that service provider can influence the flow of virtual communities, being *facilitate*, *convey*, and *filter*. The facilitating role of service provider refers to the ability to encourage or motivate the participants to adopt IS usage and actively engage in it. Apart from system features, the presence of other users in the system can be an important motivator for user engagement.

For example, users of online forums are only motivated to post new threads when they perceive that there are other active users on the forum and they are interacting through discussion threads, without social interaction, the forum will eventually wither and cease to attract users. Secondly, virtual communities can convey the social context to individual users. Users can obtain a certain level of social support and social satisfaction through online interaction, and it is especially important for disadvantaged groups such as autistic, older or other socially impaired people. And lastly, like offline society, the presence of fake or harmful information is inevitable in a virtual community. From social rumors, hate crime, cyber bully, to phishing, fake product reviews, and privacy breaches, how to filter the information and prevent the detrimental effect on user experience have become a prevalent problem in the field of IS [6, 7]. We intend to examine these three aspects in three respective studies.

2 BACKGROUND LITERATURE

Following the years after these classical theories were developed, the increasing ubiquity of technology has greatly changed the way information systems are used. The most important change is the role of the users and how information is generated. Users have evolved from purely passive consumers under a fixed service framework designed by the providers, to become the most prominent content contributors [8]. From simple forums, Q&A communities, to social media, and pooled resource hubs like YouTube and Wikipedia, users are increasingly being drawn by the quantity and variety of User generated contents (UGC), and the technological aspect of the website becomes a supporting role in the backstage. Even in some of the fields where the provider–consumer relationship remain relatively unchanged, such as e-commerce and TV/video streaming, UGCs have been present in the form of feedback, comments and reviews [9-12]

Research in IS has mirrored this trend, a diverse stream of studies have focused on the importance of user participation, such as content contribution, knowledge management, system design and implementation [13-19]. The service provider is the bridging node that connects multitude of users, while contributors and users are two sides of the same coin, participants may assume the role of either or both at any time point (sharing vs. acquiring information).

SIGMIS-CPR '17, June 21-23, 2017, Bangalore, India
© 2017 Copyright is held by the owner/author(s).
ACM ISBN 978-1-4503-5037-2/17/06.
http://dx.doi.org/10.1145/3084381.3084430

3 METHODS

In the first study, we propose to use gamification to capture the effect of social interaction as a motivation for user engagement. Gamification is the process of adding games or game-like elements to a non-game task in order to encourage participation and engagement [20]. We utilize a unique dataset at a SMART-enabled science museum open to all visitors, and employing a leaderboard to one of the interactive exhibits to display the highest scoring user in a specific learning task. We expect that the leaderboard will serve as internal motivation for accomplishment and reputation. We create several indicators of user engagement (average number of interactions, average score, rate of achievement, and subsequent web account creation), and examine the time series data to determine if gamification was associated with differences in outcomes between the pre- and post-gamification periods in a sample of 50,833 consumers.

We intend to use geriatric population as the target of the second study, as the social context conveyed by the virtual community can help older people to , and avoid becoming marginalized in society [15]. For senior users, changes in the salience of goals at different life stages may result in changes in preferences for social interactions. Because of the psychological need to feel embedded in a larger social group [21, 22], maintaining a healthy level of social network ties is critical for the emotional and physiological well-being. Through social interactions over IS platforms, it supports self-actualization and social needs of the senior population, and allow passing on of knowledge and taking responsibility for future generations. We collected survey from 235 users aged above 55 in one of the largest online community in China, and capture the important events in their life (e.g. living condition, health status, marriage status, and working status), and study the impact of virtual community usage based on their social and psychological needs.

In the third study, we adopted Signaling theory from marketing literature to breakdown the cognitive process of buyers when they face a mixture of true and fake advertisements and guarantees in the context of ecommerce, and how they perceive the signals to be honest and true. We posit that *Social Presence* signals from reviewers in the feedback system possesses the bonding ability that makes the cost/difficulty in sending fake signals prohibitively high in given feedback system. Research has shown that when users perceive that they belong to a group and their action is being observed, they display conforming behavior that are less likely to draw disagreement from other group members [23], and even take actions to defend the norms and beliefs of the group [24]. The idea is that benevolent information will eventually "weed out" harmful information by the unanimous action of the users in the community.

4 IMPLICATIONS

There has been increasing attention from both researchers and practitioners on the proactive role of users in shaping the unique online climate. However, the diverse nature of social interaction makes it difficult to summarize all user behaviors under a single unifying theory. By identifying the information systems as a node where individual users are both influencing and influenced by other users, we wish to shed light on how system designers and service providers can better leverage the social characteristics of the user community in the place of functions that are either difficult or expensive for IS system to achieve.

REFERENCES

[1] Susarla, A., Oh, J.-H. and Tan, Y. Social networks and the diffusion of user-generated content: Evidence from YouTube. *Information Systems Research*, 23, 1 (2012), 23-41.

[2] Goh, K.-Y., Heng, C.-S. and Lin, Z. Social media brand community and consumer behavior: Quantifying the relative impact of user-and marketer-generated content. *Information Systems Research*, 24, 1 (2013), 88-107.

[3] Lerner, J. S. and Tetlock, P. E. Accounting for the effects of accountability. *Psychological bulletin*, 125, 2 (1999), 255.

[4] Bakshy, E., Rosenn, I., Marlow, C. and Adamic, L. *The role of social networks in information diffusion*. ACM, City, 2012.

[5] Stieglitz, S. and Dang-Xuan, L. Emotions and information diffusion in social media—sentiment of microblogs and sharing behavior. *Journal of Management Information Systems*, 29, 4 (2013), 217-248.

[6] Dellarocas, C. *Immunizing online reputation reporting systems against unfair ratings and discriminatory behavior*. ACM, City, 2000.

[7] Jindal, N. and Liu, B. *Review spam detection*. ACM, City, 2007.

[8] He, J. and King, W. R. The role of user participation in information systems development: implications from a meta-analysis. *Journal of Management Information Systems*, 25, 1 (2008), 301-331.

[9] Dellarocas, C. The digitization of word of mouth: Promise and challenges of online feedback mechanisms. *Management science*, 49, 10 (2003), 1407-1424.

[10] Chevalier, J. A. and Mayzlin, D. The effect of word of mouth on sales: Online book reviews. *Journal of marketing research*, 43, 3 (2006), 345-354.

[11] Mudambi, S. M. and Schuff, D. What makes a helpful review? A study of customer reviews on Amazon. com. *MIS quarterly*, 34, 1 (2010), 185-200.

[12] Ba, S. and Pavlou, P. A. Evidence of the effect of trust building technology in electronic markets: Price premiums and buyer behavior. *MIS quarterly* (2002), 243-268.

[13] Rui, H. and Whinston, A. Information or attention? An empirical study of user contribution on Twitter. *Information Systems and e-Business Management*, 10, 3 (2012), 309-324.

[14] Tang, Q., Gu, B. and Whinston, A. B. Content contribution for revenue sharing and reputation in social media: A dynamic structural model. *Journal of Management Information Systems*, 29, 2 (2012), 41-76.

[15] Chiu, C.-M., Hsu, M.-H. and Wang, E. T. Understanding knowledge sharing in virtual communities: An integration of social capital and social cognitive theories. *Decision support systems*, 42, 3 (2006), 1872-1888.

[16] Hendriks, P. Why share knowledge? The influence of ICT on the motivation for knowledge sharing. *Knowledge and process management*, 6, 2 (1999), 91.

[17] Bock, G.-W., Zmud, R. W., Kim, Y.-G. and Lee, J.-N. Behavioral intention formation in knowledge sharing: Examining the roles of extrinsic motivators, social-psychological forces, and organizational climate. *MIS quarterly* (2005), 87-111.

[18] Hartwick, J. and Barki, H. Explaining the role of user participation in information system use. *Management science*, 40, 4 (1994), 440-465.

[19] Barki, H. and Hartwick, J. Measuring user participation, user involvement, and user attitude. *Mis Quarterly* (1994), 59-82.

[20] Deterding, S., Dixon, D., Khaled, R. and Nacke, L. *From game design elements to gamefulness: defining gamification*. ACM, City, 2011.

[21] Baumeister, R. F. and Leary, M. R. The need to belong: desire for interpersonal attachments as a fundamental human motivation. *Psychological bulletin*, 117, 3 (1995), 497.

[22] Snowden, L. R. Social embeddedness and psychological well-being among African Americans and Whites. *American Journal of Community Psychology*, 29, 4 (2001), 519-536.

[23] Vance, A., Lowry, P. B. and Eggett, D. Using accountability to reduce access policy violations in information systems. *Journal of Management Information Systems*, 29, 4 (2013), 263-290.

[24] Terry, D. J. and Hogg, M. A. Group norms and the attitude-behavior relationship: A role for group identification. *Personality and Social Psychology Bulletin*, 22, 8 (1996), 776-793.

Lessons on Value Creation From the Open Source Phenomenon: Understanding the Impact of Work Structures, Contracts and Digital Platforms*

Doctoral Consortium

Poonacha K. Medappa
HEC Paris
1 Rue de la Libération
78350 Jouy en Josas Cedex
France
poonacha.medappa@hec.edu

CCS CONCEPTS

•**Information systems** → **Open source software** •**Applied computing** → **Psychology** • **Applied computing** → **Economics**

KEYWORDS

Open source software; FLOSS; structures of work; open source license; motivation; superposition

ACM Reference format:

P. K. Medappa. 2017. Lessons on Value Creation From the Open Source Phenomenon: Understanding the Impact of Work Structures, Contracts and Digital Platforms. In *Proceedings of ACM SIGMIS-CPR'17, June 21–23, 2017, Bangalore, India.*
DOI: http://dx.doi.org/10.1145/3084381.3084436

1 MOTIVATION AND PROBLEM STATEMENT

In the current digitally enabled collaborative environment, free (libre) and open source software (FLOSS) projects have become ubiquitous. Increasingly, both individuals as well as organizations are adopting FLOSS as a viable mode of software development because of the multifarious advantages it offers with respect to evolved coordination and motivational mechanisms. Further, organizations are discovering that FLOSS projects are often able to create software that surpasses proprietary software in terms of quality and functionality. For example, in a 2013 study of 750 C/C++ FLOSS projects, it was found that the quality of FLOSS projects surpassed that of proprietary software [1]. Prior research has examined several aspects related to FLOSS project value and has laid the groundwork for a deeper enquiry into the subject (e.g. Crowston, Wei, & Howison, 2012; Howison & Crowston, 2014). By building

SIGMIS-CPR '17, June 21-23, 2017, Bangalore, India
© 2017 Copyright is held by the owner/author(s).
ACM ISBN 978-1-4503-5037-2/17/06.
http://dx.doi.org/10.1145/3084381.3084436

on such research, our aim is to move this salient agenda forward, which we believe will be valuable to both research and practice.

Digital transformation (eg. 3D printing, creation of sharing economy) across industries has led to non-IS disciplines becoming increasingly information oriented. This in-turn has created opportunities for organizations from non-IS industries to adopt practices that have been successful in the IS discipline. In specific, the success of FLOSS projects in creating software of high quality and innovativeness at a low cost have begun to attract considerable attention from other disciplines. For example, with biology increasingly becoming an information orientated science, some have suggested that what worked for open source software might be part of the answer to the spiraling cost of drug R&D [4]. While there is a desire to adopt the FLOSS style of development across non-IS industries, we are yet to see the kind of open source transformation that overwhelmed the IS industry in the early 2000's [5,6]. This leads us to the central question that this dissertation will try to answer – *What lessons can IS and non-IS organizations learn from the value creation mechanisms of FLOSS communities?*

2 BACKGROUND LITERATURES

FLOSS communities are nothing without the contributing participants and the question of what motivates contribution has been a central theme in studies of FLOSS [2]. Past research on the motivation of contributors have identified a mix of intrinsic [eg. fun [7], sharing or learning opportunities [8]] and extrinsic [eg. signaling [5], reputation and career benefits [9]] factors that drive contributions to FLOSS projects. While extant research has tried to understand why developers are motivated to contribute to FLOSS projects, recent studies have shown that individuals' motives are not static, but evolve over time [8,10]. Taking into account this dynamic nature of motivation of contributors, our research studies how the nature of motivation (be it intrinsic or extrinsic) changes when the characteristics of the FLOSS projects changes and how this impacts the value of the project.

In our attempt to go deeper into the mechanisms that govern the nature of motivation of the contributors, we ground our research in self-determination theory (SDT) [11]. SDT and its sub-theories postulate the existence of three innate psychological needs: *autonomy*, *relatedness*, and *competence*, which lead to enhanced self-motivation when satisfied and result in a positive affective state [11,12]. To understand how the structures of work influence the motivation to contribute, we invoke the theory of superposition [3]. Superposition is the process through which software development occurs in a sequential manner, where changes to the software are added incrementally one-on-top the other. Each change represents a task that is independently built by a contributor and has its own functional pay-off through the improvements that it brings to the application [3].

By building on SDT, the theory of superposition and integrating them with other theories from the disciplines of psychology and IS, this dissertation tries to unearth the value creation mechanisms that operate within FLOSS environments. Within this broad framework, we identify three studies that differ in the research questions being targeted and their underlying theoretical motivations. The first study tries to advance the theory of superposition by understanding the influence of superposition on the value of the FLOSS project. While doing so, we also study the influence of organization ownership on the relationship between superposition and value of the FLOSS project [14]. The second study, tries to unearth how the choice of license can impact the nature of motivation of the contributors and the important role that the structures of work play in meeting these motivational needs. The third study attempts to understand how digital platforms facilitate value creation by allowing an effective work break down structure that not only motivates contribution but also eases the problems of coordination and governance.

3 METHODS

The developed hypotheses will be tested using a mix of archival and survey data on a sample of FLOSS projects hosted on GitHub. The availability of change logs for most public FLOSS projects allows us to recreate the entire history of a project and test the hypothesized relationships. However, the promises offered by the rich FLOSS datasets come with several perils [15,16]. We intend to take careful note of these issues before we conduct the empirical analysis.

4 EXPECTED RESULTS AND IMPLICATIONS

The findings of these three studies are not only expected to advance IS theories on FLOSS, but also provide three overarching lessons that is intended to educate IS and non-IS organizations looking to adopt the FLOSS model of development. In specific, we try to integrate theories from IS and organizational studies to provide a more nuanced understanding of the value creation mechanisms that operate in FLOSS communities. We hope that our findings will provide a rich picture of the FLOSS development and allow both IS and non-IS organizations to understand how best they can extract value from participating in FLOSS projects.

5 REFERENCES

[1]   Coverity Report. Coverity Scan: 2013 Open Source Report [Internet]. 2013. Available from: http://softwareintegrity.coverity.com/rs/coverity/images/2013-Coverity-Scan-Report.pdf

[2]   Crowston K, Wei K, Howison J, Wiggins A. Free/Libre open-source software development. ACM Comput Surv [Internet]. 2012;44(2):1–35. Available from: http://dl.acm.org/citation.cfm?doid=2089125.2089127

[3]   Howison J, Crowston K. Collaboration Through Open Superposition: A Theory Of The Open Source Way. MIS Q. 2014;38(1):29–50.

[4]   Munos B. Can open-source R&D reinvigorate drug research? Nat Rev Drug Discov. 2006;5(9):723–9.

[5]   Lerner J, Tirole J. Some Simple Economics of Open Source. J Ind Econ [Internet]. 2003;50(2):197–234. Available from: http://doi.wiley.com/10.1111/1467-6451.00174

[6]   Wagstrom PA. Vertical interaction in open software engineering communities. Carnegie Mellon University; 2009.

[7]   Ghosh RA. Interview with Linus Torvalds: What motivates free software developers? Vol. 10, First Monday. 2005.

[8]   Shah SK. Motivation, Governance, and the Viability of Hybrid Forms in Open Source Software Development. Manage Sci [Internet]. 2006;52(7):1000–14. Available from: http://pubsonline.informs.org/doi/abs/10.1287/mnsc.1060.0553

[9]   Hann I-H, Roberts J, Slaughter S, Fielding R. Economic Incentives for Participating Open Source Software Projects. Twenty-Third Int Conf Inf Syst [Internet]. 2002;ICIS 2002. Available from: http://aisel.aisnet.org/icis2002/33

[10] Fang Y, Neufeld D. Understanding Sustained Participation in Open Source Software Projects. J Manag Inf Syst. 2009;25(4):9–50.

[11] Ryan R, Deci E. Self-determination theory and the facilitation of intrinsic motivation, social development, and well-being. Am Psychol. 2000;55(1):68–78.

[12] Ke W, Zhang P. The effects of extrinsic motivations and satisfaction in open source software development. J Assoc Inf Syst. 2010;11(12):784–808.

[13] Ryan RM, Deci EL. Self-Determinaton Theory and the Facilitation of Intrinsic Motivation, Social Development, and Well-Being. Am Psychol. 2000;55(February):68–78.

[14] Medappa PK, Srivastava SC. Does the Task Structure of Open Source Projects Matter? Superposition and Value Creation. In: Thirty Seventh International Conference on Information Systems. Dublin; 2016. p. 1–10.

[15] Kalliamvakou E, Gousios G, Singer L, Blincoe K, German DM, Damian D. The promises and perils of mining GitHub. In: Proceedings of the 11th Working Conference on Mining Software Repositories. 2014. p. 92–101.

[16] Howison J, Crowston K. The perils and pitfalls of mining SourceForge. In: International Workshop on Mining Software Repositories. 2004. p. 7–11.

Post-Merger IS Integration: Influence of Process Level Business-IT Alignment on IT-based Business Value

Doctoral Consortium Proposal

N. Ravikumar
Indian Institute of Management
Bangalore
Ravikumarn@iimb.ernet.in

Abstract[1]

Mergers and Acquisitions (M&A's) are increasingly popular in the last few decades. Research indicates only 40% of these mergers create value for shareholders. Research confirms that IT-Business alignment is one of the key drivers of business value creation. This conviction is seen in the M&A literature as well. The broad research interest of the thesis is to understand the influence of pre-integration process level IT-business alignment on the post-integration IT-business value. We build on the conception that the first order effect of IT-Business alignment occurs at the process level. In this thesis, we reason that the degree of IT-business alignment of the processes that are getting integrated influences the post-integration process level IT -business alignment and thereby impacting the IT-business value.

Motivation and Problem Statement

Mergers and Acquisitions (M&A's) are increasingly popular in the last few decades. Research indicates about 60% of these mergers do not create value for shareholders. Research confirms that IT-Business alignment is one of the key drivers of business value creation. This conviction is seen in the M&A literature as well. There are also indications that non-aligned successful M&A integrations can happen. These studies are conducted mostly at the firm level. The literature on IT-Business alignment at process level argues that the ambiguities in such firm level studies could be due the assumptions in these studies that firms follow a single strategy whereas the data indicates firm-level strategy is multi-dimensioned. The literature on IT-business alignment at process level argues that the first-order effects of IT-Business alignment occur at the process level. We believe that the process level IT-Business alignment study could reveal more insights to the integration problems and to understand the evolutionary nature of the strategy. In this thesis, we want to address this gap by exploring the IT-Business alignment at

SIGMIS-CPR '17, June 21-23, 2017, Bangalore, India
© 2017 Copyright is held by the owner/author(s).
ACM ISBN 978-1-4503-5037-2/17/06.
http://dx.doi.org/10.1145/3084381.3084437

process level in M&A context. The focus is to theorize on the influence of pre-integration IT-Business alignment on the post – Integration IT business alignment and thereby on IT-based business value creation(Ref: Fig1). Our research question is: *What is the influence of pre-integration IT- business alignment on the post-integration IT-business-value at the process level?*

Background Literature

We can characterize three streams in the IT integration literature in the context of the mergers – One stream explores the realization of IS integration success and its importance to M&A value [1,4,5,12]. The second stream explores the integration capabilities to manage successful post-acquisition IT integration [2,3,8,11]. The third stream of literature is about integration process [7,5]. Together these studies contribute to our understanding of how IT integration creates value in M&A. In the first stream of work, authors emphasize the importance of the concept of IT-business alignment to integration success. We build on this line of work.

The studies conducted at the firm level are with an implicit assumption that organizations pursue the single strategy, but data indicates that the firm-level strategy is multi-dimensioned [9], i.e., Organizations may follow operational efficiency and product leadership simultaneously, thus leading to ambiguous results. Also, the recent literature that involves IT Business alignment has gravitated towards process level alignment rather than firm level [10]. Hence we intend to study alignment at the process level. One of the important reasons to consider process level alignment versus firm level is the existence of mixed or multiple strategies in contemporary organizations[10].Tallon et al.,(2016) conceptualize business IT alignment at process level as the degree of IT support the business process gets [10]. They use the term IT slack and IT shortfall to explain the alignment at the process level: 1.IT fails to fully support the business strategy (IT shortfall), 2. IT fully supports the business strategy in such a way that the supply of IT resources equals the demand for IT resources (perfect alignment), or 3. IT fully supports the business strategy but does so without using the entire body of IT resources available to the firm (IT slack). They also show that the business process performance is positively linked to the level of IT business alignment. We extend this concept of IT business alignment to M&A context to formulate our research framework.

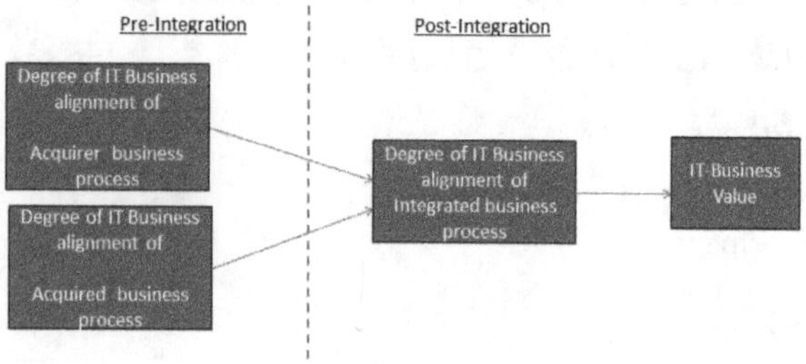

Figure 1: Conceptual model

Method

The studies in the area of post-merger integration are mostly case study based due to the data availability and confidentiality concerns. We intend to use the case study based methodology and semi-structured interviews to collect the data. We intend to do an in-depth case study and also survey to validate the understandings from the case study. We intend to identify the functional processes that got integrated – example product design and development process, key Sales processes. We will discuss the level of IT business alignment for these processes before integration and post-integration with senior IT and business executives involved in managing the IT and the integration process. We intend to do multiple case studies covering both success and failure cases.

Expected results

We expect to see a positive relationship between pre-integration IT alignment and post-integration IT alignment and further on the process performance. We intend to study the process level alignment in both scale based integration and scope based integration of the processes.

Implications

We will be contributing to the post-merger IT integration literature and to Business IT alignment literature at the process level. This topic is of importance to practitioners as it can guide them in understanding the possible difficulties that process can run into post integration due to IT Business alignment issues.

REFERENCES

[1] Giacomazzi, Franco, et al. "Information systems integration in mergers and acquisitions: A normative model." Information & Management 32.6 (1997): 289-302.

[2] Henningsson, S. (2008). Managing Information Systems Integration in Corporate Mergers and Acquisitions (Vol. 101). Lund Business Press.

[3] Henningsson, S., & Yetton, P. (2011). Managing the IT integration of acquisitions by multi-business organizations.

[4] Johnston, K. D., & Yetton, P. W. (1996). Integrating information technology divisions in a bank merger Fit, compatibility and models of change. The Journal of Strategic Information Systems, 5(3), 189-211.

[5] Mehta, M., & Hirschheim, R. (2004, January). A framework for assessing IT integration decision-making in mergers and acquisitions. In System Sciences, 2004. Proceedings of the 37th Annual Hawaii International Conference on (pp. 264-274). IEEE.

[6] Mehta, M., & Hirschheim, R. (2007). Strategic Alignment In Mergers And Acquisitions: Theorizing IS Integration Decision making. Journal of the Association for Information Systems, 8(3), 8.

[7] Merali, Y., & McKiernan; P. (1993). The strategic positioning of information systems in post-acquisition management. The Journal of Strategic Information Systems, 2(2), 105-124.

[8] Robbins, S. S., & Stylianou, A. C. (1999). Post-merger systems integration: the impact on IS capabilities. Information & management, 36(4), 205-212.

[9] Tallon, P. P. (2011). Value chain linkages and the spillover effects of strategic information technology alignment: A process-level view. Journal of Management Information Systems, 28(3), 9-44.

[10] Tallon, P. P., Coltman, T., Queiroz, M., & Sharma, R. (2016). Business Process and Information Technology Alignment: Construct Conceptualization, Empirical Illustration, and Directions for Future Research. Journal of the Association for Information Systems, 17(9), 563.

[11] Tanriverdi, H., & Uysal, V. B. (2011). Cross-business information technology integration and acquirer value creation in corporate mergers and acquisitions. Information Systems Research, 22(4), 703-720.

[12] Wijnhoven, F., Spil, T., Stegwee, R., & Fa, R. T. A. (2006). Post-merger IT integration strategies: An IT alignment perspective. The Journal of Strategic Information Systems, 15(1), 5-28

Drawing on the Underrepresentation of Women in IT-Professions: An Analysis of Existing Knowledge and Need for Research along the Stages of Educational Systems

Doctoral Consortium

C. Oehlhorn

University of Bamberg

An der Weberei 5, 96047 Bamberg

Germany

caroline.oehlhorn@uni-bamberg.de

ABSTRACT

MOTIVATION AND PROBLEM STATEMENT

Recent statistics reveal that organizations fail to fill all their information technology (IT) vacancies. Since numerous years, almost every organization in the European Union is affected by the skill shortage of qualified IT employees. Facing this challenge, the education of IT employees is considered one of the major issues by organizations and governmental institutions. Furthermore, IT professions are still dominated by men and women are widely underrepresented. From a theoretical perspective, the topic why women choose an IT career is discussed within IS research so far. Thereby, previous research also reveals that organizations often face challenges to retain female IT employees, and that turnaway and turnover of employees represent a serious issue. In the meantime, different institutions within the educational system (e.g. schools, universities, institutions for vocational education) take various approaches to give young women an understanding of IT and its work environment. On closer consideration of the educational system in general, multiple ways become apparent that enable access to IT professions: secondary and higher education as well as further education. This literature review reveals how the underrepresentation of women in IT professions is focused within IS research regarding the stages of educational systems.

KEYWORDS

Women in IS; IS education; skill shortage

SIGMIS-CPR '17, June 21-23, 2017, Bangalore, India

© 2017 Copyright is held by the owner/author(s).

ACM ISBN 978-1-4503-5037-2/17/06.

http://dx.doi.org/10.1145/3084381.3084435

BACKGROUND LITERATURE

The structure of educational systems - Today, almost every country possesses an own educational system, but it is often difficult to compare these systems. However, each educational system is constituted of multiple stages, which people pass until they are qualified to pursue a profession. Most commonly, an educational system consists of the following four stages:

Primary or elementary education. The term 'primary education' covers education on the part of institutions (e.g. kindergarten, preschool, elementary school) that provide a first elementary basis for further education at school.

Secondary education. Secondary education is realized at all secondary schools (e.g. high school, college), which students usually finish with a first graduation qualifying for a profession. The graduation at secondary schools is almost always a necessity to take up studies at university.

Tertiary or higher education. Tertiary education most closely corresponds to education at universities or equivalent academic institutions. The academic graduation is often the highest qualification for the entry into professional life.

Quarternary or further education. Further education constitutes an exception in contrast to the other three stages of an educational system. People pass this stage in general after they took up a job and do this on a voluntary, extra occupational basis. Further education is often provided by academic institutions as well as by independent and accredited organizations.

The underrepresentation of women in IT professions - The issue of skill shortages in IT professions appeared in media in the early 1990s. Initial activities are implemented by organizations to counteract the skill shortage [1], but it takes a couple of years until women are detected to be a potential group of qualified IT employees at the beginning of the 21st century. Today, the reasons why women decide for a career in IT are addressed within IS research in the meanwhile. Nevertheless, different reasons why women decide against working in an IT environment are discussed as well. Thereby, it has been well recognized that it is difficult to attract and retain women in the field of IT. Only a small percentage of young women chooses an IT-related subject in secondary school or at the tertiary level, and in the further course of education until these women take up an IT profession, this percentage continues to decrease.

METHODOLOGICAL APPROACH

To analyze a research topic in its entirety, a systematic literature review was performed. The approach conducted in this paper includes two main steps: firstly, the selection of relevant key publication outlets, and secondly, the definition of a literature search strategy that contains all relevant search terms and covers a certain period of time. This literature review refers to the eight top IS journals comprised in the Senior Scholar's Basket of Journals of the Association for Information Systems and the proceedings of the International Conferences on Information Systems as the major international IS conference and considers a time frame for from 2000 to 2017. Relevant publications are identified through searching within the databases and archives of the selected outlets using the following search term: ('skill shortage' OR 'education') AND ('information technology' OR 'information systems') AND ('women' OR 'girls' OR 'female'). After receiving the result list for the search, a first screening of the articles was performed by considering the title, abstract and keywords. A second screening of the whole content of the remaining articles led to the final selection of relevant articles. Finally, 51 papers serve as a basis for this literature review.

FINDINGS

The following paragraph shows the results out of 51 identified articles from which 14 articles can be thematically categorized into three stages of educational systems.

Secondary education: Three articles refer to the underrepresentation of women in IT professions focusing education at school. Among those, two articles address preparatory activities during school education to arouse young women's interest and provide first knowledge in IT domains. Another article draws on the enlightenment of young women about IT subjects, IT studies and future work opportunities.

Higher education: In summary, eight articles refer to the academic education in association with the underrepresentation of women in the IT sector. Thereby, four articles broach the female students' perceptions and interest to choose a career in IT fields. Four additional articles go into details regarding teaching at university and schedule of curriculums.

Further education: The last category addresses the opportunity of vocational training and education during work life in IT fields. Hereby, three articles deal with particular prospects female employees have before they decide for further training or education in this domain.

IMPLICATIONS

After completing the literature review, several contributions and a research agenda are worked out.

First, 51 relevant articles about the underrepresentation of women in IT professions published in the eight top IS journals and the ICIS were screened. In contrast to previous research that highlight the importance of this phenomenon, the topic seems to appeal to IS research so far. Especially in the last ten years, numerous articles addressing reasons to argue the underrepresentation of women in IT professions were published in IS publications.

Second, the identified articles were classified according to their content into three stages of educational systems: secondary, higher and further education. However, research about events passing the different educational stages exists only partially. Thereby, single articles address issues concerning scheduling or teaching during school and academic education in preparation of a future engagement in the IT sector or how the young women's perceptions about IT professions and their interest can be influenced. In addition, no article focuses on the first stage of educational systems, elementary education.

Third, by categorizing the identified articles, thematic priorities of existing literature become apparent. To show research gaps in relation to the underrepresentation of women in IT professions, the following research agenda for future research is proposed:

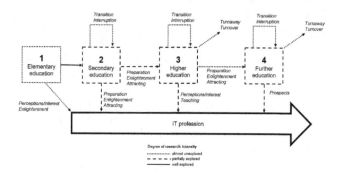

Figure 1: Proposed research agenda

Whereas the professional life of IT professionals is well explored, research about processes that can influence the young women's perceptions about working in IT during the stages of educational systems (especially during secondary and higher education) are hardly or only partially investigated. Considering the increasing skill shortage of qualified IT professionals, further research within these stages is required to investigate why only few women decide for a career in IT fields. Out of these insights, measures to increase the attractiveness of IT professions to young women can be deduced to counteract the skill shortage.

Essays on Internet Governance

Doctoral Consortium

Neena Pandey

Decision Sciences & Information Systems

Indian Institute of Management, Bangalore

neena.pandey@iimb.ernet.in

1 MOTIVATION AND PROBLEM STATEMENT

Expecting tremendous social and economic implications of digital platforms and infrastructures, firms and governments across the world are making huge investments in creating and maintaining these infrastructures, health information systems and the Internet being the two striking examples. However, with growth, concerns related to their standardization, control and governance become significant. The Internet is a global information infrastructure [5] and to restrict its unintended consequences, positive steps towards its design and governance is being sought by researchers [6] and practitioners alike. I study three different aspects of Internet governance. The three questions that I analyze in my dissertation are: *(1) What country level factors (institutional quality) impact a nation's choice of Internet governance structure and what is the role of Internet affordances in the relationship?; (2) How does the proportion of Internet-deprived population (i.e. the extent of digital divide) affect the impact which zero-rating plans can have on an economy?; (3) Critically analyzing the current discourse on net neutrality and questioning the assumptions on which it is defined currently.*

2 BACKGROUND LITERATURE

By definition, Information infrastructure is a shared, open (and unbounded), heterogeneous and evolving socio-technical system consisting of a set of IT capabilities and their user, operations and design communities[5] and it is characterized by non-linear evolutionary dynamics [3], hence making its governance complex.

Internet Governance: The primary task of Internet governance involves the design and administration of the technologies necessary to keep the Internet operational and enactment of substantive policy around these technologies [2]. Whether it should be governed in a multilateral or a multi-stakeholder form is an issue of contention among countries of the world.

SIGMIS-CPR '17, June 21-23, 2017, Bangalore, India

© 2017 Copyright is held by the owner/author(s).

ACM ISBN 978-1-4503-5037-2/17/06.

http://dx.doi.org/10.1145/3084381.3084431

Zero-rating Plans: It is a contract between Internet Service Providers (ISPs) and Content Provider (CPs) which allows CPs to subsidize the consumption of their content, i.e. the downloaded content would not count towards customer's ISP subscription cap. The impact of allowing such plans by the regulatory bodies has been studied with the assumption of full Internet penetration in the countries [1] and not when the digital divide is significant.

Net Neutrality: Analysis of net neutrality (an agreement between ISPs and CPs to prioritize the CP's content) considers network congestion as a significant parameter [4] and studies its impact on economic indicators (consumer, producer and total surplus). However, whether having a goods-dominant view which ensures accessibility to all data on Internet ensure net 'neutrality' has not been studied.

3 METHODS

The first essay is an empirical study with a nation as a unit of analysis, where I use Worldwide Governance Indicators (WGI), affordances of Internet (derived from the ICT policies of the countries) and the choice of governance structure as per the signatories at the WCIT-2012 meeting at Dubai for testing the model. The second essay performs analytical modeling and analyzes the problem using game theory methodology. Finally, the third essay will be a qualitative study for which I intend to use case study methodology. However, the essay is still in its conceptualization phase.

4 RESULTS/EXPECTED RESULTS

In Essay 1, I have established the relationship between the institutional quality (economic and socio-political) of a country with its choice of the Internet governance structure. I am collecting the data to analyze the mediating relationship of Internet affordances.

In Essay 2, we find that the amount of data that a CP will zero-rate is directly proportional to its revenue-generating capability. Moreover, contrary to the widely held perception, the ISP will not always choose the firm with higher revenue generating capability to zero-rate. In most conditions, both the competing CPs will be allowed to zero-rate their content.

In the third essay, we expect to be able to establish the need to move away from the general discourse on net neutrality to extend it to include the view of the service (user and usability)

Neena Pandey

rather than only from goods (system and accessibility) perspective.

5 IMPLICATIONS

Considering that the Internet is and hopefully will remain the most ubiquitous information infrastructure of recent times, the importance of restricting its unintended consequences cannot be emphasized enough. This research highlights a few issues of Internet governance and takes a step towards analyzing them. Whereas the first essay makes a contribution towards the academic conversation on the choice of Internet governance structure (and of Information infrastructure, in general), the second will have strong policy implications considering the hot societal debate it is analyzing. The implications are important in the context of developing countries where the governments are caught in a dilemma of freedom of expression versus narrowing the digital divide. Through the final essay, we hope to change the academic and practitioner's discourse on net neutrality by re-conceptualizing it from all dimensions towards making the Internet 'neutral.'

REFERENCES

[1] Cho, S., Qui, L., & Bandyopadhyay, S. 2016. Should Online Content Providers Be Allowed To Subsidize Content?|An Economic Analysis. Information Systems Research, 27(3) , 580-595
[2] DeNardis L. 2014. The global war of Internet governance. Yale University Press.
[3] Grisot, M., Hanseth, O., Thorseng, A. 2014. Innovation of, in, on infrastructures: articulating the role of architecture in information infrastructure evolution. Journal of the Association for Information Systems. 15(4), 197.
[4] Guo, H., Cheng, H. K., & Bandyopadhyay, S. (2012). Net neutrality, broadband market coverage, and innovation at the edge. Decision Sciences, 43(1), 141-172.
[5] Hanseth, O., Lyytinen K. 2010. Design theory for dynamic complexity in information infrastructures: The case of building Internet. Journal of Information Technology. (25:1) 1-19.
[6] Lee, J. K. (2015). Guest editorial: research framework for AIS grand vision of the bright ICT initiative. MIS Quarterly, 39(2), iii-xii.

Social Media and Online Political Participation of Citizens

Doctoral Consortium

Vidushi Pandey

Dept. of Decision Science and Systems,
Indian Institute of Management Raipur,
Raipur, India (492015)
vidushi.fpm2013@iimraipur.ac.in

ABSTRACT

This research aims to explore the role of social media platforms on citizen's political participation behavior. The three essays in this work explore the nature of political participation on social media, identify the mechanism through which social media impacts online political participation and study how technological feature of social media impact costs and benefits perceived by citizens in political participation. The results of this work will add to the literature of political participation as well information systems by identifying the link between social media's features and its impact on online political participation of citizens

KEYWORDS

Social Media; Political Participation; Social Capital

1 MOTIVATION AND PROBLEM STATEMENT

The extensive use of social media by citizens in their everyday life has influenced the social and political lives of both citizens and governments. While domains like Public Policy, Political Science and Communication Studies have primarily focused on exploring the concept of participation from citizen's perspective, focus of Information Systems domain on this issue has primarily been from government's perspective. Even in the studies of other domains that have focused on citizen's perspective, the exploration of technology's impact on participation has been limited. A large proportion of studies have considered impact of Internet as a whole on political participation[1]–[4]. Focus on impact of specific forms of Internet such as search engines, online news portals and social media platforms has been sparse.

SIGMIS-CPR '17, June 21-23, 2017, Bangalore, India
© 2017 Copyright is held by the owner/author(s).
ACM ISBN 978-1-4503-5037-2/17/06.
http://dx.doi.org/10.1145/3084381.3084427

Also, the dependent variable in most of these studies has been offline political participation. Since Internet as a platform not just provides information but also the capability to act on this information, not just offline but online forms of participation also need to be recognized and considered in literature.

It is with this motivation of exploring the role of social media in citizen's political participation behavior we have undertaken the present research work. The research questions we specifically want to address in this study are: What is the dominant nature of online civic/political participation activities undertaken by citizen on social media platforms? What is the mechanism by which social media influences online political participation? What technological feature of social media impact costs and benefits perceived by citizens in online political participation?

2 BACKGROUND LITERATURE

Majority of studies on political participation focus on exploring factors that impact participation behavior of citizen. Life satisfaction [5], [6], trustful predisposition [7] ,people's ideological identity [8], extraversion [9], [10], higher education and better socio economic status[11], [12] are a few individual level factors that have been found to have significant impact of people's participation behavior. One such factor that has gained sufficient focus in literature is the Social Capital of an individual. Positive impact of social capital on people's political participation has been repeatedly established in literature[2], [13]–[15]. It is identified that social capital that citizen develop through community meetings, interpersonal discussion, becoming members of groups and organizations enables them to exchange information, elaborate on community issues and create opportunities to participate in political activities [8], [16], [17]. Technology's role in impacting social capital and participation behavior has however been debatable. Putnam (1995) claimed that television viewership negatively impacts people's social capital thereby resulting in reduced participation. Other studies in these direction have found mixed results around technology's impact on citizen's political participation behavior. In this thesis our aim is to explore the impact of a specific form of technology (social media) on online political participation of citizen by referring to Down's theory of political participation [19] and social capital theories[20], [21].

3 METHODS

The first essay focuses on exploring the nature of online political participation on social media. We applied data mining algorithms (k-NN, Logistic regression and N-Bayes) to automatically classify user tweets into a set of categories as defined in the theoretical framework. In the second essay, our objective is to identify the mechanism through which social media impacts online political participation of citizens. A combination of focus group interviews and survey instrument was used to capture different aspects of people's participation behavior. The data was analyzed using Structured Equation Modelling technique. The third essay aims to explore the impact of free information encountered by users on their social media feed on their political participation behavior. The data for this essay contained the number of tweets a user has sent out that contains political hashtags (his online political participation) and the number of tweets that he encountered on his timeline which contained these hashtags (free political information encountered by him on his timeline).

4 RESULTS

The results of fist study revealed that the prominent form of political participation that people exhibit online was of 'Activism'. Results also uncovered new forms of participation activities where identity of participant did not play a qualifying role as expected according to our theoretical framework. The results of second study reveal that social media positively impacts the expected benefits of participation and perceived ease of participation (reflecting a decrease in the costs of participation). This effect is both direct (owing to technical capabilities of social media as a platform) and indirect (owing to social capital provided by social media). In the results of third study we expect to find a significant relationship between free information encountered by citizen on social media and their political participation behavior.

5 IMPLICATIONS

The results of first study have identified the prominent nature of online political participation. Based, on the insights from our results we contribute to the literature by suggesting that "Identity of participant" does not play a qualifying role in classifying online political participation as it did in case of offline political participation. The results of second study identify the features of social media platform that have a positive impact on political participation from citizens. This will help Governments and other stakeholders design better political participation strategies keeping the identified features in focus. The results of third study would establish the impact of free information encountered on social media on people's participation behavior online. If the results of this study are significant it will emphasize a need of better information verification mechanism on social media to prevent spread of fake news and curtail negative participation behavior.

REFERENCES

[1] M. K. Jennings and V. Zeitner, "Internet use and civic engagement: A longitudinal analysis," *Public Opin. Q.*, vol. 67, no. 3, pp. 311–334, 2003.

[2] D. V Shah, J. Cho, W. P. Eveland, and N. Kwak, "Information and expression in a digital age modeling Internet effects on civic participation," *Communic. Res.*, vol. 32, no. 5, pp. 531–565, 2005.

[3] M. Xenos and P. Moy, "Direct and differential effects of the Internet on political and civic engagement," *J. Commun.*, vol. 57, no. 4, pp. 704–718, 2007.

[4] J. Pasek, E. More, and D. Romer, "Realizing the social Internet? Online social networking meets offline civic engagement," *J. Inf. Technol. Polit.*, vol. 6, no. 3–4, pp. 197–215, 2009.

[5] R. E. Harlow and N. Cantor, "Still participating after all these years: A study of life task participation in later life.," *J. Pers. Soc. Psychol.*, vol. 71, no. 6, p. 1235, 1996.

[6] J. F. Helliwell and R. D. Putnam, "The social context of well-being," *Philos. Trans. Soc. London Ser. B Biol. Sci.*, pp. 1435–1446, 2004.

[7] K. Kaufhold, S. Valenzuela, and H. G. De Zúniga, "Citizen journalism and democracy: How user-generated news use relates to political knowledge and participation," *Journal. Mass Commun. Q.*, vol. 87, no. 3–4, pp. 515–529, 2010.

[8] H. Gil de Zúñiga, A. Veenstra, E. Vraga, and D. Shah, "Digital democracy: Reimagining pathways to political participation," *J. Inf. Technol. Polit.*, vol. 7, no. 1, pp. 36–51, 2010.

[9] A. L. Kavanaugh, D. D. Reese, J. M. Carroll, and M. B. Rosson, "Weak ties in networked communities," *Inf. Soc.*, vol. 21, no. 2, pp. 119–131, 2005.

[10] E. Keller and J. Berry, *The influentials: One American in ten tells the other nine how to vote, where to eat, and what to buy.* Simon and Schuster, 2003.

[11] S. Verba, K. L. Schlozman, H. E. Brady, and H. E. Brady, *Voice and equality: Civic voluntarism in American politics*, vol. 4. Cambridge Univ Press, 1995.

[12] C. Zukin, S. Keeter, M. Andolina, K. Jenkins, and M. X. D. Carpini, *A new engagement?: Political participation, civic life, and the changing American citizen.* Oxford University Press, 2006.

[13] J. Eveland William P, "The effect of political discussion in producing informed citizens: The roles of information, motivation, and elaboration," *Polit. Commun.*, vol. 21, no. 2, pp. 177–193, 2004.

[14] E. Katz and P. F. Lazarsfeld, *Personal Influence, The part played by people in the flow of mass communications.* Transaction Publishers, 1955.

[15] M. S. Weatherford, "Interpersonal networks and political behavior," *Am. J. Pol. Sci.*, pp. 117–143, 1982.

[16] J. Gastil and J. P. Dillard, "Increasing political sophistication through public deliberation," *Polit. Commun.*, vol. 16, no. 1, pp. 3–23, 1999.

[17] C. A. Klofstad, "Talk leads to recruitment: How discussions about politics and current events increase civic participation," *Polit. Res. Q.*, vol. 60, no. 2, pp. 180–191, 2007.

[18] R. D. Putnam, "Bowling alone: America's declining social capital," *J. Democr.*, vol. 6, no. 1, pp. 65–78, 1995.

[19] A. Downs, "An economic theory of political action in a democracy," *J. Polit. Econ.*, pp. 135–150, 1957.

[20] R. S. Burt, "Closure as Social Capital," *Soc. Cap. Theory Res.*, pp. 31–55, 2001.

[21] J. S. Coleman, "Foundations of social theory Belknap Press of Harvard University Press," *Cambridge, MA*, 1990.

Online Learning: Improving the Learning Outcomes

Doctoral Consortium

Ritanjali Panigrahi
Indian Institute of Management Rohtak
Haryana - 124001
India
ritanjali.panigrahi@gmail.com

ABSTRACT

The use of Technology to facilitate better learning and training is gaining momentum worldwide, reducing the temporal and spatial problems associated with traditional learning. Despite its several benefits, retaining students in online platforms is challenging. This paper discusses an integration of online learning with virtual communities and mobile platforms to foster student engagement for obtaining better learning outcomes in blended learning platforms as well as to understand the public sentiments regarding the pure online learning platforms and finding the factors to improve the learning outcome. The potential utility of the study is discussed in terms of the contribution to the theory and practice.

CCS CONCEPTS

• **Social and professional topics** → **Computing education**

KEYWORDS

Online learning; learning outcomes; virtual communities; MOOCs; mobile technologies

1 INTRODUCTION

Online learning and training are [1]gaining popularity worldwide, reducing the temporal and spatial problems associated with the traditional form of education. The primary factors behind using online learning are not only to improve access to education and training, and quality of learning, but also to reduce the cost and improve the cost effectiveness of education [1]. Despite several advantages of online learning, retaining students in such platforms is a key challenge with a high attrition rate [2]. As a higher amount of money is spent on infrastructure, staff training, etc., organizations seek to take maximum benefit from online learning which requires an understanding of the factors

SIGMIS-CPR '17, June 21-23, 2017, Bangalore, India
© 2017 Copyright is held by the owner/author(s).
ACM ISBN 978-1-4503-5037-2/17/06.
http://dx.doi.org/10.1145/3084381.3084434

that measures the effectiveness and outcome of e-learning. Therefore, the primary focus of research remains on how to retain online learning users, and increase the efficiency of the online learning.

Users may learn inside and outside the classroom; inside classroom learning is by instructors either from face-to-face, pure online or blended learning (combination of face-to-face and pure online learning) whereas outside classroom learning is learning by users anytime and anywhere after the class. The exponential growth of the internet along with the emergence of Web 2.0 has enabled individuals to share information, participate, and collaborate to learn from virtual communities (VC) anytime and anywhere [3]. It is essential to assess the role of a less constrained informal mode of learning such as virtual communities in the formal learning to engage and retain students.

The continuous development in mobile technology has expanded the opportunity to learn from mobile devices anywhere, anytime. The success of M-learning in organizations depends on upon organizational, people, and pedagogical factors apart from technological factors [4]. A range of mobile technologies such as laptops, smartphones, and tablets are embraced by students to support informal learning [5].

2 RELATED LITERATURE

The related literature is discussed in the perspective of (a) the factors that affect learning outcomes, (b) the role of VCs and mobile technologies in blended online learning, and (c) understanding the MOOCs (Massive Open Online Courses).

2.1 Learning Outcomes

Learning outcome is the measure of the effectiveness of a learning platform. There are several factors which determine the learning outcomes. They are learning interventions, team collaboration, virtual competency, learning engagement, formal vs. informal learning.

2.2 Virtual Communities (VCs)

A VC is a network of individuals interacting through social media to pursue mutual interests or goals. A study [6] has shown that VCs creates a sense of belongingness and keeps the members engaged which results in improving the learning outcome. Since most of the studies focus on the VC's role in improving learning, it is essential to understand the role of VCs to increase the learning outcome when integrated with online learning platforms.

2.3 Mobile Apps

The usage of mobile technology positively influences students' learning achievement and interest [7]. Students who received persuasive short messaging service (SMS) intervention performed better than students who did not receive any SMS intervention [8]. It is, therefore, essential to understand the role of mobile apps integration in the online learning platforms to increase the learning outcomes.

2.4 Understanding MOOCs

MOOCs are gaining popularity for providing online courses to a larger mass for free or with very nominal costs. Despite the advantages, the attrition rate is very high [2], and the learning outcome is scantly researched. For ensuring low attrition rates and improving the learning outcome, it is essential to understand the users' attitude towards MOOCs, and social media is the best place to understand crowd sentiments considering the massive amount of data being created. It is also vital to explore the factors that can improve the learning outcome in MOOCs.

3 RESEARCH METHODOLOGY

3.1 Research Objectives

- To study the public sentiments on MOOCs on social media.
- To understand the factors that help improve the learning outcomes in a pure online platform.
- Study the role of VCs on the performance of students in a blended learning platform.
- Study the role of mobile apps in the performance of students in a blended learning platform.

3.2 Sample and Data Collection

Objective 1: Data (tweets) are collected from Twitter based on keywords search of MOOC provider names. Data extraction is done through the web crawling on Twitter by a python program.

Objective 2: The data collection (from students with higher education qualification) would be performed through focused group interviews, and open-ended questionnaires.

Objective 3 and 4: The students (in a post-graduate course) would be facilitated by an integrated virtual community and a mobile app respectively in a blended learning course. The responses would be captured through a survey.

3.3 Hypotheses and Statistical Tools

Hypothesis (Objective 3): The integration of virtual communities in a blended learning environment improves the learning outcome of the students.

Hypothesis (Objective 4): The integration of mobile apps in a blended learning environment improves the learning outcome of the students.

Objective 1: Trend analysis, sentiment analysis, influencer analysis, association rule mining, etc. are performed. The tools used are Python, R programming, and pivot tables

Objective 2: Structural Equation Modelling

Objective 3 and 4: Experimental design and Structural Equation Modelling is used

4 POTENTIAL UTILITY OF THE PROPOSED STUDY

Theoretical contribution: Understanding the factors that can improve the learning performance of a pure online learning platform and comparing with the existing theories would contribute establishing a theory related to online learning platforms. For blended learning platforms, the study can contribute to building the theory related to an integration of virtual communities and mobile technology with online learning.

Contribution related to practice: This study can contribute to practice for (a) online learning platform organizations and (b) the educationists. For pure online learning platforms, understanding the factors that improve the learning outcome would help online learning organizations to build their platforms for better outcomes. For blended learning platforms, the results would motivate the educators to employ strategies such as to gain maximum benefits out of the integrated technology.

REFERENCES

[1]   Bates, "Restructuring the university for technological change," in What Kind of University?, London, England, 1997.

[2]   L. W. Perna, A. Ruby, R. F. Boruch, N. Wang, J. Scull, S. Ahmad and C. Evans, "Moving through MOOCs: Understanding the progression of users in massive open online courses," Educational Researcher, vol. 43, no. 9, pp. 421-432, 2014.

[3]   F. Rennie and T. Morrison, E-learning and social networking handbook: Resources for higher education, Routledge, 2013.

[4]   V. Krotov, "Critical Success Factors in M-Learning: A Socio-Technical Perspective," Communications of the Association for Information Systems, vol. 36, no. 1, p. 6, 2015.

[5]   A. Murphy, H. Farley, M. Lane, A. Hafeez-Baig and B. Carter, "Mobile learning anytime, anywhere: what are our students doing?," Australasian Journal of Information Systems, vol. 18, no. 3, 2014.

[6]   L. Zhao, Y. Lu, B. Wang, P. Y. Chau and L. Zhang, "Cultivating the sense of belonging and motivating user participation in virtual communities: A social capital perspective," International Journal of Information Management, vol. 32, no. 6, pp. 574-588, 2012.

[7]   X. Zhai, M. Zhang and M. Li, "One-to-one mobile technology in high school physics classrooms: Understanding its use and outcome," British Journal of Educational Technology, 2016.

[8]   T. T. Goh, B. C. Seet and N. S. Chen, "The impact of persuasive SMS on students' self-regulated learning," British Journal of Educational Technology, vol. 43, no. 4, pp. 624-640, 2012.

Social Presence in Social Media: Persuasion, Design and Discourse*

Doctoral Consortium

S. Parameswaran
Department of Management Science
and Systems
SUNY at Buffalo, USA
sparames@buffalo.edu

1 MOTIVATION AND PROBLEM STATEMENT

The social presence construct has gained widespread use in explaining computer mediated communication outcomes. With social information systems gaining more prominence, this construct, which has at its heart the users and their interrelationships, has gained more traction. In my dissertation, I analyze this important construct in three essays from three perspectives: consequences, "competition" aspect, and antecedents. One, while social presence has been shown to impact task performance under various contexts, there is less clarity in the mediating mechanisms, and even less research on the contingencies in social presence's impact on task performance. So, in my first essay I ask: How does social presence affect task performance? And do these effects depend on task-related, contextual and cultural contingencies? Two, in the United States, several studies of different groups of HIV-positive individuals generally show suboptimal rates of adherence. I examine the "competition" dimension of social presence, i.e. others are present but competing with the user, and its outcomes in the HIV context. I analyze the impact of a competitive gamification application in improving HIV patient medication adherence measured using a Medication Event Monitoring System (MEMS). I also analyze patients' entrainment with multiple time cycles related to technology cues, game performance, and the work life, which pose conflicting demands to patients' adherence. I also study how this entrainment is impacted by patients' perceptions around their technological and social environments. Three, with social systems providing users affordances for user-generated content, and for maintaining online relationships, it is important to study the user's online

SIGMIS-CPR '17, June 21-23, 2017, Bangalore, India
© 2017 Copyright is held by the owner/author(s).
ACM ISBN 978-1-4503-5037-2/17/06.
http://dx.doi.org/10.1145/3084381.3084428

social network structure and its impact on the social presence. In essay 3, I analyze the antecedents of social presence, particularly those pertaining to online social network structure.

2 BACKGROUND LITERATURE

The basic idea behind these essays is bringing about a social space online. The pioneering work on social presence informs my dissertation [1]. Essay 1 integrates social presence theory with the Elaboration Likelihood Model [2]. Essay 2 is rooted in entrainment theory [3], and the Health Belief Model, a widely cited model of preventive health behavior that proposes that a "cue to action" for a patient elicits health behavior change in the patient [4]. Essay 3 integrates the social network theory with social presence theory [5].

3 METHODS

In the first essay, we build a social presence model of task performance, with task complexity and system purpose as the moderators. We empirically tested our hypotheses with the state-of-the-art, rigorous Two Stage Random Effects Meta-Analytic Structural Equation Model [6]. The second essay is an experimental study. We have three main data sources for analyses – patient electronic medical record (EMR) for co-morbid conditions, our cloud setup for daily MEMS (time of use) and game app use data (time and duration of use), and four surveys for self-reported data on a variety of psychological, perceptual, behavioral, and demographic variables. We plan to use longitudinal structural equation modeling and panel data analyses to test our hypotheses. Essay 3 analyzes secondary data from a leading online health community. Text analyses and social network analyses will be used to operationalize the variables. Econometric models will be used to empirically test the hypotheses.

4 RESULTS

Our analyses from essay 1 shows that social presence's relationships with task impacts - performance and effort, are mediated by flow-based central processing, and trust-based peripheral processing. Task-complexity negatively moderates the positive social presence-flow relationship, and positively moderates the positive social presence–trust relationship. On the other hand, utilitarian system context (versus hedonic) positively moderates the positive social presence-flow relationship, and negatively moderates the positive social presence–trust relationship. Data collection for essay 2 is under progress. Essay 3 is under data analyses stage.

5 IMPLICATIONS

My dissertation contributes to the literature on social presence in three ways. One, it provides clarity on consequences of social presence through the social presence model of task performance, with task-related and contextual contingencies. Two, if positive results are obtained in essay 2 analyzing the competition dimension of social presence, then the proposed technology intervention focused on enhancing ART adherence through fun and competition could significantly enhance the standard of care with respect to poorly adherent HIV/AIDS patients in the US. This change in clinical practice may also have broader implications for the self-management of other chronic diseases as well. Three, the study of antecedents of social presence in online health communities fills the gap in the literature that has less focused on a user's social network.

6 REFERENCES

[1] Short, J., Williams, E. and Christie, B. The social psychology of telecommunications. London: John Wiley & Sons, 1976.
[2] Petty, R. E. and Cacioppo, J. T. The elaboration likelihood model of persuasion. Springer, City, 1986.
[3] Ancona, D. G., Goodman, P. S., Lawrence, B. S. and Tushman, M. L. Time: A new research lens. Academy of management Review, 26, 4 (2001), 645-663.
[4] Rosenstock, I. M., Strecher, V. J. and Becker, M. H. Social learning theory and the health belief model. Health Education & Behavior, 15, 2 (1988), 175-183.
[5] Borgatti, S. P., Everett, M. G. and Johnson, J. C. Analyzing social networks. SAGE Publications Limited, 2013.
[6] Cheung, M. W.-L. Meta-analysis: A structural equation modeling approach. John Wiley & Sons, 2015.

Exploring Factors Influencing Self-Efficacy in Information Security: An Empirical Analysis by Integrating Multiple Theoretical Perspectives in the Context of Using Protective Information Technologies

Doctoral Consortium Proposal

Dinesh Reddy

The University of Texas at San Antonio

dinesh.reddy@utsa.edu

ABSTRACT

Self-efficacy in information security (SEIS) is one of the most researched predictors of end user security behavior that hinges on end user acceptance and use of the protective technologies such as anti-virus and anti-spyware. SEIS is also modeled as a mediator between factors affecting SEIS and the end user cybersecurity behavior. However, it is not clearly established in past literature on whether SEIS is better modeled as a predictor or as a mediator. It is stressed in literature that we should find new ways to improve SEIS. Accordingly, the purpose of this research is to empirically investigate what factors influence SEIS, and to examine the relative effect of each theorized factor (including self-efficacy) in increasing information security.

KEYWORDS

Self-efficacy; security; education; training; awareness; SETA

1. [1]INTRODUCTION

Information security can be achieved through policy enforcements, awareness, trainings, and education. Information security can also be compromised by negative technologies that include the tools which could disrupt computers that process the information. (E.g.: computer viruses, spyware etc.) [5]. On the contrary, "Protective information technologies (PIT) are designed to deter, neutralize, disable or eliminate the negative technologies" ([5] pg:387). Some of the examples of PIT include anti-spyware, anti-virus etc. So it is important that computer users adhere to security compliance behavior while using PIT.

It was found that self-efficacy in information security (SEIS) is one of the top three variables affecting security compliance behavior [11]. SEIS is defined as a belief in an individual's capability to protect information from unauthorized disclosure, loss, modification, destruction and lack of availability [9]. SEIS has been modeled in prior studies as a direct determinant of end user security compliance behavior such as user acceptance of PIT [5]. SEIS is also modeled as a "mediator" where there are factors affecting security compliance behavior via SEIS [5]. Self-efficacy

as a mediator will have the explanatory power of the relationship between predictor variables and compliance behavior. Research on self-efficacy for a range of behaviors has revealed that self-efficacy is a better predictor of subsequent behavior than the direct influence of self-efficacy's predictors on behavior. Knowing how to increase perceived SEIS could, therefore, have direct implications for security compliance behavior. Eight predictor variables are modeled in this research to influence SEIS. First set of predictor variables include cybersecurity positive experience, incidents experience, observational learning, and computer anxiety which are the adapted versions of self-efficacy enhancement methods proposed by [1]. The second set of predictor variables includes cybersecurity training, conceptual and procedural knowledge, and awareness, which form the basis of security education training awareness (SETA).

Enhancement of SEIS will further gain significance, if end user security compliance is "higher" when the predictor variables affect security compliance behavior via SEIS, as compared to predictor variables affecting security compliance behavior without including SEIS as a mediator. Hence, the purpose of this research is threefold: (1) To build a research model by theorizing the factors that influence SEIS, (2) To empirically examine and determine what factors increase SEIS, (3) To empirically examine if all theorized factors (including SEIS) have a direct effect on compliance behavior or if SEIS is a mediator.

2. BACKGROUND LITERATURE

Information security refers to the protection of the three key entities of information namely confidentiality, integrity and availability, irrespective of whether the information is stored, processed or being transmitted [9]. One specific form of security compliance behavior is behavioral intention to adopt PIT [10]. According to social learning theory, individuals with low self-efficacy tend to show negative performance and remain passive in nature owing to the fact that they are not confident in their ability to perform difficult tasks. On the other hand, individuals with high self-efficacy tend to show positive performance, and remain active in nature owing to the fact that they are confident in their abilities to handle difficult tasks. Hence, SEIS is a belief in an individual's capability to protect information and information systems from unauthorized disclosure, loss, modification, destruction and lack of availability.

Cybersecurity training (CT) has been emphasized and recommended as a countermeasure to reduce IS computer abuse [12]. CT is defined as those activities that impart specific cyber

---

[1] Permission to make digital or hard copies of part or all of this work for personal or classroom use is granted without fee provided that copies are not made or distributed for profit or commercial advantage and that copies bear this notice and the full citation on the first page. Copyrights for third-party components of this work must be honored. For all other uses, contact the Owner/Author.

SIGMIS-CPR '17, June 21-23, 2017, Bangalore, India
© 2017 Copyright is held by the owner/author(s).
ACM ISBN 978-1-4503-5037-2/17/06.
http://dx.doi.org/10.1145/3084381.3084429

skills to help users make security decisions [6]. Security policies form the basis of security education training and awareness (SETA). Cybersecurity knowledge refers to maturity of security subject matters and familiarity with tasks and actions to be performed when encountered with a risk [14]. In their research, [5] state that end users who are knowledgeable about protecting their computers against negative technologies are more confident in successfully combating the negative technologies by using PIT. The steps to perform a security task involve two aspects namely knowing 'that' (content) and knowing 'how' to perform the task. The former aspect best relates to the theoretical/conceptual facts and information about the security tasks. This aspect of knowledge can be termed as 'cybersecurity conceptual knowledge'. The latter aspect relates to the skill that is needed to utilize and apply the conceptual knowledge to solve the problem and execute the steps required to perform the security task, and is termed as 'cybersecurity procedural knowledge'. Cybersecurity knowledge is considered as a combination of conceptual knowledge and procedural knowledge [8]. Cybersecurity Awareness (CA) is defined as the state of being cognizant of performing secure tasks on a computer [2]. Studies show that self-efficacy and cybersecurity skills mediate the effect of CA on security compliance behavior [7].

The repetitive nature of positive experience is highlighted by [1] as mastery performance where an individual enacts a task multiple times to gain expertise in that task. An example of a cybersecurity positive experience is to successfully recover the lost data by using recovery software. Previous loss experience in terms of how recent, how frequent and how intense is a direct measure of the cybersecurity incident experience effect. Thus, cybersecurity incident experiences lower the user confidence and beliefs in further using the anti-virus software to safeguard against new virus [4]. Cybersecurity observational learning is defined as acquiring the security knowledge and skills in a training like environment, by watching others performing an online security task. There are four dimensions to observational learning namely attention, retention, production and motivation [2]. [15] found that the observational learning construct positively influenced post-training software self-efficacy. Computer anxiety is defined as "anxiety about the implications of computer use such as the loss of important data or fear of other possible mistakes" ([13]; Pg383). Anxiety relates to emotional state of mind that signifies stress. Computer anxiety significantly negatively influenced computer self-efficacy

3. METHODS

The research model will be tested using surveys. The survey items are both adopted from existing reliable scales and newly developed on a 7-point Likert scales. Survey items are pilot tested on a small sample (exceeding 100) of undergraduate students. The criteria for inclusion of pilot test data in the initial data analysis is that the respondents in the sample should be using a personal computer or laptop which is not secured and managed by IT administrators or internet service providers. The end users themselves should have control of managing his/her personal computer or laptop. 3 items were developed for inclusion criteria. The target population for actual data collection comprises of home computer users, university subjects including undergraduate and graduate students, staff, instructors, lecturers, research assistants, teaching assistants, professors and any other computer end user in a large academic setting, and working

professionals who have a personal computer/laptop whose security tasks are managed by themselves. The anticipated sample size is 300. Post data collection, covariance based structural equation modeling will be used to conduct data analysis in order to empirically test all the hypotheses.

4. EXPECTED RESULTS

While SEIS is modeled as both predictor and mediator variable affecting security compliance behavior, it is expected that SEIS when modeled as mediator will increase security compliance as compared to SEIS modeled as a predictor variable. It is expected that Cybersecurity training, knowledge, awareness, positive experience and observational learning positively influences SEIS. Cybersecurity incidents experience and computer anxiety are expected to negatively influence SEIS.

5. IMPLICATIONS

The results will provide insights into what factors contribute to increase in SEIS, in the context of using protective information technologies, thus filling an existing gap in the academic literature. The results of this research may open up new avenues for future research on the specific skills that are most influential in predicting self-efficacy in information security. The results could also help security professionals design more focused security training programs, course content and security awareness programs, based on factors that are most influential in increasing self-efficacy in information security.

REFERENCES

[1] Bandura, A. (1977). Self-efficacy: toward a unifying theory of behavioral change. *Psychological review*, 84(2), 191.

[2] Bandura, A. (1986). *Social foundations of thought and action* (pp. 5-107). Prentice Hall.: Englewood Cliffs, NJ.

[3] Bulgurcu, B., Cavusoglu, H., & Benbasat, I. (2010). Information security policy compliance: an empirical study of rationality-based beliefs and information awareness. *MIS quarterly*, 34(3), 523-548.

[4] Claar, C. L., Shields, R. C., Rawlinson, D., & Lupton, R. (2013). College student home computer security adoption. *Issues in Information Systems*, 14(2).

[5] Dinev, T., & Hu, Q. (2007). The centrality of awareness in the formation of user behavioral intention toward PIT. *Journal of the Association for Information Systems*, 8(7), 23.

[6] Furman, S., Theofanos, M. F., Choong, Y. Y., & Stanton, B. (2012). Basing cybersecurity training on user perceptions. *IEEE Security and Privacy*, 10(2), 40-49.

[7] Hanus, B., & Wu, Y. A. (2016). Impact of Users' Security Awareness on Desktop Security Behavior: A Protection Motivation Theory Perspective. *Information Systems Management*, 33(1), 2-16.

[8] McCormick, R. (1997). Conceptual and procedural knowledge. *International journal of technology and design education*, 7(1-2), 141-159.

[9] Rhee, H. S., Kim, C., & Ryu, Y. U. (2009). SEIS: Its influence on end users' information security practice behavior. *Computers & Security*, 28(8), 816-826.

[10] Shropshire, J., Warkentin, M., & Sharma, S. (2015). Personality, attitudes, and intentions: predicting initial adoption of information security behavior. *computers & security*, 49, 177-191.

[11] Sommestad, T., Hallberg, J., Lundholm, K., & Bengtsson, J. (2014). Variables influencing information security policy compliance: A systematic review of quantitative studies. Information Management & Computer Security, 22(1), 42-75.

[12] Straub, D. W., & Welke, R. J. (1998). Coping with systems risk: security planning models for management decision making. *Mis Quarterly*, 441-469.

[13] Thatcher, J. B., & Perrewe, P. L. (2002). An empirical examination of individual traits as antecedents to computer anxiety and computer self-efficacy. *Mis Quarterly*, 381-396.

[14] Wang, P. A. (2013, June). Assessment of Cybersecurity Knowledge and Behavior: An Anti-phishing Scenario. In *International Conference on Internet Monitoring and Protection (ICIMP)*.

[15] Yi, M. Y., & Davis, F. D. (2003). Developing and validating an observational learning model of computer software training and skill acquisition. *Information Systems Research*, 14(2), 146-169

Table of Contents

NOTES